Mindfulness-based
STRATEGIC
AWARENESS
TRAINING

Mindfulness-based STRATEGIC AWARENESS TRAINING

New Approach Based on Free Energy and Active Inference For Skillful Decision-making

Juan Humberto Young

WILEY Blackwell

Registered Offices

John Wiley & Sons, Inc., 111 River Street, Hoboken, NJ 07030, USA

John Wiley & Sons Ltd, The Atrium, Southern Gate, Chichester, West Sussex, PO19 8SQ, UK

For details of our global editorial offices, customer services, and more information about Wiley products visit us at www.wiley.com.

Wiley also publishes its books in a variety of electronic formats and by print-on-demand. Some content that appears in standard print versions of this book may not be available in other formats.

Library of Congress Cataloging-in-Publication Data

Names: Young, Juan Humberto, author.
Title: Mindfulness-based strategic awareness training comprehensive
    workbook : new approach based on free energy and active inference for
    skillful decision-making / Juan Humberto Young.
Description: Hoboken, NJ : Wiley-Blackwell, 2023. | Includes index.
Identifiers: LCCN 2023000308 (print) | LCCN 2023000309 (ebook) | ISBN
    9781119766971 (paperback) | ISBN 9781119766995 (adobe pdf) | ISBN
    9781119767374 (epub)
Subjects: LCSH: Leadership–Psychological aspects. | Mindfulness
    (Psychology) | Meditation.
Classification: LCC HD57.7 .Y68454 2023 (print) | LCC HD57.7 (ebook) |
    DDC 658.4/092–dc23/eng/20230130
LC record available at https://lccn.loc.gov/2023000308
LC ebook record available at https://lccn.loc.gov/2023000309

Cover Design and Image: Courtesy of author

Set in 11/17pt KeplerStd by Straive, Chennai, India

Printed in Singapore by Markono Print Media Pte Ltd
M113879_310323

TESTIMONIALS

"For many years now I have been working with MBSAT ideas and practices and applying them in my personal life, my business and my public work, since the first training protocol based on Positive Psychology. I have participated in the second phase of the protocol with mindfulness-based cognitive training and now look forward to the third phase based on Computational Neuroscience with Positive Psychology and Mindfulness as supporting pillars. I would not have thought possible the positive impact that MBSAT is having in managing my diverse tasks."

Lukas Arnold
Entrepreneur and politician
MBA, Master in Positive Leadership and Strategy
Founder and co-owner of Mammut Shops, Cycle Store and Berg & Tal Marktladen AG
Board member of several companies
Mayor of Stans, Canton Nidwalden, Switzerland

"I have worked with Juan for a number of years and have experienced that the MBSAT protocol helps improve strategic awareness in practical terms. The new MBSAT book uses an approach based on computational neuroscience and statistical physics to advance learning capabilities of the mind in an accessible manner. This is a leap forward in training for skillful decision-making, be it in professional or personal capacity."

Name undisclosed due to confidentiality agreement
CEO at one of the largest Swiss multinationals in its industry worldwide
MBA, Probability Mathematician

"In this pioneering work, Juan Humberto Young has skillfully integrated the ancient practice of mindfulness with cutting-edge research on the predicting brain. The outcome is a book that anyone who makes decisions should read: leaders, individuals, really anyone. At the core of MBSAT is minding, that is, attentively caring for. Just like a gardener minds their plants, attentively caring for them, we learn to mind ourselves and the world around us. In so doing, we can make more skillful decisions and flourish in this world of uncertainty. In my view, there is no better resource on mindfulness and decision-making than this wonderful book."

Jochen Reb
Professor of Organisational Behaviour & Human Resources,
Lee Kong Chian School of Business, Singapore Management University (SMU)
Researcher in Decision-Making and Mindfulness Sciences
Founding Director of the Mindfulness Initiative @ SMU
Co-Editor of *Mindfulness in Organizations* (Cambridge University Press, 2015)

"I read your book Mindfulness-based Strategic Awareness Training (2017), and I am proud to have you as a graduate of our Master of Studies in Mindfulness-Based Cognitive Therapy."

Willem Kuyken
PhD., Riblat Professor of Mindfulness and Psychological Science,
University of Oxford, Department of Psychiatry
Director of the Oxford Mindfulness Centre
Co-author of the book *Mindfulness: Ancient Wisdom Meets Modern Psychology* (Guilford Press, 2019)

"I tend to be a bit skeptical of new MBPs (Mindfulness-Based Programs) and am especially skeptical about MBPs designed for the workplace, but MBSAT is truly solid and filled with integrity in every way... this is a program designed by someone who truly knows the business/corporate world from the inside out AND IS ALSO a mindfulness person with high standards and impeccable credentials!"

Steve Hickman
Psy.D., Founding Director, UCSD Center for Mindfulness,
Clinical Psychologist UCSD Medical Center, Associate Clinical Professor UCSD School of Medicine (Retired),
Author of *Self-Compassion for Dummies*, (Wiley & Sons 2021)

CONTENTS

FIGURES

PART 1

Chapter 4

PART 2

Introduction

Chapter 5 – Session 1

Chapter 6 – Session 2

Chapter 7 – Session 3

Chapter 8 – Session 4

BOXES

PRACTICES, EXERCISES, TOOLS, AND EXPERIMENTS

Chapter 10 – Session 6

Chapter 11 – Session 7

Chapter 12 – Session 8

About the Author

Juan Humberto Young was six years member of KPMG and a Senior Manager responsible for strategy and information technology projects. He was a Senior Management member and Vice-president at UBS, Zurich, and head of the Asset Management and Financial Restructuring department for many years. He is active in business and was chairman and majority shareholder of R&B Engineering, a medium-sized electrical engineering firm that designs and plans electrical systems for private clients, companies, and public organizations in Zurich.

In education, he has been teaching at various business schools. He designed a master's degree program in advanced management based on positive psychology and behavioral economics and was its academic director at a European business school for eight years. He is an affiliated faculty member of Singapore Management University (SMU), where he is also the lead teacher of the Mindfulness-based Strategic Awareness Training (MBSAT) program for MBSAT teachers. He is the author of Mindfulness-based Strategic Awareness Training, published by Wiley Blackwell (2017), and the MBSAT Workbook by the same publisher (2023).

Juan Humberto Young holds a master's in Public Administration (MPA) from Harvard University, an MBA from the School of Business at the University of Chicago, a master's in science in risk management from L. Stern School of Management at New York University, a doctorate in management from Case Western Reserve University, Weatherhead School of Management, a master's in applied positive psychology from the University of Pennsylvania, and a master's in Mindfulness-based Cognitive Therapy (MBCT) from the University of Oxford. Has also completed studies in applied neuroscience at King's College.

He maintains a private consulting practice for clients and a micro coffee farm in Boquete, Panama, where experts say the best specialty coffee in the world is grown. He holds a first Dan (black belt) in Aikido from the Japanese Aikikai Foundation and the Aikido Foundation of Switzerland.

Preface:
The Genesis of this Book

Tutto è già stato fatto.
Tutto è già stato detto.
Tutto è già stato scritto.
Però nessuno ha guardato, nessuno ha ascoltato e nessuno ha letto.
E così tutto comincia da capo.[1]

Why would a businessperson write a book on improving mental well-being and the quality of life? I am frequently asked this question. There are several reasons, but I will limit my answer to personal, concrete experiences and the conclusions I drew from them. In part, this book is also a reflection on my personal journey.

Experience has taught me that shaping one's life is about strategic awareness and skillful decision-making, and I realized that both could be trained. Strategic awareness has also helped me uncover options under challenging situations and flourish despite adversity. Repeating more of the same, as the aphorism suggests, is neither desirable nor unavoidable. When I first noticed the verse, it seemed a pessimistic worldview and somewhat a cautionary message to me. On second thought, I interpreted it as an invitation to train and teach new skills: the ability to look, listen, and mind for a flourishing life. This is what this workbook is about.

Overcoming Adversity

Years ago, I developed a neurological condition manifested by uncontrollable twitching on the left side of my face. As it persisted, I consulted with medical doctors, but they could not provide me with a precise diagnosis. Some spoke of a tumor, some of Bell's palsy, the condition that affected Sylvester Stallone. The condition worsened when I moved to Switzerland and had to cope with the stressors of a new environment, a distinct language, and foreign culture. There were moments when my face was partially distorted as the spasms almost closed my left eye and pulled the left side of my mouth towards the ear, giving me an angry look even when I was in a good mood. This often led to awkward social interactions, misinterpretations, and misunderstandings, especially in business and teaching. Over time, an uncomfortable pressure built up in the left half of my face, extending down to the collarbone, that bothered me

---

1 "Everything has already been done.
  Everything has already been said.
  Everything has already been written.
  But no one has looked, no one has listened, and no one has read.
  And so, everything starts all over again."
  An Italian aphorism on the walls of a fine restaurant in Varese, Northern Italy.

round the clock. Eventually, I met a Chinese physician and underwent painful, in-depth acupuncture for many years to control the conditions, at least to some degree. Despite this socially debilitating state, I built a prosperous professional career, reaching a high level in the hierarchy of UBS, one of the top Swiss global banks in Zurich, and launching several successful business initiatives.

I continued to expand my academic education with the freedom I gained through my entrepreneurial activities concerning time management and financial flexibility. Besides my studies and ongoing business activities, I could dedicate myself to teaching, an activity I always cherished because of the inspiring relations with students and participants, the intellectually stimulating topics, and the opportunity to contribute to society. While teaching a class on Mindfulness-based Strategic Awareness Training (MBSAT) in Zürich, a middle-aged student noticed my condition and told me she had had the same affliction, combined with incredible pain. She encouraged me to see the neurosurgeon who had completely cured her with microsurgery.

After consulting with this physician, I finally got diagnosed after over two decades of suffering. The neurosurgeon explained there was a tiny vein in the skull behind the ear, compressing a facial nerve that caused the twitching. He said the causes were unknown, and the condition could affect anyone. The good news was that it was operable. The risks involved in the procedure were losing hearing capacity or, even worse, twitching and permanent disfigurement. Both risks, he said, were manageable thanks to advances in microsurgery.

Now, things were in my hands; considering the risks, I needed to decide whether to proceed with the surgery. I set about doing my homework for the decision. First, I gathered more information about the physician and his team and discovered that they were some of the best surgeons performing this type of intervention (vein decompression). Also, now having the diagnosis, I learned more about the condition. For example, there are two types, one with unbearable facial pain. My student had this type and told me she had thought seriously about ending her life before finding a physician. The second type - which is what I had - is without pain. Here, the critical problem is that people invariably feel stigmatized, leading to social isolation and, most of the time, depression. With a certain resilience, I avoided falling into depression or social isolation.

Having decided to have the surgery, I took preventive measures with strategic foresight to cope with the next phase. First, I intensified my physical and mental training to prepare for the intervention; as a long-time kickboxer and Aikido practitioner, I was already in a relatively good physical condition. I further stepped up the training. Also, as a longtime meditator, I intensified my meditation practice to reinforce my mental strength. I had learned to meditate many years ago, as, in my search for ways to ease the condition, I had met an Indian teacher who taught meditation techniques to calm afflictions. Second, I took a radical decision in case the outcome of the surgery would be adverse. In this case, I was going to change the focus of my professional life. I prepared to abandon my professional activities, move out of Switzerland, and live on my farm in Central America. There, I would have less social interaction, intensify my agribusiness activities, and dedicate myself to writing in solitude. Luckily, I did not have to resort to this option, and my strategically aware preventive training and meditation paid off by shortening my recovery in the hospital from two weeks to 3 days.

When I opened my eyes coming out of the anesthesia, I felt a completely new person. The 24 hours of permanent pressure on the left side of my face that I had endured for decades was gone; I felt fresh in my face, and I could hardly believe how I had lived a significant part of my adult life with that debilitating condition.

The critical question is why I did not fall into social isolation or depression, despite such a severe neurological constraint in my life. How could I move forward and create a productive, flourishing professional and private life when so many others succumbed to depression, isolation, and loneliness? There are two main reasons that have to do with mindset and how I managed my adversity. First, I could separate the real suffering resulting from the physiological condition (the uncontrollable, permanent twitching in my face) from adding self-inflicted torment that would have resulted from ruminating about the disease. I recognized the situation without adding unhelpful thinking, never bemoaning the situation or lamenting. I believe it was this attitude that immunized me against depressive states. This way of minding adversity is a lesson taken from ancient Asian Psychology and part of this workbook's training.

Second, I could turn the adverse condition into a source of constructive information to help me with my social interactions, a kind of smart heuristic (Gigerenzer et al., 2022). As you will learn in this book, computational neuroscience suggests that our brain builds generative models of the world, driven by beliefs. Without being aware of it, I could create a generative model of social interaction based on beliefs about how people reacted to my twitching face; people who responded negatively in their body language I avoided socially and professionally, and those who were indifferent to or even curious about the impairment were the contacts I cultivated. I believe this "theory of mind" helped me to predict relatively well the quality of relationships, and judging by the results; it has worked well for me, as I could reduce Free Energy (avoiding decision mistakes), which, as you will learn in this book, is a critical success factor for conducting a productive professional and private life.

During my studies in positive psychology and neuroscience, I took several tests as part of my training. Three characteristics, amongst others, kept emerging as steady elements of my character. A salient feature was my strategic orientation manifested in an ability to see complex patterns, create simulations based on the patterns, anticipate difficulties, and generate solutions. A second character element that stood out was curiosity and an openness to seek new experiences and take risks to reap the gains from innovative thinking and behaviors, combined with a readiness to absorb the costs, if things did not go according to plan. The third feature that ranked high amongst my character themes was zest and vitality - a theme that comprises two aspects of human functioning: mental and physical. Zesty and vital individuals tend not to wear out. They are enthusiastic, reflecting a high level of playfulness. I do not doubt that these three elements did indeed help me cope with the tough neuro-physical and cultural challenges in my life. Not that I was born with these themes engrained in my personality; we all have these traits embedded in our personality. The challenge is to mobilize them.

Once I learned the science behind the psychology of traits, I could easily map these character elements to my BETA in dealing with my condition and situation, for example, body sensations and thoughts (the "B" and "T"), anticipating difficulties, exploring new ways of dealing with them and actions and emotions (the "A" and "E"), moving forward with drive, energy, and playfulness. The entire Part 1 of the training program (Session 1-4) is dedicated to BETA, its components, and their synchronization.

The most important about these discoveries is that all these resources can be mobilized and cultivated, and all required skills are trainable! The constraint of my situation prompted me to activate and intensify these characteristics to overcome the hurdles and become more resilient. I firmly believe that anyone can do it. Again, this is what this workbook is about.

Uncertainty in Today's Environment

Through this challenging, intense experience, my interest in brain functions and neuroscience developed not to satisfy intellectual curiosity about a fashionable, scientific subject but out of vital practical concern and the need to understand the consequences of the procedure I was planning. I spent more than a year studying and deliberating before I had the surgery. I wanted to know how my cognitive processing capacities could be affected if there could be complications. Because of my deep dive into the practicalities of brain functions, I fathomed the critical importance of the most complex organ and processing system on earth that controls our thoughts, memories, emotions, and innumerable other, mostly automatic functions, including all the processes that regulate our body, from temperature to breath to digestion and so forth. Once I grasped the intricacy of the brain, it was an obvious conclusion that the brain, and hence neuroscience, is central to our well-being. This led me to search for and design pragmatic ways to integrate related science into the MBSAT protocol.

It also dawned on me that my personal experience of coping with uncertainty, adversity, and fundamental change in life is quite characteristic of what most people go through in these turbulent and disruptive times. I discovered that many of the tools and methods I had intuitively applied on my path to achieving a prosperous life have a scientific underpinning and are well researched. In retrospect, it also became clear that there is no need to rely purely on intuition; the skills involved are trainable. These insights reaffirmed my motivation to continue teaching MBSAT and work tirelessly to make the MBSAT protocol as robust, meaningful, and applicable as possible for its active, non-clinical participants.

Today a growing number of individuals worldwide find themselves confused, fearful, and almost without direction, confronting a fast-changing world driven by the dangerous effects of microbiological organisms, climate change, acceleration of digitalization, and the related rapid cultural changes - conditions that are penetrating all aspects of post modern life. Confronted with this reality, young people ask themselves what their future will be; will they find jobs and build a family? Older individuals worry about the future of their professional life, asking themselves if they can keep their jobs and maintain their families. Many look with increased frustration to the politicians for solutions they don't have, or lack the courage to design and implement the creative solutions necessary to mitigate people's suffering.

This situation reminds me of when I moved to Switzerland to support my Swiss-German wife's desire to live closer to her elderly mother. I left behind a stable, well-organized, and promising future and moved voluntarily into an unknown environment that created states of confusion, fear, and uncertainty, similar to what many people are experiencing today. I thought about what Martin Heidegger, the philosopher, wrote about being thrown into the world to mean being thrown into our daily existence. Heidegger's concept of "thrownness", at least for me, suggested the need to find a level of understanding and effectiveness in the world that I was thrown into, implying the need to act, to cope the best I could. It reminds me as Aikidoka[2] of the Nage techniques, in which one is thrown during the training from different angles and directions, sometimes from the front, the back, etc. But as aikidokas, one also learns Ukemi techniques, meaning knowing how to fall and roll with the thrust, stand up and be ready for the next move instantaneously. With Ursula Reimer Sensei, I maintained a strict Nage/Ukemi practice routine over many years, training to always prepare for the following fall. In many respects, especially in adversity, life is like being in an Aikido dojo (gym), learning to fall, and standing up again without an aggressive attitude towards yourself and others. In MBSAT, we train and practice learning to fall and standing up by mobilizing and leveraging existing resources, abandoning non-adaptive legacy beliefs and habits, and exploring and developing new skills to cope and flourish even under demanding circumstances and environments.

MBSAT as Practical Training and the Question of Luck in Life

As an academically trained management practitioner, integrative scholar, and businessperson working towards implementing knowledge in daily life supported by science, I work at the intersection of research and practice in what could be called "implementation science": the science of translating research findings into practical applications for functional outcomes (Rapport et al., 2018). When I come across something that works well or, on the contrary, not so well, I try to understand the underlying science or theoretical knowledge related to the occurrence to better understand the issues. Therefore, in this workbook, you will often find examples of situations and experiences of others or my own in connection with theories that can explain what happened beyond anecdotal validity. In other cases, I find an interesting theoretical framework and seek to understand their practical applications in daily life. This is notably the case in this book with the Free Energy Principle and the Active Inference process, two compelling theoretical concepts I have tried to interpret and translate into practical knowledge that can be of value in our daily life.

MBSAT advances with the desire to better understand life experiences, especially challenging ones, and intends to extract practical knowledge from experiences that help people, myself included, cope and thrive in a challenging environment. Therefore, I have often reflected on my experience as a foreigner in Switzerland. After moving here, I was not sure whether I would make it; the odds were against me. My wife and I

---

2 A disciple of Aikido, the Japanese art of defense

both underestimated the difficulty and complexity I was confronting in my quest to find a good life compared to the one I had left behind in my home country. After a series of strategic moves and skillful decisions, however, I have reached a level of financial independence (if that counts as a proxy of success) that is hard to achieve. Not being a hedonic or overindulgent person, not into extravagant signs of affluence, but more into a eudemonic way of life, a life dedicated to finding the meaning of existence and helping others, the achieved financial freedom facilitated the pursuit of my development interests. The desire to understand life and my personal experiences brought me back to academic settings to learn and investigate the related issues rigorously. In particular, I wanted to better understand the conditions of flourishing. I knew my realizations were not the results of any superior intelligence. In 1987 I heard a lecture where Maturana, the influential biologist author of the autopoiesis theory of life, asserted that every human being capable of speaking is intelligent; therefore, as a speaking person, I knew I had at least average intelligence; at the same time, Maturana's insight implies that everyone has the potential for achievements and flourishing, but intelligence seems not to be the only factor. I felt I had to dig deeper for explanations.

Amongst others is the question of luck. D. Kahneman, the Nobel prize winner in economics, gives importance to a luck factor; I agree with him to a certain extent. For example, I was born in a quiet country and into a relatively affluent family, circumstances that can count as a lucky factor. Yet maybe there is a bit more than just plain luck. For example, even as my path toward senior management at UBS began with a lucky shot, more was required for sustained success. As my boss at my previous job at UBS was trying to fill a senior position as head of a department, he offered the task to various senior officials, but all declined, perceiving the job to be a dead end. The task was to merge and manage an extensive portfolio of several billions of assets with impaired value. Finally, I was offered the position. After reflection, I took this marginalized job position but asked my future boss to give me expanded authority to trade with the assets actively. He agreed. This move essentially converted what was initially a cost center into a profit center. After the first year of operation, we (my team and I) contributed several million to the bank's profit stream. My department became one of the most lucrative, using a benchmark "profit to departmental headcount" at the bank head office. Therefore, it turned out to be a lucky shot, yet engineered by me into an agency-based fortunate opportunity to make it attractive. I certainly was fortunate that my two Swiss bosses at UBS were outstanding individuals, able to understand the extraordinary difficulties I confronted on my path to building my career at UBS. They did their best to soften the impact of the odds against me as the only foreign department head.

Luck is random. I concluded one needs to engineer it and cultivate skills to hedge against its vagaries. In this context, skillful decision-making and the question of what makes some people do well despite challenging situations stayed in my mind.

Strategic Awareness is a Critical Factor in a Flourishing Life

How is it possible that some individuals embedded in a challenging environment can still do well? I hypothesized these individuals are naturally endowed with a particular sensibility manifest in a set of adaptive beliefs and a keen perception that allows them to sense what is latent in their environment and anticipate and predict the direction of environmental changes. These individuals could infuse general awareness with specific conditions, such as a natural curiosity, a broad openness to everything happening, and an ability to question and put their beliefs, prejudgments, and prejudices on hold. When these elements are integrated into general awareness, I understood that a strategic awareness emerges that allows these individuals to regain agency, hence some autonomy and mastery, despite living in challenging environments. By transforming the noisy, adverse signals from problematic situations into helpful knowledge that supports their decision-making and allows them to engage in skillful actions, they move forward and closer to doing well in their lives. Thus, strategic awareness may be the critical factor beyond average intelligence and luck that mediates and facilitates flourishing states.[3]

Eventually, my quest led me to enroll at Oxford University. The experience at Oxford University during my studies for the Master's in Mindfulness-based Cognitive Therapy (MBCT) was not what I expected; I thought I would enter an expansive learning space, with questioning and discussing leading to higher levels of understanding. However, it turned out to be a narrowly focused environment dedicated to training therapists to help people prevent the ravages of depressive relapses. It was a beautiful goal, and the teachers working there wrote the therapeutic reference protocol. Without question, the individuals active at Oxford Mindfulness Center are probably some of the best working on preventing depression worldwide. But that was not was I was looking for; I have never been depressed, and hardly any of the people I came in touch with through my work (clients, business partners, employees, etc.) had been depressed either. We may all have specific issues that need to be improved, but as I mentioned, there were hardly any clinical cases in my environment. I have to add that in my non-working environment; I have some experience with therapeutic needs because I have a bipolar daughter, a very successful businesswoman. In this regard, the issues of depression were not entirely irrelevant to me. So, during my years at Oxford, I learned groundbreaking depression-preventing techniques that helped me better understand my daughter and give her light fatherly suggestions for improving her condition. Yet the fact remained that clinical settings were not my natural environment.

Thus, my graduation project at Oxford University bore the seeds for a non-clinical protocol focusing on skills that enhance personal growth and flourishing instead of designing remedial interventions for mental health deficits. Based on my deep conviction that the elements for strategic awareness are trainable, I created Mindfulness-based Strategic Awareness Training (MBSAT) to train and develop the conditions that can lead to skillful decision-making. The protocol design started as part of my graduation project at Oxford University; after several design iterations over several years, it has taken its present form. Thus, MBSAT is the scientific substantiation of my hunch about what makes some people do well despite challenging situations.

---

3 The term strategic awareness is amply discussed throughout the book. Simply put, but not simplistically, it refers to the ability to recognize the saliency of events happening in our lives and the world around us – an ability with enormous potential to improve the quality of our lives.

Mindfulness in an Active Life and a Scientific Underpinning of Mindfulness

When thinking about mindfulness, many people associate it with a life of quiet mysticism, few external sensory impulses, and a focus on one's inner life. When I listen to the classical Indian music by Ravi Shankar and the Ragas from other Indian music masters, I can't help myself dreaming and visualizing living a simple nomadic life in ancient Asia, uncovering the deep mysteries of life. Before COVID-19, I used to go once a year or at least every two years on austere retreats to renew my spirit. Although I had many benefits from these intense, personal retreats, I also realized that a contemplative life is not my life nor my path; I enjoy being active, uncovering and creating opportunities that allow me to do well and that enable others and the environment to prosper. I am more attuned to the mindset expressed by a nun from the Nepalese 900-year-old Drukpa Lineage who said: "Lots of people think that as a Buddhist nun, all you do is just meditation, but we believe that helping others is our true religion. We think that merely sitting still in one place meditating is not the most effective way to be in the world these days."

For me, that is the actual game of life: doing well for oneself and others. In this sense, life means the challenge of living a "strategic, active, mystical, secular life." It is mystical because it is a mystery; there are no simple answers to life's fundamental/existential questions. It is strategic because in doing good to others and the environment, one also cares for oneself sustainably. It is secular; a life lived in the active, secular world instead of a monastic setting. Everyone can do it from the place we are in our lives. If you are a banker, the mystic and the mystery is to discover ways to optimize your profits and, at the same time, optimize your offerings for your customers and employees. If you are a politician, create laws and policies that benefit not only one group of citizens but all, for example, laws that help businesspeople and the workforce. If you are a journalist, present news that is truly independent of who they favor. It is difficult to put into practice what I just described; but that is the mystery of life that needs to be decoded, and it is the genuine job of a strategic, active, and aware individual to uncover and create sustainable solutions that lead to a prosperous life for themselves and others. I designed this workbook for active people in the game of life that is played in a world that is becoming increasingly volatile, uncertain, complex, and ambiguous (VUCA).

In my previous book, *Mindfulness-based Strategic Awareness Training - MBSAT*, I attempted to anchor the ideas of the MBSAT program in fundamental theories to create a rigorous foundation for the training protocol. I presented concepts from Positive Psychology, Contemplative Sciences, Cognitive-Behavioral Therapy, Behavioral Finance, Motivation Psychology, Risk Management, Systems Dynamics, and other disciplines in an integrated manner. Integrating these concepts allowed me to design a comprehensive training protocol that has proven very effective for a non-clinical population.

In writing this workbook, I continue with the motivation to present content and material anchored in accepted and validated science and combine the rigor of scientific findings and insights with a desire to find an objective function for the MBSAT protocol, intending to find an answer to the general question: What is it precisely that MBSAT trains, develops and creates? In that spirit, I expanded my research to investigate ideas from other areas that could help me find answers.

In my quest to bring scientific rigor to MBSAT, I stumbled upon an article by two neuroscientists, K. J. Friston and K.E. Stephan (2007). Reading this article changed my way of looking at life. It is a demanding piece to read for people like me who are not theoretical neuro-scientists; I read it several times and still didn't fully understand all the mathematical details. However, it set me on a path to study the ideas and work of path-breaking scientists and philosophers in Bayesian Cognitive Science (BCS) and computational neuro-scientists investigating and broadening the understanding of how carbon-based systems such as humans can live and thrive in a world where all systems are exposed to disorder and decay. All these bright minds are trying to answer Erwin Schrödinger's, the Nobel prize-winning physicist's fundamental question: how can it be explained that natural living organisms such as human beings can resist thermodynamics? The question refers to the second law of thermodynamics, which suggests in its most straightforward interpretation that all systems tend towards change and disintegration. However, living systems such as humans can combat this tendency by maintaining a level of order, keeping themselves in certain limited states that protect them at least momentarily from the certainty of total dissipation. In his 1944 book *What is Life?* Schrödinger's question, amongst others, was how is this possible? Over the past two decades, a computational neuroscientist, physicist of the mind, and psychiatrist, Karl John Friston, seems to have found a universal mathematical answer in what he calls the Free Energy Principle (FEP), formulated in its most condensed form as complexity minus accuracy (Friston, 2010). In practical terms, you can think of a situation when you enter a dark room full of uncertainty and potential complexity, as we don't know what is in front of us. What is the first thing you would do? You would switch on the light to increase the accuracy of your visual perception, thus reducing the chance of making an error by bumping into an obstacle and hurting yourself. FEP has excited serious, respectable scientists and philosophers of the mind who are actively taking part in a comprehensive research program, finding evidence to support FEP as a unifying explanation for perception, learning, and behavior and the mechanics behind human life and the mind. The research program of BCS is dynamic, comprehensive, and sophisticated, using highly complex mathematical language. However, given the far-reaching ambitions of these ideas, seeking validation for a unifying explanation of the human experience (thinking, learning, feeling, acting, perceiving), if the insights and the findings are to have relevance, they need to be made accessible to the public, who are the ultimate judges of their own experiences and can evaluate effectively if it is a workable function. I believe it is essential to design simple, easy-to-implement practices based on these ideas and principles to help people improve their living conditions.

I must clarify again that I am neither a physicist, theoretical neuro-scientist, nor an advanced theoretical statistician. Therefore, I am not looking at FEP from a pure, mathematical model but more a narrative of a grand meta-theoretical framework from which concepts with solid explanatory power can be extracted to help formulate insights to support a workable objective function for MBSAT and translate it into simple, guided applications to improve people's lives.

A Radically New Approach to the Mind

At their core, BCS models essentially suggest that we are not reacting beings getting stimuli from phenomena, interpreting them, and reacting by generating and enacting behaviors. For BCS, the opposite process is the case: the brain generates anticipations and predictions about what is going on in life that supports human cognitive and behavioral strategies.

Given that the validation of the predictions only becomes real in the near or more distant future, an essential concern for these models of the brain is the accuracy of predictions: will the predictions be close to reality? Or far away from our expectations? Or somewhere in between? The discovery of these ideas was highly liberating for two reasons:

a) They give me the feeling that my life is not entirely random and that I can shape it by volition. Thus, they gave me a sense of empowerment and of having some control over my life.

b) It confirmed what I had always thought: that inferring the future is critically important. It is a strategic mind that underlies the quality of decisions and influences the conditions of one's life.

Here I found the answer to an issue I have always had with mindfulness-based programs and their emphasis on cultivating "non-judging" and the attitude of just "being" in the present moment. I now understand why it is so hard for people to be in the present moment without judging. Suppose the brain/mind is indeed predicting. In that case, it will constantly be in the business of making predictions and updating data, beliefs, and parameters, thus preparing for more accurate predictions in the future. But given the uncertain nature of predictions, the mind can't avoid unconsciously evaluating and judging the accuracy of the predictions. Therefore, it is naturally hard for the mind not to be judging in the present moment. Recently, I spoke with the CEO of one of the three largest reinsurance companies in the world. As we were talking, he told me that every time he decided (after having enacted a prediction about what he expects to happen), he still keeps simulating alternative scenarios on how his decision could go wrong; he is evaluating the impact of prediction errors. His mind is engaged in what I call "present predictive awareness", a state equivalent to "Strategic Awareness", meaning being in the present moment and building skillful simulations about the future—in other words, evaluating the scale of prediction errors to keep a low ratio of prediction errors to predictions, as precise predictions are the basis for skillful effective decisions, which is MBSAT's primary focus.

The present moment, most mindfulness-based programs emphasize is just one of several dimensions we need to keep in mind. Decisions only take effect on a future time scale, with outcomes that may be experienced seconds later (for example, drinking a glass of water, resolving our expected dehydration) or on a longer time scale, such as decisions about whom to marry, what job offer to accept, or should you have children.[4]

After spending over two years immersed in the literature of Bayesian Cognitive Science and computational neuroscience reading scientific, technical papers with terms borrowed from physics, statistics, information theory, and philosophy of the mind, all very abstract and theoretical in their formulation, I have come to a place where I believe I have a valuable understanding of these ideas and the insight and intuition to integrate them into the MBSAT training protocol. MBSAT is an ideal practical conduit

---

4 The importance of inferring the future validates a hunch I had already as a child. One day – I was about 15 - my father asked me what I wanted to do later in life, confident that I would want to follow the family tradition of Certified Public Accountants (CPAs). To his consternation I replied: "I don't want to work as a CPA or auditor looking at the past. I want to work in the MCD (management consulting division) looking at the future."

for the Free Energy Principle (FEP) and BCS ideas. I designed MBSAT under the premise that the lack of Strategic Awareness equated to a lack of precision in perception and prediction, which leads to prediction errors, unskillful actions, and decision errors that create difficulties in people's lives. Erroneous predictions and predictions lacking accuracy often lead to unskillful contextual decisions. With MBSAT, I aim to help people improve the quality of their choices with specific training to enhance the quality of their predictions and reduce the frequency and scale of prediction errors.

The theoretical logic of FEP and BCS, combined with the practical orientation of MBSAT, appears predestined to provide a reliable intervention to improve people's lives. It would be a loss for human development to keep these ideas limited to their clinical setting and not expand them to non-clinical environments. MBSAT, since its development almost a decade ago as a skill-building, non-clinical protocol, has experienced an organic growth evoking interest in the business community, the public in different spheres, and governments. In Singapore, the government has recognized MBSAT as a valuable, innovative intervention and included it in its national skill-building program, subsidizing participants in MBSAT courses. Also, at Singapore Management University's (SMU) Mindfulness Initiative under the direction of Prof. Jochen Reb, we have designed programs for training future MBSAT teachers. In addition, the SMU Academy runs several times a year; successful government tuition subsidized MBSAT eight-week programs for Singaporeans and Singaporean residents.

I sincerely hope that this workbook will enable readers and MBSAT practitioners to recognize the beautiful simplicity and explanatory effectiveness of the Free Energy Principle operating in their lives and institutions and learn to mind its force as a resource they can leverage to improve the quality of their lives.

Necessary Caveats

I realize that in a changing world, theories and ideas also change. By placing a strong emphasis on CBS, especially on the views of specific scientists, I am taking a risk because these theories and ideas might be contested. However, I believe it is an acceptable risk. If one equates Free Energy Minimization with reduction of prediction errors, consequently with fewer decision-making errors, things will be ok for MBSAT.

Common sense suggests that excellent decisions are the ones without errors in their formulation and implementation. However, sometimes there is also something positive resulting from mistakes. In Positive Psychology, questionable mathematical or statistical validity ideas are still helpful. A friend of mine published a paper with a physicist colleague advocating the cultivation of an ideal ratio of positive emotions to negative emotions. They even suggested an optimal ratio for living a flourishing life. Years later, scientists proved that the mathematics on which they based the ratio was wrong. I spoke with my friend, who told me that the math was faulty, but that it didn't diminish the concept's usefulness. Indeed, common sense suggests that having a higher proportion of positive emotions than negative emotions in life is a valid path towards well-being. In the same vein, I argue that even if the theoretical apparatus of CBS ideas were to be dis-confirmed, the ontological soundness of the principle would remain: deciding with fewer prediction errors.

Finally, in this book, you will find references to many people's experiences; this reflects that as a practitioner academic, my lab is the general active experiences of life instead of an academic lab performing trials and experiments; life experiences are our actual trials. Sometimes they work, and sometimes they don't. The neuroscientist L. Feldman Barrett (2020) said that most psychological trials fail as they don't account for the dynamics of a predictive brain, which never sits still awaiting a stimulation, but continuously generates predictions to perceive, collect evidence, act and decide what to do next. Therefore, the anecdotes described in this book are best viewed as the result of predictive experiences in the living lab and not perfect silver-bullet solutions or expressions of life expertise.

MBSAT as a Developmental, Proactive Training for Non-clinical Participants

An important caveat regarding this program is to realize that this workbook is not a problem solver and cure-all for people with severe deficits. Individuals with serious mental issues such as depression, chronic stress, social inadequacies, or other painful conditions should seek help from other, more appropriate clinical interventions. Essentially, MBSAT is conceived as a NON-clinical intervention to improve people's quality of everyday life and to invigorate their mental health as defined by the World Health Organization, namely "a state of well-being in which the individual realizes his or her own abilities, can cope with the normal stresses of life, can work productively and fruitfully, and is able to contribute to his or her community," and this only happens when people improve the quality of their decision-making.

In this spirit, I have designed this program as a proactive strategy for thriving and growing. The book is the fruit of my journey seeking to live a skillful life balancing my desires and material ambitions with the esthetics and practicality of doing good. It is a life that reflects the essence of being truly human as reflected in all spiritual traditions: a life of honesty, integrity, and respect; genuine kindness, reconciliation, loyalty, and wisdom; not harming others nor myself or the environment. The hope is that readers understand the book as an invitation, source of inspiration, and practical guide to living an active, flourishing, and meaningful life based on these values and qualities.

MBSAT
Mindfulness-Based
Strategic Awareness Training

A Suggestion on How
to Read this Book

The challenge of this workbook is to motivate the mentally healthy target population who have no urgent remedial needs to actively engage in understanding and practicing.

The recommendation, therefore, is to read the preface first (many readers tend to skip prefaces habitually or return to them later). The preface provides you with a summary of my experience and how MBSAT came about based on the lessons life taught me. Having confronted many tough challenges successfully, these experiences stand for the essence of the proposed training and can best outline what you may expect to learn yourself from the program.

It might also be the case that you want first to understand what you embark on before committing yourself to train. For this reason, the first three chapters provide a conceptual summary of the computational neuroscience informing MBSAT, and Chapter 4 offers an overview of essential terms and concepts.

While understanding conceptually is important, practice is the key to reaping the full benefits of the MBSAT training program. Ironically, clinical populations with serious afflictions (depression, psychosis, anxiety disorders, etc.) are usually motivated at once to engage with the training interventions as they seek relief. In contrast, healthy individuals who "merely" seek increased well-being usually feel less urgency to practice and tend to be very busy, so even a few minutes of daily practice is a challenge for personal time management.

Based on my experience in teaching and training in groups as well as 1:1 and based on in-depth interviews with people who read and trained with the previous book, the *MBSAT manual*, I could identify three main learning styles and respective groups of readers and MBSAT participants. How you can benefit from reading this book and working with it essentially depends on how you build and integrate new knowledge and skills, what stimulates your interest and how your motivation gains momentum.

The three learning-style groups I came across are the following:

◉ **CO Group:**

   If you are part of this group, you prefer to first understand at a COgnitive level what you are going to engage in. Before switching on your new tv, gadget, or computer you prefer to have a look at the manual or before engaging in a new endeavor (a new diet, sport, professional association, etc.) you gather information to understand what the new venture implies for you.

◉ **TR Group:**

   If you like to TRy things out before you invest time or energy, you are typical of this group. You are more on the practical side of things. Only when you find practical value or meaning in an endeavor do you feel like going deeper at a rational level and trying to understand the conceptual ideas, underpinning science, and intricacies.

- **MO Group:**

  Perhaps you like to follow the MOod of the moment and feel neither very close to the CO group nor the TR group. In some instances, you desire to engage cognitively and study things before trying them out. On other occasions, it is the opposite: you try first and might come back later to find out why things work.

The best method to acquire new knowledge and skills doesn't exist. All three learning styles are effective, provided that you are aware of how you best learn and can sustain your motivation.

Here are some suggestions on how you can gain the most from this workbook based on your personal way of learning.

- Whatever your learning style may be, the recommendation is to read the preface first and then determine your main learning style.

- Do you recognize yourself mostly in the description of the CO group? If yes, you probably can benefit most from delving first into Part 1 and reading the first three chapters. You will learn a lot about state-of-the-art cognitive-behavioral neuroscience of human development in a condensed and easy-to-understand way. Once you move to the practices you already have a solid theoretical base.

- Are you the type who likes to try out things and experiment? If your answer is yes, you are more of a plug-and-play type or learning-by-doing individual. In this case, you can start with Chapter 4 of Part 1. This chapter provides a kind of starter kit of principles and terminology. Then you can directly engage with the practices in Part 2. You will immediately reap the benefits of the techniques.

- Finally, if you sometimes read the instructions first and sometimes prefer the plug-and-play approach, then the safe way for you to proceed is also to start reading Chapter 4. Afterwards you can work through the training sessions at your own pace and whenever you feel the need to understand more in-depth the theoretical underpinning of techniques you can find the required information in Part 1.

These are suggestions for leveraging your learning and training style. In whatever group you are, you can always move between Part 1 and Part 2 of the workbook. For example, you might have done some of the practical sessions and feel the need to understand more in detail at a conceptual level; in that case, you can return to Part 1 and read up on foundations and concepts.

To make the most of the MBSAT training program, the combination of cognitive understanding and practical know-how has proven optimal. It is vital to engage with the practices, that is to apply the doing mode of learning. Also essential in MBSAT is increasing your personal understanding of how to improve your levels of well-being and what the science is that drives this knowledge. In any case, the most important thing is to get started.

As you read the first three conceptually based chapters you will find ideas and concepts repeated in different contexts and illustrated with different examples. This is intentional. The purpose is to explain some of the more theoretical concepts from different angles to facilitate understanding and to expand and deepen the comprehension of more subtle themes in the book.

In any case, I believe that the challenge of any book on human development like MBSAT is that it needs to stretch the readers' minds and invite them to actively engage in the practices while at the same time making reading and practicing enjoyable.

About the Companion Website

This book is accompanied by a companion website:

www.wiley.com/go/young/mbsatworkbook

The website includes handout and audio files.

PART 1

FOUNDATIONS
AND CORE PRINCIPLES
OF THE MBSAT PROGRAM

*"Nothing is as practical
as a good theory."*

K. Lewin

Area of Poor
Free Energy
Minimization States

Area of Rich
Free Energy
Minimization States

Chapter 1

THE UNDERLYING BIOMECHANICS OF OUR BRAIN

Mindfulness-based Strategic Awareness Training Comprehensive Workbook:
New approach Based on Free Energy and Active inference for Skillful Decision-making,
First Edition. Juan Humberto Young.
© 2023 John Wiley & Sons Ltd. Published 2023 by John Wiley & Sons Ltd.
Companion website: www.wiley.com/go/young/mbsatworkbook

1.1 Flourishing in a World of "VUCA": Is it Possible?

We live in a world where Volatility, Uncertainty, Complexity, and Ambiguity, the so-called VUCA environment, is becoming more acute, accelerated, and pervasive. For example, the fatal effects of COVID-19, a viral pandemic, began in Wuhan province in China. In less than two weeks, its impact was felt in most parts of the world, with millions of people infected around the globe and thousands of deaths resulting from the pandemic. Another example is the widely circulated video of a police officer in the USA with his knee on the neck of an Afro-American until he died of asphyxiation, triggering a chain reaction of events and protests in the USA and worldwide. More recently the deadly European fight between two ethnically very close groups of people affecting the whole world is another more contemporary example of VUCA in the world. The notion that we live in a globalized "VUCA" world is now an accepted view widely shared by the general public and academia alike, and amply reported and manifest in the media.

The recognition that our lives are embedded in a volatile, complex, uncertain, and ambiguous world suggests an essential question: can we flourish and live to our full potential under the reality of VUCA? If the answer is no, we have no choice but to give up and wait for the final dissipation of life. However, if the answer is yes, the essential issue should be: how can we achieve a flourishing life amid an increasingly disruptive world?

A critical premise of this workbook is that one can increase flourishing levels by making wise, strategic decisions, minimizing our quota of predictions errors, and taking skillful actions that don't harm ourselves, others, and the environment. This premise suggests that continuously training and developing the art and science of strategic and skilled decision-making pays a "high quality of life dividend" as we become more autonomous, competent, and able to cultivate harmonious relations in life.

Before contemplating how to train for skillful decision-making, I believe it is valuable and necessary to first look at what our brains do. This is because the brain is, so to speak, the Chief Executive Officer (CEO) of our emotional, cognitive, and physical make-up. Nothing happens in our lives without the presence of our brain CEO; it is where the processing of all our experiences happens. We gain information and build knowledge used to decide and mobilize action through the brain. Thus, understanding the mechanics of the brain is essential to identify the elements and levers that need to be intentionally trained to increase our chances of a flourishing life by achieving a low average of prediction errors and a high level of skillful decision-making in a world of VUCA.

1.2 Free Energy Minimization: The Motivation Behind What the Brain Does

For decades, the dominant framework about what the brain does has been that it is in the business of reacting to our sensory stimuli. According to this framework, the brain responds to our impulses to accommodate its emotional, cognitive, and motoric infrastructure and make sense of what is happening in the external and internal world or in both aspects of an individual's life. This sensorial reactive paradigm has been increasingly questioned in the last 20 years, as scientists discovered that this would be an inefficient way of operating and too complex to maintain. "If your brain were merely reactive, it would be too inefficient to keep you alive. You are always being bombarded by sensory input… A reactive brain would bog down like your internet connection does when too many of your neighbors are streaming movies from Netflix… It would also be too expensive, metaphorically speaking, because it would require more interconnections than it could maintain." (Feldman Barrett, 2017, p. 60).

If the brain is not reacting to sensory inputs, what does it do then? The consensus in a growing group of neuroscience experts today is that it is predicting. What is it predicting? The anticipated needs of the human organism in a very broad sense, not only anticipating the effects of the VUCA environment but also anticipating the natural necessities of our body and of our psychological and social needs. Continual predicting is presumably the result of an evolutionary advantage designed to help us prevent the decay and degenerative characteristic of all advanced biological systems. For example, it predicts the need for hydration by recognizing an internal signal as thirst. Undoubtedly, it is easy to understand the advantage of an anticipatory action of drinking water before entering deficit states of dehydration. A deferred reaction to drinking water when dehydrated would be counterproductive in terms of survival and evolution. The advantage of anticipating is evident in all areas, whether you anticipate the reaction of persons you interact with or simply predict, whether a dish is tasty or how long it will take to go to work. All those ceaseless and often trivial predictions serve the overriding purpose of keeping us alive and well.

So, how do brain and body realize and implement the anticipation of biological needs?

The principle that rules the anticipatory process is the minimization of energy, or what is called in computational neuroscience Free Energy. The field of computational neuroscience has its own terminology and for the sake of consistency and scientific rigor this workbook will stick to it. The term "minimizing" for example stems from underlying mathematical computations; it is used here as a short form for "reducing as much as possible" in everyday language.

Minimizing Free Energy allows individuals to stay within their biological and physical requirements for their self-organization and survival and to slow down decay and dissipation, which is the goal of brain activity (Friston & Stephan, 2007; Friston, 2009, 2010).

Technically, it is a theoretical informational quantity captured by the Free Energy Principle (FEP). In physics, energy is related to accomplishing a task. You could compare it, for example, to the energy necessary to move your car from A to B, let's say, from Zurich to Milan. Free Energy as an informational quantity is conceived as the adverse effects on an individual's whole being (in MBSAT terminology on the integral BETA comprising Body sensations, Emotional sensations, Thought processes, and Action impulses); it is the energy that is created from undesirable and unexpected states or situations, for example, when you enter a room and you experience difficulty breathing because of the unanticipated poor air quality of the room. It is a negative effect on our psychological, physical, and relational self, resulting from unexpected interactions with the changing and chaotic forces of Volatility, Uncertainty, Complexity, and Ambiguity (VUCA) in the environment. When we can minimize the adverse effects of VUCA on our BETA, we are minimizing Free Energy, and it helps us flourish; it helps us thrive and become creative. However, when Free Energy is left unbounded instead of reducing it, it creates disappointing, demoralizing, and disintegrating states in our BETA. You can think of Free Energy as a chaotic and potentially destructive force that needs to be channeled and directed in constructive ways. This is what MBSAT training is about: MBSAT is a methodology to help us learn from the adverse effects of Free Energy, to domesticate and master it and lastly thrive in a VUCA world. Wrestling with Free Energy is an integral part of living and in the process we become resilient and resourceful.

An easy way to conceptualize the Free Energy principle is by looking at Figure 1.1. The mustang, a wild horse full of impetuous, untamed force, is an analogy for Free Energy. If his vehement nature is left unattended, it can seriously hurt you and cause great harm. However, if one is able to domesticate the horse, which is the equivalent of minimizing Free Energy, its strength and dynamism can be put to good use and become a valuable resource as the illustration shows.

According to Friston, the Free Energy Principle, it can take different forms, briefly described in the following paragraphs with an attempt to explain the concepts in an easy-to-understand manner. K. J. Friston is an outstanding neuroscientist and a pioneer of brain imaging who has dedicated his lifework to understanding how the human brain works.

The Nature of Free Energy in MBSAT

A wild destructive force, when uncontrolled

A valuable resource, when minimized and used well

Figure 1.1 The Nature of Free Energy in MBSAT

BIOMECHANICS OF OUR BRAIN

1.2.1 Free Energy as posterior divergence

Free Energy can manifest itself as a posterior divergence, a difference between what one perceived while it was happening and the natural causes of the sensory generating an element of surprise, when the initial perception and the feedback from the environment diverge. For example, imagine that you hear a delicate piece of music with a wonderful violin playing, and you visualize a male musician with his instrument. You ask your friend about the musician who is playing, and she replies it is Hilary Hahn. To your surprise, she is a woman. "She plays wonderfully," you said to your friend. Ok, now you know, and you make a note internally to yourself that women can play the violin as well as men. You just updated your perceptual model of violin players to include women. Your brain model of violin players is now more complete, so next time you hear someone playing the violin, your perceptual inference (your anticipated judgment of who is playing) will include both women and men as possible musicians, which leads to fewer states of surprise. You will be less subject to surprise and, therefore, will minimize Free Energy. This is an example of how dealing with Free Energy can result in a gain. In the same way as Free Energy is an integral part of life, so are surprises. It all depends what we are capable to make of them.

1.2.2 Free Energy as prior divergence minus accuracy

Prior divergence implies a difference between your anticipated beliefs about the causes of what is happening in the world and the sensory data you then observe minus an element of accuracy. The more accurate the anticipation has been, the smaller the divergence and the more success in minimizing Free Energy. For example, you can imagine the following situation.

You are looking for a home address. As you know the area, you can quickly find the address and anticipate high accuracy levels. However, as you get close to your friend's house, you find traffic signs of rerouting because of road works, prompting you to make a long detour. You lose your orientation, as it compromises the accuracy of your prior belief about getting there; therefore, you are generating free energy. To correct the situation you drive more slowly, searching for street signs and house numbers until finally, you find the expected location. Here, losing your orientation (accuracy) led to your slowing the action of driving, which corresponds to reducing the complexity of the previous predictive actions and minimizing Free Energy in the process.

1.2.3 Free Energy as expected energy minus entropy

Free Energy can also be conceived as expected energy, which implies a generative model of the world in our brains corresponding to the joint probability of a sensation and its causes happening together, minus the entropy (disorder) that might affect recognizing the causes of the sensations.

Imagine having your teeth checked, and the dentist tells you need some new filling. She explains she could give you anesthesia to make it less painful. This will cause a numb feeling that will take about half a day to wear off, and you may also experience some difficulty when eating. Or she can repair the tooth without anesthesia, avoiding the inconvenient after-effects, yet it will be a bit painful during the half-hour while she works on the tooth. You choose to go without. While the dentist is doing her work, you feel the pain (your sensation), but you have expected it because you were told about it. No surprise here, as in your brain generative model, "dental work without anesthesia" can indeed cause pain; therefore, knowing that is the fact, you can minimize Free Energy (surprise) and get over it relatively well. There is also no complexity; you are in a state of high accuracy and slowing down entropy, which is the only thing you can do in this situation. It is actually all we can do as humans in the long run. In the film *The Dark Tower*, Matthew McConaughey says to Idris Elba: "We both know that no matter who crosses the finish line first, the universe will die out of entropy. Death always wins, that's the deal". Yet, in the meantime, the purpose is to have a meaningful and flourishing life.

1.2.4 Minimizing Free Energy

As we can infer from these examples, minimizing adverse effects of the unexpected helps minimize Free Energy and vice versa. In MBSAT, when we speak of minimizing Free Energy (FE), it means reducing the adverse effects of VUCA. For practical purposes in MBSAT, FE can be conceived of as an unregulated, wild and potentially harmful energy as mentioned above and illustrated in Figure 1.1. By now you are probably also getting familiar with the term minimizing, used throughout this workbook as a synonym for "reducing as much as possible" in line with the terminology of computational neuroscience.

Here is another example from everyday life to make the concept of Free Energy as practical and hands-on as possible, while still rooted in and congruent with its highly scientific and theoretical foundations. Imagine going to your favorite Indian restaurant and ordering your favorite dishes. However, when the food is served, you notice it looks different, and when you taste it, you realize it is not as delicious as it used to be. You are disappointed and maybe upset. You take action by asking the waiter about what is happening. The waiter and the manager, who also approached, explain that there had been a policy change; they are now specializing in buffet and employed a new cook. Dishes ordered while sitting at a table are now part of the à-la-carte menu, and this is what the new cook is not so good at, the manager admits. Here, we can observe the Free Energy Principle in action. You predicted a state of satisfaction by deciding to eat at a place you know well and where you like the quality. By choosing your favorite restaurant, you expect to reduce VUCA. Still, now you find yourself in a state of dissatisfaction despite having made a careful prediction and a safe decision from your point of view by going to a risk-free restaurant with the prospect of low VUCA, enabling you to minimize Free Energy. The difference between the desirable predicted states you were expecting and the states of dissatisfaction you are now experiencing is a surprise. Whenever you are confronted with this kind of surprise or deficit, in whatever dimension it could be (a quantity, a direction, a magnitude, a certain quality, etc.), the Free-Energy Principle is at play, and the situation will obliterate more Free Energy than anticipated and desired. Therefore, to keep ourselves in a state of flourishing, one should always seek to minimize Free Energy. The goal of MBSAT is to build the strategic awareness and the adaptive skills needed to achieve this state of flourishing despite challenges and adversity.

Action and acting are essential components of the Free Energy Principle. Acting is what will help reduce total Free Energy by shaping the world around us. Action can comprise a perceptual change to minimize uncertainty (inquiring about the causes and knowing the causes of an event, such as the food not being to one's liking). With active adjustment of our beliefs, one increases the accuracy of expected events, in this case enjoying the expected tasty dishes by asking who is cooking today.

The example of the eating-out experience can also give additional insights. It shows amongst others that by minimizing Free Energy (VUCA), one is maximizing the evidence of one's prediction models; here, the belief was "eating my favorite dishes at my favorite Indian restaurant will give me a lot of satisfaction." Suppose the food conformed to your expectations, then you would have had the evidence for your prediction/ decision model: your "eating at my preferred restaurant" belief has been confirmed. However, because of the error in prediction (assuming the usual way of cooking, which proved mistaken), the belief turns out to be inaccurate.

Minimizing Free Energy by avoiding surprise and its adverse effects drives human life and functions as a unifying factor. It is a universal principle of perceiving, learning, acting, and conducting our lives. It not only shapes our existence but is also at the basis of how our institutions function and adjust and learn. Friston and Stephan (2007) suggest that Free Energy and the Free Energy Principle (FEP) are at the core of all human activities. For example, we can observe the FEP operating in one of contemporary life's most important cultural institutions: business organizations. The FEP and its functioning in the world of business merit a closer look.

In business, the overriding goal is profit: it determines the value of a company and is essential for its survival. Profits result from a simple equation: revenues less cost equal to profit (R–C = P). CEOs and managers responsible for for-profit centers are constantly seeking strategies to increase earnings by reducing the firm's cost structure, amongst other policies.

Surprise will be defined as any unexpected increase in the firm's cost structure or reduction of the revenue stream leading to lower profits, hence an undesirable outcome. Thus, business managers spend a significant amount of time and effort minimizing the magnitude and quantity of costs to build evidence for increased profits. This is a practical example of how the Free Energy Principle operates at the core of business settings.

One needs to appreciate that a manager who only minimizes costs will eventually compromise the future survival of the firm. To ensure revenues in the future, business leaders need to take actions that increase strategic costs by investing in new products, services, production capacity, etc., to stay competitive and guarantee the novelty of the company's offering. However, these particular types of strategic cost-increasing initiatives will naturally increase complexity and uncertainty (VUCA) in the business system. In evaluating the quality of decisions, CEOs or managers will need to maintain a cost function with a low average of predictions errors such as faulty products, poor services, unskillful choices, etc. Some mistakes are inevitable; the key is to stay within the optimal tolerance of prediction errors to maintain the organization's viability. This tolerance limit is called the upper bound of the Free Energy Principle (FEP). It is a type of tipping point beyond which damage becomes very impactful, if not irreversible. However, most of the time, this upper bound limit cannot be quantified precisely, especially in VUCA, when information is incomplete and changing rapidly. To avoid hitting Free Energy's upper bound, companies strive to contain and track prediction errors with strategic plans and budgets.

The equivalent of a manager focusing solely on reducing costs and never investing would be a person who locks herself in a dark room to avoid surprises. Eventually, the pervasiveness of VUCA and entropy will catch up, compromising her physical existence as a living being (Friston et al., 2012; Clark, 2017). To prevent passing from active living to lethargy or even death (an adverse phase-transition in the terminology of FEP), she will need to allow herself some prediction errors to learn to adapt to the changing environment skillfully. This implies that she will need to invest some of her "surprise expenses budget" by testing and experimenting, thus implicitly accepting some unavoidable errors. Again, in doing so, she needs to maintain the average of her prediction errors below a certain upper threshold of Free Energy, as this is the only strategy that increases her survival chances and keeps her vital integrity. Living in constant change and uncertainty, any organism, whether human or institutional, must conserve its vital force by minimizing Free Energy to survive. As Friston and Klaas write: "The Free-Energy Principle can be motivated, simply, by noting that systems that minimize their Free Energy respond to environmental changes adaptively." (Friston & Stephan 2007, p. 9).

To better grasp the Free Energy Principle (FEP), we may think of our environment as everything around us. We live in an environment, but we are not the environment. We differ from plants, dogs, buildings, cars, etc., apart from more complex phenomena like organizations or processes. It is like having an invisible wall separating us from the "out there" (everything that is not me), what neuroscientist K. Friston calls a Markov blanket. Therefore, we are not directly influenced by what surrounds us, yet the environment affects us indirectly through our senses (our BETA in MBSAT language). We habitually distinguish between things we like and dislike and things to which we are indifferent. We influence the environment with our actions by changing things we don't like or creating things we do like, thus creating an existential loop.

The German philosophers W. Weise and T. Metzinger suggest the following experiment. Imagine making a list of essential things we need to survive, and another with things that endanger our survival. The result would be a concise list of the things we need for survival: air (which is free), food and water for internal energy, a place for resting (sleep), a partner for reproduction, and a few more items. The list of potentially dangerous things to our survival is almost endless. Eating the wrong plants can make us sick; a dog can bite and infect us with rabies; we can fall from a building; a car can hit us; the air can be contaminated; a friend can betray us; we can get divorced, lose our jobs, etc., etc. All of this is chaotic energy, suggesting that we need to minimize the impact of this energy on our lives to keep ourselves alive. That is the Free Energy Principle in a practical nutshell.

So, how can we achieve the vital aim of minimizing Free Energy? The following section explains how the brain helps us in doing so.

1.3 The Bayesian Hierarchical Hypothesis of the Brain: How the Brain Minimizes Free Energy

The term Bayesian has been coined in reference to the English statistician and religious minister Thomas Bayes who wrote a pathbreaking paper on probabilities in the 16th century. Later the French statistician Pierre-Simon Laplace expanded the idea that became known as Bayes Theorem. It suggests that with new information, one can update a prior held subjective belief about an event and develop a new, evidence-based updated belief. It is a statistical approach that encourages discovery and exploration, as a person can change her previously held beliefs and opinions as she gains new knowledge and learns about new realities. This is the mindset MBSAT strives to convey.

Bayes' Theorem uses three elements to revise the probability of an event. A subjective belief called "prior" is based on experience. Another feature represents the "likelihood" of something you believe you are sensing, given your prior belief. By adjusting the "prior" based on the "likelihood" of the event, you arrive at the "posterior" corresponding to a new belief based on new observations after having taken care of some of the likely outcomes.

To illustrate these elements, imagine the following situation: John, a business executive, needs to travel to join an important meeting. As part of the requirements for travel, he takes a COVID-19 test, and it comes back positive (the posterior). It surprises him, because he doesn't have symptoms and feels well and therefore hypothesized that he shouldn't have the virus (his prior). He calls his friend Reto, a physician, who tells him that the test is very reliable and that only 1% of the population in the city is infected. Still, there are errors, with healthy people sometimes getting false positives (a positive test result, although the person is not infected). "The issue is to know," says Reto, "if your case is in the 1% of the wrong diagnosis. I needn't go through the math, but I would say that you have about a fifty-to-fifty chance of having the virus. Take a second test (new information). If the result is positive, then you know you are infected."

The illustrations below recount the conversation between the business executive and the physician and present the underlying math (Figures 1.2 and 1.3).

In simple words, one begins with an initial belief and gathers fresh evidence to lead to a new belief. In a nutshell, this leads to the formula: new belief = old belief + evidence.

For mathematically interested readers Figure 1.3 presents the detailed calculations. Obviously, hardly anybody would actually do the math. Instead of thinking in probabilities, most people think in percentages or apply rule of thumb derived from sampling the environment. Thus, our brain, more than a Bayes calculation machine, is a sampler of experiences.

Figure 1.2 Bayesian Questioning Mindset in MBSAT (I)

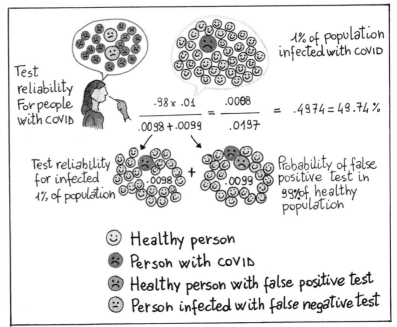

Figure 1.3 Bayesian Questioning Mindset: The Math (II)

Bayes formulations are data-driven models that have been crucial in developing and advancing modern Data Science. Amongst others, they are used extensively in Machine Learning, for example, when Netflix, Amazon, and many other online services collect data on their clients' preferences and use this information to recommend movies, books, and other products and services that they predict could be of interest for their clients. Similarly, spam systems in email programs also use Bayesian networks to classify emails as spam based on the user's prior experience. Emails sent to the trash are integrated into the learning process of the email program to recognize them in the future and send them directly to the trash bin, thus optimizing the users' email function. Self-driving cars use Bayesian predictive systems for calculating directions and regularly download satellite information for optimally updating and directing the autonomous vehicle towards destination points.

There are truly mind-boggling cases of machine learning. Google's DeepMind company developed a learning program they used to beat the Korean GO world master Lee Sedol; it was based on Bayesian Learning, using two learning algorithms to determine how helpful a move could be and another to choose actions. The playing program AlphaGo learned the moves from its opponent and updated its data bank to develop unexpected new moves, beating master Sedol four times out of five games.

At Harvard, I was lucky to study two semesters on Decision and Negotiation Analysis with the late famed Prof. Howard Raiffa who was a pioneer Bayesian statistician and the father of decision analysis. He taught us to maintain our beliefs flexible to update them when new information becomes available during negotiations. This flexibility of beliefs is now more critical than ever in times of VUCA.

1.4 The Relation Between the Brain and Bayes Theorem

As mentioned above, there is increasing consensus amongst neuroscientists that the brain is not reacting but is in the business of anticipating and making predictions about our needs to accommodate, adapt and improve people's survival opportunities in the changing VUCA environment. The critical question is, how does it do it?

The brief comment about Bayes Theorem in the preceding section presented a natural description of how Bayes' idea is used for inferring and predicting causes of phenomena, based on beliefs that can be updated with new evidence to formulate new beliefs and predictions. The Bayesian Hierarchical Brain Hypothesis in neuroscience suggests that the brain operates similarly. As we live in a VUCA world, there is no possibility of knowing all the causes of the phenomena we confront. The solution for the brain is to function as a chief prediction officer (CPO) based on prior experiences and beliefs. The brain has developed a mechanism that simply anticipates and predicts needs based on previous experiences and beliefs. As it receives new information through the senses, it either validates its predictions or updates the brain with new beliefs.

What entails this idea of a Bayesian Brain (BB)? "Bayesian Brain says that we are trying to infer the causes of our sensations based on a generative model of the world... If the Brain is making inferences about the causes of its sensations then it must have a model of the causal relationships (connections) among (hidden) states of the world that cause sensory input... It (the BB) provides a principled explanation for self-organization in the face of a natural tendency to disorder... A self-organizing system that minimizes its entropy (disorder) would appear to be making Bayesian inferences about its sensory exchanges with the environment, which of course, is just the Bayesian brain hypothesis." (Friston, 2012b, p. 1233). For the BB hypothesis, humans perceive reality under an implicit mechanism that looks similar to the principles underlying Bayesian inference, the statistical method explained above that has become very popular with data scientists. An example may help illustrate this reasoning.

Imagine that it is midnight, and you are in deep sleep. Suddenly, there is a knock on your door. You and your spouse wake up, go to the door and look out, but see nothing. Both of you wonder what it could be. You believe that someone is trying to rob you, as you remember that a neighbor was robbed a couple of weeks ago; your spouse believes that it is maybe someone in distress who needs help. Both decide that it is safer not to open the door and to abstain from finding out the cause of the knock in the middle of the night. The following day, as you pick up your mail in front of your house, your neighbor asks you, if you heard a knock last night. She tells you she also heard the knock and opened the door after talking to her husband. She found Mark, another neighbor, collapsed and suffering from a heart attack on her doorstep. They rushed him to the emergency and fortunately he is doing well now. This chain of events shows you a BB in action. The knock on the door is the initial event. A discussion about the likelihood of the cause followed it: depending on the weight or veracity one puts into a belief one can formulate different priors: a robbery attempt or a distress call. After gaining more data through the neighbor, the actual cause of the knock is revealed, namely an emergency call by another neighbor. This information now allows building the posterior.

Bayesian neuroscientists assert that this is the way our brains always work. The process relies on a generative model that has developed from prior experiences and generates inferences about the causes of phenomena and adaptive behavior patterns. Given that the brain is inside the skull, it has only access to phenomena through the senses; therefore, it is constrained to infer the causes of events (Ramstead et al., 2019). It has a de facto veil that separates it from the environment in the same way as the door in the example above separates the couple from the actual cause of the knock.

Thus, what the brain does non-stop is actively inferring about what is happening, with some subjective appreciation of trueness or falsehood about the causes, and evaluating and selecting adaptive actions to maintain viability in relation to proven states of survival. The brain is permanently inferring, thus seeking verification for our hypothesis (beliefs) to reduce prediction errors and free energy.

Here are some practical examples to further explain this process.

- You go to the office in the morning and notice your boss in the parking lot. You greet her in a friendly way; she answers back laconically and instantly turns away from you. "What is the matter?" you ask yourself. "Have I done something wrong? Or are there plans to fire me, given the difficult situation of the company?" These kinds of thoughts cross your mind. Only late in the afternoon you hear from a colleague that your boss has severe personal, non-work-related difficulties. Now you relax after spending most of the day worrying, wasting a lot of Free Energy on unnecessary apprehension.

- A manager sends an email with an attractive offer to one of the company's best customers. She hears nothing in return. Even after several more emails, still no response. She gives up, believing that the client bought the product from the competition. Only weeks later, she receives a message from the client, excusing himself for not responding earlier. He explains he has been in hospital in intensive care, fighting a COVID-19 infection. Now that he is back, he wants to set up an online meeting and discuss the offer.

The hidden causes of these situations (the terse response of your boss and the lack of response from the client) were resolved in retrospect after gaining clarity about the causes of events: family issues in the boss's case and COVID-19 in the client's case. The initial predictions were erroneous; only after sampling additional data were the individuals able to formulate new predictions ("Actually, I am not getting fired"; "I can still close a deal"). This is precisely what the brain has in common with Bayes Theorem: revising personal predictions after having sampled new information, thus moving from an initial subjective prior to a data-driven posterior. Ambiguous situations such as the illustrations above abound in daily life, often leading to errors in inferences that consume energy and create stress and unhappiness as the causes of the events remain uncertain. This makes it very hard to minimize Free Energy.

Of course the brain, as already mentioned, doesn't do these calculations in an explicit Bayesian statistical sense, but samples a couple of causes of an event. In the case of the knock on the door, the couple sampled two possibilities: some thief in front of the door or someone in distress; there could be more possible causes, but clearly, the couple couldn't represent all causes given the constraints of time, processing capacity and bounded rationality (Simon, 1991), so they settled on two possibilities each with an implicit probability. "The brain represents information probabilistically, by coding and computing with probability density functions or approximations to probability density functions." Knill and Pouget, (2004, p. 713). Simply put, this means that the reality from which we extract information to manage our life is not black and white but resembles a continuum of grey tones in an uncertain, changing, and ample VUCA space. Therefore, the best we can do is to hold helpful beliefs about the causes of reality that allow us to build good predictions as the basis of skillful decision-making (should they open their door, yes or no). And this is the Bayesian Hierarchical Brain in action. It is hierarchical because the sensory data move hierarchically from the bottom up to higher levels of cortical structures, moving sensory inputs that are then validated at each level of the cortical hierarchy. In the opposite direction it carries information as predictions, generated internally at the higher level of the cortical structures and validated at each level as they move down the sensory hierarchy. Messages pass through a cortical hierarchy in a bi-directional sense.

All this happens in split seconds. The brain with its billions of neurons that communicate at lightning-speed is a true marvel.

1.5 The Models in the Brain and Active Inference

The question, then, is how our beliefs about the causes of our sensations come about. Friston asserts as we have seen in the quote above (above Section 1.4; Friston, 2012b, p. 1233) that the brain is inferring the causes of our sensations based on a generative model of the world.

1.5.1 The brain models

Brain models are, in fact, a cluster of meanings of the things we perceive and show different values that an event can take. It relates values to decision-making; things we value trigger a decision to act and accomplish them; if we don't value certain things, we tend not to decide on them. In the example of the knock on the door, we can see that the wife and her husband attached different beliefs to the cause; thus, each of them had another value encoded in their BM concerning the event "knock on the door," but after coordinating their variational inferences they decided not to act on the signal, deciding not to open the door.

The make-up of the brain models is based on two mechanisms. One, based on experiences and beliefs about possible causes of an event and generating predictions, are the so-called Generative Models (GM); a second mechanism that observes data and recognizes causes of events is called the Recognition Models (RM).

Brain models are "a mathematical abstraction, comprising two related networks of mathematically modeled 'neurons.' One, the recognition network, works from the bottom up; it's trained on real data and represents them in terms of a set of hidden variables. The other, a top-down 'generative' network, creates values based on beliefs of hidden variables. The training process uses a learning algorithm to change the structure of the two networks to classify the data accurately. The two networks are changed alternately, a procedure known as a wake-sleep algorithm". (Stewart, 2019, p. 194) To better understand the interaction of these networks, let us contemplate Figure 1.4 Active Inference for Decisions – AID in Daily Life.

Active Inference for Decisions - AID in Daily Life

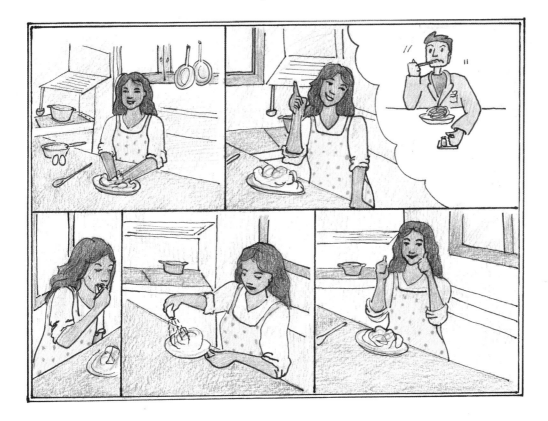

Figure 1.4 Active Inference for Decisions (AID) in Daily Life

It depicts the mechanics of the brain models, using an everyday example. A stay-at-home parent is cooking dinner for her family, the same dish she has already prepared several times before. Based on her generative model, she prepared a dish she believes will be appreciated by her family. While preparing the food, she predicts having a nice dinner with her husband (the generative model); to reduce Free Energy she tastes the dish to make sure it is well seasoned (the recognition model), makes some adjustments, and decides the dish is now ready to be served. In that scene, we witness the Bayesian brain in action: the generative models (generating several hypotheses about the desirability of the dish, the level of spice, etc.) and the recognizing models (tasting the dishes). She has used two strategies of Active Inference:

a) She used her perception skills to optimize the bound of surprise (avoiding generating Free Energy) by choosing a dish that she knows her family likes (her prior).

b) She takes actions (tasting the dish) to minimize the bound of surprise (her family complaining about the flavor of the dish). Her surprise would be the family not liking the dish.

The contrary (her family enjoying the dish), will provide evidence that her models worked, thus, she has minimized Free Energy.

Brain models have additional characteristics; in particular, they are dynamic and hierarchical (above Section 1.4), (Badcock et al., 2019a and Badcock et al., 2019b). The term "hierarchical" calls for clarification in this context, as "hierarchy" can have an adverse connotation. For example, in inefficient public administration there is usually an accumulation of socio-political power in the political sphere at the highest level of governmental hierarchy. Yet the case of the hierarchical Bayesian Brain is very different. It resembles more the political structure of a well-functioning democracy that works as a dynamic distributed hierarchy where ministers will share their specialized knowledge in a collective decision-making process, resulting joint decisions to the benefit of their citizens. Similarly, a hierarchical brain works to optimize and coordinate the work of the different hierarchies of the brain for efficient survival outcomes for the individuals.

1.5.2 Active Inference (AI)

Based on what we have discussed so far, we found out that the brain is an embodied organ acting on a Bayesian principle, inferring the causes of sensory perceptions. Now, we need to know how the Bayesian process is implemented.

Within Bayesian Cognitive Science there are several models on how the brain formulates inferences (Spratling, 2017), for example, Predictive Coding (Rao & Ballard, 1999), Predictive Processing - PP (Clark, 2016), Prediction Error Minimization - PEM (Hohwy, 2013) and Active Inference (Friston et al., 2017). What all scientific approaches have in common is the centrality of generative and recognition models as mentioned above. They also all share the same view of the primary functioning mechanism of brain activity, a process that allows us to articulate a new belief following the pattern "new belief = old belief + new evidence."

It is Active Inference (AI), a process that better fits today's postmodern active life. It argues that individuals do act on their predictions where internal states don't match the hidden external causes by acting to close the gap, thus actively minding prediction errors and minimizing Free Energy. We not only update inferences to adapt our brain models to the world, but even more essential, we take actions to change the environment itself.

Thus, AI's pragmatic orientation makes it significant, attractive, and relevant. The aspiration to minimize Free Energy is the source of the many wonders and advances we have in our lives. Cars, planes, houses, air conditioners, tablets, smart phones, computers, chairs, accounting information systems, consulting services, marketing plans, medical devices, cashmere jackets, watches, books, Facebook, Google, Wikipedia; almost everything we experience in our living niche follows the Free Energy Principle – FEP and the enaction of AI. These artifacts have been created by humankind's work as extended, enacted possibilities to minimize Free Energy in our quotidian lives. I see AI as a liberating mechanism, meaning it does not leave us to the hazard of a random destiny, but we can actively engage in building our present and future. AI provides the tool for how individuals can satisfy the elements of the Self-Determination Theory (SDT) of motivation: the need for autonomy, relations, and mastery. If Active Inference is correct, we can gain personal agency as autonomous beings and self-determine the direction of our lives, mastering not only ourselves but also masterfully acting to shape our eco-niche to our advantage.

The mathematical neuroscience principle of Free Energy offers to a world full of political, social, economic, and environmental challenges the scientific motivation to engage in the changes we need to survive as a species.

So, let's unpack Active Inference to understand its functional and integrative mechanics. We can conceive of Active Inference as a computational process of Mind Learning similar to Machine Learning for silicon systems. It involves four states (Ramstead et al., 2019):

- **Internal states** (experiences, ideas, feelings, physical aches, amongst others) corresponding mostly to beliefs about the external states affecting by sensory states.
- **Sensory states**, our perceptions through our senses: what we hear, smell, see, touch, physically feel in our body when experiencing the external states.
- **Active states** correspond to the experience of the body in the physical space: whether it is moving or static, and the internal physiological movements of our body, doing things. Also at the level of simple mental action, acting virtually in the mind.
- **External states** include everything that is not an internal state, such as other people, material artifacts, and natural phenomena.

The illustration below visualizes the four states involved in Active Inference (Figure 1.5).

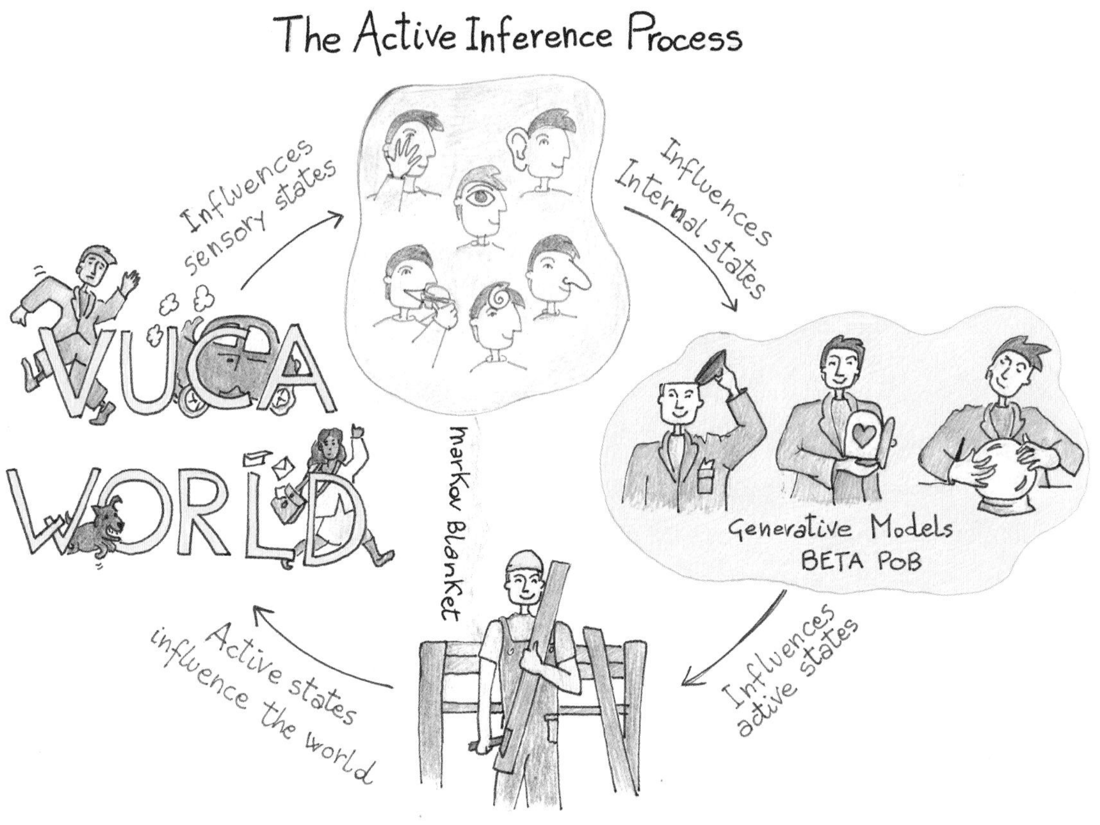

Figure 1.5 The Active Inference Process

In Figure 1.5 we see a veil, the Markov Blanket, separating internal states from external ones, accessible only through sensations and actions. The brain has no direct access to causes of events in the outer world, but only indirectly through sensations or actions of the agent, the individual. This indirectness is an additional source of VUCA, which is why MBSAT focuses on training individuals' sensations and actions to help them minimize Free Energy.

Active Inference happens at three levels of complexity and context to coordinate behavior for achieving desired outcomes and goals. The first level activates simple motivational processes. This is the case in the following sequence: you walk in the street and see a person wearing a nice jacket. Minutes later, you pass by a shop and see a beautiful jacket in the window. You go inside and buy the jacket. The appealing look of the person you saw before builds a motivating action to acquire the jacket based on a simple prediction: "With this jacket, I will look as good as that person."

The intermediate level corresponds to a semantic aspect based on beliefs prevalent in culture. For example, you are on the intercity train during the rush hour. An older adult gets on at the next stop, and you offer your seat as the train is full. Deferring to an older person is a universal courtesy rule. Therefore, you are predicting the person will accept the offer without offense and in conformity to the rules of society.

Finally, the highest level of complexity is determined by episodic or subjective beliefs connected to specific circumstances. Imagine, for example, that the person buying the jacket mentioned above lives on a restricted budget and is having second thoughts after the purchase. He is thinking about returning the item, when he remembers he will soon get his year-end cash bonus. This private episodic event outweighs his misgivings about getting the jacket, so he keeps it.

The three levels work interactively. In the example above, a higher-level episodic event - the prediction about getting the bonus - provides support to the first level motivation - the prediction of looking good in the new jacket - and also to the intermediate-level, generalized idea that he will look good in the jacket according to the fashions of the moment. (Pezzulo et al., 2018)

Under the AI scheme, the internal states are separated by a veil (Kirchhoff et al., 2018) from the external states, the former being only accessible through the sensory states and actions, which is the reason it is so essential to maintain steady and healthy internal states, as they are fundamental for keeping skillful generative and recognition models.

So far, we have discussed the computational aspect of the FEP corresponding to optimizing variational Free Energy by minimizing VUCA and its algorithmic character, corresponding to the rules behind the process of Active Inference. We now turn to how the Bayesian brain (BB) implements Active Inference (AI). Here, we will not engage in the neurobiological details of its implementation as that is beyond the book's scope. Instead, the aim is to provide an easily understandable explanation of how BB implements AI.

1.6 How the Bayesian Brain Implements Active Inference

For John R. Searle, the UC Berkeley philosopher of the mind, one of the chief functions of the mind is to relate individuals to the world by perception and action. As he writes, "by perception we take in information about the world, we then coordinate this information both consciously and unconsciously, and make decisions or otherwise form intention, which results in actions by way of which we cope with the world." (Searle, 2004, p. 179) The ability to see, hear, smell, touch, and taste lets us become aware through our senses. Perception for the empiricists comprises the raw data received by the senses; for rationalists, they add thinking to the sensory input to make sense of the percept.

In AI, perception works in reverse: the brain models predictions. "Perception is indeed a process in which we (or rather, various parts of our brain) try to guess what is out there, using the incoming signal more to tune and enhancing the guessing... the ongoing process of perceiving... is a matter of the brain using stored knowledge to predict, in a progressively more refined manner..." (Clark, 2016, p. 27) This is actually not a very recent view. As early as in the late 1980s, the British neuroscientist R. L. Gregory conceived of perceptions as hypotheses, percepts containing predictive power (Gregory, 1980). Therefore, in the scheme of AI, perceptions are predictions; they are perceptual guesses or hypotheses.

AI comprises three elements:
- Prediction
- Prediction Errors
- Precision

These elements are called the three Ps in this Workbook.

1.6.1   Prediction

Dictionaries typically define a prediction as a statement of what you think will happen in the future. In AI, predictions are expected packets of information that carry embedded beliefs, prior experiences, and an appreciation of the context of the perceived situation. They are sent down the neuro-cortical pathways of the brain with our best assumptions about the causes of the perceived phenomenon (a person's behavior, the impact of a dish we taste or a surface we touch, etc.). L. F. Barrett explains the process as follows: "We think of predictions as statements about the future, like 'It is going to rain tomorrow.' or: 'The Red Sox will win the World Series' ...but here I am focusing on predictions at the microscopic scale as millions of neurons talk to one another. These neural conversations try to anticipate every fragment of sight, sound, smell, taste, and touch that you will experience and every action that you will take. These predictions are your brain's best guesses of what's going on in the world around you and how to deal with it to keep you alive and well." (2017, p. 59)

In AI, predictions are brain activities and can cover a wide range of dimensions. Concerning time, they can range from micro-moments to long timelines, all in the service of anticipating our needs to resist entropy and help us survive (minimizing Free Energy). As we commented before, AI can also take the form of episodic predictions. The focus is on a specific event concerning us personally, for example, predicting the outcome of a friend's dinner invitation. On other occasions, it can be more semantic, that is more about the general future situation in the world, such as predictions about the development of the economy and your company's finances. Usually, it will be a combination of both; for instance, your prediction might be about your company's future (semantic) and how it will affect you personally (episodic).

In a previous book (Young, 2017), I wrote about my first and only experience watching a live football game. It was in Madrid's famous Santiago Bernabéu Stadium, and despite not being a football fan, I became mesmerized by Ronaldo's play. In that match, he alone scored all the winning goals for his team. What I found fascinating was his way of playing. Often he moved in the opposite direction to where the ball was going, while most players were following the ball. Ronaldo repeatedly stood in the middle of the field just observing, like taking a rest and pondering; then, suddenly, he would bolt in the opposite direction to his team, only to see the course of the game changing in his direction with him already in an optimal position and able to catch the ball and score a goal. That game stayed with me for a long time. Finally, while writing my first book, I made the connection and realized that this was prediction at its best. Ronaldo is simply a supreme predictor. He has the natural abilities combined with trained skills and many years of experience playing the game, thus having enough statistical data at his disposal to make accurate inferences about the ball's movement. The secret of his success was being more precise in the quality of his predictions about the ball's movements compared to the other players. This insight allowed me to see the world differently and to look at successful people (managers, tennis or golf players, successful parents, teachers, or medical doctors, to name just a few) as individuals who are on average more precise in the formulation and implementation of their predictions than the mean of the population. Therefore, they have a low average of predictive errors in their life and can flourish, given that we could conceive a flourishing life as one with a low level of prediction errors.

To become good predictors, we need to understand how predictions come about. In AI, predictions are driven by priors corresponding to beliefs, a kind of deeply ingrained assumptions or convictions.

There are several types of such prior beliefs. Zeki and Chén (2020) define two forms of priors:

a) Inherited (biological) priors result from firmly held notions we are born with and are resistant to change even with extensive experience. They can have an evolutionary origin. For example, it is clear to everybody that we cannot survive without oxygen beyond a relatively short time. Trying to stay underwater for more than a few minutes will seriously compromise our physiological state; our body will enter a state of surprise (shock), and we cannot minimize Free Energy. So most humans have a prior belief that it is not possible to survive more than approximately 3 minutes underwater without breathing gear.

b) The second type of beliefs are gained (artefactual or synthetic) priors. They are based on concepts formulated postnatally and changed by experience through life. Some authors call them empirical beliefs and relate them to the hidden causes of events (Ramstead et al., 2020). These priors are less constrained than biological beliefs. An example could be the prior belief that Latin Americans are better dancers than Europeans, although there is no solid statistical evidence of this. An important aspect is that this type of priors is influenced by moods, which are considered hyper-priors in the scheme of AI. For example, a person with a mood disorder such as depression generates pessimistic predictions that involve a high level of Free Energy, rendering it almost impossible to minimize it. (Badcock et al., 2017)

There is an additional distinction based on the focus of a prediction:

◉ Proprioceptive predictions have to do with generating actions, moving our body.

◉ Interoceptive predictions are concerned with emotional processing.

◉ Perceptions about the external world informed Exteroceptive predictions.

Figure 1.6 illustrates these three modalities of predictions. In the first case Misty Copeland, a principal ballet dancer in a famous ballet ensemble performing with her body proprioceptive predictions; the following figure represents a woman's interoceptive prediction of her probable state of pregnancy and the last is Megan Rapinoe predicting the movement and direction of the soccer ball.

Figure 1.6 Proprio-, Intero- and Exteroceptive Prediction
(Adapted from Seth & Friston, 2016: Active interoceptive Inference and the Emotional Brain)

The second part of this book will comment on these predictions in more detail.

1.6.2 Prediction Errors (PEs)

The Bayesian Brain's generative models use prior beliefs about sensations and causes of phenomena to generate predictions and then test them against the environment's inputs, using the recognition models in a directional and hierarchical process. Discrepancies between the two signals imply that there must be some kind of prediction error (Clark et al., 2018).

Predictions come with "noise"; they can be warped, blurred, or distorted to various degrees because of the hidden causes of the object of perception. In addition, the internal states of the perceiver can also affect the precision of the inferring data. The juxtaposition of perception, action, precision, complexity and the situation's context-sensitivity lets prediction errors emerge and creates surprise, an impediment to minimizing Free Energy (Hohwy 2013, p. 92). However, when these factors are skillfully combined, they can enable the minimization of predictive errors in a particular situation.

Some years ago, one of my daughters called and told me she was about to visit me, adding that she was not coming alone. "So, you're coming with your boyfriend!" I replied. "Nice! You can have your room as always. He is welcome, too." "Well," she said, "the thing is: it is not 'he' but 'she.'" "Oh, ok," I said, "no problem, come with her then." Over the years, she kept telling me how precious and vital my spontaneous response was to her. Although my internal world model led me to think of a couple as a man and a woman, I gave her a supportive response on the spot. I realized my predictive error only when she told me that her partner was a woman. My daughter's input prompted the error recognition, thus stemming from an external source and not from my reasoning. Had I insisted on the conservative, culturally driven "classical pair prior," I would have been delusional and certainly inflicted a lot of pain on my daughter.

The external world kept predictions in this account in check. Prediction errors (PEs) are the way of telling the brain that something is out of sync. PEs often occur when we try to predict fast-changing modalities in the world (for example, the new fluid concept of a pair). Our generative brain can also attempt to predict slowly changing conditions of the world (such as moving toward legalizing marriage based on a fluid concept of pairs). Here, the long-term neural connections in the brain are affected by synaptic efficacy (Hohwy, 2013).

PEs have several functions:

a) They help support perceptual inferences, as they are based on our guess about a percept/object and can be conceived as a measure of the appropriateness of our beliefs.
b) PEs can serve as red flags about the unexpected. For example, one can drive a car on a very familiar route while remaining alert to eventualities, such as children crossing the street.
c) Overall, PEs foster learning processes by integrating new data in our brain models, thus shaping our perception, attention, and motivation, ultimately shaping our beliefs and models of the world.

There are also several types of PEs. Perceptual PEs comprise errors in the sensorial channel: seeing, hearing, etc. I might, for example, swear that I saw a red cat, but it was, in fact, a brown cat. Cognitive PEs are errors in our mental elaborations. A case in point is the example mentioned above in connection with divergence (above Section 1.2.1), related to the erroneous assumption that the unseen violin player must be a man, as women cannot be such outstanding musicians. These two types of PEs are called unsigned or neutral in neuroscience, meaning they just report the surprise concerning the issue.

In contrast, the third type of PE is motivational and shows the valence of the error (big or small surprise). The motivational value stems from surprises creating a powerful motivation to learn. We prefer to avoid the unexpected, such as realizing that it was a big mistake not acknowledging that women can be consummate violinists. (den Ouden et al. 2012)

Rather than eliminating PEs, the realistic goal is to reduce them, which can be seen as a mechanism for minimizing perceptual divergence, the difference between our hypothesis about the object of our perception and the natural causes of the percept, for example, my instant assumption that my daughter's companion was a man versus the real hidden cause, the reality that her companion, unbeknownst to me, was a woman.

However, PEs are not just nuisances; they have functions as mentioned above. We need PEs; without them, nothing would surprise us or appear to us as novel; therefore, we would miss the opportunities for the brain to learn new stuff. In other words, errors are not all negative; they are part of our lives, but the fact remains that there is no use to produce errors on purpose. Some will happen anyway; so it is better to limit them as much as possible and when they happen all the same, the point is to make the best of them with strategic awareness and a well aligned BETA.

The trick is how to keep the average of PEs under a certain limit to minimize Free Energy, which makes the difference between having a hard time or flourishing in life. As people get into adulthood, their predictions tend not to be far off; otherwise, we would hallucinate. Feldman Barrett (2017) defines prediction loops as billions of tiny predictions and errors, like small droplets that join with other predictive loops in different brain regions. In her words: "The multitudes of predictive loops run in a massive parallel process that continues nonstop for your whole life, creating sights, sounds, smells, tastes, and touches that make your experience and dictate your actions." (2018, p. 63)

Figure 1.7 exemplifies the structural dynamics of a prediction loop.

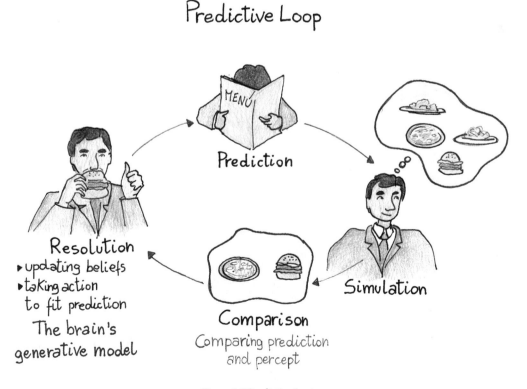

Figure 1.7 Predictive Loop

The prediction generates a simulation of sensations and actions compared to actual sensory inputs from the world. If they match, the prediction is confirmed, and the simulation becomes an adaptive experience; if not, it turns out to be a prediction error that needs to be resolved either by updating the generative model or by taking action to conform to the outer reality to the prediction.

1.6.3 The Precision of Prediction

Whether a prediction is precise is defined by the outcome in the real world. Hence it is not a mathematically exact quantity, but an approximation. In essence, you need to achieve an acceptable average of precision and keep outliers on the negative side (the variance) within certain limits to avoid major disasters.

Imagine you are driving and about to turn into a one-way street to the right. You stop at the corner and check to your left and in front of you. As you see that the path ahead is clear, you speed up and immediately hit the brake again in shock as you just barely can avoid a collision with a bicycle coming from the right side. You made a prediction error that could have had grave consequences. You assumed that the one-way rule is for all traffic and overlooked that the signals allow bicycle traffic in both directions.

In the framework of FE and AI, your oversight reflects a lack of precision in your prediction, resulting in a prediction error (PE). Given the interactive nature of this event, it must be added that the bicycle rider also made some PEs. He predicted that the car driver would stop and give him priority passage; however, he could have exercised some caution given the odd situation of the street with car traffic one way only, but bicycles allowed in both directions.

This is a case of socially constructed PEs, because of a lack of prediction precision from both the car and bicycle driver. In today's postmodern world of ubiquitous fake news, alternative facts, and media misinformation that, as some suggest, capture our attention to exploit our vulnerabilities, PEs are easily created ("I bought this product predicting it would make me happy as the commercials insinuated, but it is not the case and I ended up feeling disappointed"). What we need is a mediating element that helps reduce PEs. This is what makes precision about predictions so crucially important.

In the world of Active Inference (AI), predictions are generated by our internal model of the world; thus, implementing precision requires us to engage in another prediction process, which is the prediction about the accuracy of the prediction. It is a second-order type of prediction. First, the prediction (belief) regarding the phenomena gets created, and to reduce the possibility of PEs, we make a second prediction about the precision of the prediction (PP). AI's brain models will draw inferences from a probability distribution about the external phenomena and a second inference drawn from the probability distribution of the precision about the likelihood of the events based on observations.

To illustrate this, let us go back to the example above. The car driver's prediction is: No traffic, therefore move. The second prediction on the precision of the original prediction is: How sure is it that it is ok to move forward? Well, yes, it is ok to move, is the brain model's implicit answer, there is the one-way traffic signal on the right, no one is coming from the left and the front, and clearly, no one will come from the right. The first prediction corresponds to object awareness, and the second prediction is a meta-awareness that comprehends the quality of the precision of the predicted phenomena. "To optimize prediction error minimization, we need to learn about and predict precisions. This means predicting when, given the context, a prediction error signal is likely to be precise. It is a kind of second-order perceptual inference because it is an inference about perceptual inference." (Hohwy, 2013, p. 65) "The prediction error depends on the precision of the prediction, and the actual observation... orthogonal to the precision of the prediction is the precision of the prediction error.... Here it is important to recognize two sources of precision, the precision of the prediction and the precision of the prediction error; ... whereas the precision of the prediction is a measure of the amount of uncertainty regarding the prediction, the precision of the prediction error is a measure of the uncertainty; that is, whether it is reducible (can be decreased by learning) or irreducible (is because of the inherently stochastic nature of the world)" (Kwisthout et al. 2017, p. 87).

a) Implications of precision for attention:

It is worth clarifying that within the framework of AI, the notion of "precise prediction" is not clearly defined but described as a process. "When I hear attention is 'taking possession by the mind in clear and vivid form,...., I think: No, it's not; attention is simply the process of optimizing precision during hierarchical inference...; attention might not be the 'selection' of sensory channels but an emergent property of 'prediction'; where high-precision prediction -errors enjoy greater gain" (Friston, 2009, p. 299).

As can be seen from this quote, it equated attention with precision, which is a crucial point within the context of MBSAT, given its mindfulness orientation. Most mindfulness interventions focus on "training attention", but with an interpretation of attention that doesn't fully appreciate its neurological function and the brain processes involved. Viewing attention as the enaction of precision within Active Inference dovetails perfectly with MBSAT's prospective orientation centered on strategic awareness.

Predictive errors travel bottom-up from superficial neurological layers towards more complex neuro layers. We increase precision by paying attention to PE signals. If the signal converges with the prediction, it validates the generative model. However, suppose the signal does not match the prediction. In that case, it continues its feed-forward trajectory along the hierarchical path gaining precision by paying more attention to the signal until it matches the generative model of the world, and the latter gets either adjusted with a perceptual update, or an action is taken to conform the prediction to the percept.

Let us consider a concrete, everyday situation. For example, I predict the cup of tea is not hot. When I touch it, and it is only lukewarm, I realize a minimal PE. If the cup is hot, showing a significant PE, the signal travels upward towards the region of the generative model, where the prediction was created, simultaneously setting in motion a calibration process, gauging the precision of the tea temperature. At one point, the model gets updated through learning, so next time I will first touch the cup of tea with one finger to test the temperature or, if I predict the cup will be hot, I can directly take action to match the external world (the temperature of the tea) to the prediction, for example by putting a couple of ice cubes in the cup to cool it off. Please note that the action of putting the ice in the cup is also a prediction, albeit with a high level of precision, as we know that ice reduces the temperature of any drink including tea.

b) Interaction of prediction, precision and prediction errors

Remember that prediction, the precision of prediction, and prediction error are often referred to as the "three Ps" in neuroscience.

Here is an example of such a hierarchical interaction process. Imagine your boss offers you a promotion as regional manager in a tropical country with warm weather all year. Northern Europe was where you were born and raised. You simulate possible states in your mind; you know you go to warmer countries for vacation every summer, and you have always enjoyed these experiences. So, you predict you will undoubtedly enjoy the experience of living and working in such an environment. You talk to your family in the evening, and they are also excited about the offer. Your high cortical predictions are suggesting: "Yes, I will take the offer with joy." Later, you talk to a friend who has experience living in the tropical climate. He tells you spending vacation in a tropical country and living there permanently for work are two different things. He suggests you research what it is like to live in the tropics. Your friend doesn't want to influence you and therefore doesn't give you any specific advice, but strongly recommends you search for more information. Your investigation reveals concerns: long rainy seasons, tropical diseases, traffic jams, etc. These issues are now traveling bottom-up as simulations of sensory inputs of living in a tropical country, imagining, for example, sweating profusely, getting stuck in a traffic jam, perhaps even getting sick. These are sources of prediction errors you believe your family might be confronting. Now with more precision about your initial prediction that it will be fun to "enjoy the tropics," you engage in more realistic talks with your boss and negotiate: housing conditions, frequency of home travel, etc. - all resources that you and your family will require to be able to minimize Free Energy based on your current, more realistic predictions about what it is like to live in the tropics.

1.7 Summary: Our Brain's Essential Biomechanics

Let us summarize the key ideas presented so far and integrate them into a straightforward narrative that connects to the following chapters.

Our starting point was the characteristics of our postmodern society, and we noted the increasing Volatility, Uncertainty, Complexity, and Ambiguity (VUCA). There is abundant empirical evidence of distress in the world, even in advanced industrialized societies, as documented by Anne Case and Nobel laureate Angus Deaton in their book *Deaths of Despair and the Future of Capitalism* (2020). Amongst others, the authors document increased incidents of suicide out of despair in the USA. We can conclude at prima facie that in a world dominated by these characteristics, individuals urgently need competencies to anticipate and predict socio-economic trends and impending challenges to increase their decision-making skills for lasting well-being.

With this in mind, I presented an information-theoretic quantity: Free Energy (FE). According to neuroscientist K. Friston (2006, 2010), FE is critically involved in increasing human survival prospects across different dimensions of life (biological, social, and economic) and through time. Like any biological system, life inevitably exposes humans to the effects of attrition and eventually natural decay. To keep themselves within acceptable bounds of survival opportunities, members of our society require access to the extended benefits of postmodern life such as income-generating work, housing, health insurance, and many other necessities. Hence, being sick, losing one's job, not having a house to live in, being deprived of health insurance, living in a corrupt political system and other undesirable life conditions create distress or - in the terminology of FE - states of stressful surprise. Avoiding unwanted states of surprise in our lives equals minimizing FE. When we can minimize FE, we are doing well; the models of ourselves as a flourishing individual are working.

This discovery signifies that we can have an objective function of how humans can stay alive and prosper by minimizing Free Energy. We have looked at this principle in individuals living under the necessities of life in a postmodern society. For example, losing a job and staying unemployed for an extended period reduces the chances of maintaining an acceptable existence. Yet, minimizing FE is a universal principle. Even if an individual would relinquish modern life and move, for example, to a beautiful archipelago in the Atlantic, home to the Kuna Indians for example, thus returning to a life of subsistence with no need for a job, the person would still require minimizing Free Energy out of the vital need to hunt or fish to sustain his or her livelihood.

In the subsequent sections, we have looked at the functioning of the **Bayesian Brain** (BB) and its implications for FE. Neurological findings show that the BB, instead of reacting to inputs, builds predictions about what it perceives in the environment and its internal milieu (BETA – Body sensations, Emotions, Thoughts and Action Impulses). This process resembles Bayes' statistics and consists of updating priors and their respective probabilities when new data is discovered, allowing for the formulation of posterior probability distributions. Bayesian statistics have been crucial for the development of Artificial Intelligence, including so-called machine learning based on artificial neural networks and all the data mining processes accessible in today's digitalized world. As parallels with the neurological operation of the brain became apparent, neuroscientists built the case for approximated Bayesian inferences in the brain, according to the following algorithm:

revised posterior prediction = prior prediction + (sensory signals–prior prediction) x precision

These elements form the basis for mind learning.

While researching this material, I found a certain similarity between how the brain builds predictions and a corporate finance concept. In investment theory, there is an equation for estimating expected return: Expected return (the posterior in BB) = risk-free return (the prior in BB) + (Market return or the sensory signal–risk-free return) x a risk factor denominated as BETA (the precision in BB). I just mention this to suggest similarities between disciplines that facilitate interdisciplinary work and understanding.

Subsequently, we saw that the Bayesian Brain embodies **Generative Models** (GMs) and **Recognition Models** (RMs) of the world that are contextualized to our existential niche. They are based on our experiences and shape the circuits that generate predictions and prediction errors (Keller & Mrsic-Flogel, 2018). The parameters of the BBs are beliefs corresponding to the guesses of what we perceive with our senses (see, hear, smell, touch, or taste) and of things that loosely appear in our mind, with different values on a continuum of many possibilities or probabilities.

Then we discussed that BB models are implemented through a process of **Active Inference** (AI) composed of three elements: prediction, prediction errors and precision, the three Ps, and that it is the proper conjugation of these elements that allows minimizing FE, where minimizing Free Energy corresponds to minimizing predictive errors which can only be done in two ways: either by changing the prediction via new information or by changing the world that is by acting in the world. In brief, BB is modeled from continuous variables of recognition of events and previous subjective experiences of the observer and based on the likelihood of the observations given the earlier adventures of the person and new information.

The conceptual trio composed of the Free Energy Principle, the Bayesian Hierarchical Brain, and the Active Inference mechanism with its three computational quantities: predictions, prediction errors, and precision represent a robust theoretical framework for training strategic awareness and skillful decision making. It supports a scientifically grounded, powerful, and practical approach that can guide people in their search for a flourishing life. Precisely when we are confronted with the challenges of our VUCA world, we can continually update our Generative Models and refine our Recognition Models using Active Inference to mind our internal and external world.

Finally, these theories are a tightly researched line of reasoning about the mechanisms of the brain and its influence on the life of individuals. The ideas conform to Marr's three levels of analysis (Marr, 1982, p. 24-27):

1) computational:

   optimizing Free Energy/minimization of prediction errors

2) algorithmic:

   the process of Active Inference and

3) implementation:

   continuous implementation of the 3 Ps: enaction of Prediction, Prediction Errors, and Precision.

Also, at a practical level, the theories stand for a regulatory mechanism that skillfully guides the interface between people and their environment. "Every good regulator of a system must be a model of that system... the living Brain, so far as it is to be a successful and efficient regulator for survival, must proceed, in learning, by the formation of a model (or models) of its environment... Now that we know that any regulator must model what it regulates, we can measure how efficiently the brain carries out this process. There can no longer be a question about whether the brain models its environment: it must." (Conant & Ross Ashby, 1970, p. 82)

These insights confirm the potential for strategic awareness training. They show that awareness training to update our brain models is necessary for productive functioning and living in our existential niche.

Chapter 2

FREE ENERGY, ACTIVE INFERENCE AND THE PREDICTIVE BETA MIND IN MBSAT

2.1 MBSAT's History and Evolution

2.1.1 Designing a program for an active, non-clinical population

There exist several mindfulness-based programs for specific purposes that are well designed and effective for what they are supposed to do. For example, there are excellent interventions to reduce stress resulting from physical afflictions and effective programs to reduce the incidence of episodes of depression (mental anguish), to name just two. However, when scanning for comprehensive interventions that could be of help to non-clinical individuals, I discovered a plethora of interventions that seemed poorly focused and unspecific, in part adaptations of clinical and spiritual programs, mainly intended to assist individuals to relax, handle stress, and in a subtle, implicit way even suggesting becoming less active. I knew first-hand that these approaches were maybe convenient but not sufficient for dealing with the critical challenge active people confront in their daily lives: avoiding decision errors.

There are many sources of decision errors. A quintessential, common one is to decide in favor of things we like, despite their harmful consequences. For example, most people like sweet foods; they give us a momentary, pleasurable kick; however, in the long run, they affect our physical health: weight problems, diabetes, etc. Or deciding to avoid things we don't like, despite the fact they could be good for us. For example, not liking vegetables we try to avoid dishes with vegetables; however, it is widely recognized that a balanced diet including vegetables is of great importance. Another pitfall is making decisions without having relevant information, thus out of ignorance. These three conditions - things we like, those we don't like, or are ignorant about - are often at the source of mistakes we make in our daily lives, getting people in trouble. The influence and misapplication of these conditions lead to narrow-mindedness with binary implications such as self-interest vs broader interest or short-term vs. long- terms interest. While active in a VUCA world plagued with misinformation, fake news, and intentional distortions, even of scientific truths, one can easily imagine how the potential for decision mistakes gets amplified.

I contend that in such an environment, we all need Strategic Awareness (SA), which can be delineated as a capacity that brings clarity of mind by observing reality with a discerning, evaluative quality, thus enabling wise choices and skillful decision making. It allows us to see what is contextually skillful in our private and professional lives to benefit ourselves, others, and society.

SA comprehends a series of capabilities:
- Embodied, continuous-time observation.
- Seeing connections between disparate phenomena.
- Anticipating consequences and long-term effects of what we are observing.
- Understanding oneself as part of social systems and our environment.

SA enables us to:
- Perceive potential risks and develop solutions and countermeasures.
- Recognize favorable trends and take advantage of them.

- Anticipate the behavior of others.
- Anticipate the consequences of our actions.

SA leads to desirable outcomes:
- Wise and skillful decisions to reduce Free Energy in our life.
- Seeing and seizing opportunities that facilitate our flourishing.
- Noticing potential problems and preventing them before they get us in trouble.

It is SA that mediates the quality of our decision-making. Since the quality of our decisions has such a significant impact on the quality of our daily lives, I firmly believe that an effective mindfulness program for active, non-clinical individuals should have as the primary outcome the capacity to improve both SA and decision-making skills. Decisions flawed by prediction errors can lead to a miserable life. Therefore, it is essential to keep the rate of decision errors as low as possible if they can't be avoided altogether. A low rate of decision errors can still lead to a flourishing life. This is not a convoluted scientific assertion; it is merely common sense that mistakes in decision-making are not conducive to a desirable, fulfilling life; being a skillful decision-maker will lead to a good life not only for the decision-maker but also the world surrounding this person, the fellow human beings and the environment in which we are embedded.

As we all live in an increasingly VUCA (volatile, uncertain, complex, and ambiguous) world that confronts people with more risks, the probability of making errors in predictions and decisions is also higher. At the same time in VUCA opportunities abound; it just requires a strategic eye to spot them. In Chinese, the symbol of crisis also means opportunities, implying that it depends on whether a person's Strategic Awareness either perceives problems or primarily possibilities. MBSAT aims to assist its dedicated participants in developing personal capacities that increase SA and decision-making skills. With the abilities and competencies gained in the program *Mindfulness-based Strategic Awareness Training–MBSAT*, they can sustainably enhance their well-being.

MBSAT seeks to help people cultivate the ability to see opportunities, even in adverse situations and circumstances by training them to stay calm despite relatively volatile environments, to maintain clarity of mind despite the uncertainty and ambiguity of problems and to cultivate a caring attitude that allows seeing the interconnections and the complexity of local and expanded world realities. These are all trainable abilities and competencies that enable the materialization of equanimous perception that lets Strategic Awareness emerge, enhancing people's ability to make more precise predictions and wise, skillful decisions.

To casually reflect on the ubiquity of the role of decisions in our lives, just observe what you do every moment of your life. We spend all of our awake time making decisions, often very trivial ones such as getting up early or staying a few more minutes in bed, taking a single cup of coffee or serving yourself one more; leaving for work on time, opening your computer, sending emails to your client, family or friend, deciding what to eat for lunch, for dinner. It has been estimated that an adult human being makes over 30,000 decisions a day. Many of these choices are automated decisions, becoming habits of behavior, performed with little awareness. Yet sometimes, trivial decisions like washing our hands can become critical, like during the COVID-19 crisis. Decisions vary in their importance and impact on our lives; the crucial ones we can think of as strategic decisions. These are the decisions that, if one errs, the effect on the quality of our life will be enormous. Here are some examples: who to marry, what profession to choose, where to work, what company to work for, when to have children, an important question for a couple, what sectors of the economy to invest in, etc. These are decisions where predictive errors have a considerable cost: divorce, job dissatisfaction, bankruptcy, and so on.

MBSAT, as a mindfulness-based protocol, has at its foundation a robust triangulation of various disciplines: positive psychology, cognitive-behavioral science, business strategy, behavioral finance and economics, systems dynamics, contemplative sciences. In addition, Self Determination Theory (SDT), a scientifically robust motivational theory, is also anchored in MBSAT. SDT suggests that individuals have three fundamental needs: autonomy, mastery, and relationships. For details, please refer to my previous book (Young, 2017).

What the current book adds is up-to-date material about my understanding of the most promising concepts from computational neuroscience on how the brain works: The Predictive Brain (PB), also defined as Bayesian Brain, Free Energy (FE), and Active Inference (AI), all notions discussed in the previous chapter. The following section intends to relate these concepts to MBSAT. It provides a conceptual and functional understanding of how MBSAT can help non-clinical, active individuals improve their quality of life and support their natural desire for flourishing.

2.1.2 MBSAT and computational neuroscience

Grounding MBSAT in computational neuroscience follows a clear-cut, intelligible rationale. In MBSAT's approach, Strategic Awareness and skillful decision-making are forerunners of wise actions and the foundation for building a flourishing life. Decision-making requires the ability to anticipate outcomes; hence, computational neuroscience with its core idea of the brain as a predictive organ is central to the design logic of MBSAT.

> A skillful strategic decision-maker can be defined as someone who makes accurate predictions most of the time, maintaining a low average score of prediction errors and ensuring that the brain's recognition and generative models are accurate and continuously updated.

This predictive orientation is a distinctive feature of MBSAT. Mindfulness programs usually strongly emphasize being in the present moment. From MBSAT's wide-angle point of view, all dimensions are critical: the present moment, the future, and the past because all three contribute in their specific way to sustainable flourishing in life. When we look at practical interventions, we will return to this topic below in more detail (section 2.4 The Predictive BETA Mind). As discussed in the previous chapter, humans need to reduce surprises by acquiring information about the past, present, and future environmental conditions. This implies generating predictions/hypotheses that are driven by our beliefs about the causes of sensory data. By perceiving changes in the environment and engaging in cognitive processes (thinking, inferring, planning) we can gauge the consequences of changes and take action accordingly, either by changing the hypotheses or beliefs or influencing changes in the environment to conform them to the predictions.

2.1.3 Phases of MBSAT program development

Designing, testing, teaching, adjusting, and updating the MBSAT program has been a process spanning over a decade.

It started at the University of Saint Gallen in Switzerland, where I taught an elective graduate course on Corporate Finance and Business Strategy. During one of the financial crises that shook the Western economies, I noticed the students were stressed and worried about their future. So I incorporated some practices I have used myself in challenging times to help them cope with uncertainty. This clearly fulfilled a need, because the class was oversubscribed in the following semester; while the university limited elective courses to 30 students, there were twice as many registrations. The students then submitted a petition to the university's administration to raise the limit of participants for the course and got it approved. At the end of the semester, the class received very favorable reviews. One of my students from Germany then requested permission to write his master's thesis with me and got the approval of the Dean's office. He studied the effects of some practices they learned in the course. The results revealed students were more confident and dedicated to their studies and less stressed, consequently achieving better grades. Inspired by the course outcomes and my student's success in their studies, I changed the course's name in the next semester to "Becoming a Strategic Leader with Mindfulness-based Strategic Awareness Training (MBSAT)." It was the first time I used the name MBSAT, about a decade ago. This experience propelled me to design MBSAT as a non-clinical protocol for active individuals and leaders.

One of the beautiful things about teaching brilliant, curious individuals is learning from them. This happened to me with a student in my Strategy & Finance classes who also attended the MBSAT course I taught subsequently at a European university. A brilliant Russian mathematician and Data Scientist with a PhD from Stanford University, he was an Associate Partner at McKinsey at the time and today is the Chief Data Officer (CDO) of a large global bank. Over time, I have become a sort of mentor for him. Through our long personal conversations, my interest in Information Theory was reawakened and I began reviewing the notes of an Information and Control Systems course I took at MIT as a cross-register graduate student from Harvard. For Professor McInnes, the course instructor, information systems are ways of resolving complexity and uncertainty and to reduce cognitive dissonance. Yet there is also the human factor. My former student explains in our ongoing conversations that most of the difficulties he encounters with Data Science projects aren't with the systems per se but with the rigidities he often sees in managers' mindsets. While the projects are transformative in processing and delivering information, managers keep their legacy mindset models, which, in his view, create frictions for the progress of the projects. Therefore, we discuss how MBSAT, with its orientation towards transformation and skillful decision making, could be conceived as a deep-learning mind technology for transforming people's minds in a similar way as data science projects are deep-learning and transformation processes of organizations' strategies, procedures and information processing technologies involving functional organization processes (marketing, production, human resources, etc.) that firms need to change in an age of digitalization.

MBSAT operates with a similar logic, as it seeks to support people in transforming their brain-mind information processing abilities, which will assist them in processing the continually growing body of data effectively and efficiently and in building more accurate predictions with fewer prediction errors while maintaining good generative models of what is happening in their inner biological space and the outer VUCA environment and ultimately helping them make skillful decisions that support their personal, organizational, and societal goals.

Motivated by the intellectual interactions with my Russian student, my curiosity to investigate the connection between Data Science, Machine Learning, and MBSAT was spurred. The extensive research I engaged in has been ongoing for years and resulted in new material for this book. It complements and extends the MBSAT approach as presented in the first MBSAT book (Young, 2017).

2.1.4 Reflecting on the latest developments

When my dad passed away at the age of 85, he was using a Sony VAIO PC. My 93 year old mother, still alive, spends most of her day with her Apple notebook watching the news, Netflix movies, receiving and sending emails from her family and friends. They both updated their external silicon brains for processing information and interacting with a post-modern society.

We keep computers relevant in a competitive information technology environment by regularly updating and innovating software, hardware, and the main architecture components. To keep ourselves relevant, we humans also need a mechanism that allows us to update and innovate our mind's software in the form of beliefs, perceptions, and judgments as they constitute the mind's operating system that feeds our brain's generative model of the world. We could even argue that our biological "hardware" is also renewed in this updating process, when new neuronal connections and networks emerge in our neurons.

I see MBSAT as a human updating technology for our information processing designed to facilitate carbon-based systems (humans) updating their brain's generative and recognition models of the world. We live in a digitalized, knowledge-based society that continually generates massive amounts of data that have the potential to be noisy (non-relevant and distracting) or, on the contrary, crucial for our survival.

Strategic Awareness (SA) as a trainable capacity allows us to discern and extract the critical and essential information from the VUCA sea of trivial and noisy big data in which we all live our lives. Given the changing state of the world, we need to continuously refine our generative models in our minds to optimally navigate our post-modern world and make skillful decisions to help us cope with the VUCA environment we live in.

Recently, an Oxford University epidemiologist said this in an interview, answering a journalist's question about COVID-19: "We are experiencing a 9/11 casualty level every single day in America. This is an emergency that vaccine can't help us with today; the only thing that can help us today is to be smarter about decisions: masking, distancing...". I believe the answer says it all as it establishes the central role of decision-making for people's well-being.

There are three (non-exhaustive) categories of decisions that people engage in:

a) Standardized and habitual decisions

This type of decisions is mostly routine based or of the kind where the process is well defined, for example, updating a corporate information system with the newest technology, replacing your worn-out sofa, changing the oil in your car after a specific mileage, all the habitual decisions related to our daily necessities of life, etc.

b) Impactful decisions

This is a category of situations that fall into what we could define as critical decisions, for example, buying a house, marriage, having children, etc.

c) Transformative decisions

This third and increasingly frequent type of decisions has to do with novel and adaptive situations.

Regarding the first two types of decisions, there are models, support systems, and criteria to support us, and we can learn to use them more effectively. Besides, we can simply correct the decisions ex-post without major consequences other than passing irritations sometimes. Obviously, impactful decisions are more challenging than standard decisions given the switching costs involved in the corrections: divorce, custody battles, loss of savings, etc.

The third type of decisions is becoming more recurrent in a VUCA environment as we more often confront novel situations where we cannot draw helpful information from experience. This kind of decisions often challenge our deeply held beliefs, ideologies, and judgments. Take, for example, the decision to wear a mask during the COVID-19 pandemic, a simple hygiene measure that the scientific community strongly recommended as a practical step to reduce infections; however, it became politicized and controversial, sometimes with deadly consequences for people who decided not to use a mask. Or think of washing hands frequently for prevention: it is another case of a seemingly trivial decision that turned into a strategic, adaptive decision in a particular context. The changing and evolving world that we live in requires that individuals update their views of the world to live a life that supports their needs and desires for a healthy and pleasant existence.

Building a skillful decision-making capacity that is up to the task in the VUCA world requires a particular type of learning. It must be based on first-person experiences and allow one to observe and recognize the impediments to moving forward and adapting to emerging changing conditions.

Thankfully, computational neuroscience provides a concise answer for navigating successfully in VUCA times:

> In VUCA times, you need to keep your brain's generative and recognition models updated to be a skillful decision-maker.

Our brain models are key to flourishing. There is growing evidence from the clinical literature that most mental afflictions result from poorly operating generative and recognition models in the brain. Let us look at depression as an example. Although I do not practice as a therapist and have never experienced depression, I spent several years at Oxford University studying how to help people prevent the recurrence of that affliction; thus, I have a good understanding of the disorder. It is now recognized from a computational psychiatry point of view that in depressed individuals, there are depressed beliefs as persistent priors ("I am a failure," "I am not attractive," etc.) that have become hard to update and that populate the generative model of the individuals concerned. These beliefs lead to fuzzy inferences, faulty perceptions and consequently unskillful decision-making, causing inept actions or inaction.

In the same manner, but with much less dramatic effects, unskilled decision-making in non-clinical individuals is connected to generative models lacking the required updating capacity.

Figure 2.1 details the MBSAT Free Energy Active Inference Model and the focus of the training. The protocol starts with interventions and practices to refine our recognition models by cultivating awareness of our sensory states: visual, earing, touching, smelling, tasting (the signals we receive from external states) and enhancing the perception of our internal states (BETA). This is the main focus of Part 1 of the MBSAT protocol (Sessions 1-4). Then we focus on training how to maintain reliable generative models (beliefs) for supporting our internal states, for example, to like what is necessary and good for us and to dislike what is objectionable and harmful. This leads to developing the ability to act skillfully, that is to make skillful decisions and take skillful actions that will positively impact the external states. The cultivation of our generative models and ability to act skillfully with strategic awareness is the focus of Part 2 of the protocol (Sessions 5-8).

This training cycle creates an existential loop that begins with the generative process set in motion by external states and culminates in our actions to influence the external states with the goal of reducing Free Energy and promoting flourishing states and well-being.

The MBSAT Free Energy Active Inference Model of Human Experience

Figure 2.1 The MBSAT Free Energy Active Inference Model of Human Experience

2.2 Contextualizing MBSAT Under the Free Energy Principle (FEP)

MBSAT is a human-centered development technology to hone the skills necessary to process relevant and disruptive information. It seeks to fortify people's immunization of BETA (Body sensations, Emotions, Thoughts, and Actions Impulses) from disruption by supporting an active calibration of their portfolio of beliefs. Calibration is the adaptive transformation that balances people's body sensations, emotions, thoughts, and actions in ways that support their flourishing needs. With a balanced BETA, people can better cope with the mounting challenges of living life in a rapidly changing and complex environment.

To ensure coherence in its method, MBSAT has its own specific vocabulary and logic that follows from the Free Energy Principle (FEP) and Active Inference (AI). Therefore, participants in MBSAT need a basic understanding of the notions of FEP and AI and their functioning. In the academic literature, Free Energy (FE) is a highly abstract subject, treated in intricate mathematical formulas by theoretical researchers, making it difficult to follow, even for scientists. One of the leading researchers in the field, mentioned in Chapter 1, is K. J. Friston. There is a telling anecdote of a group of scientists at a university in the USA, who, after pouring hours over an academic article on FE without arriving at a clear understanding, end their meeting with the shared sigh: "God help us understand Friston's Free Energy Principle!"

It may not come as a surprise that a group of specialists like the one in this anecdote finds it hard to agree on a novel approach; especially when a subject is formulated in such a complex way as the Free Energy Principle, reaching a clear common understanding becomes utterly challenging. This is the main reason these important ideas are not more widely known. But suppose that minimizing FE is recognized as a general principle that explains the survival imperative of life. In that case, I believe such an essential principle needs to be widely accessible to the larger public and not restricted to a self-selected community of well-intentioned academics. Currently, this community operates primarily at the theoretical level, although with the view of eventually translating their ideas into more practical applications, mainly to relieve individuals with mental afflictions (depression, schizophrenia, ADD, etc.). MBSAT has set out to operationalize FEP and make it applicable also for a non-clinical population.

The logic is straightforward. If the FEP can demonstrate that minimizing FE is a survival imperative of life, then it can suggest ways to optimize people's living needs. Therefore, under the premise that the FEP is correct in explaining how living systems such as human beings can resist harmful forces, there is an obligation to make these ideas available for all. And this means stripping them down from complicated jargon and formulations to expand their understanding and availability to the general non-clinical population. This is the task that MBSAT has taken on to fulfill by designing understandable and straightforward, practical FEP-inspired interventions that can assist individuals in moving towards flourishing in their lives by helping them make decisions that minimize Free Energy.

In MBSAT, Free Energy Minimization (FEM) is equivalent to minimizing decision errors, which requires accurate generative models of the world. This implies having accurate beliefs and realistic recognition models that help us capture on-time deviations from skillful decisions and take corrective measures when the evidence in the world does not support our decisions. In such situations, one can either update the model with new beliefs thus adapting our BETA to fix the evidence. Or, alternatively one can take actions to adapt the world to our beliefs, recognizing that the world is wrong but that our models/ beliefs are still correct, which is a possibility.

As I have already mentioned, I don't pretend to understand Free Energy and Active Inference totally; after all, it is an evolving scientific project. However, after several years of studying them I believe, I can now translate them into practical interventions to let more people benefit from these pathbreaking ideas.

2.2.1 MBSAT's Objective Function

Ever since writing the first book, Mindfulness-based Strategic Awareness Training - MBSAT (Young, 2017), I felt the urge to define an objective function for the program, a straightforward formula that captures the essence of what MBSAT strives to do, comparable to the objective function in business. An objective function catches, in a nutshell, the connection between input (costs) and output (objective) and, in this way, facilitates the motivation to do the work required to reap the benefits MBSAT offers.

Yet I knew firsthand that formulating an objective function accurately without oversimplifying is difficult. While studying for an MBA at the University of Chicago Booth Graduate School of Business, I discussed the objective function of finance and of the manager's role with a distinguished professor. He argued that the objective function of managerial finance was solely to maximize profit (Friedman, 1970), and its functional correlate of shareholder value (Jensen, 2000). Profits and shareholder value are of course vital objectives for business organizations, but I was intrigued by the implications of the professor's statement. I pointed out that in asymmetrical situations, an organization's gain may imply losses for others in society, making it difficult for a manager to implement such a single-minded mandate. In political economics, so-called externalities and market failures are well-recognized problems caused by discrepancies between individual and collective rationality. What is suitable for the firm or some individual entities is not necessarily good for society as a whole, as J. Tirole, the 2014 winner of the Nobel prize in Economics, explains in his book *Economics for the Common Good* (2017). Today, we witness that Friedman's and Jensen's ideas are questioned to the point where Jensen found himself compelled to issue an apology for the adverse effects his views might have caused by contributing to some of the economic crises. Hence, more sophisticated thinking than simply maximizing profits may require a more adaptive approach to maintaining balance and sustainable equilibrium.

Because of this experience, I have been cautious about offering an MBSAT objective function. However, I can see its need and usefulness for guiding the BETA training protocol and supporting MBSAT course teachings. The discussion in the previous chapter about Free Energy Minimization as the imperative for biological systems to maintain their viability (their existence) may be helpful in this respect. The theoretical foundations of these ideas stem from observation of the natural biosphere and, thus, in principle, are less susceptible to subjective appreciation. The argument is that the principle, propositions, and theories underlying Free Energy and Active Inference are undisputable, science-based facts resulting from scientific research on brain behavior and brain functions.

This allows me to propose the minimization of Free Energy (FE) as one of the critical metrics for MBSAT, conceived and operationalized as a quantity necessary for human survival. In individuals, Free Energy varies depending on the quality of the individual's BETA - particularly the cognitive-emotional processes and actions - and the environment.

The account I am about to present on the practical application and operationalization of FE in MBSAT can make sense for everyone to improve their quality of life. With this in mind, I rely also on functional managerial quantitative expertise and experience that is straightforward and not intimidating, based on finance, accounting, and risk management.

Let us begin by looking at Figure 2.1.

The illustration presents the world divided into two areas. An area below a certain limit corresponds to beneficial FE minimization states, thus a space attractive to human beings: having a job, being in good mental and physical health, enjoying good relationships, and many other attractive FEM states. The upper area corresponds to a space of poor FE minimization states which are naturally unattractive to human beings: unemployed, divorced, homeless, and other non-FEM states (Bruineberg & Rietveld 2014).

It is easy to see that individuals spending more time in the lower space of rich FEM possibilities are doing something well: their decisions are working out well. Regarding those who stay in the opposite upper space, one can assume something is wrong with their decisions. From this point of view, the goal of MBSAT is simply to help individuals spend more time in the lower area of rich FEM (a space of low entropy) and spend less time in the upper poor FEM space (as space of high attrition) with the skills gained from MBSAT and its practices.

While it may be unavoidable for human beings to land sometimes in the upper space during the trials of life, the trick is to keep the visits to the poor FEM areas short and sporadic. This doesn't exclude that one might consciously take a decision that requires a temporary passage in the upper, inhospitable space, for example, in the search for meaning or special knowledge or as a kind of investment to later move to the rich FEM spaces. In the illustration above the letters in parentheses relate to the Self-Determination Theory (SDT) (Ryan & Deci 2018) and correspond to the three needs: competency, autonomy, and relationship that are necessary to keep an authentic intrinsic motivation in our life according to SDT. For example, being married helps fulfill our need for relationship indicated by (R) and having good mental health helps us be autonomous and competent, indicated by (A, C).

From this narrative, it is easy to see the importance and necessity for training decision-making skills. Through the quality and skillfulness of our decisions, we can build the conditions to stay longer in the

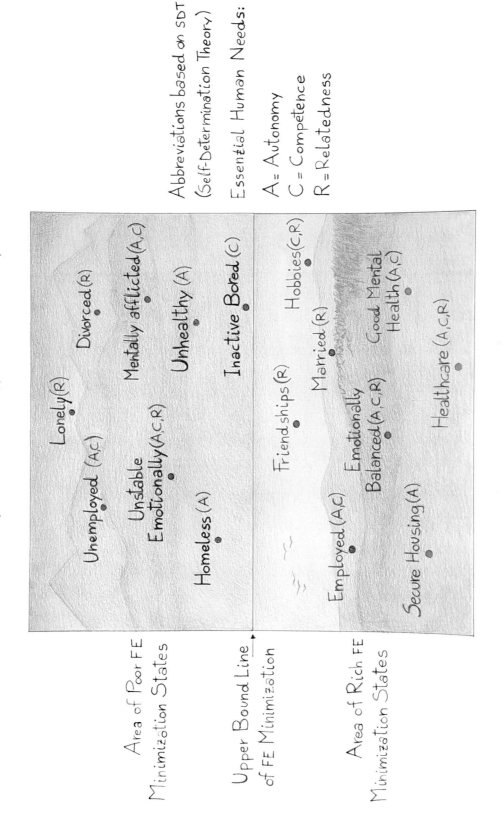

Figure 2.2 The Landscape of the Free Energy Minimizing Principle

rich FEM spaces and have shorter visits to the poor FEM places, although they may sometimes be necessary or inevitable.

Skillful decision-making as a practical meta-outcome of MBSAT subsumes two additional aspects:
a) an aware, strategic mind that can sense beyond the obvious.
b) a contextualized BETA (Body sensations, Emotions, Thoughts and Action impulses), that is adequate to prevailing events at hand. Having a happy BETA in a situation of danger might not be skillful.
What drives these two components of a person's experience are their beliefs shaped by their personal, biological, and cultural backgrounds. Therefore, running behind every decision we make are our beliefs as subjective priors with a constant question: Do I genuinely believe that this decision will get me the desired reward and enable me to stay in the rich FEM space?

Essentially, it all boils down to making few decision errors, which is a practical way to keep track on how well we minimize Free Energy. A low score of decisions errors to predictions means one is on the right track for minimizing Free Energy. When our predictions and decisions are often right on target, it also means that our models of the world and ourselves are effective.

Based on this analysis, we arrive at the following formulation for the objective function (OF) of MBSAT:

> MBSAT's Objective Function:
> Assisting individuals in optimizing their BETA and Portfolio of Beliefs to make skillful decisions that help them stay in Free Energy Minimization spaces.

2.2.2 Operationalizing Free Energy Minimization (FEM) in MBSAT

Many devices are a well-established part of modern life, and we use them well without understanding the underlying mechanics or physics of how they work. Think of driving a car; most people don't understand the mechanical engineering and combustion physics of a vehicle; however, we all do a reasonably good job of driving. Similarly, most people don't understand how their refrigerator works. We travel thousands of miles by plane confidently without knowing aeronautics. Or think of the ubiquitous computers and mobile phones; except for a small group of experts, the large population of users doesn't know about their technical designs, and yet computers and mobile phones have become so critical in our lives that we can't imagine how to cope without them.

In the same fashion, I don't believe that to apply Friston's ideas in practice a person needs to understand its complex mathematical architecture. I think we can grasp the Free Energy Principle and its corollary process theory of Active Inference for practical, hands-on applications when presented in clear, user-friendly prose. To begin with, the notion of energy is ancient and has occupied brilliant minds ever since. Over 2,000 years ago, the Greek Stoics spoke of vital energy coming from the sun. Last century the French philosopher Henri Bergson coined the term "Elan Vital" (vigor) for energy that helps in the perception of life, and the Polish-French psychiatrist Minkowski spoke of "vital energy" that helps understand emotional aspects of life. Later, the subject has been taken up by others, for example, the psychoanalyst S. Freud who wrote about libido as inner energy, the repression of which can, sometimes, lead to mental afflictions (neurosis).

Friston's concept of Free Energy is related to information. In the previous chapter, I have explained that the brain is a continuous information processing organ. It sends signals (predictions) using a generative model based on beliefs accumulated from previous experiences about the causes of sensations collected through its recognition model. It predicts empirical signals from the environment to confirm the predictions as accurate or indicate prediction errors. Between the two signals, the input from the environment and the prediction generated by the brain, a computing discrepancy analysis is going on. If it corroborates the predictive signal, it is evidence that one possesses a good operating model of the causes of sensations. However, suppose it disproves the signal from the environment, meaning the empirical signal is more accurate, then there must be some predictive error that needs to be accounted for, in which case there are two possibilities. The first option is to add new information to the inventory of experiences (updating the generative model) so that the next time something with similar characteristics occurs there is already information (a belief/prior) at hand ready to process the sensation more precisely. The other option is to take action and modify the environment by adjusting the source of whatever is generating the sensation sent to the brain.

Both activities consume energy. Updating the generative model requires energy to learn new information, for example, realizing that, contrary to a chauvinist belief ("only men can be excellent violin players"), a woman played the fabulous piece just heard (the anecdote in Chapter 1). Depending on how strongly the belief is held, the prediction error can cause different degrees of irritation. If the irritation is mild, the response could be: "Ok, my mistake. Now I know women can play violin as well as men." Or, if it is a hard-held belief, it can engender more intense emotional states: "Now women want to challenge men as violin players." In the case of an active strategy, where the prediction error is countered by taking action, energy is used to influence the environment. An example from everyday life could be the following chain of events: coming home hungry to have dinner and believing the soup is ready, taking a spoonful in a hurry and finding out that it is too hot to eat; then pouring a bit of cold water into the soup to cool it off. Here, although one can adjust the cause of the sensation to accommodate the original prediction, one still consumes energy, first to soothe the burnt tongue, then to get cold water and cool the soup, and finally, in all certainty, one will be under some adverse emotional state.

For Holmes (2022), FE is an adverse concept and represents mental pain. In MBSAT, the goal is to avoid adverse energy and pain originating from prediction errors. Therefore, in MBSAT, the main Key Performance Indicator (KPI) we use for optimization is the **Free Energy Minimization Metric**, because FE and its expectation can be broadly construed as metrics of cognitive activity (Ramstead et al., 2021) and operationalized as the long-term average of prediction errors (Wiese & Metzinger, 2017), a value that needs to be kept low as evidence that a person's generative models of the world and skillful decision-making capabilities are effective and supportive of a path towards flourishing. When we speak of FE in MBSAT, we refer to the variational Free Energy that results from a discrepancy between the outcomes observed in the environment and the outcomes predicted by the decision maker's generative model. We also speak of Expected FE referring to the minimization of FE one would expect in the future, resulting from predictions and decisions taken now and their effects in the future.

In this way, the Free Energy Principle FEP is entirely compatible with the intention of MBSAT as a program designed to improve the living conditions of individuals; it allows participants to study their belief-driven BETA (body sensations, emotions, thoughts, and actions) and to calibrate their generative models. According to the FEP, internal states keep parametrized beliefs about themselves and the external states operating as random variables.

Figure 1.2 and 1.3 in Chapter 1 above present a model of how MBSAT can improve people's decision-making skills based on Bayesian cognitive science principles and theories. A well-trained BETA is essential for the brain's recognition models to recognize and capture what is happening in the environment with a high level of accuracy. Balanced beliefs are the basis for effective generative models that produce good predictions. In combination they allow Strategic Awareness to emerge and foster skillful decision-making as the illustration below visualizes (Figure 2.3).

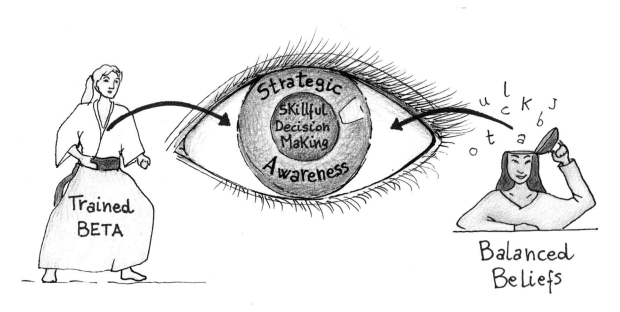

Figure 2.3 The Core of MBSAT

2.3 Active Inference (AI) in MBSAT

2.3.1 Operationalizing Active Inference in MBSAT

In Chapter 1, we looked at Active Inference in relation to the brain and its predictive processing capabilities. Here in Chapter 2, we are making the connection between Active Inference and MBSAT. Utilizing Active Inference (AI) doesn't require understanding its technical terminology, and even less its complex mathematics. After all, AI theories result from functional and descriptive models of processes existing in people's brains and how the mind works. Therefore, in MBSAT, understanding AI is enabled by easy-to-understand frameworks with the objective to help us with our experiences in life.

MBSAT conceives of AI as a process of inference geared towards facilitating decisions that will bring about actions capable of moving people closer to their desired states. A convenient example of operational AI that occurs to me is a home automation system, in which an autonomous system gathers information to take action and produce desirable states. There is a European standard automation system in my house in Zurich that allows managing the lighting, blinds and shutters, displays, compatible audio-video equipment, and security systems. It also has an integrated weather station that measures wind speed, rain, humidity, and temperature. The entire system is hosted on a server, generating and taking orders to regulate the house environment; for example, it manages the home temperature to stay within desired bounds, manages the timing of switching the lighting on and off and regulates the alarm system, amongst other functions.

But the system does also something more sophisticated paralleling decisional AI. If you look at Figure 2.4, you notice two switches labeled "Markise W." (West) and "Markise S." (South) that control the automatic sunshades. Here they display a red

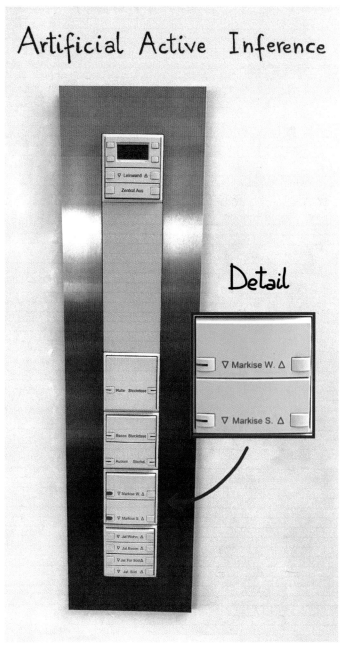

Figure 2.4 Home Automation

warning light, a perfect example of Active Inference in a silicon-based system. The weather station is constantly monitoring and sensing changes in the external environment of the house. An algorithm compares pre-established parameters with the actual readings of wind speed, humidity, rain, temperature. When the values deviate from the parameters and reach certain boundaries, the system activates specific actions and safety measures. Here, it has turned on the red signals, showing that it has blocked the sunshades as a precaution because the wind has reached a pre-defined strength; that is the system intervenes to avoid the wind ripping the shades apart and possibly causing collateral damage, even harming a person with the pieces flying around.

We can interpret the logic of this automation system as a light, easy-to-understand version of active inference. It has a generative model that operates with priors (the pre-established values of the parameters); a recognition model (the weather station) that samples the environment for events such as rain, changes in temperature, wind speed, etc. When events are above the pre-established bounds the system is programmed to tolerate, it takes protective action to avoid damage.

With some imagination, we can view the parametrized reference values (wind speed, frequency of rain, etc.) that activate the system as beliefs. Here, it is actually what the system's designers or operators believe is necessary to keep the functions running smoothly and safely.

The example of the automation system also illuminates another subtlety. The automated sunshades effectively minimize FE for the users by protecting them from the harmful effects of sunlight. In addition, from the system's point of view, its action to block the sunshades as a precautionary measure to avoid damage means the system is minimizing FE for the benefit of itself.

Nowadays, there are many examples of artifacts supporting AI processes. Increasingly, smart watches take on this function. Friends of mine who practice martial arts and sometimes train by themselves use smart watches to keep track of their workouts and monitor their condition to safeguard their health. For example, in case of a hard fall, the device recognizes the impact and asks if they have experienced a fall. Touching the "Yes" key on the watch starts an emergency call which could be a life-saving action. Similar measuring devices attached to the upper arm, around the waist, or on other body parts are used in many sports today. These are great examples of what the philosopher of science A. Clark calls Extended Active Inference (Constant et al, 2022), an AI process beyond the skull, outside of the human brain. As the internet of things becomes pervasive in our daily lives, we can expect more outsourcing of our AI processes to intelligent artifacts.

In contrast to extended AI, MBSAT supports a personalized, self-minding type of AI by training strategic awareness to process information accurately and support clear perceptions and skillful actions. There is an urgent need for this kind of personal AI capacity in today's environment, as risk and volatility create conditions where people are in far from desirable states (where FE is hard to minimize). We saw this in the rapidly aggravating environment of COVID-19 with its significant impact on job loss, suicide, divorce, family violence, etc., all distressing states preventing people from minimizing FE.

AI operationalizes the brain models in MBSAT training. It is a corollary of the FEP, involving two essential processes: perception and action. Perception within MBSAT is interconnected with updating our BETA states and our Portfolio of Beliefs in response to external and internal signals and triggering an AI process that hopefully leads to a more reliable predictive iteration.

2.3.2 Differentiating types of Active Inference

It is worth noting that, in MBSAT, AI can vary depending on the evidence and the type of reasoning prompting the prediction. For example, imagine your preschool child asks you: "Mom, where do I come from?" and you answer your son or daughter: "You come from inside me; I had you growing inside my belly, taking care of you for nine months until you were born." Your child continues to ask: "And mom, could dad have had me inside his belly, too?" "No, sweetie, only mothers can have kids inside their bellies; dads can't." This is the case of a Simple Active Inference process: a general prior with a high level of truthfulness (only women can have babies) allows for precise predictions with practically zero prediction errors.

There is another type of situation where there is no certainty of truthfulness, and the only information is a specific observation. Let's say you are visiting a new town and go out for dinner not knowing much about the local food but wanting to have a FE minimizing experience (wanting to eat a dish you like). After looking at the menu, you can't decide. You look around in the restaurant and notice the same dish on many tables. You ask the attendant about it and find out that it is a popular local dish. You keep asking the attendant different questions: What are the main ingredients? Is the dish popular also with foreigners? etc. The attendant tells you to try it. So, you order the dish, and you don't enjoy it. The attendant tells you that it can happen that a guest doesn't like it on the first try; for some it seems an acquired taste. She asks how long you will be in town. Hearing that you will stay about ten days she suggests you come back soon and try again. She says she is sure you will grow to like the dish. Here is a situation where from a single observation (the same dish on many tables) one is expected to enact a prediction: If this dish is so popular, even with foreigners, I can expect to like it, too. However, this turns out to be a prediction error, as you don't like the dish, and are unable to minimize FE. This type of inference can be defined as Complex Active Inference. In the example you probed the environment by asking questions of the attendant before ordering and you were aware that there could be different outcomes from absolute dislike to fully loving the dish and everything in between the extremes.

In cases of complex AI, the decision-maker often has the choice to do more observations, like going back to the restaurant as suggested by the attendant and ordering the dish again. Perhaps you find to your surprise that you like the dish this time, and now you can build general predictions about the dish based on a posterior belief (when I order this dish, most probably I will like it). In other words, you are now able to reduce uncertainty and risk and in a position to minimize FE (the average of prediction errors). However, in this case one is still left with the possibility that predictions and outcomes might not always match, whereas in the first example it will always be true that only women can give birth to children.

In both examples, reduction of FE happens in stable (only mothers give birth) or relatively stable environments (trying the same food another day). However, there are also circumstances in which the decision-maker finds himself in an unstable environment and in addition has incomplete observations to support predictions, thus facing multiple uncertainties and even higher complexity. Imagine the following situation. Your boss calls you and tells you of an opening in a remote country in the southern part of the globe, a region with socio-economic and political difficulties. He tells you that this could be your ticket to a higher position later back in the main office, if you take the assignment. Based on predicting your states in the future, do you think you will be able to minimize FE reasonably well in that country? First, what are your beliefs about the life you can have in that country? The other consideration you need to pay attention to is your beliefs regarding the genuine prospects of a top-level position coming back from the overseas assignment.

To engage with this type of inference, one needs to build deeper simulations, projecting and anticipating possible future states one might find oneself in under different scenarios and simulating the consequences of different decisions or actions, thus projecting the expected FE of diverse decisions and outcomes. This type of AI requires projecting oneself into the future and asking "what if" questions. For example, what if you choose to take the assignment and when the time comes for repatriation to the main office, there is an economic recession, and the chances of a big promotion are gone? These inferences are called Deep Active Inferences in MBSAT; they presuppose a quality of self-observation at a high meta-level, observing the states of one's BETA under different scenarios. This is where mindfulness approaches can be beneficial as they support the conditions of the mind necessary for lucid prospective perception/simulations and skillful decision-making and action.

There are similarities between this higher level of AI and strategic planning. People who work on strategic planning are familiar with "what-if" questions; they help them design multiple future scenarios by tweaking some parameters (price, quantity, quality, etc.), learning iteratively about different potential outcomes associated with different levels of risks and ambiguity. The questions asked in this type of AI are no other than questions about the precision of planners' beliefs. J.K. Friston called this version of AI sophisticated inference (Friston et al., 2021).

2.3.3 Active Inference (AI) as a process in MBSAT

The MBSAT protocol and AI as predictive process emphasizing action form an ideal partnership. This is highlighted by their shared meaning of inference as a process of accumulating evidence to reach a conclusion or help decide what action to take. AI in MBSAT is a spacious cognitive process where abstract ideas as well as practical issues can be worked out, such as "If I take this job, I might be in a secure position for the next five years". It is concerned about means ("If I exaggerate a little about my professional experience, I might get the job") and also value ("This harmless exaggeration will get me the position and then I can do a great job for the benefit of my employer"). Active Inference in MBSAT is beyond deductive (general truth to specific conclusions) or inductive (from specific observations to general truth) inquiry; it is more an artistic form of thinking based on abductive inquiry (from incomplete observations to educated guessing) trying to guess the right paths forward with incomplete data. AI is according to Friston (Friston et al., 2017) a process that captures the biological systems capacity to survive and flourish in VUCA environments. AI also assist people prevent entropy (disorder, dissipation) and help them with allostasis, which is a way of anticipating people's desired outcomes and to assist them in modifying the structure of the environment to accommodate their desired goals, while keeping their homeostasis balance (regulating their internal milieu to function at optimal levels) (Sterling, 2012).

MBSAT is about training our BETA through AI. This involves gaining agency and influence over the course of life by reducing the uncertainty affecting generative and recognition signals, optimizing decision-making and minimizing FE, thus maximizing flourishing and well-being states. The four first sessions of the program focus on training the brain's recognition models to observe with precision the causes of sensory phenomena. The sensory states influence internal states and they then can influence active states, which comprise the generative models, where predictions are activated based on beliefs (priors). This is the focus of the second half of the MBSAT training program (Sessions 5-8). Finally, the active states influence the external states by taking actions that affect the environment.

Inference processes are distributed throughout MBSAT's process of Active Inference Decisions (AID) (Figure 1.4, Chapter 1) as the mechanism that activates all the BETA components in a continuous-time dimension. This allows maintaining a predictive BETA that is based on robust but flexible brain models given that the context and content of people's states (sensory, internal, active and external) are constantly changing. The illustration of AID in the previous chapter illustrates a stay-at-home parent continuously tasting and seasoning the food she is preparing for her family, finding the optimal seasoning combination to decide when the dish is ready. This is an easily understandable example of the process of active inference for decision-making in a daily routinized activity.

Figure 1.4 shows there are four states of AI: internal states (predicting), sensory states (tasting, collecting evidence), active states (correcting discrepancies), and external states (in this example: the finished dish). Let's illustrate the process and its four states again with another example.

Imagine that you are going for a walk with a friend, and suddenly, you see two men holding a woman to the ground. You and your friend become agitated and both sense pressure on the temples. The scene (part of the generative process, the environment where the scene is generated) corresponds to the external states which impinge on your sensory states through the visual and auditory senses as you hear the woman shouting: "I have done nothing wrong." The men holding her down shout in return: "Relax, keep calm." Notice the direction of influence from the external states to the sensory states and from the sensory states to the internal states (for example, sensing pressure on the temples). It is essential to recognize that the scene impacted the sensory states (the seeing and hearing), not the internal states directly. It was the sensory states that then affected the internal states (the agitation in the BETA and the state of the generative model where beliefs are embedded).

So, what to do? It depends. Imagine you firmly believe that men should not grab women; for you, the sight of such a scene means the men have terrible intentions. The belief triggers a prediction about the woman being attacked; you might rush to defend the victim. Now imagine the following: you hold the belief that the woman must have stolen something from the men. This might lead to a prediction that the guys need help to hold the woman down, so you ask the men: "Hey, guys, do you need some help?" After investigating the event's causes, you find out that the woman had an epileptic attack. The two gentlemen were simply trying to calm her. In both cases, you could not minimize FE (avoiding a prediction error).

Your friend also witnessed the event but didn't engage with the situation. He went to a pharmacy to buy an aspirin to reduce his chance of getting a headache. Based on experiences, your friend acted on his belief that pressure in his temples equates to an imminent migraine. He minimized personal FE by reducing the probability of getting a headache. Perhaps one could question your friend's behavior and his indifference to situations requiring minimizing social FE, such as bullying, sexism, religious extremism, and other unharmonious social situations. Here is an important point to recognize: people's BETA can only be self-regulated by engaging actively with the environment, and this is because humans are open systems that are materialized within a larger system that is the environment.

Tutoring individuals to refine their Active Inference processes and become more contextually precise is a key training goal of MBSAT. It implies helping participants refine their abilities to formulate good predictions with fewer prediction errors, developing their competence for making skillful decisions that minimize FE (disappointments, frustrations, errors, the effects of VUCA, undesirable BETA) and supporting them on the path toward a flourishing life.

2.4 The Predictive BETA Mind (PBM)

2.4.1 The Predictive BETA Mind as personal laboratory

In MBSAT, the Predictive BETA Mind (PBM) is conceived as a personal laboratory where the individual is its own subject of experimental trials, permanently researching, probing, learning, and actively searching answers to the vital question: How can I enhance the value of my decisions to sustain and enrich the quality of my life? With the attitude of a scientist but more of an artist, the active MBSAT person carries a private lab in his/her head, devising predictions about the causes of internal occurrences (for example headaches, heart palpitations, strong feelings, spontaneous thoughts, impulses to act, and other happenings) and about external events in the environment (fluctuations in the job market, social interactions at work and in the family, changes in legislation, and many other types of events) that can affect the direction of his/her well-being. In effect, the MBSAT buddy engages in a vital ongoing research project about all the events (remembering past events, observing current events, and anticipating future events) that could impact her existence and compromise her capacity to reduce VUCA (Free Energy). In other words, the MBSAT buddy is optimizing his/her learning rate as she comes across more events in her life and gathers more experiences.

In Figure 2.5, the MBSAT buddy is embedded in a system of resources (possibilities offered by the environment), a family, a car, shopping facilities, a pet, communication by phone, working in the office and online, traveling, etc. His predictive BETA mind (the union of body sensations, emotions, thoughts, and actions that forms the brain models) is continuously and actively inferring and optimizing his/her three computational quantities: prediction, prediction error, and precision and looking for optimal strategies and policies that allow to minimize FE for avoiding decision mistakes The predictive BETA mind (PBM) comprises our whole human being, symbolized in the illustration of Figure 2.5 by the Greek letter ß surrounding the entire MBSAT buddy. In finance the letter ß is associated with risk and volatility. Living means indeed managing risk and volatility; therefore, it requires a well-trained predictive BETA mind to ensure sustainable well-being.

Figure 2.5 The Predictive BETA Mind

In most mindfulness-based programs, the present moment is praised and sought-after. "Being in the present moment" is actively cultivated and perceived as something that needs to be achieved. Buddhist monks made the idea famous and J. Kabat Zinn (2013) spread it in the West; it suggests that individuals cultivate an absence of cognitive content about the past or future to be more mindful in life. MBSAT is based on a Bayesian view of the brain that implies a mind that holds priors (beliefs, preconceptions) and continuously samples the environment for either updated or reinforced beliefs to help minimize FE (equivalent here to uncertainty). Thus, for MBSAT, the mind will always be consciously or unconsciously actively loaded with content about the past and future, sampling the present to generate more accurate predictions and reduce prediction errors. In MBSAT, I call this the state of "present predictive awareness" which represents strategic awareness. In connection with practicing in Part 2 we will return to this issue and find out that trying to get rid of thoughts actually results in trying to control them, rather than learning to understand them.

2.4.2 The Predictive BETA Mind and its interconnection with the nervous system

From MBSAT's perspective, what is needed to help us progress on our vital path towards flourishing and well-being is a healthy "Predictive Beta Mind" (PBM). As shown in Figure 2.5, this is the view that the mind not only resides in the central nervous system (the brain and the spinal cord) but that through the peripheral nervous system, the mind is distributed and permeates the whole body, with such a huge number of neurons that, if connected end to end, would circle the world two and half times, despite their microscopical size. The PBM's generative and recognition models are then conceived as mind processors to capture data and process information from bodily sensations, emotions (feelings or moods, if you like), mental percepts or thoughts, and action impulses. The latter are the carrier of signals that are potentially important for our well-being. Inspired by David Marr's framework of three levels of analysis, mentioned in Section 1.7, I am interlinking the FE Principle, MBSAT, and the Predictive Beta Mind as they are connected by their joint purpose and function of improving and optimizing the human capacity to process information to enhance the chances of survival. The three levels can be described as follows.

At the **computational first level**, the task is to define what one intends to optimize. As to the FE Principle, one seeks to optimize FE minimization, which in MBSAT corresponds to a low average of prediction errors, as this is what allows us to refine our decision skills. This in turn corresponds to optimizing beliefs by the PBM as apposite beliefs are the basis for skillful decision-making. At the **algorithmic level**, the question is what process can help us achieve optimization of our decision skills. The answer is the eight-week MBSAT training with its specific practices for precise Active Inference processes included in the protocol that allow for FE minimization, effective beliefs, and low prediction errors. Finally, at the **implementation level**, we have to ask where the computational and algorithmic processes get implemented. After regular training with the practices of MBSAT during a long enough period, the processes will be engraved in the cortical microcircuits (Bastos et al., 2012). Following a Hebbian learning process (neurons that fire together learn together) and with the frequent application of the MBSAT practices, the Predictive Beta Mind (PBM) will build habituation routines apt at generating skillful predictions and recognizing predictions errors with increased, calibrated precision.

It may be worthwhile to point out that MBSAT's concept of predictive BETA mind is compatible with the concepts of the widely accepted, classical cognitive psychology model. Figure 2.6 connects BETA as the focus of training in MBSAT with Beck's renowned cognitive model (Young, 2017, p. 128 and 143-5).

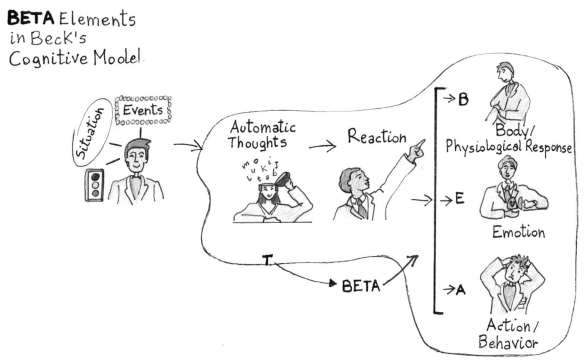

Figure 2.6 BETA Elements in Beck's Cognitive Model

2.4.3 The Predictive BETA Mind in decision-making

The MBSAT training model based on the FE Principle requires individuals to find a happy balance between the mandate to minimize FE to sustain our path towards flourishing and well-being, and the intentional but occasional situations in which one needs to build, invest and even consume FE. And here is where strategic awareness plays a crucial role in guiding our BETA to make skillful decisions. Although it is not my desire or preference to use personal examples to illustrate concepts, given that this is a workbook oriented towards applied theory and practical application, personal examples could help clarify ideas. Besides, it is compatible with one of the primary learning vehicles in MBSAT: experiential learning. In MBSAT programs, we invite participants to test the interventions and share the results of their experiences as a mechanism for collaborative learning. In that spirit, I share an incident that happened years ago. It was crucial in my life, yet I grasped the actual nature of the experience only recently with the help of the FE Principle.

When I arrived in Switzerland, I had an excellent position as Director of Planning and Management Control of the international division at the largest Swiss hospitality and gastronomy enterprise in Switzerland at the time. After a little more than a year, it became clear that my performance was severely impaired because of language barriers. Most members of the executive level were not yet fluent in English, and I could not speak German. My planning initiatives for the future of the company were not understood; it was, for me, a demotivating environment. I remember proposing acquiring the USA-based McDonald's franchise for Switzerland. The response I got was: "Mr. Young, it is obvious that you don't understand the Swiss mentality; we will never eat with our hands; we eat hamburgers with knife and fork." Just for the record, McDonald Swiss is one of the largest food businesses in Switzerland today and has surpassed my former employer's turnover years ago. After the disappointing experience, I decided to speak with the owner and the chairman of the company, and we agreed that I should stop working and concentrate on learning German. The CEO instructed the human resource manager to formulate a separation letter that would qualify me for unemployment benefits (80% of my compensation as Director of Planning for two years). With this documentation, I went to the Zurich unemployment office, where they told me to come back at the end of the month to receive the first of the payments. Later I returned to the office, but when they presented me with the amount, I simply couldn't accept the money. Confronted in earnest with the situation of taking money for not working, I backed off.

My refusal led to a discussion with the officer, a gentle lady; she told me that it was my right to have the money, that it was the provision of the law and perfectly normal in Switzerland.; She even called her boss who repeated that I was entitled to the money and that it was a large sum because my pay rate was very high. He even recommended saving some of the money and then going to the very best German language school. Despite all of these arguments, I refused the money and gave them three reasons. Firstly, I believed in getting paid for work, not earning money without having to work for it. Secondly, as long as I was healthy, I believed I could do some kind of work, if necessary below my qualifications; a less qualified job at a low salary was still better in my view than getting paid for not working. And finally, I argued, Swiss people had been making contributions for years to the unemployment fund, whereas I was less than two years in the country. Accepting the enormous monthly benefits was for me like abusing the country's institutions. I believed this would not be fair to the people of this country and it didn't feel right to me. They told me this was the first time in all the years they had been working at the unemployment office that a person refused benefits. We ended up shaking hands, and after closing the door behind me and leaving the building, I remember thinking: I hope things go well and I have made the right decision. The harsh truth was that I had hardly any savings; in fact, it was the first time that I had debt as I borrowed money to pay for the last semester of my studies at Harvard.

This very concrete example can help understand and illustrate the PBM. My decision to reject the benefits was based on the prediction that I would be able to find a job and based on my belief that even being employed below my qualifications was more desirable than getting paid essentially for not working. It was difficult to know under the circumstances how accurate the precision of the prediction that I had made was. I had never before experienced being unemployed and didn't have previous knowledge of how long it could take to find a job given the multiple obstacles (foreigner, without knowledge of the country's language, zero social capital, and almost no financial capital). The precision of my predictions was informed by beliefs inherited from my parents: one works for one's money; one delivers more value than expected; any job is good providing that it is honest work. Soon afterward I started to look for a job, which proved to be a challenging task; during that time, I often asked myself if I had made a mistake (prediction error) in refusing the unemployment benefits. Eventually I found a job, although not at my level, but the beginning of what turned out to be a rather successful and fulfilling working and professional trajectory to this day.

For years I have been thinking about this crucial decision and its consequences in my life, seeking meaning in what happened on the grounds of classical attributes: luck, courage, hard work, honesty, fairness, ... and yes, while these factors played a role at a deeper level the explanation felt incomplete. As mentioned earlier, it is only recently, from the perspective of the Free Energy Principle that I have come closer to a better understanding of my action, when I voluntarily created a situation of increased FE and VUCA in my life contrary to the normal reaction to try to minimize it. It would have been easy to accept the benefits and avoid the uncertainty that I created with my refusal to take the money.

An argument that has been used as an objection to the Free Energy Principle is the so-called "Dark Room Problem". It stipulates that if the goal is to reduce Free Energy (uncertainty, complexity, the entire VUCA), the easiest way is to simply reduce the impact of sensory inputs by shutting yourself up in a dark room where the probability of being able to minimize Free Energy is as high as possible. This argument is flawed, however; it may work for a mole or a deep-sea fish species that can exist in dark environments, but not for humans who need to interact with their environment to maximize their survival chances.

In hindsight and enlightened by the Free Energy Principle I could re-interpret what happened at the time of my crucial decision to refuse the unemployment benefits. I became aware of my unconscious belief that accepting the compensation was equivalent to entering a dark room and that the risk might be to become complacent and lose the drive to look for new opportunities. By refusing the benefits, creating entropy, and augmenting Free Energy (VUCA), I felt that the personal costs (economically, psychologically, and socially) associated with the additional uncertainty were in reality an investment. I firmly believed that eventually I would be able to find an honest job - perhaps for a while below my experience and training, but still capable to create a sustainable way of minimizing VUCA in my life in the longer term.

This experience can be seen in the framework of "exploitation versus exploration", a classical strategic problem. Taking the benefits would have meant exploiting an easily accessible offer from a system (the unemployment benefits scheme). Not using the system, on the other hand, pushed me out of my comfort zone, forcing me to explore innovative ways to ensure my socio-economic survival in an unfamiliar environment. I unambiguously chose the latter, with no regrets.

We move now to Chapter three which is dedicated to the design of the MBSAT program and its distinctive features.

Chapter 3

THE MBSAT PROGRAM AND ITS DISTINCTIVE FEATURES

Mindfulness-based Strategic Awareness Training Comprehensive Workbook:
New approach Based on Free Energy and Active inference for Skillful Decision-making,
First Edition. Juan Humberto Young.
© 2023 John Wiley & Sons Ltd. Published 2023 by John Wiley & Sons Ltd.
Companion website: www.wiley.com/go/young/mbsatworkbook

3.1 The Predictive Brain in MBSAT

MBSAT is conceived as a mind learning protocol similar to machine learning. It intends to help participants capture valid data as they interact with the environment (family, work, etc.), help them efficiently process all data or experiences, train their recognition and generative models in the brain and learn from this process to formulate reliable predictions as the basis for skillful decisions with minimal prediction errors. One of the most salient distinctive features of the MBSAT program is seeing the brain as a prediction organ, which requires a fundamental paradigm shift from participants. Most people view the brain as a reactive nerve center triggered by external stimuli.

MBSAT's conception of the brain as an information processing organ follows the view that the brain engages in computations necessary for anticipating our biological and cultural needs. In this program, we are interested in four types of computations reflecting the core elements of the MBSAT protocol. The **first set** of computations is related to our body sensation, emotions, thoughts, and action impulses (**BETA**); the goal is to reach balanced, calm states to generate smooth, reliable BETA computations.

The **second set** of computations relates to our **beliefs**, especially in dealing with adversity and financial needs. The goal is to generate computations to inform and maintain flexible beliefs and facilitate counterfactual analysis supporting our predictions within the context of ongoing events or situations.

The **third set** of computations relates to social computations in **relational** settings. Here, the intention is to generate wholesome computations infused with respect for others that can support our predictions about our fellow human beings and facilitate formal and informal social interactions capable of generating trustworthy, valuable social environments.

The **fourth group** relates to strategic computations that enable effective **decision-making**. It is about embracing the value of satisficing instead of maximization as a strategic criterion for decision making, recognizing and accepting that life is all about negotiating compromises.

Reliable computations are the basis for skillful predictions and maintain low prediction errors. This is the essence of MBSAT training: learning to refine mind computations for making accurate, precise predictions that support skillful decision-making and reduce decision errors.

As discussed in the previous chapter, the brain has two computational models: the generative and the recognition model (Ramstead et al., 2019 & 2020). They embody encoded beliefs about our internal states and the external environment. The beliefs guide our sensations, feelings, cognitive processes, and actions reflected in our BETA (body sensations, emotions, thoughts, and actions impulses). Therefore, keeping these two models in an optimal state is central to minimizing Free Energy (FE). From this point of view, MBSAT is a training protocol on how to reduce FE for helping individuals stay in states of sustainable well-being and flourishing. It implies learning to mind computational information reflected in the four structural components of the MBSAT training program:

- Minding - BETA.
- Minding the Portfolio of Beliefs – POB (Section 3 of this chapter).
- Minding our Social Experiences – SoE (Section 4).
- Minding the Strategic Adaptation of Life – SAL (Section 5).

3.2 Minding Our BETA: The Recognition Models in MBSAT - Valence and Feeling Tone

3.2.1 The recognition models and their interplay with valence and feeling tone

MBSAT trains the brain's recognition models by focusing on attention training. By strategically paying attention, one can increase the ability to recognize accurately and thus increase the precision of one's recognition model. In the framework of the MBSAT program, attention is equivalent to precision: one needs to be attentive and strategically aware to make precise predictions. In MBSAT, we build the capacity to be precise and strategically aware in perceiving and interpreting both internal and external phenomena by continuously refining our evaluation of interior states and external states (environment).

The recognition models help generate posterior beliefs encoded in the internal states representing the best guesses of the causes of sensory states once new information has been observed. Therefore, recognition models are crucial as they provide the mechanism to update beliefs, which is essential for transformative learning. To function optimally, they need to be supported by adequate BETA states that are influenced by feeling tone or valence in the terminology of neuroscience. Valence or feeling tone has been recognized as an essential mediator of the states of the BETA that support people's recognition models.

Exciting findings from laboratory experiments in neuroscience reveal the influence of emotions on our predictive brain's optimal functioning and FE minimizing. This confirms the teachings in Buddhist psychology that our experiences are driven by feeling tones or Vedana in the ancient Pali language. Feeling tones are conceived as having three essential qualities: pleasant, unpleasant, and neutral. Suffering in Buddhist psychology, or Duhkha in Pali, is generated when these fundamental basic tones are maladaptive; for example, when pleasant sensations and emotions become an addiction, unpleasant emotions turn into hate, and the neutral feeling tone becomes apathy.

3.2.2 The Free Energy Principle (FEP) and valence in MBSAT

The pioneering work of Alice Isen on the value of positive emotions showed the adaptive effects of positive emotions on cognitive flexibility (2004), decision-making (2015), and self-regulation (2000). Also, Seligman (2012) illustrated the importance of positivity for flourishing states; he created the field of Positive Psychology, now a well-established branch of psychological science, with a considerable allegiance of researchers and applied professionals. And what about negative emotions? They exist, of course, and have a defensive function that mobilizes "fight or flight" responses when we sense danger and existential threat (physically or mentally). For this reason, MBSAT views both positive and negative sensations, emotions, thoughts, or actions composing BETA as adaptive, depending on their context. They are all necessary and potentially have a useful function in minimizing FE. From this perspective, it may be helpful to think of Adaptive Psychology instead of Positive Psychology.

From the point of view of the Free Energy Principle (FEP), emotions are considered beliefs with an encoded expected precision about the consequences of active inference and related actions. Here is an example of the interconnection between belief, emotion, and active inference in the following simplified reasoning: "If I work hard, I will get a large bonus, and I will be pleased." Based on the FEP paradigm, Active Inference posits that emotions emerge or are influenced by our beliefs. In this example, working hard (the belief) will be rewarded with an outcome (a promotion, more significant bonus, salary increase, etc.) that will make the individual happy and able to minimize FE (complexity, uncertainty, etc.).

Underlying the specificity of emotional states is a general tonality, defined as mood. In general psychology, moods are conceived as containing a general valence that lasts longer than an emotion. A mood could be, for example, a joyful or playful mood or, conversely, an angry or fearful mood. What becomes apparent is a standard duality of goodness with positive outcomes, hence with desirable states and undesirable states with negative valence and adverse outcomes.

Under the FEP scheme, moods parallel emotional beliefs; they are hyper-priors. Moods are a type of belief about the emotional consequences of actions (Clark et al., 2018). The mood reflects the overall momentum or expected direction produced by prediction errors. A positive mood suggests things are going well and will even continue well. A negative mood means the opposite, that things are not going well and might even get worse. (Kiverstein et al., 2020). In MBSAT, we conceive emotional valence as a proxy for the rate of change of FE over time, both its direction and velocity. When minimizing FE, one increases the probability of being in valuable states (a good job, a good marriage, reliable friends, etc.). We associate positive valence under this view with emotions that decrease FE and resolve VUCA. In contrast, we associate negative valence with increased FE and lack of resolution of VUCA. More than being in a positive or negative emotional state, its valence takes a dynamic view associated with the direction, the velocity, and the rate at which one can reduce prediction errors (Joffily & Coricelli, 2013).

Studies of negative emotions and stimuli reveal they increase reactivity by activating in the brain the amygdala, the hippocampus, and the anterior pole of the PFC (prefrontal cortex), with physical manifestations observed by an increase in the heart rate and respiration rate, detectable via hyperventilation. Positive emotions reveal the opposite, less reactivity and less activity in the amygdala, hippocampus, and the PFC, which allows for gentle adaptive states to emerge, for example, cognitive reappraisal, allowance, acceptance, as strategies that support emotional regulation and prevent overreaction, (Goldin et al., 2019). Not that one type of emotion is superior to another; what is necessary is to match the contextual situation to emotional regulation and skillful decision making. For example, suppose you are driving, and a car is heading in your direction, out of control. In that case, the best emotional strategy is to leverage fear supporting a rapid reaction to avoid a collision and minimize FE (getting hurt). Here, the way out of this unpredictable situation is by following the direction of our unpleasant emotions (fear).

It can help predict the origin and orientation of the expected uncertainty and help engage actions that decrease expected FE, the uncertainty about the consequences of occurrences and actions. Here, one should react fast as the action must happen without delay (Solms, 2019), as FE minimization results in emotional balance. (Demekas et al., 2020).

In one of his interviews, K. Friston argued that a reasonable person from the point of view of her existential goodness would be good at minimizing FE or maximizing the evidence of her generative models. This means that the person, when confronted with new information, will process and assimilate the information in an efficient thermodynamic way. A reasonable person will have a cool brain, where her prior beliefs are already quite close to her posterior beliefs, meaning that the person already has a good idea of what is going on, so the probability of a surprise is low, the person can minimize complexity costs (the price that she would need to pay to provide for the accuracy of some information). Thus, the person can smoothly optimize her belief updating.

MBSAT's entire design accords with this line of reasoning. BETA training, the cultivation of strategic awareness, and the softening of beliefs through transformative learning reduce surprises and close the gap between priors and posteriors, effectively minimizing FE. MBSAT helps maintain a minimum adaptive set of prior beliefs that can easily be updated without overhauling the entire portfolio of beliefs. Also, individuals with such a handy set of beliefs are in a suitable position to optimize the return of their total portfolio of beliefs in the form of lasting well-being.

3.2.3 Free Energy, BETA states and valence in MBSAT

Referencing the psychoanalyst Holmes (2022), we can state that FE is aversive and represents pain, while reducing FE is rewarding and motivating, with feeling tones and valence acting as the drivers of the FE minimization processes and gradients. Figure 3.1. summarizes the relations between the valence of BETA states and FE minimization and visualizes the notion of gradients.

In the upper left corner, the illustration shows a person in distress whose BETA is in a low FE minimization state, needing to direct her state to higher minimization states, perhaps by allowing, accepting, or resigning to an aversive situation, hoping that a solution will emerge later. The red gradient visualizes this adjustment in direction. A person in an unrealistic, Pollyannaish positive state is depicted in the lower-left corner. Although this person is in a BETA state of low intensity, she cannot minimize FE, as problems will probably remain unresolved. She will need to engage in mobilizing the direction of her positive states to regions of higher FE minimization, corresponding to the green gradient

The following example highlights how impactful existential feeling tone can be. One of my MBSAT students, an executive in Madrid, Spain, with Syrian roots, told the class about the survival story of one of his friends who was imprisoned under horrific conditions with three inmates in the same cell. His friend said he made it a habit during his time in jail to go daily on imaginary "beach strolls" whereby he would sit with his eyes closed and imagine himself walking along the seashore, using this daydream as a positive recharging strategy to cope with the traumatic circumstances. One of his three companions died in prison; the other two became seriously affected mentally. In contrast, my student's friend is now out of jail and working in a good position in a more peaceful country. This story has much in common with Viktor Frankl's observations in concentration camps during World War II. Individuals with an optimistic mindset, including Frankl, were more likely to survive and overcome the horror in a relatively adequate state than individuals with a more pessimistic outlook.

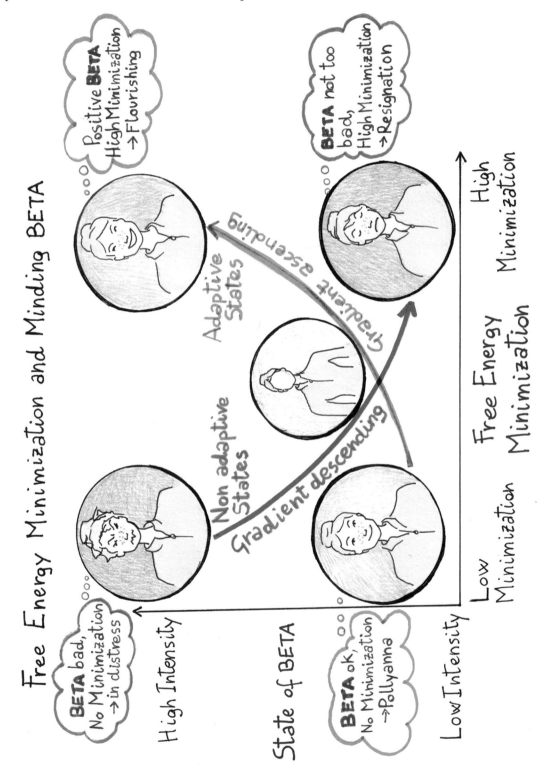

Figure 3.1 Free Energy Minimization and Minding BETA

Nevertheless, it is worth reiterating that an essential aspect regarding valence or feeling tone is that no particular feeling tone, emotion, or valence is superior to others. Positive or negative valence feeling tones are all adaptive, provided that they minimize FE and are part of contextualized processes. As seen in the example of an imminent collision, negative emotions such as fear can also be lifesaving, depending on the circumstances.

Minding our BETA is about recognizing and minding the interoceptive, proprioceptive, and exteroceptive signals of BETA, either generated and related to the body's internal conditions or emanating from the environment. It is about bringing integrity and stability to Body sensations, Emotions, Thoughts, and Actions impulses. A stable BETA can survive in an adverse environment, whereas an unstable BETA can't survive even in friendly environments (Wiese & Metzinger, 2017). Predictions are related to both interoception (internal signals) and exteroception (sensory signals from the environment) and movements of our body (proprioception). However, it is often more critical to avoid unexpected interoceptive states, like finding oneself with loss of oxygenation, than unexpected exteroceptive sensations, like being confronted with a foul odor (Seth, 2015).

Minding our BETA is the focus of the first phase of the MBSAT training program to assist the brain in achieving balanced, relaxed computations. In Minding Beta, we have two steps:
a) Recognizing the states of the BETA by observing and watching each element: the body sensations, the emotions, the thoughts, and the actions impulses.
b) Contextually vectorizing or directing BETA towards FE Minimization zones either by amplifying a desirable direction of the BETA or by decelerating an undesirable direction of the BETA.

Once participants in MBSAT training have gained some practice with this skill, they move to the next phase. Using curated data that have been precisely recognized and stabilized during the Minding BETA phase, participants can proceed to Minding their Portfolio of Beliefs which form the basis for reducing VUCA and increasing the accuracy of their generative models necessary for resolving uncertainty and making precise predictions and skillful decisions.

While the first phase of MBSAT centers on the recognition models, the second phase centers on the generative models of the brain. These are the focus of Section 3.3.

3.3 Minding our Portfolio of Beliefs (POB): The Generative Models in MBSAT

"All that we are is the result of what we think; those who shape their mind after selfish thoughts bring misery wherever they talk and go... All we are is the result of what we think; those who shape their minds after selfless thoughts bring joy wherever they talk and go." (Easwaran, 1985, Twin Verses) These famous Twin Verses are the beginning of the Dhammapada, the collected teachings by Buddha, a source of wisdom that goes back more than 2000 years. They point out from time immemorial the importance of the quality of cognitive processes in creating experiences. Modern neuroscience and psychology corroborate the ancient wisdom scientifically. Minding BETA relies on scientific findings from Applied Neuroscience and Psychology for balancing body sensations, emotions, thoughts, and action impulses while Minding the Portfolio of Beliefs relies on robust evidence from Applied Neuroeconomics and Cognitive Behavioral psychology to transform and update beliefs.

Our individual experiences, culturally shaped patterns, and evolutionary tendencies form our generative models, which are parametrized and formalized as beliefs about what is causing our experiences. They are operationalized with an initial prediction, with prima facie inferences about the most probable hypothesis about a sensory observation. It is a naïve calculation of a joint probability of sensing (in the example below, a classical music piece) and its possible hidden causes. The following illustrative anecdote can clarify this process in practical terms.

Imagine a person fond of impressionist composers hearing a particular piece and exclaiming: "What a lovely tune!" then turning to a friend and saying: "Who is this? It must be Lang-Lang playing Gabriel Fauré." This is her recognition in action. Her friend tells her that it is Helene Grimaud playing Lili Boulanger, a French impressionist composer and one of the very few women writing music at the beginning of the last century.

Now the generative music model of both persons is activated as both make a prediction. The person asking generates an implicit prediction: "I would like to know the composer's name as I may want to listen to this music again in the future." Epistemic value guides her question (acquiring new knowledge). She is about to enrich her generative world model by incorporating new beliefs or priors related to her knowledge of impressionist music. Next time she listens to similar music, she is likely to formulate a more precise question: "Oh, wonderful music! It sounds like an impressionist composer, doesn't it?"

Let's assume this time her friend answers it is by Gabriel Fauré, a late French romantic composer contemporary with the impressionists. Thus, the person asking just made a prediction error. Still, now she can update her generative model with a richer set of priors: "Late French romantic composers may sound like impressionist composers given that their artistic work period overlaps for 10 to 20 years around the end of the romantic period and the beginning of impressionism." Correcting a prediction is equivalent to updating an existing prior, generating a posterior belief that will serve as a new prior. The hindsight inspires the next foresight in a kind of inverted sequence. The example also shows how the generative model shapes the recognition model and vice versa.

The illustration in Figure 3.2 visualizes this recognition sequence (symbolized by music notes), prediction, prediction error, and belief updating. An opaque screen in the center of the image indicates the difficulty and uncertainty in making predictions based on our recognition models. The outcome of the interrelated models always carries a certain degree of uncertainty and probability of error, so the screen is labeled Markov Blanket in reference to mathematical statistics focusing on randomness and probability. It also represents the fact that persons recognizing the environment and generating prediction or actions are separate from the milieu or generative process.

The generative models activate impulses and give them a direction originating from prior internal beliefs, in this case, guessing the causes of an external stimulus that triggered the sensations. However, the prediction that Fauré was the composer was inaccurate; only after finding out that it was Lili Boulanger is the actual cause of the musical sensation revealed.

The practices of MBSAT help individuals optimize their portfolio of beliefs by becoming aware of their beliefs and understanding how they have been shaped by personal experiences, cultural influence, and biological conditioning. MBSAT seeks to assist individuals in maintaining a robust set of adaptive beliefs that increases the quality of their predictions. Having accurate predictions is key to staying in the desirable states on the right side of the landscape of FE Minimization (Figure 2.2). In the prediction error case regarding the composer, losing Free Energy is trivial; however, imagine making the same prediction error in an important, prize-winning quiz. If you guessed the composer's name correctly, you could have won a free lifelong subscription to all the concerts in the city. Here, not getting the prediction right would undoubtedly be an economic loss and a setback in well-being.

At the beginning of this chapter, we saw the quote from the Dhammapada that we are what we think; in reality, we are what we believe. Indeed, our beliefs are what drive our BETA. This points to the importance of having adaptive beliefs that function well in our private lives and society. There are always beliefs behind thinking, behaving, feeling, and acting. Let's say a person buys a house in the countryside, considering that the quality of her life will be better than in an urban environment. Not only her cognitive process is driven by a belief (the quality of life is better in the countryside than in urban settings), but also her action (buying the house in the countryside will increase my well-being) and her feelings (I will be happy in the countryside).

One of the goals of MBSAT is to assist participants to discover and identify their beliefs associated with the themes of each session. This is challenging; often, beliefs run hidden behind the scenes doing the heavy lifting for our activities. The aim is to review and, if necessary, readapt, refine or even replace beliefs to make them conform to the changing reality of today's environment.

Behavioral research has demonstrated that individuals are risk-averse concerning their possessions, meaning they want to conserve their possessions and have difficulty disposing of them (Kahneman 2012; Kahneman and Tversky 1979). This finding has extremely far-reaching consequences and ramifications. One of my friends, a highly trained economist, once heard an explanation by Lee Kuan Yew, the late prime minister of Singapore. In an address to a small audience, he described how he observed people doing the impossible to save their possessions during the catastrophic Bukit Ho Swee fire in Singapore on May 25th, 1961. The then prime minister said that experience gave him insight into what was required to achieve a well-functioning democracy. People needed to have a stake in it, and for that, people needed to have possessions and assets, especially their own home. This led to a housing policy in Singapore that resulted in over 90% percent of homeowners and a very stable and prosperous state.

Beliefs are like possessions, as Abelson concluded (1986). If this is the case, one must act as an investor and skillfully manage one's portfolio of beliefs. This is precisely MBSAT's point of view and the focus of Part 2 of the training program: Minding our Portfolio of Beliefs (MPB). It comprises three phases:

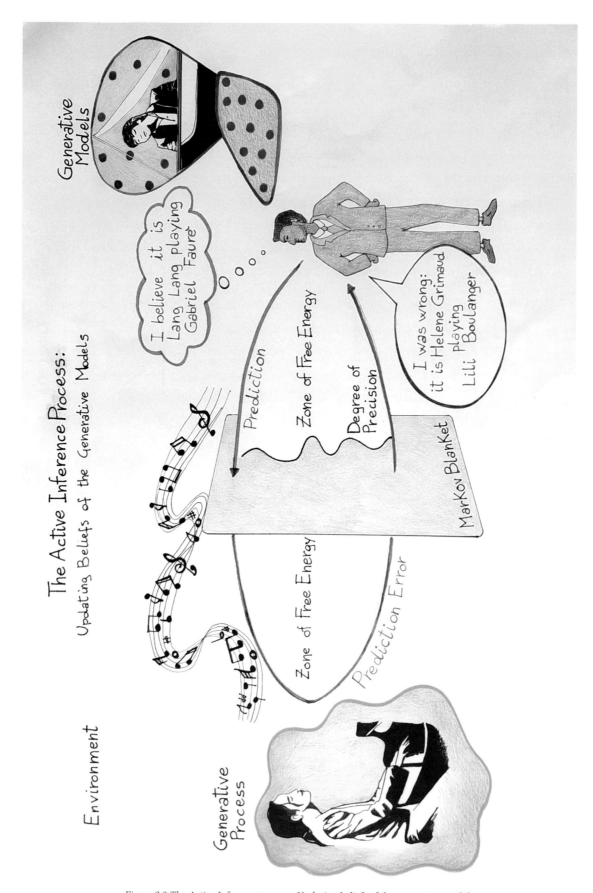

Figure 3.2 The Active Inference process: Updating beliefs of the generative models

⊚ Phase I of Minding our Portfolio of Beliefs: Recognizing our beliefs

The intention here is to acknowledge our beliefs or priors in the language of the Predictive brain. This phase is challenging because beliefs are often obscure and invisible to our daily awareness while running the show of our life, making us automatons without consciousness and agency over our own experience. Here we seek to leverage our brain's recognition models to help us catch beliefs in different aspects of our lives.

⊚ Phase II of Minding our Portfolio of Beliefs: Understanding the function of our beliefs

Here, the intention is comparable to managing a financial portfolio where it is standard practice to assign risk weights to each asset. In MBSAT, the goal is to understand each belief's risk profile by assessing their potential contribution to minimizing FE. Some beliefs will help us reduce FE; others will not. Still, we must grapple with all of them to understand the added value or added risk they bring to our lives. It is essential to have the strategic awareness to recognize the impact that some beliefs (priors) entrenched in our brain's generative models exert on our lives.

⊚ Phase III of Minding our Portfolio of Beliefs: Recalibrating our beliefs

Finally, having identified our beliefs and gained a deeper understanding of our beliefs' functionality, the last step is to take action to recalibrate our portfolio of beliefs. For that, we use the MBSAT FE Minimization Action Quadrants (FEMAQ). Some beliefs are likely to be dropped, such as the belief that a married couple is always a man and a woman, and new beliefs may be formed, such as "marriage is possible between persons of a different gender and persons of the same gender." We can also recalibrate a belief upwards or "up-recalibrating" it; for example, the belief about not liking fetid fruits like Asian durian; after testing the fruit, one might find it pleasant. The belief becomes, "well, certain fetid fruits are ok."

Conversely, one can also "down–recalibrate" beliefs, for example, the belief that it is hard to control overeating when you taste something delicious. When you eat something you particularly like with full senses (mindfully) instead of the usual mindless way, you might discover that you can moderate your intake and still feel satiated and happy. The belief becomes: "Favorite treats should be eaten very mindfully to avoid excessive consumption."

Figure 3.3 presents the four types of belief updating concerning the intensity of effort involved. Creating a wholly new belief or discontinuing an existing belief completely (the upper quadrants of the updating matrix) are the two types that stand for high-intensity and require greater motivational energy and determination. In contrast, reducing or increasing belief exposure (the lower quadrants) are updating modes of low intensity and involve less incisive modifications. However, this doesn't necessarily mean that the updating process is easier; the beliefs concerned might simply be less urgent or less critical.

Given the critical role of beliefs in our lives and their importance to fully leveraging the benefits of MBSAT, a good understanding of what beliefs are and how they function in our lives is vital. In MBSAT, we look at beliefs from three perspectives: general psychology, behavioral economics, and computational neuroscience, to ensure a comprehensive understanding and adequately mind our Portfolios of Beliefs.

For readers who would like to go deeper into this topic, there is a more detailed analysis from the three perspectives at the end of this chapter (below Boxes 1-3).

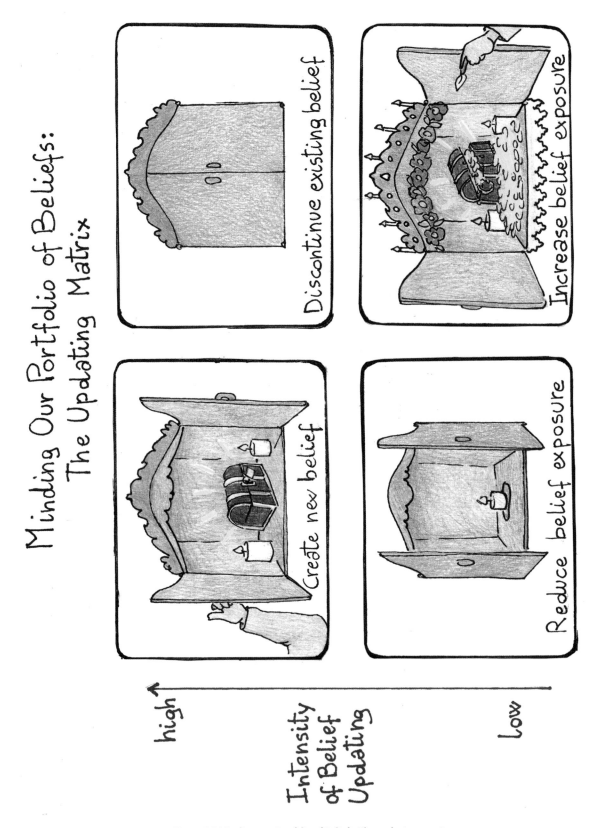

Figure 3.3 Minding our Portfolio of Beliefs: The updating matrix

3.4 Minding the Portfolio of Beliefs: People, Self, Adversity and Money

A significant part of beliefs stored in our generative models cluster around three central themes pervasive in our lives: people (including ourselves), adversity, and money. In practice, these themes are closely interwoven: adversities are often related to money issues or conflicts with people, and the corrosive force of money often seeps into our relations.

In the following sections, we focus on beliefs about people and ourselves as encompassing theme. We conclude with a brief outlook on training in Part 2, where adversity, money, and relations are treated in individual sessions.

3.4.1 Minding beliefs about people

"Other people matter" is a central belief in MBSAT. These were words often spoken by one of the architects of Positive Psychology, Christopher Peterson, who passed away shortly before teaching the inaugural class of a positive psychology leadership program in a business school where I was the academic director. Chris's phrase "other people matter" has reached iconic status amongst positive psychologists. One of the distinctive features of MBSAT is the set of practices designed for minding and caring not only about oneself but also about others, including nature, flora, fauna, and the climate. In one of the dinner conversations with Chris in Philadelphia, we discussed whether one could be happy caring only about oneself. The clear consensus was that it was not possible. However, we all recognize that we are dismally failing as human species, just looking at the state of things: economic turmoil, social inequality, ethnic relations, climate change, and many other grave matters.

Another friend, Steven Hickman, who created the Mindfulness Center at the University of California, San Diego, joined me several years ago to teach in the first MBSAT Teacher Training program. He wrote how uncomfortable he was with the tribal mentality he observed in the mindfulness community, seeing and feeling a sense of "us as counterpoint to them" in the mindfulness field whenever someone is doing something differently or acting in different ways, which leads to attitudes of exclusion or lack of recognition of the other. Although these are generalized human condition frailties, in his view, however, it is an odd behavior that mindful individuals and teachers should be concerned about as "we need to maintain an even higher standard of care and awareness of bias, discrimination, selfing and ethics in general." (Hickman, 2016, p.294).

Our social brain (Molapour et al., 2021) builds social computations necessary for minding ourselves and others in relation. The practices in MBSAT train to frame and integrate these computations for skillful predictions in social relations.

Seven types of social computations have been identified:

1) Social perception:
   Perceiving social signals like facial expression, body movements, speech.

2) Social inference:

Integrating verbal, body, and contextual information, including thinking about the mental states of others and inferring their beliefs.

3) Social learning:

Supporting passing information to others and lowering the costs of acquiring knowledge when learning from others, which is one of the goals of this book.

4) Social signaling:

Referring to the ability to transfer information via different cues: voice intonation, body posture, gaze, intensity, direction. These computations, amongst others, signal intentions, individuals' images, desires, and even the content of their beliefs

5) Social motivation:

Managing rewards (things people like and want) and rejections (what they find undesirable) as members of a social environment.

6) Group identity and bias computations:

Building and modulating dynamics in the group. These computations are vital for individuals living in more diversely integrated worlds. They assist individuals in transforming and opening up new patterns and paths of interactions, facilitating relations beyond homogenous groups.

7) Social integrative computations:

Minimizing the production of Free Energy (surprise, uncertainty, entropy) in a group, reducing social prediction errors, and maximizing socially shared generative models that facilitate social predictions in groups through fine-tuned socially active inference process.

When these computations are framed and modulated healthily, they contribute to building generative and recognition models shared by others as these computations are good at inferring BETAs generated by others and predicting BETAs caused by others, functioning like duets and choirs, developing socially skillful decision making. (Friston & Firth, 2015, Moutoussis, et al., 2014, Molapour, et.al., 2021). Minimizing Free Energy in social decision-making and policy design emerges as the superior metric, superseding, to some extent, classical utility maximization. Members of a group will still seek personal utility and keep their options open as freedom of choice to balance their self-centered ambitions with other-centered desires, thus generating less stress and more cooperation in groups. Training individuals to develop socially practical computations is at the center stage in MBSAT.

In a world that is becoming more integrated and diverse than ever, the importance of formulating and implementing effective social computations has become a critical success factor for people. Humberto

Maturana, the Chilean biologist and renowned co-author of the theory of autopoiesis [1], stated that the emotion required for well-functioning human systems is respect for the other, specifying that respect is essentially different from tolerance. He made a firm rejection of tolerance as an enabler of good life in groups. It is an unusual distinction, as most people think these two qualities are synonyms. In fact, the terms are far from being equal. Respect is an emotion that elevates attention. One pays more attention to something one respects; tolerance on the other hand establishes a permissible limit on differences one can accept, but tolerance can turn into negation or aggression once a certain threshold is crossed. With respect, Maturana suggests, understanding is possible even amongst people who hold different views; tolerance does not give the other person genuine attention. Our ideas prevail while waiting for the moment to negate what we have merely tolerated (Maturana, 2009).

3.4.2 Minding our self

The late Chris Argyris, who taught at Harvard Business School HBS, Harvard Kennedy School, and Harvard Education School, maintained that human beings hold two types of theories: one they espouse, representing what they believe and value, and another that they use and implement, reflected in their actions (Argyris & Schön, 1978). Argyris's research suggests that inconsistencies between the two theories lead people to act inconsistently. For example, people may believe individuals should be compassionate, but they cannot notice it when they act without compassion. Simply put, people regularly lack the awareness to observe themselves in action; it is only after the facts that they perhaps realize their actions. This is due to what Argyris called "defensive reasoning," creating a "Model I" way of thinking that builds defensive routines and prompts people to defend their worldviews and actions and to limit their learning to "single loop" feedback, where only ideas and actions that are self-serving and self-referential are admitted.

The way out of this trap for Argyris is to adopt a "productive reasoning" attitude that generates a "Model II" way of thinking, seeking to find the truth and understanding the reality about the world and our happenings. Based on double-loop learning feedback, not defensive knowledge creation, productive reasoning allows the constant renewal of our world views to be more consistent with a changing VUCA reality and the practical philosophy of MBSAT.

3.4.3 Focal points in training the Portfolio of Beliefs: adversity, money, and relationships

MBSAT's goal is to intentionally leverage Free Energy Minimization and Active Inference processes to help people eliminate the mismatch between their espoused theories and their theories-in-use and experience their lives consistently with more accurate predictions and fewer prediction errors. The training focus of our portfolio of beliefs is on difficulties with adverse situations, economic issues, and relationships. Sessions 5, 6, and 7 of the MBSAT program are specifically dedicated to assisting indi-

---

1 Maturana developed the theory of autopoiesis together with his student Francesco Varela. It is a wide range theory suggesting principles how living systems are capable of self-regulating and maintaining their own boundaries, thus their existence. The German sociologist Niklas Luhmann later expanded the theory to social systems to signify amongst other the capacity of social systems for communication and consciousness in order to allow for meaning-based self-reproduction practices.

viduals in identifying, updating, and minding their beliefs related to adversity, coping with money, and building relationships that support flourishing states.

With a finetuned Portfolio of Beliefs, we gain freedom and agency in our lives. Often, freedom is perceived as an individualistic enterprise. For the Korean-born Swiss-German philosopher Byung-Chul Han, freedom is social. He writes: "... being free originally means being with friends. Freedom and friend have the same linguistic Indo-European root. Freedom is basically a relationship word. One feels truly free only in a successful relationship, in happy togetherness with others." [2] Thus, freedom for oneself is only achieved in relationships with others.

3.5 Minding the Strategic Adaption of Life (SAL): Skillful Decision-Making

Decisions are, by definition, controversial (Karnani, 2008), just like business strategies that are formalized decisions setting the direction for a business. There are no perfect decisions that satisfy all desires; they always involve compromises: gaining something and losing/conceding something. Often, people are not aware of these trade-offs in their decision-making processes, which invariably cause dissatisfaction at some point. Refining people's decision-making skills can prove a sensible and effective strategy for more well-being for individuals and the world. Leaders and individuals consciously shaping their lives (self-leadership) aspire to increase their well-being and are called upon to promote the well-being of the people they are responsible for.

The states of people's lives result from the quality of their decisions. Today's world results from people's choices in the past; thus, a key focus of MBSAT is on improving the quality of decision-making by participants, as skillful decisions will enable FE minimization. From the perspective of computational neuroscience, what we need to improve life is to train the decision-making process concerned with selecting beliefs and actions amongst a range of options and possibilities. Decision-making is a process of selection that suggests three essential qualities: anticipation, simulation, and evaluation to choose wisely amongst alternative options.

At Harvard, I studied with the late Pierre Wack (1985), the French oil executive who accurately predicted two oil crises and later supported Nelson Mandela with a post-apartheid South Africa scenario. I enjoyed his classes very much, not only because of his extensive erudition and academic knowledge, but also because of the realism of his course deriving from his experiences in business. In one of his lectures he said that managers and people should think like paddlers steering a canoe in the middle of river rapids with steep gradients that create turbulence and high-velocity currents. In such situations, the paddler must make continuous decisions that impact the success or failure of reaching the destination alive and healthy. Wack already anticipated today's VUCA conditions and needs. We all have to skillfully surf the waves of

---

2 Original German text: "Frei-sein bedeutet aber ursprünglich bei Freunden sei. Freiheit und Freund haben im Indogermanischen dieselbe Wurzel. Die Freiheit ist im Grunde ein Beziehungswort. Man fühlt sich wirklich frei erst in einer gelingenden Beziehung, in beglückendem Zusammensein mit anderen." (2016, *Psychopolitik*, S. Fischer Verlag GmbH, Frankfurt am Main, p. 11)

chaos in an increasingly VUCA world. In such environments, the most important ability we have is our agency, which we need to keep refining to become more precise about our predictions, not only about what may happen but also about what needs to be decided if the future states of our predictions, once realized, are to be desirable adaptive states that enhance the chances of minimizing Free Energy.

Strategic awareness allows one to build counterfactual options and investigate a wide range of choices to evaluate decisions under different scenarios. When we introduce counterfactual capacities into our Active Inference process, we add to our decision-making arsenal a prominent feature often used in strategic management and planning ("what if" questions). For example, we can ask questions like: What do I expect to experience if this decision becomes a reality based on my prediction? Will I experience the desired state I am predicting now? Will my expected utility/state (*expected* FE Minimization) coincide with my future experienced utility/state (*actual* FE Minimization)? These questions make it apparent that precision is the key driving force for skillful predictions and decisions and the critical requirement for lowering prediction errors.

What is the specific nature of decision-making in MBSAT?

Teresa Amabile of Harvard Business School (1998) proved that extrinsic motivation often hampers creative decision-making as external incentives impede the free flow of ideas. In her research, she explains how explicit reward cues such as a bonus or the threat of being fired do not prevent creativity altogether but don't boost it either. In contrast, intrinsic motivation from inside the person encourages creativity, creating states similar to the conditions of flow (Csikszentmihalyi, 1991) that are achieved when the challenges of a task are congruent with the interests and skills of the individual performing the task. This kind of conditions are very encouraging for skillful solutions and decisions.

The prevailing, maximization-driven decision-making follows patterns of reinforced learning. Decision-makers follow impulses from their BETA related to external rewards such as bonuses or record shareholder value. A motivation based on external rewards restricts BETA and leads to restricted decision-making that may benefit the decision-maker but harm the social and natural environment, possibly compromising the longer-term sustainability of the system.

MBSAT decision-making follows an Active Inference process. It seeks not only to optimize an external reward function but equally to optimize an internal FE function of adaptive beliefs for making decisions that minimize expected FE (Sajid et al., 2021). Active Inference decision-making could solve the lack of creativity and inclusiveness observed in external-reward-driven processes by internalizing beliefs as parameters that optimize decisions from a wider angle and minimize FE for self and others, equal to reducing prediction errors and decision mistakes.

One can safely say that decisions begin with beliefs motivated by the desired future. Hence, beliefs are the logical entry point for MBSAT's practical decision-making training. MBSAT's approach is a strategic understanding of beliefs by systematically posing: "How do the concerned beliefs support the individual, the social and natural systems in minimizing FE?"

The concern is to train MBSAT course participants to develop a specific competence for decision-making that provides sustainable well-being. Decisions vary from skillful. The degree of skillfulness is mediated by the level of precision of people's BETA and their Portfolio of Beliefs (POB). Combining precision parameters and skillfulness derives a matrix with four outcomes, illustrated in Figure 3.4.

In the illustration, the precision of BETA and POB are aggregated under the term Strategic Awareness as their two main constituents.

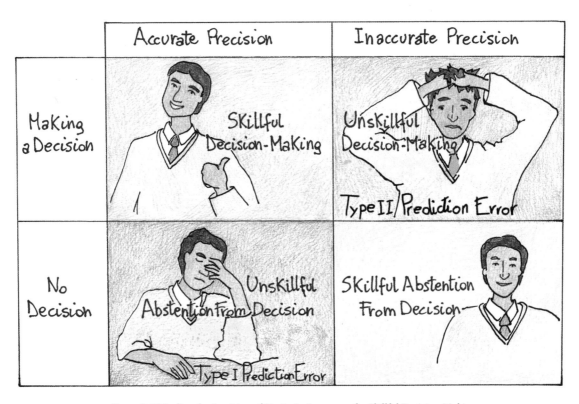

Figure 3.4 Minding the Precision of Strategic Awareness for Skillful Decision-Making

The four outcomes can be characterized as follows:

● Upper left quadrant (skillful decision):
  Skillful decision-making results from deciding with a good precision level of BETA and the POB combined.

● Lower right quadrant (skillful abstention from the decision):
  This is the case of a person skillfully refraining from deciding because BETA and POB are not precise enough, and the decision-maker is aware of the lack of precision.

● Lower left quadrant (unskillful abstention):

Here an individual abstains from deciding, although the precision of the BETA and the POB are relatively accurate. However, the individual does not trust his/her perceptions, resulting in a decision error (not deciding when a decision was required), for instance, not buying a company's share that is doing well on the stock market but has weak fundamentals (low earnings, poor market share, etc.). This type I prediction error is unskillfully abstaining from deciding and acting. This type of error is hard to spot as noise, and fake data distort decision-making.

● Upper right quadrant (unskillful decision):

In this case, the person unskillfully decides, driven by the inaccuracy of her BETA and POB. It is a typical case of overconfidence in false beliefs, resulting in Type II decision error (making a decision when it would be skillful to abstain from deciding). Although a job candidate would have been the best choice for a particular position, rejecting the person because of fixed false beliefs is typical of this sort of error.

In MBSAT, there is no prescribed cutoff rule to distinguish skillful from unskillful decisions. The guiding principle is FE minimization. It is a richer aspiration as a guiding principle for choice behavior beyond the classical economic model of maximizing utility or reward and incorporating the adaptive criteria of FE minimization. A series of experiments by Schwartenbeck et al. (2015) support that belief-based utility and its orientation towards FE minimization may be more adaptive and robust than simple classical economic-based utility maximization. The following experience can elucidate the meaning of these findings in real life.

A banker, a personal friend and MBSAT training participant, was left by his wife. When he asked her why, she told him he was constantly stressed out, and unhappy with his work, and his unhappiness had pervaded their marriage. Stunned, he said, he made all the sacrifices to provide her and the children "a top-quality life." She replied that she never asked for expensive houses, luxury cars, etc. "What is the purpose of all that luxury if you cannot enjoy it?" she told him. "I would have preferred a simpler but happier life with you."

These situations are more common than one would wish for.

MBSAT's skillful decision-making approach is a diffusion model[3] of processing information: it collects, integrates, and chooses amongst competing sources of data the decision and action that crosses an evidence precision threshold faster and more accurately.

Ultimately, skillful decision-making requires establishing personal criteria to evaluate options based on an adaptive portfolio of beliefs reinforced by a well-aligned BETA. Given our inherent limitations due to bounded rationality and information processing capability (Simon, 1982) and the impossibility of fully maximizing decisions (March, 1991, Forrester, 1968), individuals need to define a level of satisfaction

---

3 In computational neuroscience diffusion models are used to extract useful data from a noisy environment. Diffusion models are also used in machine learning and a series of other fields such as thermodynamics.

they will accept. Thus, instead of striving for states of maximization, one needs to establish satisfaction standards by finding "possible best solutions" along the lines of "this is just-good-enough." (Clark, 2020).

This reconnects to MBSAT's essential dimension of Minding the Strategic Adaptation in Life (MSAL). In the age of fake news, deep fakes, and other distractions, SAL helps us build a counterfactual capacity to find balance in our aspirations and our beliefs parameters. These are the elements we use for making decisions by acknowledging that complete fulfillment or perfect optimization of desires, ambitions, and goals are mostly confabulated deceptions. SAL helps formulate realistic and satisfying decisions that elevate people and at the same time protect others and the environment.

Session 8 in Part 2 of this workbook is dedicated to the crucial capability of Minding Strategic Adaption in Life.

3.6 Belief Updating and Attention

Given the significant role beliefs have in our lives, one of MBSAT's central challenges is helping individuals generate adaptive beliefs and continuously update them. Flawed beliefs do not render reality correctly quickly, leading to unskillful decisions, sometimes with enormous costs and regrets. Conversely, adaptive beliefs regularly lead to skillful decisions that create the conditions for people to flourish.

According to the neuro-computational approach of MBSAT, neuronal activity encodes beliefs, conceived as probability distributions in response to sensations. This suggests that people's precision in their beliefs is an essential determinant in how predictions and errors are reduced. This finding shows the importance of focusing efforts on minding beliefs by training the precision of our subjective beliefs to be as close as possible to reality in the environment. Precise, adaptive beliefs are the key to minimizing FE as they keep the average of decision errors low.

Attention is the focus of training in most mindfulness and meditation programs by emphasizing being in the present moment and disciplining the wandering mind. In MBSAT, attention training is trained to refine precision. For computational neuroscientists, "attention refers to the optimization of the precision of beliefs about the causes of sensory data, relative to the precision of those data; in order words, attentional selection is in the game of selecting the right sort of sensory information for beliefs updating." (Vasil et al., 2020 p. 8) Attention is conceived in MBSAT as an optimization quantity of precision required to adequately interpret the signals produced by the VUCA world and to balance and update our generative models continuously. Therefore, it is essential to hone precision to investigate what is happening based on the information from our body sensations, emotions, thoughts, and actions in our BETA in MBSAT terminology (Hohwy, 2020).

Clark (2016) suggests that precision is more than a process of fine-tuning; it is a dimension of the brain's generative models concerned with the external causes of incoming sensory data and the information derived from it.

From MBSAT's perspective:

> Adding precision estimations to our predictive BETA allows us to be more precise about when to suppress or enhance signals affecting our BETA, thus becoming more skillful in minding our BETA.

Attention as precision has essential functions:

a) Attention generates value by helping us reduce uncertainty in our BETA caused by signals from the environment.
b) Attention modulates the influence of our predictions and prediction errors.
c) Attention also helps optimize the precision of the Active Inference process and, by doing so, assists us in coping adaptively with uncertainty.

Precision is critical for people living in a VUCA world because it reduces the impact of noisy and ambiguous signals on our sensory inputs. The precision of the brain's internal models reduces ambiguity and complexity, making predictions more accurate and providing the desired stability by reducing volatility.

The fundamental challenge in updating beliefs is whether and when to update them. Essentially, there are two types of potential mistakes in choosing, analog to the decision-making errors type I and II depicted in Figure 3.4: not changing our beliefs when we should have changed them (type I error) and changing our beliefs when we should have kept them (type II error). The analogy to statistics and decision-making is evident, as type I and type II statistical errors are like decision-making errors. Type I error means rejecting the null hypothesis of an experiment when the hypothesis is true or in managerial decision-making, not deciding to pursue a deal when one should have gone ahead with it. Type II errors consist in not rejecting the null hypothesis when the experimental results should have been repudiated —or in management, deciding to go ahead with a business that one should not have pursued.

From the point of view of FE minimization, the practices of MBSAT help to sharpen the accuracy of people's predictions and keep the complexity of the models used to generate predictions in check to reduce the probability of errors. We cultivate the precision of attention to mind our prediction BETA mind and update our beliefs. The intention is to nurture the adaptive precision of our beliefs, especially about the present and the future, our expectations, and other vital determinants of our lives. Thus, from the lenses of computational neuroscience, (Fazekas & Nanay, 2021), attention is not primaryily about selecting what to attend to but has a precision function to help modulate the impact of sensory inputs either by amplifying or attenuating the sensory signals, thus a calibrating function for the quality and precision of prediction.

However, it is worth emphasizing that in constantly changing VUCA environments, precise non-adaptive beliefs can be an obstacle in moving forward, innovating, and adapting. Managers, for example, who hold on to precise, but obsolete ideas, products, services, or processes face a considerable challenge when indications from the environment point to new directions.

Two interrelated processes strengthen the human tendency to cling to obsolete motivational beliefs. Firstly, there is often a personal motivation in defending beliefs. Self-centered reasoning usually upholds beliefs that justify and preserve privileges, even when morally unsustainable. Secondly, to use management terms, significant impediments are sunk costs and switching cost fallacies. As beliefs are often the result of personal experiences that have absorbed resources (learning time, effort, etc.), these investments make it more difficult for the belief holders to let go of their convictions (putting up with sunk costs) and invest fresh energy and resources to update their Portfolio of Beliefs (assuming switching costs).

This is, for many, a difficult transition even in the face of clear evidence that their beliefs are no longer adaptive and affect their lives negatively. Continuously minding our Portfolio of Beliefs can smooth the updating process considerably. The following section explains the notion of minding and its importance.

3.7 Minding: A Key Quality of MBSAT

Minding as a caring practice is an age-old phenomenon. In the West, there has been a tradition of caring going back to the ancient Greeks and Romans with the writings of the Stoics and Marcus Aurelius, an epoch when philosophy was a way of life (Hadot, 1995).

In his work *Care of the Self* (1988), the French philosopher Michel Foucault studied the Greco-Roman philosophy, focusing on the seriousness of the work on oneself to enhance self-development. Reflections on the self also have a long tradition. The Roman philosopher Seneca beautifully described the stance of self-development that became Foucault's concern, calling for a process of self-examination:

> *"The mind must be called to account every day. Sextius's practice was when the day was spent, and he had retired to his night's rest, he asked his mind: 'Which of your ills did you heal today? Which vice did you resist? In what aspect are you better?' Your anger will cease and become more controllable if it knows that every day it must come before a judge. Is there anything finer than this habit of scrutinizing the entire day? When the light has been removed, and my wife has fallen silent, aware of this habit that's now mine, I examine my entire day and go back over what I've done and said, hiding nothing to myself, passing nothing by."* [4]

It is clear from this practice that the intention goes beyond paying attention to the present moment, but the aspiration is for attention to understand ourselves with an active disposition.

In the MBSAT protocol with its FE and Active Inference orientation, practices for cultivation of the self aims at minimizing FE, that is, increasing desirable states and reducing the amount of prediction error, also described as a variational approximation to the surprise generated by the discrepancy between data from the environment and an internal model an individual may have (Friston, 2012a).

---

4 From an undated article by John Seller, entitled "Roman Stoic Mindfulness: An Ancient Technology of the Self", p. 2-3, discussed by M. Foucault in his 1981 lecture in Louvain, Belgium, based on the translation by Kaster and Nussbaum (2010).

In MBSAT, the intention is to cultivate a personal caring and self-observation attitude captured by the term "minding." According to the Cambridge Dictionary, the verb "to mind" means "to take care or be careful of or about something or pay attention to something." MBSAT uses the verb in its gerund form as **MINDING** to mean a constant action of self-observation and caring for oneself, others, and oneself in relation to others. My wife Monika inspired me to come up with the notion of minding as a powerful metaphor for the kind of mindful caring that we aspire to impart in teaching MBSAT. Monika has created a beautiful garden by grooming and looking after the plants with great care and persistence, living in the center of Zurich in a penthouse with a large terrace all around. Despite challenging weather and soil conditions, the plants and flowers keep growing and thriving yearly. Some plants are several decades old, traveled with us to different countries, and still flourish. While writing this book, I often watched her toiling with pots and tools from my window and bringing her magic to our terrace garden (Figure 3.5).

It occurred to me that the way she minds the flowers and plants is how we should mind and care for our BETA, our Portfolio of Beliefs, our relations with others, and the environment – in brief, creating an encompassing minding attitude. Minding how it is understood in MBSAT creates the conditions to flourish and prepare ourselves to weather harsh conditions and withstand adversity and disruptive changes.

MBSAT's notion of minding is reminiscent of teachings by the Buddhist monk Ashin Tejaniya: "If you do not look after your garden, it will soon be overgrown with weeds. If you do not watch your mind, then greed, hatred, and delusion will grow and multiply. The mind does not belong to you, but you are responsible for it".

Minding under MBSAT is related to four processes that create conditions for continuous-time self-observation, caring for our BETA needs, and updating our beliefs. It begins with training the precision about the state of our BETA to help us weed out unhelpful beliefs, sow new beliefs, and fertilize those beliefs in need of our consideration.

Thus, **Minding our BETA** is the first process. It is related to synchronization. Often, we live with imperceptible dissonances and conflicts between our body sensations, emotions, thoughts, and actions impulses in what is called neuronal homolog conflicts. Here the intention is to reduce these conflicts between the different constituents of our BETA and attain coherent harmony to prepare people for the critical work of learning about their beliefs and changing them when necessary.

The second process is **Minding our Portfolio of Beliefs (MPOB)** means minding the basic set of beliefs that builds the foundation of our generative models and governs our predictions' quality. An integral part of MPOB is also to keep readjusting our portfolio of beliefs as required by the changing contexts of our lives.

The third process is **Minding our Social Experience (MSOE)**. The training's intention with this process is to be aware of the need for caring and celebrating others (Sampson, 2019). It includes a deep respect for others; only by respecting and minding people can we fathom who they are and their inten-

Minding-
A **MBSAT** Core Principle

Figure 3.5 Minding – A MBSAT Core Principle

tions. Essentially, MSOE seeks to create a better theory of the mind[5] and accurate social predictions.

The fourth and last critical process is **Minding Strategic Adaptation in Life (MSAL)**. It helps us build a counterfactual capacity to balance our aspirations and desires in the age of fake news, deep fakes, and other distractions. To make skillful decisions, it is essential to recognize that the complete fulfillment and total maximization of our desires, ambitions, and goals is an unrealistic and untenable aim. MSAL helps formulate realistic and satisfying decisions that elevate people and, at the same time, protect others and the environment.

3.8 Mindfulness in MBSAT

In contemporary Western societies, mindfulness strongly emphasizes two main themes:
a) The importance of paying attention to the present moment.
b) not-judging states.
Purser (2019) warned us that if pursued one-sidedly and disproportionately, the present moment can undermine critical forethought and ethical awareness of the consequences of past, present, and future actions.

In thinking about the form of mindfulness practices in MBSAT, just relaxing and focusing on the modes of the mind in the present moment will not build conditions for participants' self-development and transformation, especially for active individuals living in a VUCA world. Skillful action is what individuals living in rapidly changing environments need to improve and increase their survival and prosperity odds - to keep their jobs, relations, health, and other resources necessary for life.

Mindfulness attracted me years ago not to find peace, happiness, or spiritual enlightenment; I was more interested in resolving life dilemmas that we all have. Growing up with discretely Sybaritic parents who, besides their appreciation for beauty, also had a highly developed sense of fairness and honesty, I became imbued with their sense of aesthetics, fairness, and integrity. For example, I developed an appreciation for fine objects without losing self-control. I still have the Rolex GMT watch my dad gave me for my fifteenth birthday. I am also fond of high-performing German cars. One of them is a classic and more valuable today than when I purchased it over 20 years ago. It conjures memories of my dad's red sport MGA car that he allowed me to drive from time to time. But at the same time, I also have a strong sense of self-restraint for improper actions that might affect my integrity and well-being and the well-being of others. My dad was a wonderful man, a CPA (Certified Public Accountant), and had a strong work ethic. He was good at earning money and equally good at spending it, but not at saving it. There was never the expectation that I would have material inheritances; my dad didn't believe in wealth transfer, but in building your ways as he did from a very young age, despite the relative affluence of my granddad.

With this biography, I approached Mindfulness to help me find skillful ways of coping with the challenges of my active life. In particular, mindfulness helped me to balance my desires: in times of financial

---

5 Theory of the mind is a term used in psychology to refer to the ability to understand other people's minds.

restriction, it helped me muster strategic awareness for avoiding actions that could levy my soul, and I might later regret, and in better times, it prevented me from extravagancies and excesses. I persistently searched for proportionality and measure to design a life that would balance my hedonistic tendencies with my inclination to do good for others. In an interview with CNN on the occasion of Independence Day, celebrated in the USA on the 4th of July, the American historian Jon Meacham said the following about the importance of democracy:

> *"The civil war didn't change enough minds... one of the tragedies of American history,*
> *if not the central tragedy of the American history, is that we are founded on an ideal*
> *of equality that we professed far more often with greater passion than we practiced,*
> *the struggle for justice, equality and the history of which we can be proud is a daily*
> *one, I will argue... in everybody's soul... It is an arena of contention in which our worst*
> *instincts do battle against our better angels... and I know that my worst instincts win*
> *hell lot more often than my better angels do."*

Addressing these daily arenas of contention that everyone has: at workplaces, in social life, in political spaces, and in other areas of contention in our lives, is one of the core motivations of MBSAT, to help people mind their worst instincts. MBSAT seeks to assist people to cultivate their better angels through more adaptive beliefs. The hope is that with MBSAT training, individuals can align their espoused theories and their theories in use and become more skilled FE minimizers with more precise predictions and fewer prediction errors in their lives.

Professor Jeffrey Sachs, Director of the Center for Sustainable Development at Columbia University, asserts that mindfulness is crucial in eight dimensions of people's lives (Sachs, 2012, p. 165):

⊙ Mindfulness of self: personal moderation to escape mass consumerism.

⊙ Mindfulness of work: the balancing of work and leisure.

⊙ Mindfulness of knowledge: the cultivation of education.

⊙ Mindfulness of others: the exercise of compassion and cooperation.

⊙ Mindfulness of nature: the conservation of the world's ecosystems.

⊙ Mindfulness of the future: the responsibility to save for the future.

⊙ Mindfulness of politics: the cultivation of public deliberation and shared values for collective action through political institutions.

⊙ Mindfulness of the world: the acceptance of diversity as a path to peace.

As a complete mindfulness training-based program, I contend that MBSAT can assist individuals in developing an encompassing mindfulness mindset incorporating Sachs's eight crucial dimensions in their lives, thus reducing Free Energy and facilitating sustainable states of flourishing.

More than thinking of Mindfulness in the sense of paying attention and non-judgment, mindfulness in MBSAT is conceived of as a capability for skillful decision-making infused with a strategic awareness that needs to be trained similarly to how people train their physical body to have an active and healthy life, with fewer physical ailments in the present and the future. With its focus on the predictive BETA, MBSAT perceives mental well-being as the principal enabler of cognitive, emotional, somatic, and behavioral well-being. In the same way, as one can gauge physical well-being by measuring an individual's physical attributes, such as muscle mass, fat composition, and metabolic or vascular age, mindfulness can serve as an indicator of mental health. We can expect an individual with a more mindful mental life to be at the higher end of a mental health curve. In contrast, individuals with a less mindful orientation are likely to reflect lower mental and even physical health levels. Thus, mindfulness increases well-being by positively influencing mental health, which fosters the well-being of the entire BETA.

Therefore, in MBSAT, mindfulness has a specific significance: training for strategic awareness to support skillful decision making. MBSAT's mindfulness orientation takes an information processing approach. As Parr et al. (2019) write, it is about "attending to those sources of information that help us form accurate beliefs about the states in the world and our body." The expectation is that after finishing an MBSAT course, participants have a higher level of zest and curiosity to explore and exploit their abilities and what the world can offer them to continue on their path toward flourishing. Raising their strategic awareness and reflective thinking will foster their self-efficacy and mental health (Smith et al., 2022).

3.8.1 Mindfulness in active environments

One of the first who spoke of Mindfulness in the late 90s and early 2000 was Karl Weick, emeritus professor at the University of Michigan. He saw mindfulness as a critical capability needed for executives and professionals in high-performance positions to succeed in an age of complexity. He wrote: "By mindfulness, we mean the combination of ongoing scrutiny of existing expectations, continuous refinement, and differentiation of expectations based on newer experiences, willingness, and capability to invent new expectations that make sense of unprecedented events, a more nuanced appreciation of context and ways to deal with it, and identification of new dimensions of context that improve foresight and current functioning." (Weick & Sutcliffe, 2001, p. 42) Weick himself called this a somewhat extended definition. As he said, sometimes it takes a few lines to explain a significant idea that captures a sizeable, complex phenomenon, in this case, how to live with minimal, adverse FE (few prediction errors and decision mistakes).

Some authors have attempted to describe Mindfulness. Krieger (2005) asserted that mindfulness is a psychological state where individuals engage in active information processing while performing current tasks. They are actively analyzing, categorizing, and making distinctions in data. Levinthal and Rerup (2006) see Mindfulness as achieving high perceptual sensitivity, equivalent to having excellent recognition models and a high level of behavioral flexibility equal to having skillful active states that respond adaptively to changing VUCA stimuli. They also suggest that mindfulness helps to convert experiences into the reconfiguration of assumptions, frameworks, and actions, thus facilitating belief updating.

Bhante Gunaratana (2011, p. 141-142) maintained that "Mindfulness is non-superficial awareness. It sees things deeply, down below the level of concepts and opinions. This sort of deep observation leads to total certainty, a complete absence of confusion. It manifests itself primarily as constant and unwavering attention that never flags and never turns away." John Peacock, an outstanding scholar on secular Buddhism and my tutor at Oxford University, once told me: "My impression of you business-people is of individuals in states of permanent agitation, so I keep asking myself how they can produce quality thoughts and ideas in such states." His comment was made in relation with a passage of the Abhidhamma, the ancient Buddhist text, explaining Mindfulness's intention as stabilizing people's attention, to cultivate an attentive mind that is not "wobbling" and doesn't jump from one thought to another; instead the aim is to enable a steady mind, neither distracted nor agitated, and not wandering around. A stable mind is more precise, has more accurate perceptions and inferences, and formulates predictions with few errors.

An answer to John's rhetorical question is found in the classical book *A Primer on Decision Making* by the late Stanford professor James March (1994). He writes that "time and capabilities for attention are limited. Not everything can be attended to at once. Too many signals are received. Too many things are relevant for decision, and because of these limitations, decision-making theories are often described as theories of attention or search rather than as a theory of choice. They are concerned with the way in which scarce attention is allocated" (p.10). Because of the overflow of signals and the fixation of businesspeople on controlling their business, their minds are prone to jump from issue to issue, which understandably leads to a wobbling and agitated mind. To avoid wobbling, we need to pay "attention to attention" (Ocasio, 2011), to become more precise about when and what we allocate attention to. Mindfulness helps with this process of honing precision, which in MBSAT is called precisification (see Chapter 4, Figure 4.2).

Fiol & O'Connor (2003) show that mindfulness has a powerful influence on decision-making in band-wagon contexts, where people shape their decisions under the impression of a trend. This is the case, for example, when managers copy so-called best practices without a thorough understanding of how they apply to their companies. It is also the case of people following fashionable ideas on social media simply because everyone does so. Mindfulness can help modulate these types of copycat decision-making by expanding managers' and people's strategic awareness and motivating them to engage in counterfactual learning about the value of copying other companies or people's decisions. Many of the problems we have are because people engage in non-adaptive routines, following either wrong ideas or wrong leaders.

In Ellen Langer's view, mindfulness is essentially sensitivity to or awareness of contexts. As she points out, when we are mindful, we are more sensitive to others' perspectives than when mindless, a state where routines and habits rule our BETA. It is about seeing the similarities in things that are thought to be different and seeing the differences in things taken to be similar, as Langer suggests (2005). It is about training ourselves to strategically, yet gently and compassionately, notice everyday happenings in action, without necessarily having to sit still for extended periods but by being continuously sensible to contexts for allowing strategic awareness to emerge to find solutions even to challenging situations and still be able to flourish in life.

3.8.2 Mindfulness in computational neuroscience

Given MBSAT's foundation in computational neuroscience, it is helpful to look at what computational neuroscientists say about mindfulness and how it matches MBSAT. As discussed in the previous chapters, one of the primary goals in MBSAT is learning to minimize FE by reducing prediction errors. We reviewed two essential mechanisms to attain this goal: either changing the parameters of internal generative models, the beliefs so that the following predictions will be more accurate, or conversely aligning a stimulus to the prediction taking action to change the state of the stimulus to conform to predictions. Pagnoni and Guareschi (2017) call these two modalities "revise" (altering the model's parameters (beliefs) that drive perception and learning) and "confirm" (adjusting the environment to confirm our predictions, discussed above as the Active Inference process). A question that arises is knowing when to revise or confirm. Mindfulness can facilitate making this distinction by increasing mental flexibility and creativity.

In the ordinary course of life, events typically unfold and occur according to pre-established beliefs, routinized behaviors, and familiar settings; this certainty gives people a sense of self (Deane et al., 2020). Life for most people is infused with high precision as they limit their life to recognizable spaces of low Free Energy (work places, family homes, familiar eating places, etc.). However, as it has been ascertained, we live in a fast-changing VUCA environment where a sense of familiarity might engender dangers for the future; therefore, one needs to be attentive to potential changes in life.

This necessity for anticipating what could happen presupposes an attitude of curiosity and structured learning to generate psychological insights that allow beliefs to improve predictions and reduce prediction errors (Carhart-Harris & Friston, 2019). A critical factor is the creation of epistemic spaces as safe learning areas (Lutz et al., 2019) to update beliefs, habits, and behaviors more adapted for a changing world. MBSAT's approach to Mindfulness provides spaces where people can safely test their beliefs or hypotheses. Thus, the mindfulness approach in MBSAT creates deontic value (potential and permission to change) with deliberate practices designed to shift habits and non-adaptive BETAs by cultivating meta-cognition, strategic awareness, and curiosity to learn.

MBSAT's Mindfulness practices are conceived as disciplined, volitional processes of allocating attention, for example, by focusing on our natural breath or on any external object such as a flower, a candle, or concentrating on any element of the BETA: Body sensations, Emotions, Thoughts, or Actions impulses. Here, mindfulness and FE Minimization (FEM) become clear; as in FEM, attention becomes equivalent to the precision assigned to predictions and prediction errors (Pagnoni 2019). Precision is a second-order prediction; it means asking how accurate the precision is I am attaching to my predictions. Underlying the precision of predictions are beliefs of varying degrees of firmness. In general, high precision correlates with firmly held beliefs that imply stability or inflexibility, depending on whether the beliefs are adaptive or non-adaptive. Given that in MBSAT's mindfulness practices, we occupy the mind by following and building precision of the practice instructions, the mind cannot attend to other phenomena. This creates opportunities for reducing the precision of already established beliefs and behaviors, thus, opening up a window of opportunity to reframe people's experiences with new beliefs and behaviors and away from their habitual conditioning.

Let us examine an example of how this happens. One of the most salient challenges in sitting meditations requires practitioners to remain motionless; however, attention invariably gets distracted by a desire to move, scratch, cough, or get sleepy. Imagine, for instance, the desire to move slightly to ease some numbness, an action animated by the belief and the prediction that moving will lessen the discomfort. By resisting the urge and staying with the practice instructions, we allocate high precision to the intention and goal of the practice (not moving for the next couple of minutes or longer). Concurrently, the precision of the habitual belief: "Movement provides relief" gets attenuated. We train participants how to regulate craving (the desire to move) and simultaneously train them to reduce the average of prediction errors (by fulfilling the prediction "sitting still"). If the person completes the practice of fulfilling her prediction ("I will sit still following my breath for x minutes"), a sense of accomplishment and a satisfied BETA are likely to be experienced, contrary to what may have been the outcome, if the person had followed her habitual belief and generate a prediction error: "Moving will calm my numbness," probably resulting in a sense of frustration ("I shouldn't have moved") and in an unbalanced BETA.

3.8.3 Mindfulness, transparency, and opacity for updating beliefs

Because of the advances in computational neuroscience, MBSAT contends that instead of running after desirable things or moving away from undesirable ones, it is more effective and less metabolically costly to avoid decision mistakes. Active Inference (AI) is the process that helps us avoid making mistakes; it enables us to perceive realistically and act optimally in our surroundings and helps us reduce FE. Nevertheless, decisional mistakes are a constant plague, ubiquitously affecting people, making life hard for ourselves and others. But why is that the case? People are not purposely making mistakes of judgment; indeed, when they decide, they expect adaptive outcomes.

The German cognitive philosopher T. Metzinger (2003) has an explanation that concurs with Computational Neuroscience and MBSAT's training approach. He describes two mental states that drive peoples' lives: transparency and opacity. Transparent modes make it possible for us to perceive the world; we are aware of the content of our mental activity, without being clear about how the transparent cognitive content comes about. It is like seeing things through a clean windowpane without knowing how things are formed. Paradoxically, opaque mental states allow a higher level of perception that enables access to the formation of mental states. Instead of seeing right through the window, we realize that there is a glass panel. It is like using binoculars with a focusing wheel that allows us to increase the precision of our sensory signals, thus observing how percepts are constructed in our minds. Another way of looking at the distinction of these mental states relates to an analogy from cognitive therapy. From this perspective, transparent mental states correspond to the so-called second wave of cognitive therapies, focusing on the *apparent content of thoughts*. In contrast, opaque mental states reflect the third wave of cognitive

Opacity for Updating BETA

Figure 3.6 Opacity for Updating BETA

therapy, focusing on *how we relate to our thoughts*. The emphasis on the relation to our thoughts creates a naturally emerging dynamic towards transforming mental states.

Understanding this distinction is fundamental. Opacity drives updating beliefs, growth, and transformation processes. Transparent mental action is not susceptible to change as it is invisible; one can't change what is not visible. Thus, to change beliefs or opinions, one needs to make them visible – like a windowpane that becomes visible when it turns opaque by rain or dust. Figure 3.6 illustrates the windowpane in front of my desk where I worked on this book. The opaque spot on the upper left corner calls attention to the glass separating the viewer from the landscape. I live within 10 minutes walking distance of Zurich's downtown square "Paradeplatz." Still, from my home, when I look through the window, I see nearby trees, houses, roofs, and the Zurich hills. This view is unobstructed and transparent, not requiring any effort, but on occasions, part of the view becomes opaque, requiring cleaning that windowpane area. In those moments, I become conscious of the glass panel, the need to keep the windows clean, and the effort needed to keep them spotless. Figure 3.6 illustrates the concept of opacity in the form of a smudge on the window pane in the upper left corner.

Here is a practical example that helps bring home the understanding of transparent and opaque mental states. One of my students, a South-African of European descent, executive vice-president of a large bank, self-described as a liberal and progressive person, was having difficulties with some of the non-European members of his staff, in particular an African female with a MBA. He described how he felt tension in his belly every time this woman spoke. During the inquiry phase, after one of the MBSAT practices, reviewing his relations with other staff members, all highly educated, it turned out that it was only with this person he had issues with. As he kept investigating, he realized that despite having an idealized view of himself as a liberal progressive person, he still had deep-held beliefs about this person's ethnicity. By introspective observation, he could create the necessary opacity of his experience with this person. More precisely, he could see how his conditioning growing up in an apartheid society affected his relationship and prevented him from building a productive collaboration with this team member. He became really sad about this realization, as it contradicted his self-image of the progressive, post-modern person he aspired to be.

For Limanowsky and Friston (2018), opacity is a capacity to infer or predict with confidence and precision. Rendering the content or quality of the BETA and its underlying beliefs opaque is referred to in MBSAT as making them observable and noticing them. Opacity, therefore, is desirable; it results from an intentional process that requires personal engagement. In contrast, transparent manifestations of BETA states and beliefs are more easily accessible to conscious experience. Opaque mental representations require more effort than transparent representations. Consequently, people tend to have more transparent representations because of their low metabolic cost.

Thus, opacity is a capacity that enables awareness of habitual BETA modes and makes us more conscious. The practices in the MBSAT protocol are specifically designed to develop and foster this capacity. They build on mindfulness techniques that enhance thoughtful attention and precision estimation and ultimately lead to increased strategic awareness, a high-level awareness with high precision, thus, with high levels of opacity allowing for more precision in minding the BETA and the Portfolio of Beliefs while reducing prediction errors.

The Minding practices of MBSAT are designed as liberating instruments to free people from the burden of their non-adaptive conditioning and unfold their potential for flourishing.

3.9 The Free Energy Minimizing Self (FEMS)

One of the signature interventions in MBSAT has been the Mindful Positive Self (MPS) (Young, 2017), designed to assist participants in constructing a personal strategic plan for deploying their strengths and dispositions in life to achieve higher levels of well-being. I have reformulated the intervention for this workbook with the science and insights from the neuroscience of prediction and the Predictive BETA Mind approach. Instead of encouraging participants to aspire to higher levels of well-being, the Free Energy Minimizing Self-FEMS consists of planning to reduce prediction errors and decision mistakes using people's abilities. The FEMS, therefore, reflects a low-level prediction errors personal plan for the participants.

The FEMS is an intervention combining narrative psychology (Hirsch et al., 2013) with Active Inference. It places the aspirations of the participants in the context of their social environment. Every society has its social narratives that guide what people aspire to be in particular settings. It is about building "beliefs or premises that enter the narrative..." (Bruner, 1990, p.39). The FEMS provides structured guidance for the participants in MBSAT courses to review and update their BETAs, beliefs, and their generative models' authenticity and reliability. It allows them to practice recognition modeling and building simulations of their strategic plans under different generative narratives to define what they want to achieve in their environment.

The Mindful FE Minimizing strategic plan leads to deeper self-knowledge of the BETA and strategies for aligning the BETA elements: Body sensation, Emotion, Thoughts, and Action impulses, thus reducing the chances of unsynchronized predictions. FEMS provides a systematic self-introspection exercise, allowing participants to optimize and update their portfolio of beliefs with newer, more comprehensive information and data. As proposed in MBSAT, Minimizing FE and Active Inference are ideally suited to help formulate the FEMS. Minimizing FE involves updating beliefs to conform with the perceived reality and increasing the precision of predictions; or aims at changing the states of the world by taking action to fit our prediction, thus taking skillful actions.

The FEMS provides a framework that guides participants as they engage in the two main tasks in shaping their journey. The first is a review of their Portfolio of Beliefs. There are many options to render a Portfolio of Beliefs more adaptive and effective. New beliefs can be created or existing beliefs increased; conversely, existing beliefs can be attenuated, substituted, or eliminated. The second task consists of developing an implementation strategy. The FEMS includes a structured approach as a naïve algorithm useful for accurate predictions and to solidifying skillful decision-making.

Participants start to think about their FEMS early in the MBSAT training, as early as the first or second week of the eight-week program.

We spend most of our time and energy trying to reduce the incidence of undesirable states, unhappiness, stress, and anxiety and increase our desirable conditions, pleasure, and happiness. However, not uncommon are cases where what we believe is undesirable turns out to be good, and equally, what we thought will bring us joy turns out to be a source of dissatisfaction. Hence, the impediment to living a life without regrets and more satisfaction is often a flawed mindset. Could there be a way of reducing this harmful confusion?

I believe MBSAT's distinctive features at the service of one essential aim – minimizing FE and its equivalent of reducing decision errors – can help anyone disentangle the decision-making confusion, increase strategic awareness and improve the quality of life. The FEMS provides excellent support for this. Instead of chasing illusions of elusive pleasure and running away from fantasies of aversion, a FE Minimizing individual will simply concentrate on reducing decision-making errors, a natural imperative for minimizing FE and diminishing the likelihood of finding oneself in states that impede our flourishing: lack of job, divorce, social isolation, poor health or any other situation compromising our mental and physical health.

Box 3.1

Beliefs from the Perspective of General Psychology

From a broad, psychological perspective, beliefs can be defined as the mental acceptance, conviction, and integrity one has concerning ideas and phenomena. For cognitive psychologists in particular, the main characteristics of beliefs are the following (Connors & Halligan, 2015; Seitz & Angel, 2020):

a) Beliefs have different origins; they can be derived from our own experiences ("Based on my experience, I believe an average individual can't run 100 meters in 10 seconds") and can be also accepted coming from an authority ("I believe one should eat more greens, as suggested by nutritionists").

b) Beliefs can depend on the level of evidence, but the connection is fairly loose. For some beliefs such as "Smoking can affect your health" there is ample evidence. Other beliefs are carried without paying attention to the evidence, for example, believing that wearing a mask isn't effective in preventing COVID-19 infections despite ample evidence to the contrary.

c) Beliefs can be conscious so that individuals are well aware of their beliefs; religious beliefs are always conscious. However, beliefs can also be unconscious, meaning that people are unaware of having them.

d) Beliefs can be held with different degrees of conviction. Some individuals will believe with complete confidence that there is consciousness after death; others might be very skeptical and still others might hold the belief with less conviction.

e) Beliefs can differ in their resistance to change, for example, the resistance to change views and beliefs on issues of faith can vary greatly. For example, some Catholics resist the marriage of priests, while others don't.

f) Belief can drive behavior. A case in point is the storm on Capitol Hill in the US in January 2021 that happened because some citizens believed that the November 2020 elections were stolen by the opposing party.

g) Beliefs can have emotional consequences; for example, if a person believes that she deserves a promotion and doesn't get it, not getting the promotion can have enormous emotional costs (depression, anger, sadness, etc.).

Beliefs are formed into a system with some of the characteristics mentioned above (Connors & Halligan, 2015). When adaptive, they build the conditions for strategic awareness to emerge, leading to skillful decision-making.

Box 3.2

Beliefs from the Perspective of Political and Behavioral Economics

After looking at the psychological view, we now proceed to the economic perspective of beliefs. The emergence of the economic view of beliefs results from the evolution in economic thinking that started from the viewpoint that human behavior follows rational expectations. From this viewpoint, individuals build rational expectations about the future based on the information available and seek to maximize their expected utility (Lucas, 1981).[6] Kahneman's and Tversky's (1979) experimental studies found numerous, substantial violations of the argument of rational expectations and generated evidence that individuals do not always maximize expected utility. Their work revealed that people could behave differently; for example, they may behave conservatively, preferring lower utility when coupled with high certainty instead of higher utility with less certainty. As they discovered, people also prefer to take a loss with certainty instead of finding a solution that could be more satisfying but also is potentially more costly. This led to the field of behavioral economics and the study of biases and heuristics.

In recent years economists have started to incorporate beliefs into their analysis and to expand their view from the individual to markets and institutions. The Nobel prize laureate D. North (2005) writes: "There is an intimate relationship between belief systems and the institutional framework. Belief systems embody the internal representation of the human landscape. Institutions are the structure that humans impose on that landscape to produce desirable outcomes. Belief systems, therefore, are the internal representation and institutions the external manifestation of that representation. Thus, the structure of an economic market reflects the beliefs of those in a position to make the rules of the game." (p. 49) Bénabou and Tirole (2016) also write that "beliefs often fulfill important psychological and functional needs of the individual." The question that started to interest economists is understanding "beliefs-based utility," that is the value deriving from having beliefs, which means essentially looking at people's behavior concerning their supply and demand for beliefs.

From an economic point of view, what is of particular interest is understanding how individuals manipulate their beliefs by repressing, forgetting, or reinterpreting information unfavorable to themselves. Nobel prize laureate J. Tirole and his colleague R. Bénabou (2002) describe the self-manipulation of beliefs as the equilibrium of a game between different selves of the same individual – a game in which the individual may try to forget or repress data and information that might harm his self-confidence. But why will anyone want to lie to him- or herself, given that having reliable information is the basis of precise predictions and skillful decision-making?

---

6 There is a joke that Professor Lucas' best student was his ex-wife. She negotiated rationally a divorce settlement that included an option with the expiration date of 31st of October 1985 to 50% of any future earnings from a prospective Nobel prize award. Lucas was awarded the Nobel prize on the 10th of October 1985.

Tirole (2017) identified three reasons for people to be delusional about their beliefs:

a) The effects of a lack of willpower could lead to procrastination. For example, an individual from a minority group tells himself that as a minority, he has little chance of success. While working in Zurich, a mostly protestant city, I saw Catholics working in organizations where they thought they didn't have the same opportunities as Protestant colleagues. This prevented them from being very active in their jobs and their careers stagnated, while on the other hand, more active Catholics were progressing in the same company.

b) Expected utility (believing an activity could be painful) is different from experienced utility (the feeling of actual pain generated by an activity). It can prompt reasonings along the line of: "I have this pain in my shoulder. I believe I should maybe see a doctor about it. Nah, it is certainly nothing," only to find out later that it was indeed a condition serious enough to require a surgical intervention. Under certain conditions, people often choose not to process certain information to update their beliefs:

c) How we consume beliefs about ourselves also creates distortions. As people care about their image, they process more willingly information supporting their self-image. For example, a CEO might congratulate himself on the wonderful job he does: "Our company gets public acclamation. Sure, I am a super clever manager." On the contrary little appetite is shown for updating beliefs that contradict beliefs about ourselves.

From the supply side of beliefs, Tirole (2017) suggests three ways how people manipulate the formation of their beliefs:

a) Manipulating memory:
For example, an individual tells her partner: "I believe our deal was to share the profits of the business 50/50; now it looks more like a 70/35 profit-sharing scheme." The partner responds: "You seem to forget that in our last discussions, the agreement was defined as 2/3:1/3 and you agreed." Both partners draw on their memory selectively to process information in line with their asymmetrical motivations.

b) Refusal to hear, process, and pay attention to information that compromises our beliefs.
For example, an individual firmly (with high precision, in the language of the Bayesian brain) believes that her country's elections were fraudulent; however, she seems oblivious to the widely available and highly reliable information to the contrary.

c) Choosing actions that signal particular character traits.
For example, "I don't believe that masks help against disease, and they create discomfort, so I don't wear them despite the appeals by the government. I am also demonstrating that I am an independent, freedom-loving person."

While there is leeway in what people choose to believe, facts and evidence set certain limits. As Loewenstein and Molnar write, "there must be limitations on what they (people) can persuade themselves to be true. Thus, to model human behavior with the economists' apparatus of constrained utility maximization, we need to understand the constraints people face in choosing their own beliefs." (Loewenstein & Molnar, 2018, p. 166-7)

An answer to this issue, I think, can be found in Karl Friston's Free Energy Principle by asking, whether a belief minimizes Free Energy for the individual and society? If the answer is yes, then the beliefs could be adaptive and useful; if the answer is no, it is time to update them. And this leads us to the third view of beliefs from a computational neuroscience perspective.

Box 3.3

A Neuro-computational View of Beliefs

The general understanding of beliefs consists of a proposal that is seen as accurately driving the behavior and thinking of individuals; in order words, a belief is an assumed truth. Beliefs then are created to facilitate our understanding of the world around us. They are based on experiences with some reflections, or they can be founded on pure acceptance, like most religious beliefs. In the computational Bayesian brain view (Knill & Pouget, 2004), beliefs are seen as probability distributions; in other words, they are seen as a hypothesis (Gregory, 1980) over the hidden states of the world and encoded in our physical brain states.

The consequence of looking at the world as probabilities is that people's inferences result in forming a set of probabilistic beliefs that a person seeks to optimize vis-à-vis the truthfulness of the causes of sensory perceptions to minimize uncertainty (Free Energy). "Free Energy is essentially a measure of surprise about sensation ..., where conscious beliefs are unpacked hierarchically to predict sensory experiences. Crucially, this means that conscious beliefs have a measure of theoretical underpinning... one can quantify the attributes of beliefs and make some clear statements about how attributes will change over time... Variational Free Energy is not an attribute of physical states; it is an attribute of a probability distribution (belief) entailed by those states. In other words, conscious processing is equipped with a measure that is an attribute of beliefs." (Hobson & Friston, 2014, p. 18).

Given that variational Free Energy is an attribute of beliefs as mentioned in Chapter 1, Free Energy Minimization can be expressed as accuracy minus complexity, suggesting that accurate beliefs effectively minimize Free Energy and reduce the rate of prediction errors, making decisions more accurate. In MBSAT, beliefs are treated as hypotheses which is a helpful way of looking at them in a fast-changing VUCA world. Hanging on to non-adaptive outdated beliefs would be detrimental to survival and sustainable well-being. In the section on belief updating, we will discuss the mechanics of the belief's formation process in more detail and how updating beliefs can be trained. For now, it may be sufficient to point out that beliefs with higher precision weights are harder to update, and require more evidence to change.

To conclude this section, it is helpful to summarize the role beliefs play in life. Rather than a clash of civilizations, ideologies, or lifestyles, life can be conceived as a clash of beliefs between people and the institutions they represent. For example, take the adversarial stance we are witnessing in the global political arena, with each party claiming to be the bearer of truth concerning how better to organize society. Over the past several decades, what we have been observing is that each group has been strengthening their prior beliefs, unable to incorporate and process new evidence or information, thus unable to build posterior beliefs that might be more congruent with what is happening in the fast-evolving society. In the realm of business, the maximizing shareholder value mantra has been the holy grail for decades, and shareholder value maximization the ultimate goal every manager, arduously pursued in the effort to ensure their organizations' sustainability. In the economy, there is a parallel in the form of the long-lasting credo of non-intervention strategies by the government, letting markets do what they supposedly do best and waiting for trickle-down effects for all. Who could believe in earnest that attending exclusively to one party in a social system comprising different groups would be beneficial for the whole system in the long-term? Pure common sense evokes at the very least some reservations about the logic of these beliefs.

Studying for an MBA at the University of Chicago, it never made sense to me that highly educated, intelligent instructors were preaching unilateral shareholder value maximization. "What about the other stakeholders?" I would ask, a question that got me in trouble, especially in discussion with one instructor who aggressively shouted me down and forced me to double my studying efforts that semester to get a good grade in his course. Gradually, these monolithic beliefs are eroding. Recently, the Business Roundtable, the influential business association of CEOs, declared that businesses should be more inclusive, attend to all stakeholders, and take a more long-term view of their operations. In 2022, President Biden proclaimed that "trickle-down economics" don't work and advocated for vigorous and robust government interventions in society. Likewise, at the individual level it is also necessary to maintain and cultivate flexible, agile and authentic beliefs, as opposed to opportunist beliefs that reflect the flavor of the moment. The goal in MBSAT is to help individuals identify the beliefs that are fully amortized, having produced value for some time and helped to cope with challenges, but are now at the end of their productive life cycle. What may be needed are fresh investments in new beliefs to facilitate coping with current and future challenges in life.

Box 3.4

Mindfulness for Decisions and Actions

MBSAT is an intervention designed for non-clinical people with an active life. It takes a very different orientation than most mindfulness interventions that are more restorative in intention, supporting individuals who are out of balance to regain more equilibrium. The underlying assumption in MBSAT is that participants are getting on with their lives and what MBSAT offers them is added value by enhancing their ability to make skillful decisions and further improve their quality of life. Decision-making is one of the most constant and impactful actions in our lives.

The MBSAT program has its own terminology, methodology, and rationale and therefore requires a shift in mindset from conventional views of mindfulness that emphasize equanimity and moment-to-moment presence. MBSAT fosters precise inference about the future and skillful actions. Thus, MBSAT's distinctive configuration may constitute a disruptive innovation that requires reorientation. For participants, it is important to realize that MBSAT is an innovative approach to mindfulness to enhance personal growth and agency.

An example may be useful. In one of my classes, a senior student and advanced practitioner of classical mindfulness became quite upset and criticized me in class in a fairly aggressive tone, arguing that I was not teaching true mindfulness. She had just spent six months in a retreat and claimed to know what real mindfulness was. Despite her dissent, she kept coming to the classes because she was somehow intrigued. Several months later I received an email from her apologizing that she had not understood the power of MBSAT at the time, and that in the meantime she had gained firsthand experience of MBSAT's positive impact. She wrote that she had been working with mothers of autistic kids, and shared with them MBSAT's signature interventions with amazing practical results. For example, one of the mothers had previously been unable to cut her son's hair without harrowing tantrums. However, when she did the signature practices before entering the room where her son was, the kid reacted in a very different manner and for the first time she could cut his hair in a serene atmosphere. This anecdote exemplifies the value of these practices: facilitating sensible decisions (to go ahead with the haircut) and following up with skillful action (gently and calmly cutting the hair of the usually agitated child).

Naturally, getting the full benefit of MBSAT's approach requires open-mindedness and flexibility, especially from people who are already familiar with classical mindfulness practices. As is the case with most innovations, incumbents of traditional methods might be more resistant (Christensen et al., 2008). Ultimately, the choice of practice depends on the practitioners' needs.

Chapter 4

INTRODUCTION TO THE MBSAT PROGRAM:

ESSENTIAL FOUNDATIONS TO MAKE YOUR MBSAT TRAINING EFFECTIVE

Mindfulness-based Strategic Awareness Training Comprehensive Workbook:
New approach Based on Free Energy and Active inference for Skillful Decision-making,
First Edition. Juan Humberto Young.
© 2023 John Wiley & Sons Ltd. Published 2023 by John Wiley & Sons Ltd.
Companion website: www.wiley.com/go/young/mbsatworkbook

Welcome to the MBSAT training program!

During the next eight weeks, you will learn about the most advanced concepts of how the brain and the mind work to lay the groundwork for shaping your life skillfully. You will also practice during this time with interventions designed to help you enhance your decision-making skills. Your decisions are at the center stage of your life. Everything you do is based on decisions. Whether they are impactful and transformative or simply standard, they determine the state and direction of your well-being. You will learn what governs skillful decision-making for supporting your desires and aspirations without negatively affecting other people and the environment.

> *"There are three things extremely hard:*
> *steel, diamond, and to know oneself."*
>
> Benjamin Franklin

4.1 The Journey You Are Embarking On

To fully benefit from training with MBSAT, you need to become familiar with the program's key concepts and notions, as MBSAT has specific terms with precise meanings. The terminology facilitates your understanding and reminds you to cultivate desirable states associated with the terms. For example, a term widely used in MBSAT is BETA, which is related to a desire to balance your body sensation, emotions, thoughts, and actions states. This chapter explains the most essential principles and expressions. Throughout the program these concepts and notions will be further reviewed for a deeper understanding of their appropriate usage.

First and foremost, it must be clear that MBSAT is mind work. So it is crucial to understand what the mind/brain does.

> Do you believe you are reacting to stimuli happening in your life?
>
> Most people believe this to be the case. But according to the most recent and advanced theories in neuroscience, what your brain does is constantly anticipating and predicting your needs for your survival and well-being. You and I are all organic prediction machines.
>
> This is a fundamental change of perspective. The implication is that we must train differently to achieve aspirations of well-being and flourishing in life.

4.2 Key Concepts to Understand How Our Brains Work

The following paragraphs provide an introduction to essential terms that are repeated throughout this workbook and are crucial for a thorough understanding and effective training. In order to make them more easily recognizable and facilitate remembering them, they are highlighted.

4.2.1 Prediction, prediction errors and precision: The three computational elements of the brain's biomechanics

There are three elements that your brain computes: **predictions**, **prediction errors**, and **precision**. Skillful decisions are a function of optimizing these elements, while unskillful decisions result from wrong computations of at least one of these three elements. The key is to build accurate predictions, keep a low level of prediction errors, and maintain high levels of precision/veracity. And that is the essential work of training.

While you cannot be sure of the future, you still need to anticipate what could happen as some occurrences might negatively affect your life and well-being, and that needs to be avoided. Your brain swiftly engages in anticipation, often without you being consciously aware of it.

Your brain builds predictions based on what you are learning and the likelihood you attach to it. Here is a simple example. You meet a person who greets you: "Hi, I am Hans. I come from Switzerland." At school in your country in Latin America, you learned that all Swiss people are polyglots; they speak German, French, Italian, and a unique language, Rumantsch. This is all you know about Swiss people. "So, you speak four languages, that is cool," you reply. Hans tells you he actually only speaks German; he understands basic French, Italian and Rumantsch, but speaks none of these languages well. Your prediction that all Swiss speak four languages lacked precision, resulting in a prediction error. This results in two adjustments. First, your model of polyglot Swiss people gets more refined (not all Swiss speak four languages). Second, based on your new model of Swiss polyglots, next time you meet a Swiss you know she might or might not speak all the languages of her country; thus, your prediction will be more precise.

Making appropriate predictions is not about becoming clairvoyant; MBSAT can't teach you to become a wizard able to see the future. Given that the brain is in the business of anticipating the outer and inner environment (your needs), predictions are more about how to better anticipate with insufficient information or unreliable, even fake data, a frequent condition in fast-changing societies.

As the world constantly changes, predictions are conceived in a continuous spectrum from highly precise to unprecise with recognizable, potential prediction errors. Knowing that the intention is to approximate what is contextually more likely is a way of thinking that facilitates the updating process of perceptions and actions.

4.2.2 Free Energy (FE): What our brain seeks to minimize

Except J. K. Friston, the theory's creator, almost nobody fully understands the mathematics of Free Energy Principle (FEP), a far-reaching idea using notoriously complex mathematics to explain human life. When I started reading about FEP several years ago, its logic immediately captured my attention, perhaps because of the principle proposed: reducing the effects and the impact of VUCA to better succeed in life. It made intuitively sense. As a person active in the world of business, I am always attentive to the future direction of our societies, the development of our economies, organizations, companies, investments, and many other aspects of life. FEP instantly resonated with what I do; practically, FEP is about reducing prediction errors, thus, trying to correctly anticipate what is happening in the world in order to make skillful decisions.

Free Energy (FE) in physics is a well-accepted principle, recognized as energy available to finish a job. However, in neuroscience, FE is formulated under the discipline of information theory. Here, FE is equal to the information embodied in neurological patterns in the brain as neural transmissions. Predictions misaligned with the causes of people's perceptions and sensations build surprising states that create informational disorder conceived as adverse FE.

FE is a crucial concept in MBSAT. After pondering incessantly on how to practically integrate the logic of FEP into the curriculum of MBSAT, some unexpected directions came to me through a dream I had. It was about being in an unfamiliar, dense, dark forest, struggling to move forward on a narrow path, and seeking to survive. Suddenly, a giant bear[1] appeared and threatened me head-on, from behind, and from all sides. The danger sometimes forced me to stop in my tracks and retreat into an epistemic learning state to find out what to do next. At other times, it made me run faster or forced me to catch my breath while I continuously strained to move forward, finally making it to the edge of the forest and out into the open. Reflecting on this dream, I understood it was an allegory about mastering difficulties and deciding to advance with resolve toward my goals. It captured a difficult time in my life after arriving in Switzerland. The dream taught me to stay in moderate states (catching my breath), to reduce Free Energy (adverse surprises), for example, by keeping myself employed even by accepting jobs below my qualifications while learning the language and always staying attentive to my unfamiliar surroundings (the path in the dark, dense forest) to arrive safely in the open (a good place with fewer perils and uncertainty). I realized that the movements in the dream symbolized decisions I was taking in real life to build a new existence as an immigrant in a new country.

By analogy, I realized the path for practical integration of FEP in MBSAT was through training for skillful decision-making, which has been the principal intention of MBSAT from the beginning (Young, 2017, p. 68). People decide all day long; however, decision outcomes can be beneficial or not. Unskillful decisions are a source of unhappiness; they drain you of your mental, emotional, and physical energy. The opposite is true of skillful decisions with fewer prediction errors; they are the basis of mental health and well-being. So, to have an adequate good life, one needs to reduce decision errors. Therefore, in MBSAT, FEP has been operationalized as the average of decisions errors, which everyone needs to minimize to have a good life. When the average of decision errors is lower, less FE is generated.

---

1 A bear is the mascot of Bern, the capital of Switzerland.

One of the difficulties in understanding FE and FEP is the counterintuitive meaning of "free" in this context. The word "free" is normally associated with freely available or available at no cost, and typically people want more of it instead of minimizing it, as the FEP stipulates. To overcome this linguistic barrier, we can think of two views of the word "free":

a) Free can be something given to you for free, like the air you breathe your whole life, the sea water you can swim in for free on public beaches or the hills outside your window that you can look at freely.

b) Another view of "free" relates to the idea of something wild, untamed and potentially harmful. Concerning a living being, you might think of a wild mustang, kicking out and lashing about, if you try to saddle it. However, once trained, the horse is highly helpful as Figure 4.1 below illustrates. Or you may think of a wild, little creature like your puppy, a young dog full of energy, capable of destroying things important to you and creating chaos in your home. Free Energy can also be related to natural forces, for example, the free and ferocious energy generated by hurricanes.

The Nature of Free Energy in MBSAT

A wild destructive force, when uncontrolled

A valuable resource, when minimized and used well

Figure 4.1 The Nature of Free Energy in MBSAT
(Duplication of Figure 1.1 for Ease of Reference)

FEP relates to the second meaning of FE. Free Energy is an energy that, when not restrained, creates disorder, which is why you need to minimize it; otherwise, it creates misalignment between you and your environment. From this point of view, FE is a measure of misalignment that needs to be minimized. It is the unwelcome surprise or disappointment one experiences, when outcomes are not in line with the expected results of our predictions.

In MBSAT, **Minimizing FE is operationalized as the average of prediction errors**, the quantity you need to keep as low as possible to safeguard your mental health. The higher the number of prediction errors, the more misalignment with the environment and distress ensue, hence the higher FE. A lower average of prediction errors signals that your prediction models are well-aligned with the context you live in and that you are able to minimize Free Energy. Free Energy is then the difference between your decisions and the world reacting to your decisions. If they are compatible, things are well and Free Energy is not created. The goal is to avoid incompatibility between your decisions and the world by minimizing Free Energy.

A simple way of understanding all these ideas is to relate Free Energy to a motivation to keep oneself in states where one can avoid the common disorders of life (unemployment, break-up relationships, illness, and any other adverse situations).

To achieve this goal, people use Active Inference to help them:
a) Keep refining their perceptions to optimize their predictions about what is happening in the environment.
b) Take correcting actions that help them minimize prediction errors.
The objective is always to keep prediction/decision errors low.

In MBSAT

- Free Energy is conceived of as the untamed, harmful force of adverse states ensuing from prediction and decision errors.

- Minimizing FE is operationalized as keeping the average of decision/prediction errors low.

4.2.3 Free Energy Minimization (FEM): Application in MBSAT

Our brains are biologically programmed to seek FE Minimization as part of our potent survival instinct and our instinctive drive to foster our well-being. Our lifelong pursuit of pleasant experiences and avoiding distress is FE Minimization in action, without being aware of the complexity of neuronal biomechanics. However, we often get entangled in contradictions and other pitfalls or fail to be aware of longer-term effects and implications of our decisions and actions.

The entire MBSAT protocol with all its interventions is ultimately geared toward minimizing FE more effectively and sustainably. Moreover, there is a comprehensive intervention that tackles FE minimization directly. It consists in developing a personal strategic plan that enhances clear-mindedness about aspirations and defining concrete actions to work towards the goals. The intervention is called Mindful Free Energy Minimizing Self (FEMS). It reflects a desirable personal path for essential aspects of our life with low prediction errors. Section 4.8 below highlights the purpose this intervention.

4.2.4 Active Inference (AI): How we perceive and act in the world

There is a boundary between you (your internal states) and the environment (external states): you, as an entity, differ from everything else. For example, you are not a chair, and a chair is not you; otherwise, you would not exist as you are right now. In Luc Besson's film *Lucy*, the main character is transformed into a black matter after injecting herself with CPH4 (a drug) and absorbs everything in the room as she moves into a spacetime continuum without boundaries. When people in the room ask her where she is, she answers through a phone device: "I am everywhere."

But as you and I are not everything or everywhere, but are separate entities, we are not absorbed by things around us, or conversely absorbing everything around us like Lucy. There is a persistent boundary between us and everything else, which gives us our identity. You are not the car you are driving or your home; you are a distinct human being, different from your mother, your employees, or boss.

However, you, like anyone else, need the environment for survival. Parts of it may be harmful to you (a bad-tempered boss, an unfortunate marriage, poisoned food, and dangerous animals). Still, the environment also presents resources for your survival (a good job, loyal friends, a pet you love, nutritious foods). This leaves us with the need to make decisions that support our survival in an environment that offers both dangers and possibilities. Knowing this, the brain desperately tries to anticipate the nature of things. Is what we confront a foe or friend? Anticipation and action are the crucial issues, as it might be too late if you just sit and wait for whatever happens before reacting. Good predictions are the foundation for having a less hazardous life.

Active Inference is the process your brain uses to implement and regulate predictions, deal with prediction errors, and increase precision. It involves a cycle of four states:

(1) **External states**: the environment where things materialize: jobs, car manufacturing companies, banks, government bureaucracies, animals, plants, and other phenomena.
(2) **Sensory states**: your senses that connect you to all the phenomena in the environment.
(3) **Internal states**: your experiences, memories, knowledge, and beliefs that are connected to your sensory states.
(4) **Active states**: your interactions with the environment ensuing from your internal states.

Based on this circular dynamic, your brain builds predictions based on beliefs about what you infer is happening outside your brain. Your brain engages in evidence-seeking predictions to **update** your beliefs and brain models, or you can try to **adjust** your actions and the environment to conform to your predictions, such as adding an ice cube to cool off a scalding hot coffee cup. Figure 1.4. illustrates a similar example related to cooking.

In essence, Active Inference allows you to exercise your agency by aligning your brain models with the environment and adjusting to the world. It enables you to re-engineer and rectify errors by improving the precision of your predictions and actions.

> In MBSAT, Active Inference is the process of interaction between our brain models and the environment.
>
> It is the process our brain uses to regulate predictions, prediction errors and precision, consisting of iterative loops of perceiving, inferring, predicting and acting.

4.3 BETA in MBSAT: Body sensations, Emotions, Thoughts, and Action impulses

4.3.1 BETA: How we experience the world

Everything that you experience enters through four gates: your Body sensations, your Emotions, your Thoughts, and your Actions. They form the BETA, the basis of your experience in life. Every individual perceives and senses things, has feelings about what is happening, learns new valuable things, unlearns unhelpful legacy ideas, and acts in the world through the BETA.

BETA is our human system of experiencing comprising four interdependent and interacting elements that require minding for adaptive functioning and skillful decision-making.

Lack of integration of these four elements leads to prediction and decision errors. For example, prediction errors and unfavorable outcomes will result if body sensations, emotions, and thoughts are well integrated and point in the right direction, but the action impulses are not aligned and synchronized with the other elements. Lack of integration and synchronization amongst the four factors leads to increased Free Energy and unskillful decision-making. When out of balance, these elements result in corrupted BETAs, similar to corrupted files or programs in a computer that lead to failures in a computer system.

Taking continuous care of the BETA states is a principal goal of MBSAT to keep a well-balanced, synchronized, uncorrupted, and functional Free Energy Minimizing BETA, which is critical to maintain excellent quality of the Active Inference processes.

4.3.2 Interoception, exteroception and proprioception: Three types of predictions driven by BETA

Your life results from continuous-time decision-making of three types of predictions and inferences.

When you tell a friend that you believe you are catching a cold, you just made a prediction based on an Inference deriving from the internal state of your body, your body's signals (maybe a slight headache or a chill in your body). This type of inference is called **interoception or interoceptive prediction** and is the domain of your body sensations and emotions.

Learning to build skillful interoceptive predictions by recognizing with more precision the internal signals of your body sensations and emotions is the focus of the first two sessions of the MBSAT program.

"Did you see Gaby?" asks your friend, and you reply: "Yes, but she didn't look well. She seemed upset. I greeted her, and she didn't answer." In this brief exchange, you just made a prediction concerning Gaby based on what you believe is not her usual state: not welcoming, looking worried. These types of inferences or predictions are called **exteroceptive inferences or predictions** and are based on external signals.

Increasing the precision of your perceptual inferences to build more precise generative models with fewer prediction errors is the focus of the third session.

"I am going for a walk with the dog," you tell your partner. You just predicted that by moving your body precisely and in a particular direction, you would fulfill your prediction of going for a walk with your dog. This type of prediction is called **proprioceptive inference or predictions**. It is about acting in the world to realize your predictions, ambitions, desires, and goals.

Perhaps the easiest way to grasp the concept of proprioception is by thinking of dancing or sports, where you need to anticipate your actions (movements) in synchronization with music or some object such as a ball or a baseball bat, etc. This is the focus of the fourth session.

4.4 Minding: The Core Function of MBSAT

4.4.1 Minding our life as continuous practice in action

In MBSAT, you learn to cultivate self-observation and caring that manifest in a minding attitude. The Cambridge Dictionary defines the verb "mind" as "take care or be careful of or about something or pay attention to something." In MBSAT, we use the verb in gerund (an active form in linguistics) as **MINDING** to mean a constant action of self-observation, attending and caring for oneself, others, and oneself with others.

If you are a parent, you care for your baby's well-being; as a daughter or son, you care for your elderly parents; if you have a pet, you care for your dog or cat; if you own and love plants, you care for them. All these caring behaviors of caring and attention are manifestations of minding. Figure 3.5 nicely illustrates the attitude as the person depicted bends forward to groom her garden. Minding means being concerned about creating the conditions for growth and well-being.

The eight sessions of the MBSAT program comprise three training phases of minding: Minding BETA, Minding the Portfolio of Beliefs, and Minding the Strategic Adaptation in Life as follows:

Phase I:

Minding BETA

Minding BETA I: Body sensations: Session 1

Minding BETA II: Emotions: Session 2

Minding BETA III: Thoughts: Session 3

Minding BETA IV: Actions impulses: Session 4

Phase II:

Minding the portfolio of Beliefs – MPOB

Minding the Portfolio of Beliefs I: IRIMI–Confronting adversity: Session 5

Minding the Portfolio of Beliefs II: POMO–Financial Beliefs: Session 6

Minding the Portfolio of Beliefs III: Social Experience (SoE)–Beliefs about self and others: Session 7

Phase III:

Minding Strategic Adaptation in Life – SAL

Minding SAL: Strategic Adaptation in Life: Session 8

By fully embodying a minding attitude minding turns into a continuous practice in action. Figure 4.2 illustrates the ongoing sequence that evolves:

Minding oneself and others implies observing attentively. When we note that our BETA is agitated or unbalanced, we need to find ways to recollect and regenerate (BETA Desaturation) or to revise and update our beliefs, making them more adaptive and flexible (Beliefs Liquification). Both measures help us to become more precise in our predictions and decisions (Honing precision/Precisification). This process results in more effective minding, and the cycle continues in iterative loops, creating the Continuous Minding Sequence. The process is visualized in Figure 4.2.

The terms mentioned (Beta Desaturation, Beliefs Liquification, Precisification) are part of MBSAT's specialized terminology. Knowing the meaning of the key terms that are frequently used is very helpful for effective training. The key lies, however, in applying and practicing.

Some individuals who are familiar with Asian philosophy might recognize minding as an inquiry mode equal to what is called in advanced Buddhist psychology "dhamma vicaya"; which is a mind that constantly inquires and investigates what and why things are happening in the internal BETA mind and in the external environment as well. Seeking to have a more precise understanding of the natural reality of life.

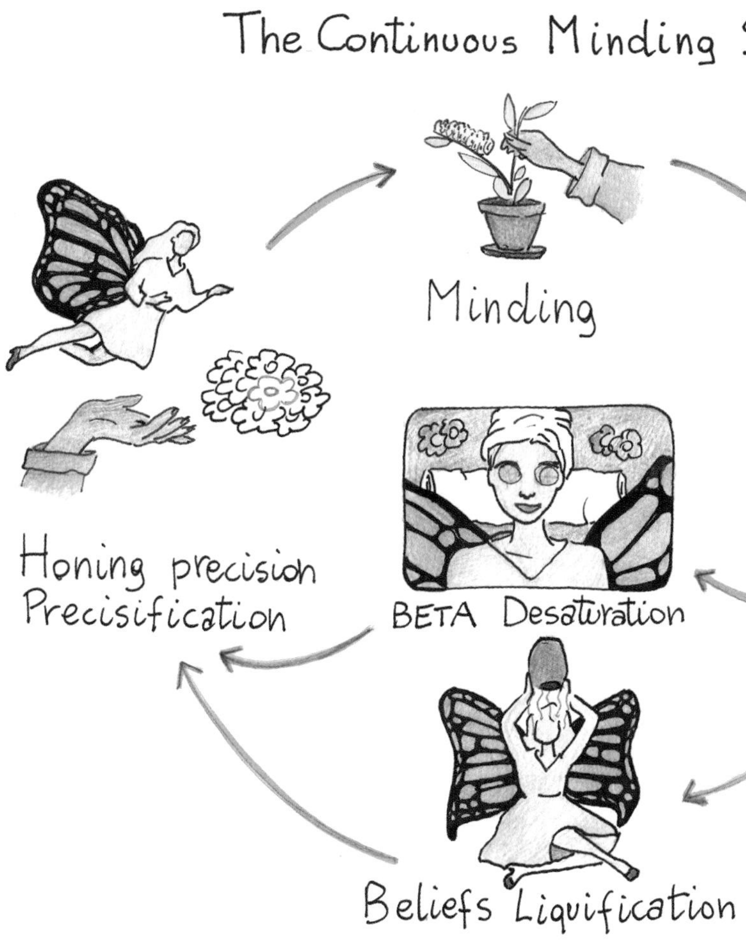

The Continuous Minding Sequence

Minding

Observing

Honing precision
Precisification

BETA Desaturation

Beliefs Liquification

Figure 4.2 The Continuous Minding Sequence

4.4.2 Mindfulness in MBSAT as the practice of minding

When people think about mindfulness, the conjured image is of an individual in a bliss state, reflecting its eastern monastic meditation traditions in search of serene living. Although not negating the value of serenity, in MBSAT, mindfulness takes a dynamic orientation; it is about achieving stability and equanimity that allow cultivating a practical and wise, active life in a volatile, uncertain, complex, and ambiguous world.

MBSAT's view of mindfulness takes inspiration from the work of the great Burmese Vipassana (analytical mindfulness) guru, Sayagyi U Ba Khin, who, besides teaching meditation, was a tireless public figure, working as Minister of Commerce and at several other ministries in cabinet-level positions. The mindfulness approach of MBSAT similarly takes inspiration from my Vipassana teacher, a retired general from the Indian army.

Mindfulness in MBSAT is not about pursuing a beatified life in a withdrawn setting, but about becoming strategically aware of one's active life and the world around us, knowing when your BETA states are appropriate - not only pleasant, uplifting, or enlightening ones but including the opposite, depending on your circumstances. It is learning to live in a fast developing, post-modern world, doing your best to adapt to life-changing conditions and thrive.

Therefore, mindfulness in MBSAT does not require years of meditation to achieve higher levels of consciousness; it is more about continuously minding our BETA and updating beliefs to notice all kinds of phenomena with fresh eyes and open-mindedness. It is about training ourselves to gently and strategically observe everyday actions (mental and physical) without sitting still for extended periods to know what is going on. Continuous sensitivity to contexts allows for strategic awareness to emerge. With strategic awareness, we can generate solutions for challenging situations to improve our lives without negatively affecting others and the environment.

Mindfulness practices in MBSAT therefore seek to increase the precision of predictions and decision-making based on strategic awareness. Becoming a more thoughtful decision-maker will help mitigate many negative effects such as stress, unhappiness, and conflicts; it will increase positive qualities that encompass all aspects of well-being: physical, mental, and emotional.

Based on Sandved-Smith et al. (2021), Figure 4.3 illustrates four phases of meditation and two states of the mind during the training, forming a systemic loop to train strategic awareness and enhance precision in perception, predictions, and decision-making actions.

There are two objective states: focused or distracted, labeled as TS or "True state" in the picture. In other words, a person can be either focused on the object of the training, for example, on the breath or thoughts, or the person's attention can be away from the breath or thoughts that are the focus of the attention, that is distracted.

Equally, the person can be in either of two subjective states: aware or unaware of being distracted, labeled in the picture as SS for "Subjective State". It is possible that a person subjectively believes himself/herself to be focused on the object of the practice, but is objectively distracted. It is about gaining autonomy, as the German philosopher Thomas Metzinger formulated it in a 2018 conference: "Mindfulness, in reality, is a systematic and formal practice for increasing people's mental autonomy."[2]

The combination of objective and subjective states generates several situations.

● The true state (TS) can be distracted, although the subjective state (SS) is perceived as focused on awareness. The combination of "TS-distracted" and "SS-focused" often happens at the beginning of the practice, when a person strives to focus on the object of the meditation, but the awareness is still distracted. It also occurs often at different times during the whole practice in moments, when the meditators' self-autonomy is waning. In the illustration, this situation is visualized by the individual sitting in practice posture while losing the mind in vacation memories (upper right corner).

● The true and subjective states can coincide when the person notices being distracted. This is a valu-

2 Verbatim: "Meditation in Wirklichkeit ist: Eine systematische und formale Praxis zur Erhöhung der eigenen geistigen Autonomie."

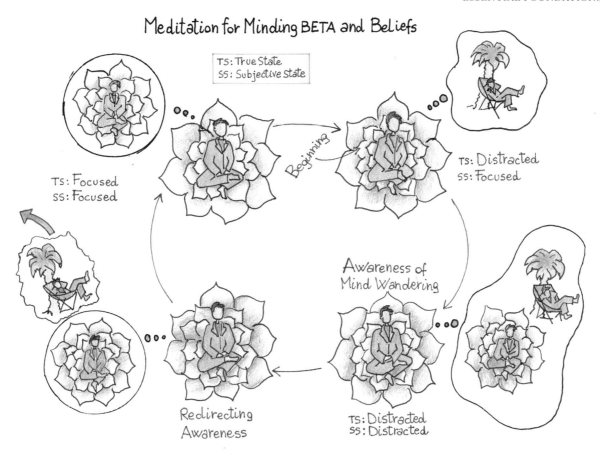

Figure 4.3. Meditation for Minding BETA and Beliefs

able occurrence for the training, as it trains the recognition models of the brain, refining the precision of the perception processes by precisely aligning both subjective and objective states. This can repeatedly happen during the practice and is indeed welcomed as part of the learning process for strategic awareness training.

◦ When the person recognizes the distraction, and objective and subjective states converge, the individual has two options: giving in to the distraction, losing the intention of the practice; or gently returning the awareness/attention to the focus/object of the practice, thus continuing to practice the precision of her attention/awareness. These are moments of autonomy and volitional control, allowing the practitioner to exercise and train skillful decision-making. Figure 4.3 refers to this stage as "Redirecting Awareness".

◦ The aspired goal is for the objective and subjective states to coincide in a state of focused awareness (upper left corner of the illustration).

To be effective, Minding meditation has to self-attenuate[3] (adjust) the precision of attention to overcome mind wandering that is related to three common challenges:

3 Here the term self-attenuation is used in a broad sense to include both moderation and intensification. Thus, if you enter a very bright room, you may want to attenuate/soften the light, but the contrary may also occur: if you enter a very dark room, you may want to attenuate/turn up the light to be able to see. Hence self-attenuation in the context of Free-Energy minimization has the more comprehensive meaning of adjusting.

- Interoceptive challenges: sleepiness, numbness, physical or emotional unease.
- Proprioceptive challenges: impulses to move, scratch, look at the watch.
- Exteroceptive challenges: distractions from the environment and our own mental proliferations.

The physicist Amit Goswami said in a TV interview that most people's brains are constricted, but that genuine mindfulness training expands the brain's consciousness. Although the MBSAT training does not require long sitting meditations, this kind of attention/consciousness training and self-observation of one's mindset is crucial. The reduced duration of the practice has to be compensated by sitting regularly so that a cumulative training effect can set in over time.

4.5 Practices and Practicing in MBSAT

MBSAT practices and exercises of MBSAT fall into three categories:

Behavioral experiments:
The focus of behavioral exercises is on motivating people to try new ways of relating to the environment by changing behavior, for example, trying new dishes, including those of which we might have negative preconceived notions. These practices and interventions have their origin in the Behaviorism movement of the early part of the last century, representing the so-called first wave of behavioral therapies. The rationale is to integrate the whole BETA in practicing, here in particular the A (Action), B (Body) and E (Emotions) of BETA. Experimenting with a change by implementing it instead of thinking about it can raise self-awareness and soften a fixed mindset.

Cognitive Interventions:
With the advent of the cognitive revolution in the mid-part of the last century, the locus of psychological therapies shifted towards cognitive therapies. This so-called second wave focused on assisting people in changing the content of maladaptive thoughts and helping them reframe their beliefs and thoughts to support well-being. In MBSAT, cognitive interventions can be useful, because thoughts are often relatively accessible to our consciousness.

Metacognitive interventions:
These practices and exercises concentrate not on changing the content of thinking but on adopting less rigid ways of processing information by adopting more accommodating attitudes and allowing events, even distressing ones, to be in awareness without generating Free Energy, that is committing predictions errors and decisions mistakes with the usual negative fallout. This view has been called the third wave of therapies. It is the type of interventions I was trained in at Oxford University. The link between processing information, mindfulness and minding in MBSAT is easily recognizable.

No artist has fallen from the sky yet, as the saying goes. But the burden on your time management for the practices of the MBSAT training is less than you might think. All that is needed in MBSAT is to maintain a concise daily practice. Provided the practice is constant, only 10-15 minutes per day are required – just a tiny fraction of your waking time.

Assuming 8 hours of sleep, eight hours of work, and 5 hours or 300 minutes for necessary personal activities such as eating or cleaning and meeting your family, there are still 3 hours or 180 minutes left for leisure such as TV watching, internet surfing, and other voluntary activities. Using 10-15 minutes for mind learning skills with MBSAT practices signifies 5-8% of the 180 minutes of freely disposable time and just about 1% of the combined leisure and work time. Representing 1.5 hours a week (15 minutes a day), this is a small investment for something as important as your mental health and overall well-being and as decisive as increasing your mind's capacity to reduce Free Energy and improve decision-making outcomes. It is also very modest compared to what is commonly recommended for physical training: 150 minutes or 2 1/2 hours of moderate training per week.

According to the World Health Organization, mental health is a state of well-being in which individuals realize their abilities; it refers to cognitive, behavioral, and emotional well-being and affects how people think, feel, and behave. In MBSAT terminology, it relates to the BETA. Good mental health helps individuals cope with the everyday stress of life, improves relations with others, and enables them to make better decisions. It even influences your physical health positively.

While it is pretty normal today to see individuals investing considerable time in their appearance and physical health, it is slowly being realized that it is probably even more critical to invest time in training and maintaining the most vital organ in the body, the brain. With only 2% of the body's mass, it consumes 20% of its energy and handles almost all functions in the body. Like muscles that grow as they get trained, the brain also gains capacity and power; it gets more effective and productive when it undergoes training by intentionally learning new things. With MBSAT, the intention is to train the brain by learning to recognize and update patterns (conditioning, habits, beliefs, and other routines) that drive our lives. This ability is crucially important to maintain good mental health and enable flourishing.

By using MBSAT's structured practices we gain brain power in the form of adaptive neurological patterns that generate better physiological, emotional, behavioral, and psychological outcomes and maintain higher levels of mental health. The practices enable reducing the uncertainty of our desired future outcomes and avoid disappointments as a source of stressful surprises. If left unchecked, maladaptive patterns will lead to mental health issues and adverse physical conditions (heart diseases, diabetes, and others).

From a neuroscience perspective, the interventions in MBSAT activate groups of neurons that, when repeatedly activated through regular, disciplined practices, build new neurological connections that are more easily mobilized for minding BETA or making good decisions. For example, practicing reframing unpleasant emotions into more adaptive ones yields a faster reframing cycle time when one wants to redirect a feeling of anger into an emotion of conciliation. Similarly, suppose you have trained the ability to mind your BETA and find yourself in a situation, where you urgently need to balance. In this case the minding BETA practice gets activated faster and more efficiently as the neurons are more sensitive to the routine of minding your BETA, so the benefits of minding BETA will become tangible almost immediately. In other words, to improve and change your recognition and generative models of your mind there needs to be a physical change in your neural pathways, which happens in response to a new discovery (insight) and an increase in attention density which is essentially practicing round your new discovery. For example, imagine that out of your systematic routine of the CEO of BETA (a mood-changing practice) you realized that you have the tendency to get angry easily. Based on that insight, you can begin to train by practicing to become more equanimous by systematically engaging in practices of relaxing your BETA, thus, developing over time new neurological pathways to deal less angrily with normal irritations in life.

4.6 Beliefs: The Drivers Behind Our BETA, Predictions and Behaviors

Beliefs are central in the MBSAT; they are the linchpin for changing our BETA and, ultimately, our life. Changing beliefs is how a person changes her life for the best or worst.

Underlying the beliefs are often likes and dislikes, making updating beliefs a more significant challenge. As ancient wisdom reminds us: "Attraction has conditioned the senses to the pleasant and aversion to the unpleasant: they should not rule us; they are obstacles on our path." (Easwaran, 2007)

Beliefs are based on prior knowledge about what we know about the world. As neuroscience suggests, they have statistical properties that represent probabilities about the causes of actual phenomena we perceive.

There are different beliefs. Biologically formed beliefs are part of the biological phenotype of an individual, which is mostly genetically determined. For example, believing and knowing that humans can't fly because of human physical morphology constitutes a universal biological belief that requires no evidence even for small children. Socialization processes form culture-based beliefs; for instance, in the COVID-19 pandemic, some people refused to get vaccinated because of their belief that governments cannot be trusted, while others with beliefs based on the science supporting the vaccine were eager to get vaccinated. There are also beliefs based on personal experience; for example, on average, humans can't hold their breath underwater for over 1-2 minutes; however, a sports diver may believe she can stay 6-8 minutes underwater because of her unique training.

Culture-based beliefs that are the result of social conditioning are often unconscious. In everyday language, this kind of belief is often referred to as bias, or prejudice (which are beliefs without evidence) whereas the term conviction usually refers to explicit, outspoken beliefs. Becoming aware of one's beliefs is one of the central goals of the MBSAT training. Awareness of beliefs is the basis for strategically aware decision-making and enables agency to orient one's personal development.

The process of updating beliefs in MBSAT is influenced by the precision individuals hold about their beliefs. Beliefs with a high level of accuracy constitute a subjective certainty, meaning that the holders are fully confident that they are accurate. Thus, high-precision beliefs are difficult to change. Learning to keep a curious attitude about one's beliefs and a willingness to revise them in the face of fresh evidence is at the core of Minding the Portfolio of Beliefs.

Figure 3.3 above illustrates various degrees of intensity in updating beliefs.

The following factual anecdote is an indicator of how deep-rooted and unconscious beliefs can be. When the world-famous orchestra in Cleveland decided to recruit more female musicians in an effort to increase diversity, it first seemed that there was a shortage of talented women (the belief). Then they changed their audition proceedings and let candidates play their instruments behind a curtain, so that the selection committee could not see, who was playing. Miraculously this increased the female proportion of orchestra musicians relatively quickly.

4.7 Decisions: Orienting and Shaping Our Lives

4.7.1 Skillful decisions: Drivers of Free Energy Minimization (FEM)

Skillful decision-making (SDM) is what facilitates and mediates Free Energy minimization. Learning how to increase the capacity for SDM requires a particular type of learning based on first-person experiences, allowing for strategic awareness to emerge and for self-recognition of the impediments to moving forward and adapting to changing conditions in the world around us.

The training model detailed in Figure 4.4 represents the training logic in MBSAT for improving strategic awareness and skillful decision-making.

The program is a triangulation of several scientific disciplines (left column of the graphic) that facilitates the training of a Free-Energy Minimization Self through three specific Minding processes: Minding BETA I-IV, Minding the Portfolio of Beliefs I-III (POB; related to IRIMI/confronting adversity, POMO/financial beliefs, Social Experience-SoE) and Minding Strategic Adaptation in Life (SAL) (for an overview, please, see Section 4.4.1).

These minding processes build strategic awareness as a core competence, depicted center stage in the graphic. Strategic awareness for its part feeds into three computational skills:

a) Building adaptive and valuable mental models.

b) Increasing the precision of predictions and actions.

c) Reducing the level of decision errors.

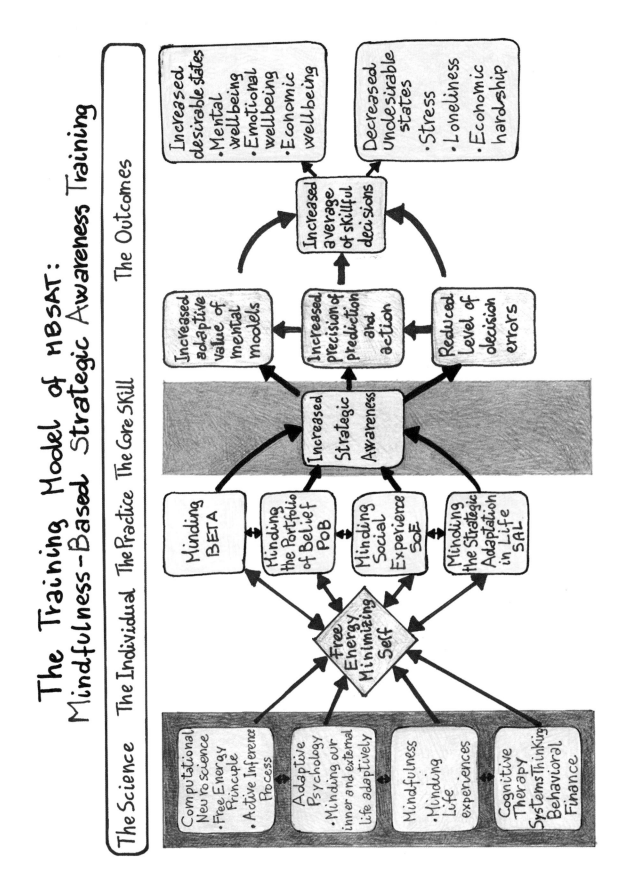

Figure 4.4 The Training Model of MBSAT: Mindfulness-based Strategic Awareness Training

The principal outcome of the training process is an increase in the average of skillful decisions that raises our desirable mental, physical and emotional states and reduces undesirable states such as stress, loneliness and economic hardship, amongst others, depicted at the far right of Figure 4.4.

Decisions generate facts that form part of the causal links shaping our lives. As Figure 4.5 below shows, the outcomes of our decisions are part of a dynamic cycle of causal links. The world of VUCA influences the state of our BETA, which influences our decisions, resulting in outcomes affecting our lives and impacting, in turn, the environment (VUCA world), thus forming ongoing loops of causal links that affect us all.

These loops of causal links highlight the importance of minding our BETA and its influence on our decision-making process.

The interdependence between the state of our BETA, the quality of beliefs we hold, and our decisions also suggest that in order to change and improve the quality of our life we need to continuously keep adjusting the direction of our BETA, avoiding tendencies that hinder minimizing Free Energy and orient our BETA and beliefs towards states that foster skillful decisions.

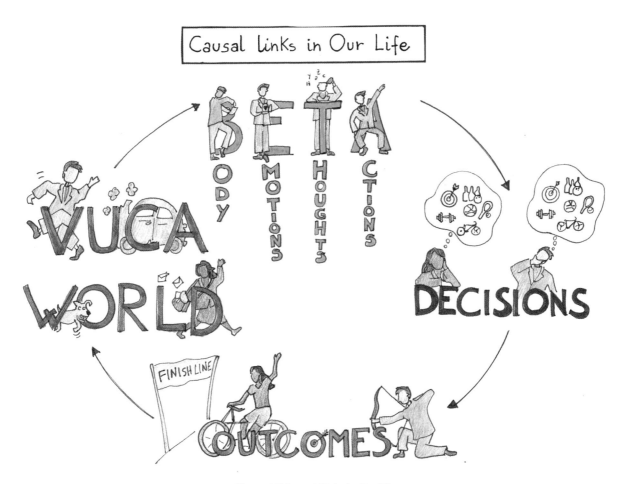

Figure 4.5 Causal Links in Our life

Orientation and momentum of the BETA are decisive for updating our beliefs and other vital abilities such as perception, action and learning. Figure 3.1 above provides a visual of the dynamic force of BETA.

4.7.2 Strategic Awareness: The lifeblood of skillful decision-making

Strategic Awareness (SA) means being aware moment by moment of what is happening in the world around us with curiosity and attention. In MBSAT in particular, Strategic Awareness means a unified, integrative way of navigating our inner and outer worlds by using different sensorial receptors to capture and process data as valuable input for minding our BETAs and adjusting our beliefs. Strategic Awareness also integrates the dimensions of time. It combines compelling memories from the past (priors) with precise perceptions in the present to formulate skillful predictions about what might come.

Strategic Awareness is an integrative skill crucial for decision-making. It is driven by abduction thinking, a form of hypothetical inferencing. Our perceptions and predictions in a changing world are in fact hypotheses (Gregory, 1980) with embedded levels of uncertainty, therefore implying the necessity to keep investigating and observing. Abduction as a thinking process is in essence continued hypothesizing on what is being observed until a hypothesis is found that is considered satisfying for an adequate update to form new beliefs. Defined as a posterior belief in Bayesian terminology, the updated hypothesis enables individuals to avoid prediction and decision errors.

There are two types of abductive inquiry in generative creative thinking: exploratory and innovative. With exploratory abductive inquiry, one senses the environment searching for evidence of one's predictions to validate the recognition models and match them with the generative brain models. In innovative inquiry, an individual/predictor creates conditions that support predictions for skillful actions in the environment. For example, in an exploratory abductive inquiry, the individual will simply test the temperature of a cup of coffee to validate her initial hypothesis and reiterate the tasting experiment until the desired temperature is reached. She can, however, take an active-creative abductive approach by, for example, adding some cold milk or water to her coffee, or an ice cube, thus acting on the environment and changing the conditions of the coffee to accommodate the situation and achieve the desired temperature, acceptable for her to drink the coffee.

Strategic awareness is facilitated by a constant and continuous abductive way of thinking. Entrepreneurs, designers, and architects are often strategically aware individuals; typically, they have a predisposition for abductive thinking and reframing questions. They tend to spend time observing, investigating, testing and building counterfactual arguments about what they are trying to achieve. They like to keep things in fluid states, probing and advancing ideas until there is consensus about adequate solutions to the job. They are natural exploratory-hypotheses builders about what might work, without having all the information required to formulate solutions.

In MBSAT, these cognitive skills are an integral part of in Strategic Awareness and need to be cultivated. They help individuals build skillful generative and recognition models and find solutions with low prediction errors to issues they confront in their lives. In reality, the private life of a flourishing person has much in common with a successful entrepreneur active in business. They both have achieved a state where their predictions are generally accurate with a low incidence of prediction errors. They have minimized Free Energy and established a good fit between their generative models and their contextual generative process.

In combination with abductive inquiry, Strategic Awareness with its capacity to and mind sensory and cognitive states that support a skillful life and sustainable well-being. A flourishing life is the ultimate goal of training and cultivating Strategic Awareness.

> *"Making decisions is
> a fundamental life skill."*
>
> Hammond, Keeney, and Raiffa (2002)

4.8 The Free Energy Minimizing Self–FEMS: Your Personal Plan to Implement Free Energy Minimizing Strategies

The Free Energy Minimizing Self (FEMS) is a personal plan for sustainable well-being starting from your strengths, assets and opportunities and culminating in strategies and concrete actions to realize your aspirations. It is developed over the duration of the MBSAT training, with the program's final session dedicated to it, and remains a practical tool for you when the course ends. You can then continue to refer to it and update it anytime as your life evolves.

Designing your FEMS comprises several building blocks. It includes feedback from people who know you well and perceive you from different viewpoints (friends and family, colleagues and supervisors at work, contacts from social activities and hobbies, etc.). It finishes with a dynamic FEMS strategic plan similar to the ones organizations establish to manage their activities and achieve the desired goals.

Thus, the FEMS becomes is a mental image of your aspired anticipated self as a person strategically aware and knowledgeable of the importance of minimizing Free Energy. The self is so to speak the interface between your brain and the external world; it is the locus that is at the center of your discernment for understanding the world and making decisions that reduce Free Energy and improve the quality of your life.

One of the principal benefits of having a FEMS is its function as a powerful magnet; it fuels the motivation to realize your aspirations. It is a concrete virtual image of your potential combined with tangible strategies and actions to make the image your reality. The clearly defined vision of one's possibilities to enact a conscious Free Energy minimization way of life serves as the blueprint for attaining authentic well-being. It then nourishes the BETA with a sense of what a person can become.

In Section 3.9 of Chapter 3 above, you can find more detailed information about the FEMS.

4.9 Core Learnings to Remember

The concept of BETA, with its four doors of human experience, is in essence a unified model of perception. It is the foundation of our recognition model. Its task is information gathering.

The generative model, on the other hand, is a unified model of understanding and acting, enabling us to grasp a situation at hand. The function here is information processing and acting.

Together the recognition model and the generative model constitute the core of our existence. They drive our brains, behavior, and experience. In brief, together they shape our lives.

Mental modeling in MBSAT and the MBSAT training of our mental models are designed to improve the precision and veracity of information gathering and processing.

The key goals of the MBSAT training program can be summarized as follows:
- Understanding the functioning and interdependence of the recognition and the generative model.
- Synchronizing BETA with the generative model.
- Minding the predictive BETA mind and keeping it updated.

Understanding, synchronizing, minding, and updating are all recursive, continuous processes for life-long vital energy optimization that sustain strategic awareness and skillful decision-making.

Box 4.1

Active Mindfulness in MBSAT

A recent TV series carries a scene where two detectives have a conversation while driving. One of them says: "So, this morning I open the app and I am doing my exercises… and my wife comments she doesn't believe in mindfulness. I reply that mindfulness is not like Tooth Fairy or UFOs; it exists, how can you not believe in it? And she says she thinks mindfulness is evil." "That escalated quickly," his colleague remarks. The detective explains: "Her theory is that mindfulness perpetuates the idea that all our problems are 'within ourselves' and can be fixed with a few minutes of meditation every day. In her view, this distracts us from the truth that the world we're living in is the real problem and we're being screwed over by corporations and governments all the time." His colleague mutters: "F…, she might have a point." "That's what crossed my mind, too," the detective says, "and now that's all I can think of when I'm doing my exercises. She's ruined mindfulness for me." This sparks laughter from both of them and then he jokes: "I wouldn't mind, but the app cost me 15.99 bucks." And they keep laughing together.

It seems there is wisdom in the assertion of the detective's wife. Ron Purser (2019), a business school professor at San Francisco State University and an ordained monk in the Korean Zen Taego order, has been a longtime critic of the contemporary mindfulness orientation or what he calls "McMindfulness", in essence pretending that with a few minutes of practice to calm the mind and be in the present moment we will solve all of our problems. This leaves out the most important aspects of true mindfulness: learning to recognize ourselves, others and the world around us as it is, and training to cope with the often-uncomfortable reality skillfully and with agency without harming others, the environment or ourselves.

MBSAT's approach to mindfulness is comprehensive as it embraces both the need for equanimity and the necessity of action. In the first four sessions of the protocol MBSAT seeks to train participants in maintaining a calm and equanimous BETA as the precondition to confront reality. The following four sessions build the necessary strategic awareness that supports a better understanding of reality and allows for dealing more skillfully with what we encounter in life. MBSAT's two main notions: the Free Energy minimization principle and the Active Inference process underscore this comprehensive view of mindfulness. The first notion tells us that we need to do reduce the level of prediction/decisions errors in order to increase our chances for having a good life. The second notion tells us how to achieve this and maintain the level of prediction errors low, that is by training to use active inference processes skillfully.

The Active Inference process is key for mindfulness in MBSAT. Figure 1.5 deconstructs Active Inference in four states: the external states of our VUCA world trigger our sensory states (recognition models) which then influence our internal states (generative models) that generate predictions and lead to actives states that can impact the external states or the world, thus closing the loop. MBSAT mindfulness practices follow the logic of Active Inference. Therefore, it is imperative that our recognition models are not affected by aberrant sensory states, for example distorted by depressive or psychotic dispositions or by an all-too-common unwillingness to work on ourselves to soften and update inadequate beliefs and biases. This inflexibility to reduce fixed non-adaptive internal states impedes renewal processes of our recognition and generative models, so necessary in our fast-changing VUCA world.

Especially in the global North issues of material subsistence (food, shelter, and other necessities for physical survival) are to a large extent resolved. It is the more subtle necessities (friendship, meaning, belonging, satisfaction, well-being) that generate most difficulties in life and are at the origin of most of our prediction errors.

Figuratively speaking, what MBSAT seeks to train is people's capacity to stay on the right side of a hypothetical normal distribution curve of prediction errors as depicted in Figure 4.6. Persons living in the zone of very high error levels on the far left live in distress. Persons living in the above average prediction error zone, still on the left of the center, live arduously at best. Only right of the center well in the zone of below-average prediction errors individuals start to live well. Finally, there a small group of persons living optimally by living in the zone of very low predictive error. In order to live on the right side of the curve people not only need to be good at keeping their recognition models/BETAs in shape but also to be able to constantly update their generative models (beliefs).

In other words, the goal is to avoid the evilness in mindfulness that the detective's wife in the conversation above is concerned about (the distraction from the truth) in so far as mindfulness in MBSAT becomes a liberating force by promoting agency and encouraging skillful action when required. Many problems we have are indeed caused by a generative environment that is unhelpful and problematic and don't originate within ourselves.

MBSAT stimulates an active type of mindfulness in several ways (Kim et al., 2022):
- MBSAT trains the attention and precision of people's perceptions (the recognition models).
- It assists people relativize inadequate beliefs.
- It facilitates liquifying non-skillful generative models, making them easier to update.
- It helps people create new, more adequate beliefs.

For additional perspectives of Mindfulness in MBSAT such as its role in computational neuroscience and updating beliefs, please, see Section 3.8.

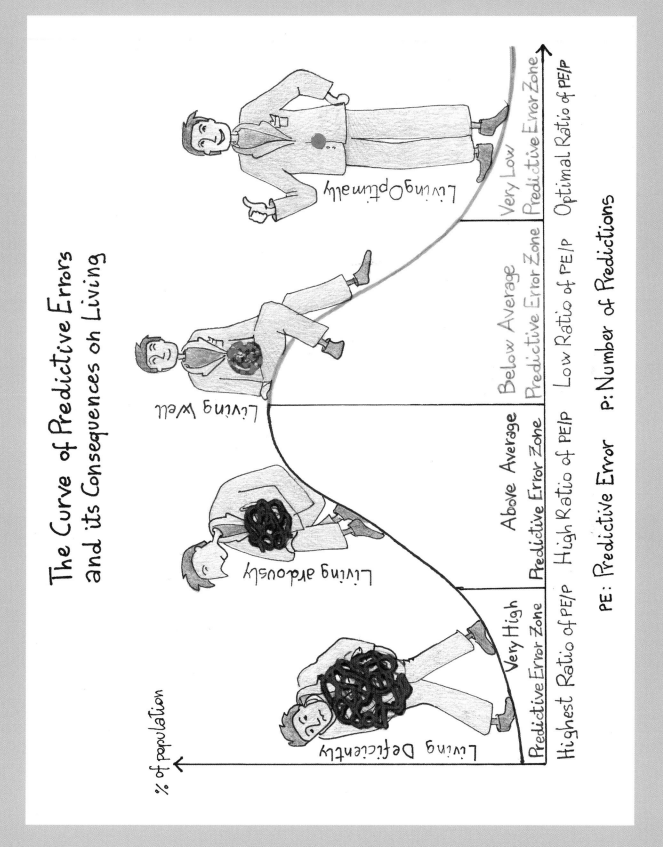

Figure 4.6 The Curve of Predictive Errors and its consequences on Living

Box 4.2

Structural Design of the MBSAT Training Program

The MBSAT training program is structured into two main blocks of 4 sessions each.

The first part of the MBSAT training program, consisting of Sessions 1-4, is dedicated to BETA (Body sensations, Emotions, Thoughts, and Action impulses). The rationale is that a well-balanced and synchronized BETA is a precondition for effective learning and personal development. Each of sessions 1-4 focuses entirely on one of the BETA components.

The second part is dedicated to updating beliefs and cultivating Strategic Awareness, a key capacity as the name MBSAT indicates, standing for Mindfulness-based Strategic Awareness Training.

Sessions 5-7 in Part 2 are about belief updating as beliefs are the drivers of our brain models and behaviors. The topics of the three sessions concentrate on three realms that are decisive for sustainable well-being and the quality of life for human beings: coping with adversity, dealing mindfully with money, and maintaining good social relationships.

The training program concludes with Session 8 which offers a brief synopsis and then focuses on the SOPA exercise. SOPA stands for Skillful BETAs and Beliefs, Opportunities, and Positive Actions and is a blueprint for establishing a personal strategic plan. Its objective is to serve as a companion for further personal development once the 8 sessions of the training program are completed, meaning that MBSAT trainees can continue to refine and update their individual SOPA plans after the conclusion of the training program.

The rationale of Session 8 "Minding Strategic Adaptation in Life" is that life often throws situations at us we didn't wish for. To achieve flourishing despite these unexpected challenges we need a mindful, constructive attitude and the strategic ability to recognize opportunities and make the best of what we have. Therefore, minding strategic adaptation in life is the epitome of MBSAT's active, developmental spirit. Instead of resignation, the essence of adaptation in MBSAT is far-sighted, creative coping with the conditions we encounter to achieve Free Energy minimization and sustainable well-being.

Figure 4.7 provides a comprehensive view of the structural design of the MBSAT training and the topics of each session. The purpose of the overview is to serve as a roadmap and help trainees navigate through the program.

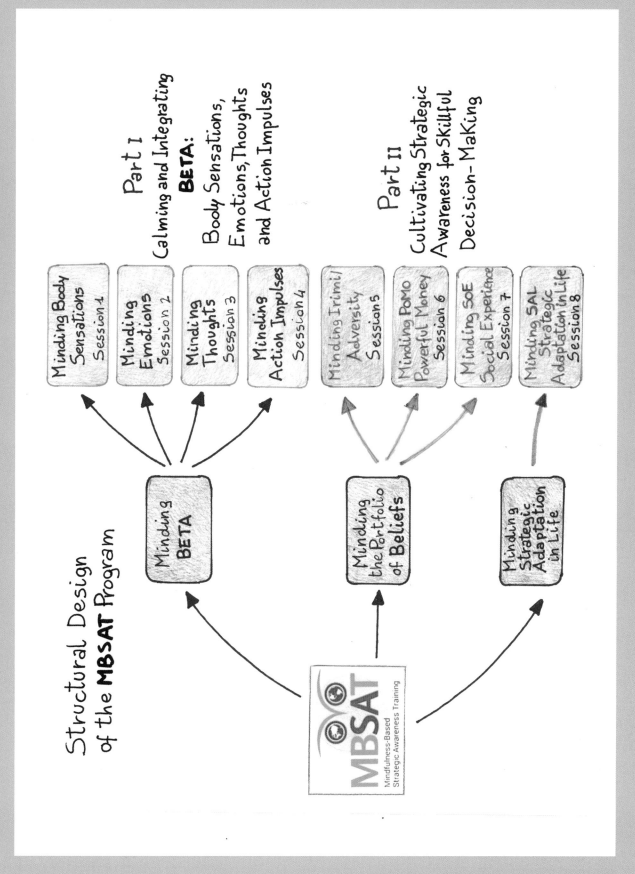

Figure 4.7 Structural Design of the MBSAT Program

Box 4.3

Strategic Awareness in Support of Skillful Decisions

Skillful decisions follow three channels: maximization, optimization, and coping conduits.

The maximization conduit: in some cases, if one is conscious of the limits, it is possible to maximize. For example, this may be the case of a sportsperson who knows well the limits of her physical condition and can then decide to go for a maximum outcome—like Felix Baumgarten who trained his body for six years to be able to execute a maximum jump from the stratosphere.

The optimization conduit: in many social interaction situations, conflicting interests impede maximizing outcomes. Optimizing decisions seems the ideal response in such cases; each party gets some benefits.

The coping conduit applies to the alarming situations we are increasingly exposed to where we see distressing things happening but cannot respond, for example the exposure to the myriad of fake news and aggressive tendencies between people and countries. In such cases, we resort to coping decisions using abducting thinking, seeking alternative information in the case of fake news or avoiding taking fixed viewpoints in the cases of conflictive dynamics.

Strategic Awareness allows us to distinguish these different situations and contexts and adapt our decision conduits in a skillful way.

MINDFULNESS-BASED STRATEGIC AWARENESS TRAINING (MBSAT)

THE TRAINING PROGRAM

*"The best way to understand
something is to try to change it."*

K. Lewin

Introduction:
Purpose and Meaning of Part 2

> *Happiness is neither virtue nor pleasure*
> *nor this thing nor that, but simply growth.*
> *We are happy when we are growing.*
>
> W.B. Yates

M. Porter, the Harvard Business School professor who revolutionized strategic management with his ideas on competitive strategy, explains that when he started to study the field of strategy, he believed that most strategic failures were caused by external factors. But after many years of studying corporate strategies, he realized that most strategic errors stem from internal factors. The firms impair themselves.

The same is the case of individuals, I believe. Despite today's volatile uncertain, complex, and ambiguous (VUCA) environment and the obvious challenges it poses, there is a subjective agency dynamic that is ultimately the decisive factor for thriving and flourishing. It depends on whether we perceive the environment as a source of numbing, in Friston's terminology Free-Energy producing events that we consider as adverse and dangerous and usually make us feel hopeless. Or whether we perceive adverse situations as occurrences to be re-engineered into Free-Energy minimizing possibilities and options capable of supporting our aspirations as illustrated in Session 5 (Figure 9.6).

The German philosopher Peter Sloterdijk writes: "The only fact of universal ethical significance in the current world is the diffusely and ubiquitously growing realization that things cannot continue this way." (2013, p. 442). Intro Part 2 Figure 1 captures the sorry state we are in.

If this is the case, we then need a systemic approach to how people can change their lives. Governments around the globe are responding to the manifold crises (wars, scarcity of energy and other resources, climate change, etc.) by resorting to nudging methods to motivate their populations to change their

"Growing realization that things cannot continue this way…"
(Sloterdijk, 2008)

Intro Part 2 Figure 1 Growing Realization

lives (saving energy, recycling, using water more judiciously, etc.). The fact is that everything is evolving, sometimes for the better (modern medicine, faster communication, etc.), sometimes for the worse; just witness the drama of migrants, fleeing violence, poverty, and starvation in search of a better life, usually to the more prosperous global North that is increasingly wary of welcoming strangers.

But if things cannot continue this way and the success of government interventions is questionable, what can we as individuals do (Intro Part 2 Figure 2)? This is the larger, most pressing question.

Intro Part 2 Figure 2 What can I do?

Seeking for an answer suggests additional inquiry, what specifically should one do to improve the conditions of the world? Sloterdijk's answer can be found in the title he gave his book *You must change your life* (2013).

In MBSAT's more concrete terms this means changing oneself, our beliefs, and behaviors, in other words changing our BETA (Intro Part 2 Figure 3).

I have to change myself.

I must change
my beliefs,
my BETA,
my life

Intro Part 2 Figure 3 I have to change myself

Coming from the Global South, living in the Global North and having worked at a senior level in the finance industry, I made a profound experience of having to change my life in order to survive in a competitive, unfamiliar environment.

When I told one of my friends, an Argentinian Jew of Easter European descent, a wonderful person, that I was planning to support my wife's wishes to live in her home country in central Europe, his immediate response, was: "Oh no, Juan, you will not make it there, you are too sensitive. These people have a hard heart, they are merciless. Look what they did to my tribe!" Still, I decided to go along with my wife's desire. Besides being curious about the perspective of living in another country, unlike my friend, I optimistically predicted that I was able to make it there. It was not that I was expecting benevolence from the environment, but I felt certain somehow that I would be able to change my life practices to adapt to my new situation, and more importantly, I had the confidence that I could generate value and growth for my new country and for myself, thus, in the words of Yates, I would be able to grow and be happy. Van de Cruys et al. (2020) assert: "Effective PP[1] agents must form optimistic yet sufficiently realistic expectations about their own future states and behaviors."

So, as a biological system of recursive decision-making, growing in my new environment meant in practical terms making no decision errors, thus minimizing Frcc Energy. Although I thought that some of my assets, such as my education at some of the world's best universities and my previous managerial experience in responsible positions could help me, I also knew that I needed to learn new skills, develop new life practices and eliminate others. This is not unusual. It happens to anyone working at a high-level, visible position anywhere in the world. Naturally, it can become more acerbic, if the person is not native. The objective recognition of my subjective reality led me to change my life in profound ways. I realized that I had to carefully concentrate my cognitive, emotional, and kinetic resources on designing decisions around three main concerns:

- **Understanding the culture of the new place where I lived.**
  Knowing its history and above all learning the country's three main languages as a strategy to facilitate my integration and social life. This indeed allowed me to minimize Free Energy (mistakes) in my socialization process in the new country.

- **Maintaining the important principle of not having conflicts at work, in my social interactions and my family.**
  This involved developing an inner capacity to stay calm despite the tensions that could build up in my environment. Decisions taken with this guiding principle in effect allowed me to avoid harming myself and others.

- **Achieving independence in my life.**
  This suggested to me a necessity to look out for, and even more importantly, to self-create business

---

1 PP stands for Predictive Processing in the neuroscience field concerned with Free Energy. In this context, the term "PP agents" means simply "persons" or "people" as human brains are by nature predictive processors.

and investment opportunities within a voluntary, self-imposed set of high ethical and moral standards in order to build financial and economic capital. I understood the decisions around this area as a mechanism of hedging and protecting myself against the vagaries of future economic hardships and as my ticket to gaining financial and personal freedom.

Having a clear compass around these concerns enabled me to make realistic predictions and decisions that supported my desires and ambitions for achieving the required changes and a thriving life in my new environment.

In today's circumstances it is clear that at some point, people must start asking questions about how to shape their lives if they are to survive and thrive - as individuals but also as a society. Certainly, they will conclude that they must avoid making decision errors in these times of change where every individual faces the challenge of designing a personal path on the shifting tectonic plates of society and economy. This is why a personal strategic plan is so important. The MBSAT training program, therefore, includes the design of a Free Energy Minimizing Self (FEMS) that helps participants to plan their lives with minimum decisional mistakes. **I believe in today's changing VUCA environment it is imperative for success to learn the fundamentals of how to change your life** when it is required. Every person has the agency to give adverse situations a more favorable turn for the benefit of themselves and of mankind.

> *"We are having dinner together to celebrate the last day of the program, but you keep leaving the group to talk on your mobile. What can be so urgent that you can't enjoy this last get-together?" I asked my student. He answered: "It is indeed serious. This program has opened my eyes; so I decided to* **change** *my business plans. With the full support of my family, I decided to withdraw from a lucrative, government-approved project in the defense and war industry. My partners are very upset and threaten me with legal action." Now laughing, he added: "You see Juan, you are responsible for this."*

This is the focus of the book's second part: assisting participants in training and practicing for keeping their brains' recognition and generative models the most accurate possible to support skillful decision-making. This part of the book is the practical manual, a handbook with practices and instructions for becoming a skillful decision-maker.

The critical success factor that will determine whether you can fully benefit from the training program is establishing a disciplined routine with regard to practicing. This requires self-control, determination and staying power to do the practices regularly. Absolutely nothing will happen without practicing the interventions recommended in this program. Naturally, the level of success will depend on your key performance indicator (KPI). MBSAT's KPI to success is a practice of at least 1.5 hours per week, that is a minimum of 15 minutes a day. This is a tiny investment of time and effort compared to the huge benefits resulting from the practices. Thus, it is merely a question of incorporating 15 minutes of high-value innovative practices into your current daily routines. By improving your decision-making skills these practices have the potential to help you grow and to intentionally move in the direction you choose to go, ensuring long-term, sustainable well-being.

Everyone is already practicing something; life is essentially enacted practice. Practice is in reality an action to achieve certain goals, like learning Aikido self-defense, playing piano, grasping mathematics, or brushing your teeth. When you carry out an activity repeatedly, you learn to perform it skillfully (playing the piano delightfully, earning a belt in Aikido, becoming adroit in mathematical calculations), and the actions become automatic, almost without effort, involving very little noticeable energy. With MBSAT the learning is to become a skillful decision maker, smart at minimizing Free Energy (minimizing prediction and decision errors).

Figure 4 of this introduction illustrates the changes that happen in our brain as we practice based on the work of James Zull (2002), professor of biology at Case Western Reserve University. Before the practice, our synapses are plain and relatively short. After engaging in the practice rudiments of new synapses start to appear and keep expanding after 15-20 minutes of sustained practice. Eventually, with regular, disciplined practice, the synapses form new connections and enrich the brain's neuronal networks. These are changes at a microscopic level that have an enormous influence.

Aristotle, the Greek philosopher, once posited: "We are what we repeatedly do." This suggests that, if we keep training to become more equanimous, eventually we will become more equanimous. Or, if we are training to recognize false beliefs, we will ultimately discard them and replace them with more accurate ones (see below Box 1 Intro Part 2, Minding Our Perception and Brain Models).

Intro Part 2 Figure 4 Practicing Increases Your Brain's Network

So, Sloterdijk maintains that there is a widespread, diffuse consensus that things cannot continue in the same way. But what exactly needs to change? We all have prejudices and beliefs without evidence. Some are legacies from past experiences and no longer adequate in today's changing reality; some are biases from our cultural and societal context we have adopted as part of our brain models. These are our blind spots that we need to constantly search for, detect and examine. Thus, we all need to change at a personal level by revising and updating the beliefs driving our lives. If we are responsible for others (as parents, managers, therapists, coaches, psychiatrists, etc.), this need is even more critical, because otherwise we might unconsciously contribute to the persistence of inadequate ideas, and beliefs.

The next critical question then is: How can we change? Here, Sloterdijk's answer is: "A human can only advance by following the impossible."

By practicing with MBSAT the hope is that people can find their personal "impossible" for contributing to the advancement of a more friendly and sustainable world. Hopefully the world will look like the future imagined in Intro Part 2 Figure 5.

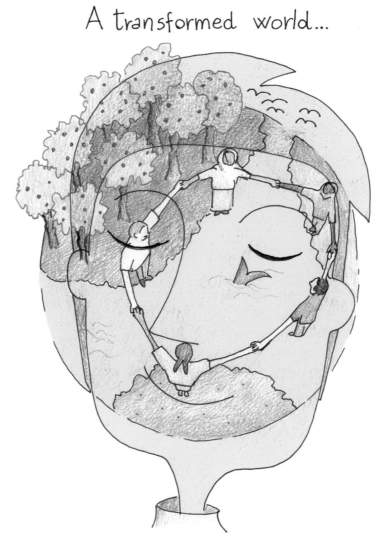

Intro Part 2 Figure 5 A Transformed World ...

Box 1 Intro Part 2
<u>Abductive Mindset and MBSAT Signature Terms for Learning and Transformation</u>

In order to thrive and flourish it is necessary to align prior beliefs (based on past experiences) with new evidence from the changing world, allowing to grow in today's VUCA environment (the generative process). This is how we minimize Free Energy, operationalized in this book as making skillful decisions with minimum prediction errors. That is the essential message of Part 1 of this book that provides a theoretical and conceptual understanding of the program.

In the second part of the workbook, the goal is to move beyond theories and concepts and into the applications and practices necessary to become a Free Energy Minimizer Self (FEMS) (a person with a lower quota of decision and prediction errors).

My academic education is based on two differing orientations: at the University of Chicago Business School, using theory to draw conclusions to explain events, and at Harvard Kennedy School and Harvard Business School, using cases and events to draw generalizations and build conclusions and beliefs. My conviction is that we need both; theory informing practice and practice informing theory. It is not one or the other; they are synergistically complementing each other.

There is a joke at UChicago: "If you want an education get a Chicago MBA; if you want a job, get a Harvard MBA or MPA, and you will learn to talk yourself into a good job." On the other hand, what is the purpose of having a good theory, if one can't communicate it well? Common sense suggests we need both; which is why MBSAT addresses both approaches (deductive and inductive thinking) in the form of a way of reasoning defined as abductive thinking. It means formulating creative ideas and tentative hypotheses without disposing of evidential support, launching an active inference process in search of probabilistic precision. Friston views "the brain as a statistical organ, engaging in an abductive inference of an ampliative nature." (Friston 2018, p. 1019)

While studying with Richard Boland, my thesis advisor at Case Western Reserve University, I first heard of abductive thinking. Dick is an advanced thinker and erudite; unknown to many he was the first to introduce the idea of management as a design profession (Boland & Collopy, 2004). His insight of conceiving managers as designers resulted from his collaboration with the star architect Frank Gehry during the design and construction of the university's Peter Lewis building.

Frank Gehry and his team were using abductive thinking to overcome all sorts of challenges (structural difficulties, space limitations, resistance to novel ideas, etc.) to realize the beautiful avant-garde building home to Case's management school (Intro Part 2 Figure 6).

Intro Part 2 Figure 6 Peter Lewis Building of the Weatherhead School of Management,
Case Western Reserve University, Cleveland, Ohio, by Architect Frank Gehry.
(Steven Litt, cleveland.com)

When Frank found out that there was a Panamanian doctoral student from the same country as his wife, he asked to meet me. To this day I remember how he told me that for lasting success one needs to keep trying with different ideas until one finds the key that opens the door to possibilities. Dick remarked, "and that is abductive reasoning". Frank says that when he creates a building he tells the clients that they are going to be in a liquid state for a long time; being liquid, he says, allows for more choices. His ideas inspired me to create the concept of liquification for MBSAT as a useful approach to updating beliefs. In a liquid state people can suspend their BETAs and beliefs and build more easily new and creative abductive guesses, hypotheses, and inferences that either support their initial belief or refute it. In liquid states, it is easy for people to begin a recursive process of data mining to update their generative mental models with new beliefs more aligned with their reality.

The expected outcome of the practical and experiential training in MBSAT's second part of the workbook is an improvement in the quality of people's decision-making and a concomitant reduction of decision mistakes. In this program, the two-pronged goals of improved decision-making and reduced decision mistakes are conceptualized as minimizing Free Energy given that Free Energy is the adverse side effect of unskillful decisions, resulting from inaccurate perception (poor planning and set-up) or ineffective action (poor implementation). MBSAT rests on the commonsense assertion that people's quality of life is a function of their decision-making quality. As McCann writes: "Making good decisions in increasingly uncertain times requires thinking in probabilistic terms. And obviously, the quality of choices resulting from probabilistic decision-making approaches depends on the accuracy of the probability estimates themselves... estimating probabilities for managerial [*and personal*][2] decisions requires forming initial subjective estimates based on existing knowledge and prior experience, even when data are sparse, while systematically updating those estimates as you learn more." (2020, p. 2).

In the following eight sessions of the program, participants learn to balance their BETA and transform their lives by updating their beliefs as they learn to master abducting thinking (acquiring an abductive mindset) and Bayesian updating (an active inferential process) as a path to better decisions in a VUCA environment.

There are several singularities of MBSAT, for example the use of signature terms, in particular the notions of liquefication, precisification and minding that are in part interconnected.

Liquefication means staying in a liquid state à la Frank Gehry with respect to our recognition models and facilitates minding the BETA. **Precisification** reflects a state of continuous inquiry à la Karl Friston to achieve higher precision in our perception, prediction, belief updating, and behavior. Finally, **Minding** is a state of active caring as practiced by the Tibetan nuns referred to in Chapter 8 Session 4. It goes beyond the usual understanding of mindfulness as being in the present moment non-judgmentally. Minding in MBSAT involves an active stance by taking action for the care of oneself, others, and the environment.

The cultivation of these three MBSAT signature states takes center stage in the MBSAT training program. Moreover, they are fully compatible with computational neuroscience and its focus on active inference processes.

Perhaps you ask yourself what this means for you as you are about to engage in the MBSAT training program. Most importantly, the invitation is to remind yourself of staying in liquid states, especially in the first four sessions. In the next four sessions the priority is on keeping yourself in states of precision. And throughout the whole program and beyond the main commitment is to mind yourself, others and the environment.

2 Author's note.

Chapter 5, Session 1

MINDING BETA I - BODY SENSATIONS

The Body as Source of Interoceptive Signals and Experiences

Mindfulness-based Strategic Awareness Training Comprehensive Workbook:
New approach Based on Free Energy and Active inference for Skillful Decision-making,
First Edition. Juan Humberto Young.
© 2023 John Wiley & Sons Ltd. Published 2023 by John Wiley & Sons Ltd.
Companion website: www.wiley.com/go/young/mbsatworkbook

5.1
Getting Started

Task of Session 1, Investment and Benefits

Task of Session 1:

Becoming fully aware of the body as the locus of interoceptive signals and experiences.

Training the capacity to recognize interoceptive bodily sensations/signals with speed, accuracy, and precision as they encoded vital data required for skillful decision-making.

Training to recognize interoceptive signals and make them more accurate and precise.

Minding skill trained in Session 1:

Increasing the precision in observing, describing, and interpreting body sensations/signals.

Expected benefits of this session and corresponding practices are:

A richer, more satisfying social life and fulfilling relationships via:

· Increased understanding of own body sensations.

· Increased ability to interpret body sensations as information signals and data points for decision-making.

· Ability to better recognize body sensations/signals, thus reducing prediction errors and decision mistakes.

Investment required to reap the benefits of this session:

● Time to read the material: for one time less than 3% of the time you spend awake per day, equivalent to 30 minutes maximum (depending on your reading skills)

● Time for practicing: on average 1.5% of your waking time or approximately 15 minutes per day.

"Inform the client, please, that we will not finance his operation," my boss said. "Why?" I asked. "I don't have a good feeling about this man. I felt a physical tension in me in his presence that I couldn't resolve. I don't want to go against my inner voices," was his answer - an odd argument for declining a deal in a highly rational financial environment, especially in light of the operation's profit potential and low-risk profile. A few months later we received a call from the country manager of our institution informing us that the prospective client was in great difficulties related to tax deception and had gone into exile.

5.2
Introduction and Concepts

PREDICTION TYPE: INTEROCEPTION

In this session, the focus is on learning to recognize and interpret the sensations in your body as interoceptive signals (coming from the guts and the heart). If they are precise and properly recognized, they carry information that can help you make skillful decisions, just as my boss did with his bodily interoception-based prediction, saving our institution a huge amount of money and headaches.

Everyone can learn to tap into this source of information and so can you. It is learning to recognize your body's interoceptive signals and what they mean in the context of a situation. Sometimes bodily signals can be detected easily due to quite distinct manifestations such as fast heart palpitations, sweaty hands, headache, or tensions in the shoulders or neck; at other times, they are more subtle, requiring more attention and precision.

Let's first begin by warming up our observation muscles and becoming more alert to what our body tells us. Remember, you not only observe with your eyes but with all your senses. In this exercise, you want to open up all five physical senses: seeing, smelling, hearing, touching, and tasting. Moreover, you need to open up also your sixth sense, that is your extrasensory perception – what you perceive in your mind, for example saying to yourself: "I don't like the smell or the color of this fruit" when the task is to simply observe the smell or color of the fruit. Being alert to the connotations of your sensory perception is key for precise observing and recognizing.

This training improves the learning rate of your recognition models, that is their ability to continue to learn and hone the skill of recognizing signals from the body beyond this session, throughout the whole program, and long after its completion.

NOTE:

Throughout Part 2 of this workbook you will encounter numerous *speech bubbles*.
They contain verbatim testimonies from MBSAT students and course participants.

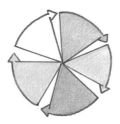

5.3
Aspects of Bodily Sensations

There are four areas of observation for all sensations.

a) The **tonality** of sensations. All sensations come with one of three possible tones: **liking** (I love the taste of mango, the looks of a person, the smell of cologne, the touch of cashmere, the sound of the song, etc.), **disliking** (I can't stand being around my boss, I hate cauliflower, I don't like rock and roll music) and **neutral** (I can sleep before or after midnight, I have no preference; I eat papaya - it is not that I like or dislike it, but it is good for digestion.)

b) The **intensity** of sensations. A sensation can be strong, mild, or medium, in a continuum between these states.

c) The **location** of sensations. It can be felt in a single place or in several areas. For example, when you are eating, you often have a sensation in the palate and at the same time you notice the smell of the dish.

d) The **rate of change** of sensations. Sometimes when one begins to observe a sensation, it can be quite strong, but as one keeps observing it, it is possible that the intensity declines or alters in some other way. At times these changes are slow, and at other times they are faster.

Figure 5.1 provides compelling visual examples of the four aspects of bodily sensations and the areas to observe.

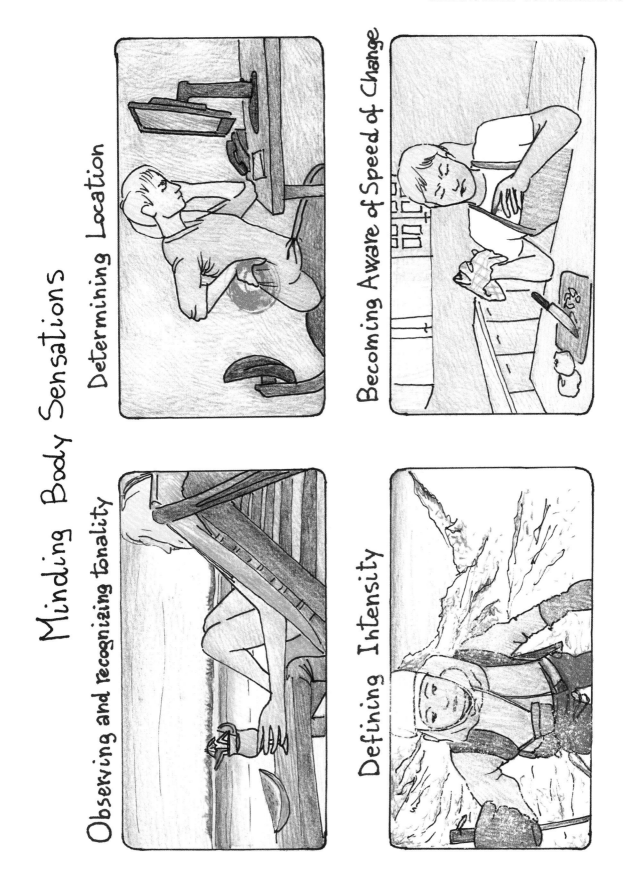

Figure 5.1 Minding Body Sensations:: Tonality, Location, Intensity, and Speed of Change

5.4
Exercises

5.4.1 A preliminary note on the notions of exercise and practice

There is a slight difference between practices and exercises in MBSAT. Practices are mainstay interventions in MBSAT training and are designed to be long-term components of personal practice, while exercises are more sporadic and designed to facilitate insights for specific themes, often in relation to the main topic of a session.

The full-senses exercise below, for example, is an invitation to experiment with personal likes and dislikes using fruit and then reflect on your insights. Awareness of one's likes and dislikes is an important aspect of self-knowledge, but the exercise with the fruit or any dish you like or dislike can be a stand-alone experiment.

5.4.2 The Full-Senses Exercise

This exercise has three experiential parts and concludes with a reflection.

Part 1: Fruit you like

Take a fruit you usually like to eat and hold it unhurriedly in your palm or between your fingers. Take your time to discover it, as if you had never encountered this fruit before.

Start by giving it a close look, visually observing all the details of its shape, color, surface and any other aspect of its appearance that you can observe with your eyes.

Moving it now gently in your palm or between your fingers you may notice its weight, the texture of its surface at the touch and many other sensations on your skin that you may discover.

Next, moving the fruit close to one of your ears and gently squeezing or rubbing it, you can perhaps perceive a very subtle noise. If you have chosen a dried fruit for this exercise, it may be easier to detect a sound. If you are using fresh fruit, you might omit this step depending on the type of the fruit.

Moving to the sense of smell, you can bring the fruit close to your nose and observe its fragrance, staying with the experience of its scent for a few moments.

Then, as you place the fruit on your lips, you may notice that the touch in this area feels different. As you go on to place the fruit inside your mouth, you may start by moving it around a bit with your tongue and notice the sensations that emerge.

Finally, you may begin to chew the fruit slowly, savoring it and observing its other qualities such as consistency, taste, juiciness, etc. As you swallow it, follow the sensation as long as you can through your throat and esophagus.

Part 2: Fruit you don't like

Repeat the same steps as before, but using a fruit you don't like, observing carefully and concentrating on registering your sensations without getting lost in evaluations and judgments.

Part 3: Fruit you neither particularly like nor dislike

Repeat the previous steps with a third fruit, and keep observing and discovering all the details you normally would not pay attention to.

Part 4: Reflection

After you have done all three parts of the exercise, which will take several minutes (max. 15 minutes), please, sit quietly and reflect on your experience. The focus is on your sensual impressions, since we are training our capacity to recognize information and interoceptive signals from the body. You can also write your observations in your diary, if this is helpful. At this stage of the program the main point is to avoid judgments. Instead of thinking "I like this fruit, because it is very sweet," just notice its sweetness. Or instead of saying to yourself "I don't enjoy this fruit, because eating it is messy", simply notice its messiness.

Later in the program we will specifically observe judgments, and you will be asked to detect possible causes of your judgments. For now, the goal is to train the sensitivity of our senses to interoceptive signals and enhance our awareness of bodily experiences.

5.5
Practices

5.5.1 Practice 1 - Following autonomous body sensations:
The breath

The breath is the essential body sensation often unnoticed yet key for survival; life ceases without breathing. As an object of attention, the breath is a great companion for precision training, because it is easily accessible and with you all the time.

Being mindful of your breath or, in MBSAT terms, minding your breath, means focusing your attention on your regular breathing, thus, the normal respiratory rate. In this practice, there is no need for a special breathing technique. The goal is simply to follow, intentionally and attentively, the rhythm of your breathing.

Here are some suggestions to practice observing your breath/respiratory rate:

a) Preparing to practice:

First find a quiet place and a precise,[1] yet comfortable posture that allows you to stay still and focus on your breath for some time. Settle into an erect posture with the head, neck, and back aligned and upright, without straining.

b) Finding the proper stance for practicing:

Begin your practice by becoming aware of the sensations involved in sitting. Then simply remain still in what is called the "being mode", a state of physical and mental stillness.

---

1 In computational neuroscience, precision is an important calculation quantity and quality related to accuracy. In MBSAT we train our precision knowing that we will never achieve 100% precision. Life is too random to achieve total precision; however, we train our precision to continuously improve the quality of our perception and predictions, and reduce the level of prediction errors. The intention is to enhance our precision skills and to enjoy the process of training and learning as much as possible.

c) Following the breath with precision:

It is essential to find a balance between a state of comfort and wakefulness. Invite yourself to focus on the breath in different parts of the body where you can feel the flow of air and the rhythm of breathing: the belly, the nose, the chest, or the throat. This can facilitate the precision of your attention. As you keep breathing, enhance your strategic awareness by following the proprioceptive movement of your breath with an action. For example by placing your hands on the abdomen or chest, observing the expansion with in-breaths, and the contraction with the out-breaths. If you decide to follow the breath with your nose, then just place a finger below the nose and feel the inhalation and exhalation of air. You can also follow your respiration rate by placing your fingers on your throat. (See Figure 5.2 below for an illustration of this practice.)

Figure 5.2 Interoception (I) – Following Autonomous Body Sensations/Signals: The Breath

d) Remembering to avoid imprecise attention:

When you become aware that your attention is not on the subject of the practice, in this case, your breath, simply recognize the distracted state, acknowledge it without judging, and gently re-establish the precision of your attention, as many times as needed, with patience and perseverance. By returning your attention again and again to the focus of the practice, you train the precision of your attention that is the pre-condition for reducing prediction errors.

e) Counting the respiratory rate:

When you are ready, the suggestion is to start counting the respiratory rate to train your precision awareness. Counting is an effective way to discipline your attention and hone the precision of observation.

BETA precision awareness training uses a training set format similar to fitness training or body-building. Simply put, the practice consists of counting in- and out-breaths in batches or sets where each set is composed of a number of repetitions and a certain number of sets then constitutes the practice. The number of sets to complete depends on the desired length of the practice and intensity of training.

A standard respiratory rate of an adult is 12-16 breaths per minute. To follow your respiratory rate, the recommendation is to begin with sets of 60 to 80 breaths, corresponding to approximately 5 minutes of attention/precision deployment training. You may count in the way most convenient to you: on in-breaths or out-breaths or in pairs of in- and exhalations; it doesn't matter. If you wish to train for 10-15 minutes of continued practice, for example, you should aim to complete 2-3 sets, that is between 120 and 240 breaths counted in one continuous, seated practice. Of course, these numbers are just approximative guidelines. As mentioned, the goal is to breathe normally and simply follow the breath by counting.

Remember also that you might occasionally lose concentration and get carried away by mind wandering. When this happens simply recognize where you are (dreaming about the next vacation, thinking of things to do at the office, wondering about what to cook for evening dinner, etc.) and gently come back to the focus of the practice: observing the respiratory rate by counting the breaths. If you remember the last counted breath, you can continue as if there had been no interruption. If you remember for example that you last counted 45, then continue with 46. If on the other hand, you cannot remember at all what number you arrived at, start afresh.

f) Practical concerns:

It is important to ensure a place that is conducive to practice, that is not noisy and neither too bright nor too dark (facilitating calmness while avoiding drowsiness), comfortably warm in winter and fresh in summer. The duration of the practice can vary from a minimum of a few minutes to as long as half an hour or more, depending on your needs and your situation.

5.5.2 Practice 2 - Following autonomous body sensations: The pulse

Another practice to train our attention and awareness of bodily sensations/signals is to follow the pulse. Like the breath, it involves an autonomous body movement we are not conscious of under normal circumstances. The pulse is also an ideal anchor for training the precision of attention and for the redeployment of attention from mind wandering.

It is easiest to follow the pulse in the following three different parts of the body:

a) On the wrist, using your first and second fingers gently pressing on the arteries.

b) On the inside of the elbow.

c) On the side of the throat.

Figure 5.3 provides visual guidance. In case you prefer option three, please, make sure not to press simultaneously on both sides of your throat as this could obstruct the blood flow. In any case, it is best to press gently, just enough to feel the blood pulsing.

Interoception (II)
Following Autonomous Body Sensations/signals:
The Pulse

Following the Pulse...
a) on the wrist   b) inside of the elbow   c) in your throat

Figure 5.3 Interoception (II) – Following Autonomous Body Sensations/Signals: The Pulse

In this practice, there is no universal standard at hand to establish training sets that would be meaningful. To train the precision of your attention the recommendation is to simply count up to a certain number, for example, 30 or 50, and then start again. The main purpose is staying with the pulse and recognizing when the attention strays away, in which case the goal is just returning to observe the pulse again and again, as often as necessary.

5.5.3 Practice 3 - Observing bodily sensations in stillness: Lying or sitting

Now it is time for you to observe sensations in your body. Let's begin by finding a convenient position, maybe lying flat on your back with your legs and feet slightly falling apart and your arms alongside your body. Alternatively, you might sit on a chair in an upright position with your feet firmly on the floor and your hands on your knees, whatever position works best for you. Make yourself comfortable. If you have a quiet moment at work and would like to do the practice, you can do so in the office, a conference room, or some other location where you won't be disturbed.

Take a few moments to settle into the posture, become aware of where your body touches the floor or chair, and feel how you are supported. If possible, close your eyes.

Now starting to pay attention to your breathing and the gentle movements of your body as you inhale and exhale. Feel the slight expansion and contraction of the abdomen, chest, nose, or neck with each breath.

After following your breath for some time, moving your attention and the precision of your perception to the big toe of your left foot. What sensation can you detect? Maybe you feel the blood pulsing or notice warmth or coolness. Whatever it is, just take note of it with interest. In case you cannot feel anything in particular right now, it is ok, too; you are still training the precision of your attention and your bodily awareness. Then do the same for your other toes.

Next, you may experiment with "breathing into your foot," that is inhaling and imagining the oxygen from the fresh air flowing down from the lungs through the leg and into the foot and the toes. As you exhale, imagine the warmth returning from the toes and the foot upwards through the leg and out of the nose. This idea is, in fact, not fantasy. The blood actually transports oxygen from your lungs down to the tiniest blood vessels at the tip of your toes. It is likely that you will notice slight changes after further inhaling and exhaling while focusing your attention on the toes.

When you feel ready to move further up your body, you may disengage from the toes with an out-breath, engaging your attention on the next in-breath with the other parts of the foot, one by one: the sole, the instep, the heel, the top of the foot, and the ankle, exploring with curiosity what you can observe in these regions and keeping "breathing with them," sending them some extra oxygen in your imagination.

With the next in-breath we continue our body observation by expanding our attention and starting to scan the lower left leg, the knee, and the upper leg, always in the same fashion, exploring and breathing. Continue with your right foot and right leg.

By now, you might feel drowsy as you start letting go of tension. If this is the case, you can open your eyes to help you stay awake. The primary purpose of observing body sensations in this practice is not relaxation, although this may be a pleasant side effect.

You might also feel an urge to adjust your position. If you need to, you may do so consciously and mindfully by moving slightly, making sure to notice what you sense at this moment and acknowledging it. If your mind wanders, thus loosing precision, the point is to become aware of where it took you and bring the precision of your attention gently back to the focus of the practice.

We continue to move gradually further up in the body. Next we scan the pelvic area, breathing in and out, then, one after the other we scan the buttocks, hips, abdomen, and lower back. As we continue to breathe, moving up through the torso, directing your attention/precision to your chest, ribs, upper back, and shoulders, continuously observing the sensations in these parts of the body with care.

When you reach the shoulders, experiment with moving your attention/precision downwards again and focus on your fingers, hands, and arms in the same way you observed your feet and legs, only this time focusing on the left and right sides simultaneously. And always remind yourself to keep breathing, while you shift the attention from one part of your body to another.

After the finger, hands and arms we move our focus to the neck and head and give them the same detailed attention/precision, with gentle curiosity exploring all the sensations in the jaw, face, eyeballs, forehead, and scalp, proceeding carefully.

Whenever it is feasible, keep also breathing into the part of your body you're focusing on in the same way we started to do it with "breathing into your foot".

The last focus is on the top of your head. Perhaps you can identify the crown of your head, a sensitive spot in the center top of the skull, exploring any sensation you can detect. You can stay there for a few breaths.

Now that we have reviewed the whole body from toe to head, we breathe through our entire body by imagining that air is seeping in through the crown of the head and provides the whole body with fresh oxygen. We exhale through the soles of our feet and then invert the flow—inhaling through the feet and exhaling through the crown. Give yourself some time to keep breathing in this way.

To complete the practice, the suggestion is to slowly return to normal breathing, lying, or sitting for a few more moments with the awareness embracing the entire body, sensing its wholeness.

Then, when you feel ready, you may start to move gently and resume your normal activities as calmly and mindfully as possible.

Variations to the bodily sensations practice:

Once you have learned to regulate your attention/precision and shift it at will as you observe sensations in your body, (a special ability you have either newly learned or lifted to higher levels), you can play around by inviting images to your mind that recall specific bodily sensations as another training method geared towards recognizing different types of sensations – pleasant, unpleasant and neutral ones.

a) Pleasant body sensations:
   Bring to your mind desirable situations in your life. It can be the image of a dish you enjoy eating, going out for a concert with your partner, or fantasies about your future vacations or a job promotion – in brief, any image that helps you evoke desirable bodily sensations.

   Once you have a distinct image in your mind, enjoy it and begin to observe the sensations along the four dimensions of observations mentioned above: location, tonality, intensity, and rate of change.

b) Unpleasant body sensations:
   Repeat the same process for unpleasant sensations.

c) Neutral body sensations:

Complete the practice with body sensations that are largely indifferent to you.

> *I have been teaching the body scan for many years as I am a certified MBSR teacher at one of the best-known, university-based mindfulness centers; yet I have never experienced my body sensations as clearly and intensely as with this particular practice. As I concentrated on pleasant body sensations I felt that I was floating, that the pleasant sensations were carrying me on a luscious trip. It really felt good, thank you.*

5.5.4 Practice 4 - Massage for bodily awareness and well-being

Research at several universities (the Wyss Institute at Harvard, the University of Lyon in France, and others) suggests that people benefit from manual massage for recovery and performance. In line with these findings, the following exercise is intended to train the ability to observe physical sensations by giving your body the treat of a massage.

Begin by finding an appropriate position, either sitting or lying on the floor or in bed and bring your attention to your breath, breathing in and breathing out for a few moments.

Then choose a part of your body that you may want to massage, perhaps because it feels strained, tired, or numb or perhaps you noticed that you don't have much sensation in this particular location. It could be your feet, hands, face, neck, knees or any other part you might feel would benefit. You can choose a small area, for example, the fingers of your hands and the toes of your feet, or a larger area, for example, your arms or legs, simply choosing a place in your body that you feel needs some extra attention.

Begin massaging by concentrating on your sensations, both in your hands and the area you have chosen. You don't need a special technique for this practice, we all know instinctively how to rub ourselves when some sensation bothers us such as numbness, itching, or discomfort. Here in this practice, we are seeking to generate a pleasant sensation in order to train our awareness of the body and its signals.

Depending on where you are and what situation you are in you can also sharpen your observation skills with minor unpleasant sensations. If you happen to be on vacation in the tropics and get bitten by a mosquito, you can use this experience to observe the discomfort it is causing. If, however, you are fond of skiing or some other winter sports you might experiment with cold or stiff limbs. The main point is to practice observing body sensations with precision.

5.5.5 Practice 5 - Training for decision-making: Identifying and observing body sensations while deciding

In this practice, the goal is to learn to recognize body sensations as carriers of information that can support your decision-making process.

- Find a comfortable position bringing your awareness to your breath.
- When you are ready, begin by directing your awareness to an issue that requires you to make a decision. Begin with a routine decision you take every day. It could be at what time to get up in the morning, deciding what to eat for breakfast, or any other decision you need to take.
- Now, see if it is possible to observe your body sensations as you are in the process of deciding. See for example, if you can capture any sensations in your belly, your neck, and shoulders, or in any other part of your body.
- Staying with the sensations observe a possible connection between what you are about to decide and body sensations that could be possibly connected to the decision.
- After some time, returning to the focus on your breath before and ending the practice.

After you have practiced this a few times, you are better prepared to observe your body sensations, when you are making more impactful decisions during the day. Is your body telling you something that helps you to take a skillful decision: a hunch, a warning, or an indication to take more time to decide? How does your bodily sensation influence the decision you make? Can you perhaps discover a pattern of bodily sensations, each time you are about to take a decision?

This type of awareness is essential to cultivating Strategic Awareness which is at the core of the MBSAT training program.

Figure 5.4 visualizes why it is worth practicing – in this session and in all the following sessions: research shows that our well-being can be boosted to a great extent by intentional activity, in this case by practicing for skillful decision-making.

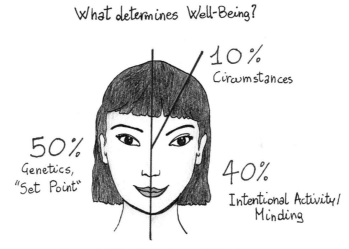

Figure 5.4 What determines well-being?

5.6
Learnings from Session 1

There are several training intentions and potential learnings in Session 1, Minding BETA I - Body Sensations. After teaching MBSAT for over ten years, I have learned to comment on just a few of the possible outcomes; it is more effective, if participants find out about helpful learnings on their own. The participants' own conclusions will be more impactful and lasting.

Here are some salient benefits I have encountered frequently over the years, all of them consistent with the design intention of the session.

- Learning the significance of minding your BETA (Body sensations, Emotions, Thoughts, and Actions) signals, each representing a channel of data and information for supporting strategic awareness and skillful decision making.

- Training and enhancing your interoceptive capacity by cultivating the observation of bodily sensations.

- Beginning to recognize the influence of body sensations in decision making.

- Increasing bodily awareness, thus laying the foundation for better integration of BETA components, so crucial for overall health and a balanced, flourishing life.

- Beginning to train the precision skills of noticing and observing as a mechanism of improving your concentration, attention, and integrity of your perceptions.

- Ability to induce pleasant body sensations as a technique for flourishing and coping.

> *"Training to be aware of body sensations has greatly improved the quality of my life. I used to suffer from frequent and intense migraines. Now I can recognize early warning signals long before the actual attack sets in and differentiate between a series of triggers (e.g., low blood sugar, stiff sitting position, tensions, irregular sleep, etc.). This allows me to take action early on. Now I have only rarely migraines and they are much less intense. I'm so grateful."*

Furthermore, in combination with reading the foundations of the MBSAT program in Chapter 4, Session 1 leads to the following far-reaching learnings:

- Radically altering the participants' view of the mind/brain from a reactive to a prediction organ, intent on assuring your survival and well-being.

- Practicing with interventions designed under the Free Energy Principle that can assist you in reducing errors in decision making.

- Beginning to learn about some of the most advanced findings from applied neuroscience in the form of the three brain/mind's computational quantities: prediction, prediction errors, and precision as well as the circular dynamics amongst these three components.

> *"You can listen in any case with every part of your body. The body tells us what is important. From organs such like our heart, lungs, and our intestines we get signals that we define and grasp as heart palpitations, unease and desire for example. They are special because they come from regions of our body than we can't see. And everything that comes from our inside world is the core of our feelings and emotions."*
>
> António Damásio, Neuroscientist

5.7
Action Plan (AP)
for the Week of Session 1

The action plan for the first week is straightforward.

- Practice every day; limit the practices to a maximum of 15 to 20 minutes.

- The first and second days begin by observing your breath for 5 minutes, then use the rest of the time (10 to 15 minutes) to observe your body sensations following the instructions of Practice 3 above, remembering to notice the four dimensions of observation: location, tonality, intensity, and rate of change.

- On the second day, proceed in the same way but recall a desirable image to observe its manifestation in the body sensations as described in "Variations" of Practice 3. Use the 5/15 minutes split: 5 minutes for breath observation and 10-15 minutes for pleasant body sensations.

- On the third day, practice in the same way as the previous day, this time with an unpleasant image.

- On the fourth day, do the same with a neutral image.

- On the remaining days of the week just alternate as you like. In addition, see if it is possible to recognize the body sensations related to a decision you are making.

- When you happen to walk, for example on your way to the office, use the opportunity to train body sensations in movement by walking mindfully and observing the sensations that the movements generate. It is also a special opportunity to become aware of your feet. We so often ignore and neglect them. It is a good moment to thank our feet for carrying us everywhere.

- To write down your observations you can use the space provided in the next section below (5.8) or use a personal diary that pleases you, depending on what you find more appealing and inspiring to keep track of your practice.

5.8
Personal Notes and Insights
The Writing Space for Your Experiences and Observations

Making notes is an effective method to reinforce learning and clarify insights.

The idea is to write briefly and matter-of-factly what you experience each day as you train your mind consistently. It is important to be terse because when you make short notes, you are more likely to keep up practicing and journaling. Your notes will help you to fortify your learnings and hone the precision of your observations. In addition, having something visible in hand in form of your diary will motivate you to be more consistent in your mind training.

Your diary can become a dear friend. It is completely private. There is no need to evaluate your progress or your practices; on the contrary, the recommendation is to abstain from judgments or critical remarks. Whatever your experience is, it is part of your learning and thus a step forward.

Examples of possible entries:

This morning during my body sensations observation practice, I noticed a certain numbness in the palm of my right hand. So, there is numbness in my body. (example of a desirable entry)

Today I had an insightful practice (judgment). I observed and recognized several body sensations; I noticed the stiffness in my neck muscles and a funny feeling in my stomach. I wonder, what this means (worrying). (example of a comment to avoid)

Chapter 6, Session 2

MINDING BETA II - EMOTIONS

Emotions as Source of Interoceptive Signals and Experiences

Mindfulness-based Strategic Awareness Training Comprehensive Workbook:
New approach Based on Free Energy and Active inference for Skillful Decision-making,
First Edition. Juan Humberto Young.
© 2023 John Wiley & Sons Ltd. Published 2023 by John Wiley & Sons Ltd.
Companion website: www.wiley.com/go/young/mbsatworkbook

6.1
Getting Started
Task of Session 2, Investment and Benefits

Task of Session 2:
Training the learning rate[1] of the recognizing models for emotional interoceptive signals as encoded vital data for skillful decision making.

Minding skill trained in Session 2:
Increasing the precision in observing, describing and interpreting emotions.
Learning to recognize, when emotions are a positive force and when they are counterproductive and need to be kept in check.

Expected benefits of this session and corresponding practices are:
· Increased understanding of own emotions.
· Increased ability to be aware of emotions as drivers influencing decision-making.
· Ability to better regulate emotions, thus reducing prediction errors and decision mistakes.

Investment required to reap the benefits of this session:

◎ Time to read this chapter: about 30 minutes, depending on your reading skills

◎ Time for explicit practicing: on average approximately 15 minutes per day.

◎ Time for implicit practicing during the day: As you go through your day pay attention to your emotions and how they shift. This requires awareness but no extra time.

◎ Time to organize feedback responses for your Free Energy Minimizer Self (FEMS) (6.5.3 Exercise 2 below): at your discretion.

---

1 The learning rate refers to the speed and accuracy of recognizing the elements of BETA; this in turn allows for more precision in decision-making and facilitates updating of beliefs.

"At first I was very happy. I wanted to sell my investment and knew that it could take months or even years in the current environment. So, when I got an offer after less than two weeks I was delighted. The buyer came to see me with his partner and made a large deposit. However, soon after uncomfortable feelings of distrust and fear were creeping up on me. My sleep became uneasy and I was irritable. The internal malaise went on for almost three weeks while waiting to close the deal. Then, one day I suddenly woke up in the middle of the night with a clear resolve to back off from the contract. I communicated my decision in the morning and returned the deposit. A few months later I learned that the group was engaging in questionable practices. The decision I took based on an emotional hunch saved me a lot of headaches, legal disputes, and potential losses."

6.2
Quiz

Session 1: Minding BETA I and Chapter 4 Essential Foundations

This is a voluntary quiz to reaffirm your understanding of MBSAT's foundations and core elements.

1) What are the three computational elements in MBSAT?

- _____
- _____
- _____

2) How do you understand Free Energy within the framework of MBSAT? Check one of the following:

☐ A desirable, unlimited quantity like the air you breathe.

☐ An unlimited, undisciplined energy that has consequences, similar to the energy of a puppy dog.

☐ An unlimited energy with the potential strength of natural forces such as a hurricane.

3) Understanding Active Inference:

a) Active Inference is the process human beings use to interact with the environment, how they act and update their inferences/predictions.

☐ Correct   ☐ False

b) Name the four states that comprise the Active Inference process.

- _____
- _____
- _____
- _____

4) What are the three types of prediction in people's lives?

- _____
- _____
- _____

5) What are the four components of the Acronym BETA?

- _____
- _____
- _____
- _____

6) What does "Minding" mean in MBSAT? (you may choose several answers)

☐ Cultivating a desirable BETA

☐ Paying attention

☐ Indifference (like I don't mind)

☐ In your own words: _____

_____

7) What are the intentions of the Mindfulness practices in MBSAT?
Rank them by using the following coding:
Explicit intention: Exp-I; Implicit intention: Imp-I.

	Exp-I	Imp-I
Improving the precision of the Active Inference process	☐	☐
Reducing the level of decision/prediction errors	☐	☐
Improving the precision of decisions and predictions	☐	☐
Reducing levels of stress	☐	☐
Improving subjective well-being	☐	☐
Improving equanimity	☐	☐
Improving Strategic Awareness	☐	☐

If you are not sure of your answers, you may take it as an invitation to go over Chapter 4 once more and/ or do some additional reading in Part 1 of this book.

6.3
Introduction and Concepts

PREDICTION TYPE: INTEROCEPTION

Emotions and beliefs are closely interconnected. From the point of view of the Free Energy Principle (FEP), emotions are considered beliefs with an encoded expected precision about the active inference consequences of thoughts and actions along the following sequence: "I feel energized; if I work hard, I will get a large bonus, and I will be pleased." The Active Inference/FEP paradigm posits that emotions emerge from and are influenced by our Bayesian beliefs. In this example working hard (the belief) will be rewarded with an outcome (a promotion, more significant bonus, salary increase, etc.) that will make the individual happy (a positive emotion) and able to minimize Free Energy (uncertainty, complexity, etc.).

Underlying the specificity of emotional states is a general tonality, defined as mood. In general psychology, mood is conceived of as containing a general valence that lasts longer than an emotion; for example, she is in a playful mood; he is in an angry mood, a fearful mood, and so on. Here we see the standard duality of attractive goodness associated with positive, desirable outcomes on one hand and negative valence associated with undesirable states on the other.

Under the FEP scheme, moods are regarded as running parallel to emotional beliefs; they are hyperpriors. They are beliefs about the emotional states of the consequences of actions (Clark et al., 2018). More specifically, mood reflects the overall momentum or expected direction of prediction errors. A positive mood suggests that things are going well and will continue to go well. A negative mood means the opposite, that things are not going well and might even get worse (Kiverstein et al., 2020).

Emotional valence is conceived as a proxy for the rate of change of Free Energy over time, such that when minimizing Free Energy, one is also increasing the probability of being in valuable states (a good job, a happy marriage, reliable friends, etc.). Positive valence under this view is associated with emotions that decrease Free Energy and resolve VUCA, while negative valence, on the other hand, is associated with increased Free Energy and lack of resolution of VUCA. In other words, more than being in a positive or negative emotional state, valence takes a dynamic characteristic associated with the direction, the velocity and the rate at which one can reduce prediction errors (Joffily & Coricelli, 2013).

Studies of negative emotions and stimuli reveal that they increase reactivity by activating the amygdala, the hippocampus, and the anterior pole of the prefrontal cortex, with physical manifestations such as increased heart and respiration rate, detectable via hyperventilation (see Figure 6.1). Positive emotions, on the other hand, reveal the opposite, less reactivity and less activity in the amygdala, hippocampus, and the prefrontal cortex, which allows for adaptive states to emerge, for example, cognitive reappraisal, allowance, acceptance, as strategies that support emotional regulation that prevents overreaction (Goldin et al., 2019).

This is not to say that one type of emotion is superior to others; what is necessary is to match the contextual situation to skillful decision-making. For example, suppose one is driving, and a car is heading in your direction out of control. In that case, the best emotional strategy is to leverage fear to support a rapid reaction in order to avoid a collision and minimize Free Energy (hurt to one's existence). In this case, the way out of this unpredictable

Figure 6.1 Reactive MBSAT buddy

situation is by following the direction of our unpleasant emotion (fear), as it can help predict the origin and orientation of the expected uncertainty and help engage actions that will decrease expected Free Energy, thus, the uncertainty about the consequences of actions, and this should happen fast to avoid permanent negative states transitions: death or injury. (Solms, 2019). It is, therefore, Free Energy minimization that results in emotional balance. (Demekas et al., 2020).

Figure 6.2 Clear-minded MBSAT buddy

In one of K. Friston's talks, I heard him say that a reasonable person from the point of view of her existential goodness will be good at minimizing Free Energy or maximizing the evidence of their generative models, which means that the person, when confronted with new information, will process and assimilate the information in an efficient thermodynamic way. In other words, a reasonable person will have a clear mind/brain, where her priors beliefs are already quite close to her posterior beliefs (Figure 6.2). This person already has a good idea of what is going on and will not have to confront surprises, hence he or she is able to minimize complexity costs (the price that one pays to provide for the accuracy of some information). As such, the individual can smoothly update and optimize beliefs. In MBSAT, we work hard at having an adaptive and flexible minimum set of prior beliefs that makes it possible to update without having to costly uproot the whole set of beliefs. This way we can optimize the return of our total portfolio of beliefs.

The psychoanalyst Holmes (2022) asserts that Free Energy may be aversive and represent pain; however, binding Free Energy is rewarding and motivating with feeling tones acting as the drivers of the FE minimization gradients and processes. An illustration of the gradients and their relation to the BETA (Body sensations, Emotions, Thoughts and Action impulses) can be found in Chapter 3, Figure 3.1. As mentioned above, it is also important to recognize that no particular type of feeling tone, emotion, or valence is superior to others. Positive or negative feeling tones can all be adaptive, if they support minimizing Free Energy as part of a contextualized decision-making process.

Minding our BETA, a core value of MBSAT, includes emotions as an integral part; it is about bringing integrity and stability to Body sensations, Emotions, Thoughts, and Actions impulses. A well-aligned and stable BETA can survive an adverse environment, whereas an unstable BETA can't survive even in friendly environments (Wiese & Metzinger, 2017). Minding BETA implies recognizing and minding interoceptive, proprioceptive, and exteroceptive signals of BETA, generated by internal conditions and the environment. Predictions apply both to interoception (internal signals) and to exteroception (sensory signals from the environment). It is, however, more critical to avoid unexpected interoceptive states, like finding oneself in loss of oxygenation than to unexpected exteroceptive sensations, like being confronted with a foul odor. (Seth, 2015).

The popular view of emotions suggests five main features:
- Emotions tend to be quick and short-lived, but combined with cognitive input they can be prolonged.
- They respond to external as well as to learned internal stimuli.
- They are subject to appraisal.
- They are motivated to avoid pain and seek pleasure.
- They guide behavior and choices.

This implies that emotions are complex phenomena affecting people's thoughts, behaviors, and body sensations and thus are important components of human experience. Taking these characteristics into account, it becomes clear that the kind of emotions an individual chooses to cultivate become an important determinant of that person's quality of life.

As a positive psychologist, I am aware that positive emotions tend to be neglected compared to negative emotions that command higher attention, as their consequences can be devastating for people. But positive emotions have many values and benefits. The pioneering work of the late psychologist Alice Isen demonstrated adaptive effects on cognitive flexibility (2004), decision making (2015), and self-regulation (2000).

In the TV show *Scorpion*, Happy Quinn, one of the main protagonists, represents an unshakeable belief in positivity and the optimism that things will go well no matter how difficult the circumstances. In the series she plays an ace mechanical engineer who always manages to find a solution even in the most desperate circumstances, whether by using an improvised tool or applying intricate scientific knowledge. By facing and embracing difficulty with hope and confidence she taps into her personal emotional reservoir of positivity (optimism, hopefulness, joyfulness and resilience) that allows her to broaden her awareness and activate all her cognitive, behavioral, and emotional resources. Not surprisingly, honoring her name Happy, she always manages to find a way out of the most challenging or threatening situations.

And what about negative emotions? They exist, of course, and we have to reckon with them. They have a defensive role. They are the forces that mobilize our fight-or-flight responses, when we sense danger to our (physical or mental) survival. They have a high metabolic cost for the individual and enormous economic costs in society.

"Every gun that is made, every warship that is launched, every rocket fired signifies, in the final sense, a theft from those people who hunger, who are not fed, people who are cold and are not clothed...The cost of one modern heavy bomber is this: a modern brick school in more than 30 cities. It is two electric power plants, each serving a town of 60'000 population. It is two fine, fully equipped hospitals...This is not a way of life at all, in any true sense."

D. W. Eisenhower, ex-President of USA and General of the USA army

6.4
Practices

6.4.1 A preliminary note

There are two constants in all MBSAT practices: finding a comfortable, upright position and observing the breath.

In Session 1 the very first practice was dedicated to breathing (Practice 1 - Following autonomous body sensations: The breath).

As the intention of Part 1 of the training program (the first four sessions) is to observe our BETA, the breath is ideal for the purpose. Breathing is a biological autonomous process where you can exert some degree of control by slowing or accelerating the rhythm of your breath, which can't be done with some other autonomous biological process (for example, with blood pressure or digestion). The breath is an interface between your internal states and the external states, that is everything that is going on within yourself and what is happening around you.

6.4.2 Practice 1 - The full emotions observation meditation (FEOM)

This practice has three parts:

Part One: Observing a likable, desirable positive emotion

Examples of positive emotions:					
Gratitude	Serenity	Pride	Inspiration	Compassion	Empathy
Interest	Hope	Amusement	Awe	Love	Joy

> *Before we began this practice, I was feeling listless and tired. There are some issues going on at the office. In addition, my aunt just had surgery because of cancer; so it has been rough these past days. As you mentioned to concentrate on a person or object that we love and watch the emotions arising, I brought my son to my mind and it immediately changed my mood. I felt full of love and tenderness toward him. It made me feel more upbeat and energized. It is amazing how switching the focus of my awareness can change the state I'm in so fundamentally and so fast.*

This practice consists of several steps:

⊙ Find a place and position where you can practice for 15 minutes quietly.

⊙ Begin by bringing your attention to a positive emotion (see examples above).

⊙ You can use any of the five senses to support the observation of your positive emotions. You can for example use the scent of your preferred eau-de-Cologne, maybe lightly wetting a cotton pad with the scent. In analogy to the full senses exercise in Session 1 you can also savor some fruit you like. Or use a photo reminding you of a pleasant experience (a vacation, meeting with friends, etc.). You can also listen to music (preferably an instrumental piece, as a song with words can distract you and reduce the precision of your observation).

⊙ Once you are able to induce a positive emotion, begin to observe it without adding mental narratives or analyzing. Simply observing the emotion.

⊙ To help the precision of the observation you can observe:
  a) The intensity of the emotion (strong, mild or medium).
  b) The location of the emotion, for example the area around your chest, your entire body or some part of your body you are able to identify and observe.
  c) You can observe the changing dynamic of the emotion during the practice; maybe it is stronger at the beginning and becomes gradually less intense or vice versa.

Part Two: Observing an aversive, undesirable negative emotion

Repeat the same steps for a negative emotion, perhaps from this list:

Example of negative emotions:						
Anger	Emptiness	Frustration	Inadequacy	Helplessness	Fear	Overwhelmed
Guilt	Depression	Loneliness	Resentment	Loneliness	Sadness	Failure

My new boss called our department and me as department head to the conference room to present his new strategy. As he outlined the new goals he had set for us I realized that his calculations were not realistic even if we stretched all resources to the limit. I immediately saw red for me and my team and clearly made my point right then and there. Soon afterwards I was fired, despite many years of experience and an impeccable track record. Being middle-aged I haven't been able to find an equivalent position with comparable pay. Ever since. I have regretted my spontaneous outburst, driven partly by anger and partly by worries. It is of little comfort that I was actually right. The goals were indeed unrealistic, and the boss had to resign about a year after I lost my job.

Part Three: Observing a neutral emotion

Repeat the same steps for a neutral emotion such as indifference or boredom. You may facilitate the observation with a boring piece of food, song, movie, etc.

After you have done all three parts of the exercise, which will take several minutes to complete (max. 15 minutes), sit quietly for a few moments. It is recommended that you write down a few words about the experience in your diary, focusing on the process of observation and avoiding evaluating the quality and the effects of the emotions, more concentrating for example on whether you were able or not to identify and observe the emotions.

Most probably the observation of negative emotions will be more salient, as they have a stronger, neurological effect and might be easier to notice.

6.4.3 Practice 2 - Training for decision-making: identifying and observing emotions while deciding

In this practice the goal is to learn to recognize emotions as carriers of information that can support your decision-making process.

- Find a comfortable position, bringing your awareness to your breath.

- When you are ready, begin by directing your awareness to an issue that requires you to make a decision. Begin with a simple or even with a routine decision you take every day. It could deciding to go ahead with your daily fitness routine, despite feeling tired, or any other decision you need to take.

- Now, see if it is possible to observe your emotions as you are in the process of deciding. See for example, if you can capture any sensations in your belly, your hands, around your chest or in any other part of your body.

- Continue to observe, whether you notice perhaps a connection between what you are about to decide and the emotions emerging that could possibly be connected to the decision.

- After giving it some time, you can return to your breath before ending the practice.

6.5
Exercises

6.5.1 A preliminary note

As mentioned in the previous session (paragraph 5.4.1), MBSAT distinguishes between practices and exercises. Practices are long-term components of personal practice and intended for regular, repeated training. Exercises tend to be stand-alone interventions, designed to facilitate insights for specific themes.

The difference is fluid, however, as someone might choose to do an exercise repeatedly over a prolonged period. The exercise "Three good things" below is one of the popular interventions that MBSAT participants tend to maintain as part of their regular practice.

6.5.2 Exercise 1 - Three Good Things

This exercise fosters not just the positive emotion of gratitude; multiple studies have demonstrated that cultivating gratitude also strengthens optimism and resilience and improves sleep quality, while reducing worrying and low mood. Furthermore, a positive mindset is known to broaden awareness and stimulate creativity (Young, 2017, pages 17-21).

The Three-good-things Exercise consists of two steps: (1) a brief daily reflection and (2) making notes in your diary to record the highlights.

Step 1: Brief daily reflection

Take a few minutes every day to think about three good things in your life. The choice has no limits. It can be something small, perhaps recent or ongoing, or something from the past. You can choose an event or a relationship; a fortunate circumstance you are grateful for or something beautiful you enjoyed. Experience shows that the best time of the day for this short practice is either in the morning as you prepare for the day or in the evening, when you are reflecting on the day's events.

Step 2: Brief notes in your diary

Write the three good things you identified in a journal and reflect on why they are special to you. It is known that journal writing amplifies the positive impact of the practice and helps to produce a calm and more mindful disposition. There is abundant scientific literature on the benefits of journal writing. Reflecting on why something feels good to you also has an enhancing effect and can strengthen links to other people in your life.

Figure 6.3 shows a person full of gratitude and contentment in conversation in a simple rural setting with a Vietnamese nun.

Goal: Increasing gratitude and moments of contentment for our BETA.

Figure 6.3 Moments of Contentment with Nun Viên Thế'

6.5.3 Exercise 2 - Building the Free Energy Minimizer Self (FEMS)

a) Introduction

We all have moments in life when our BETA (Body sensations, Emotions/feelings, Thoughts, and Action impulses) are harmoniously aligned and synchronized. At those times we feel complete and happy, we are inspired and able to mobilize our best qualities. These are moments, when we are able to minimize

Free Energy, thus reducing prediction errors and decision mistakes, and those around us who witness the experience notice the extraordinary outcomes (Figure 6.4).

The FEMS is a narrative document that captures the characteristics of these experiences, the personal qualities, and the conditions in the environment that brought forth the best in ourselves. In other words, we use these great experiences for data mining in order to formulate policies and action plans of our desirable self, one able to minimize Free Energy (Bouizegarene et al., 2020; Hohwy, 2021; Kiverstein, 2020).

A FEMS is enacted by a combination of equanimous BETAs and right beliefs about the causes of what is happening in the internal and external environments, which give clarity of mind that result in skillful decisions. When these elements come together they build an adaptive BETA capable of facilitating the attainment of strategic awareness, reducing Free Energy, and implementing skillful decision-making.

Figure 6.4 Free Energy minimizing buddy

The main benefit of having a FEMS plan is its function as a powerful magnet. Having a clearly defined vision of one's possibilities to function without incurring in decision-making errors serves as a blueprint for attaining authentic well-being. It then nourishes our BETA with a sense of what we can become. And that represents a motivational force moving us towards the vision (Apps & Tsakiris, 2014).

The process of creating your FEMS consists of several building blocks and includes feedback from people who know us well and perceive us from different vantage points (friends and family, colleagues and supervisors at work, contacts from social activities and hobbies, etc.).

The sequence of the main steps to create a FEMS is as follows:

1. Collecting feedback about decisions from people who know you.

2. Writing down your own narratives of those incidents.

3. Analyzing the data gathered and combining it with other sources of information.

4. Creating the FEMS narrative of who you are when you are making optimal decisions and minimizing Free Energy.

5. Creating an action plan that allows to leverage your BETA for skillful decision making.

b) Guidelines to start the FEMS strategic plan

Collecting feedback is the first task in establishing a Mindful FEMS strategic plan. In this session we start with collecting data from others. From the range of feedbacks you will learn important things about yourself:

- The responses from your contacts will generate awareness of how others perceive you, when you are making decisions.
- The responses will enhance your understanding of what kind of work and life situations bring out the best and the worst of your abilities in decision-making.
- The responses will help you create a personal development plan and implement actions based upon the reflections that your FEMS portrait generates.
- The responses provide a resource for future challenges, when you may be discouraged and need to get back on track.
- The responses can strengthen your ties with the people you ask for honest feedback.

Here is what you need to do in concrete terms:

1. Identify respondents:

Identify people who know you well. These may be colleagues (former or current), friends (old or recent), family members, customers, or anyone who has had extended contact with you. Think about who will give you an honest opinion: the more diverse the group, the better. Ideally, you need at least ten responses to get a sufficiently rich picture of yourself deciding in different situations, so ask enough people to ensure at least ten responses, taking into account that not everyone might get back to you in time.

2. Compose a short text to ask for feedback:

Formulate a brief feedback request that you can adjust for each person you write to. It should explain what the feedback is for and why the person's input is important. It will be most helpful, if your contacts could provide you with two examples: one of a situation where they think you took a good decision and another of a decision they think did not turn out well. An example of such a text for more formal relationships is below. It can easily be adjusted for closer, more informal relations.

Sample email request for feedback:

With the goal of continued learning and personal development, I am currently participating in a training program called Mindfulness-Based Strategic Awareness Training (MBSAT). It is based on mindfulness practices and exercises based on more recent advances in Neuroscience. As part of the program, I have the task to establish a narrative of myself in my best moments, when my human qualities shine through and I'm making good decisions. I'm looking for stories and anecdotes, where my decision-making was effective, and also

---

where I was not so effective, and the outcomes did not meet expectations. The stories will serve later as basis for an action plan to help me improve my decision-making skills, make the best of me as a person and foster satisfaction in life.

To generate an accurate story of myself, I need the input of people like you who have known me for some time. I would very much appreciate it if you could recall three anecdotes, when you could observe me in decisive moments, for example preventing an undesirable situation from occurring, overcoming a challenge, making a good or suboptimal decision in a critical situation or perhaps refraining from taking a decision, when the circumstances required one, etc. Please provide stories and examples rather than just characteristics, so I can understand the situation and what it is that you have observed. You could say for instance something like this: "I remember the time when you ...," or you could say something like: "I saw you handling this or that situation and I think it shows..."

I would very much appreciate, if you could take the time to respond as I have always valued your opinion. Could you possibly provide a feedback within a week or 10 days? The training program has a deadline that I have to meet.

Thank you very much for your support and warmest regards.

3. Get in contact:

After adjusting the sample text if necessary to your personal circumstances, you are ready to mail or email your request to the people you have identified. Although this request may at first seem a bit awkward, experience has shown that most people are happy to assist with the exercise. Depending on the people you choose, you might also call them and ask them for the answers in writing. Respondents who are very close or who you have difficulty emailing might be receptive to an interview. Then you can write down the stories you are given. This should be an exception, however.

Once you have sent your requests, it is important to keep track of the answers so that you can gently nudge respondents who are behind schedule. **Timely answers are essential, because your Mindful Free-Energy-Minimizing strategic plan will be the focus of Session 8. Time flies quickly and you also need some time to evaluate the responses.**

6.6
Learnings from Session 2

There are multiple learning and training intentions in Session 2: Minding BETA II. Emotions can have a significant impact on your life.

Salient benefits are the following:

- Radically altering your view of the role of emotions from seeing them as reactive coping mechanisms to understanding emotions as anticipatory signals to assure your survival.

- Learning how the emotional interoceptive information affects your internal states. For example, the presence of a positive emotion easily translates into softness in the muscular physiology.

- Learning the significance of minding your emotions as an important carrying channel of data and information for supporting strategic awareness and skillful decision making.

- Learning to recognize the influence of the breath as a supporting focus of concentration that helps observe the dynamic of emotions. For example, slow breathing accompanying positive valences helps regulate the body's parasympathetic systems.

- Beginning to recognize the interface between body sensations and emotions by observing changes in the body's states.

- Begin training your precision skills as a mechanism of improving your concentration, attention, and integration of your emotions.

- Practicing with emotion-oriented interventions designed under the Free Energy Principle, intended to assist you in reducing errors in your decision making. For example, positive emotions reflect the expectation that prediction/decision errors will indeed be minimized. They can, however, also lead to over-confidence.

- Seeing that no matter what emotion you are experiencing, it will change over time, either the tonality, the intensity or the location. It will change, that is the nature of life.

6.7
Action Plan (AP)
for the Week of Session 2

The action plan for the second week is quite easy, direct and short as you can distribute the different steps of practices over several days.

- Practice every day; limit the practices to a maximum of 15 to 20 minutes.

- The first day begin with Practice 1, the emotions observation meditation, by concentrating on positive emotions for about 15 minutes. Use as focus a person or something you like, a favorite dish, scent, or piece of music, etc., while remembering to use three stages of observation: location, intensity, and rate of change of the emotion as the tonality is given by the positive emotion. Make some notes in your diary.

- Next day do the same with negative emotions, beginning with relatively light aversions and avoiding intense negative emotions. Practice again approximately 15 minutes and remember to write down your observations.

- On the third day do the same with neutral emotions. This may be more challenging than you think, so give it the same attention.

- On day four choose freely an emotion you would like to practice observing. Practice about 15 minutes, and at the end of the practice do a Three-Good-Things exercise for 5 minutes.

- On the following days just alternate as you wish and incorporate observations of body sensations. For example, use 15 to 20 minutes, using half of the time for body sensations and the other half for emotions.

- Every day after finishing the practices, jot down some comments and reflections in your diary

- Start sending the requests for your Mindful Free Energy Minimizer Self (FEMS).

6.8
Personal Notes and Insights

The Writing Space for Your Experiences and Observations

Making notes of your daily experience intensifies your training and sharpens your perception. Remember that it is better to be brief and consistent than elaborate and sporadic. It is also unnecessary, even counterproductive, to rate or evaluate your experience. Whatever you observe is part of your learning and your personal growth.

This morning during my emotions observation practice, I noticed a certain calmness and I felt my heartbeat more slowly. So, there was calmness in my body. (example of a desirable entry)

Today I had a good practice (judgment). *I observed and recognized several of my emotions; I noticed my pulse accelerating as I watched a negative emotion.* (example of a judgment to be avoided)

Chapter 7, Session 3

MINDING BETA III - THOUGHTS

Thoughts as Exteroceptive Signals Influenced by Interoceptive States

Mindfulness-based Strategic Awareness Training Comprehensive Workbook:
New approach Based on Free Energy and Active inference for Skillful Decision-making,
First Edition. Juan Humberto Young.
© 2023 John Wiley & Sons Ltd. Published 2023 by John Wiley & Sons Ltd.
Companion website: www.wiley.com/go/young/mbsatworkbook

7.1
Getting Started
Task of Session 3, Investment and Benefits

Task of Session 3:

Training the learning rate[1] of the recognizing models for cognitive signals, that is thinking and cognition (the third element in BETA, the "T" for thoughts). The signals can be exteroceptive as well as interoceptive signals or states and encode vital information for decision making.

Minding skill trained in Session 3:

Being aware of thoughts and observing them.

Observing the triggers of thoughts and the associations they set in motion.

Observing how thoughts shape and influence the other components of BETA: Body sensations, Emotions and Action impulses.

Observing how emotions, body sensations and action impulses generate and influence thoughts.

Expected benefits of this session and corresponding practices are:

· Increased self-awareness and increased autonomy and agency.

· Increased understanding of the interconnection of BETA components.

Investment required to reap the benefits of this session:

The investment in time is the same as in Session 2. It is limited in time and easy to integrate in your daily schedules. What is most important is regularity: To reap the benefits you have to practice every day – briefly but daily.

● Time to read this chapter: about 30 minutes, depending on your reading skills.

● Time for explicit practicing: on average approximately 15 minutes per day.

● Time for implicit practicing during the day: as you go through your day, pay attention to your thoughts and how they evolve. This requires awareness but no extra time.

---

1 The learning rate refers to improving the speed and accuracy of recognizing the elements of BETA; this in turn allows for more precision in decision-making and facilitates updating of beliefs.

"Observing my thoughts has helped me to become more serene because I better understand their origin and whether they are founded or unnecessary. Sometimes I can smile at my thoughts... I also quickly understood that MBSAT works with minimal intervention. Once you have taken the hurdle to integrate the MBSAT practices into your daily routine, lots of things improve with relatively little effort. This is what makes MBSAT so efficient for me."

All we are is the result of what we think; people who shape their thoughts after self-interest bring misery whenever they speak and act... All we are is the result of what we think; people who shape their minds after selfless thought bring joy and happiness wherever they speak and act.

Dhammapada by the Buddha

Thoughts of themselves have no sub-stance; let them arise and pass away unheeded. Thoughts will not take form of themselves, unless they are grasped by attention; if they are ignored, there will be no appearing and no disappearing.

Ashvaghosha

7.2
Quiz
Session 2: Minding BETA II – Emotions

This is a voluntary quiz to reaffirm your understanding of MBSAT's foundations and core elements. Emotions are crucial in human lives.

1) How does MBSAT conceive emotions? Summarize your understanding in a few words of your own.

_____

_____

_____

_____

_____

2) How does MBSAT distinguish between an emotion and a mood?

_____

_____

_____

_____

_____

3) What emotions help people reduce Free Energy? Choose one of the following:

☐ Positive Emotions

☐ Negatives Emotions

☐ both

4) In MBSAT the concept of valence is introduced as a metric to help evaluate the rate, the direction and the velocity at which one can reduce prediction errors. Summarize your understanding of this concept in a few words.

Positive Valence:

_____

_____

_____

_____

Negative Valence:

_____

_____

_____

_____

5) What areas of the brain get activated with emotions (negative and positive emotions) and what is the consequence?

Areas in the brain and effects related to negative emotions:

_____

_____

_____

_____

Areas in the brain and effects of positive emotions:

_____

_____

_____

_____

6) In your own words, what would you say is the value of minding emotions in people's lives?

_____

_____

_____

_____

_____

7) Which of the three of types of prediction and inference is activated by emotions? Choose one of the following:

☐ Interoceptive

☐ Exteroceptive

☐ Proprioceptive

Recommended solutions of the quiz can be found on the companion website: www.wiley.com/go/Young/mbsatworkbook

7.3
Introduction and Concepts

PREDICTION TYPE: EXTEROCEPTION

We are what we predict more than what we think; inaccurate prediction leads to unhappiness not only for you but also for those around you. We are what we predict; skillful prediction leads to higher subjective well-being for you and others around you.

Some 2000 years ago the Buddha didn't have all the neuroscience apparatus and scientific support that we have today, which has revealed that what the brain/mind does is predict and anticipate our needs for survival. Nevertheless, the Buddha's wisdom expressed in the quote of the Dhammapada before the quiz is in its essence timelessly true.

The brain, as explained[2], is always several steps ahead, trying to anticipate what our needs are and how to satisfy them. It is constantly engaged in an ongoing prediction process. The challenge is that the environment, where we live and act, is just as continuously changing. This creates uncertainty that our brains seek to minimize.

In the previous session, we were concerned with establishing the appropriate direction of the emotional valence of the BETA and we described that finding the appropriate emotional valence in the context of an experience is key to having a Free-Energy minimizing BETA. For example, for an individual involved in a confrontational, hostile experience, most probably the appropriate direction of the person's emotionality should be at the least defensive, to protect herself and avoid harmful consequences. In the same manner, thoughts also require an appropriate cognitive state to support the minimization of decision-making errors.

Thoughts are mental representations within an inferential network (Vosgerau & Synofzik, 2010) that facilitate content and interpretations of other elements of BETA. For example, a person feeling irritable without apparent reason might realize after some reflection that she hasn't eaten. Now with thoughts of being hungry in her mind, the person is able to decipher her emotional state. This is how thoughts can provide content and interpretation of emotional processes. "I am irritable, because I am hungry and haven't eaten." The thoughts in this case provided the cause of the unease. Given the versatility

2 Part 1 of this workbook, in particular Chapter 4 above (synopsis).

of thoughts, they can bring clarity and equanimity to all elements of the BETA's inferential network and reduce agitation. Thoughts and emotions often are in a kind of peculiar reciprocal relationship, a thought can often be spontaneously generated by external perceptions, thus exteroceptive predictions. It can be any signal generated by the environment that is captured by any of the senses. We can add to the signal an additional emotional input thus creating an "extero-intero" signal that influences our BETA.

For Cognitive Behavioral Therapy (CBT), one of the most effective non-drug induced therapeutical interventions for the treatment of depression is interpretations in the form of thoughts about events and experiences that determine and influence emotions, actions, and body sensations. Part of working with thoughts is to uncover the emotional voice embedded in the thoughts. While writing this text I received an email from M. Seligman[3] sent to the community of positive psychologists, informing us that Prof. Aron Beck just passed away at 100 years of age. In my previous book, I wrote about an encounter between Beck and the Dalai Lama (Young, 2017, p. 126-127) in which he gave the Dalai Lama a description of his CBT method with an example of how he helped a patient, a Nobel Prize candidate who became depressed after missing the prize. After some guidance by Dr. Beck, the man left the consultation office feeling relieved and with more appreciation for his family. The Dalai Lama, in his customary joyful and playful way, started to laugh saying that Dr. Beck's method was very similar to the analytical mediation used in Tibetan Buddhist Psychology, consisting of guiding a suffering person with a question-and-answer process that elicits self-healing insights. The process is also known as Socratic Questioning, a mirroring approach of questions and answers used by the Greek philosopher Socrates with his students to uncover the truth. Socrates called his method Maieutical to draw an analogy between the process used by midwives (his mother was a midwife) in helping women give birth, and the inquiry of a therapist bringing out the truth from inside the patient.

As thoughts often are generated automatically, the focus of MBSAT is on training for minding the quality and contextual relevance of thoughts to support the Free Energy minimization of decision making, in other words, reduce decision mistakes. As life evolves, people need to maintain a certain mental stability by staying in states that favor their imperatives for survival and aspirations of prosperity in an entropic, fast-changing VUCA world. As amply discussed in Part 1 of this workbook, having a brain able to anticipate one's needs and guide BETA towards states that help process information for optimal decision-making is key for well-being; it is the way to protect mental, social, and physical health.

For mental well-being it is necessary to mind the consumption and production of cognitive material (ideas, thoughts, news, stories, plans, beliefs, and other mental inputs); they need to be truthful for maintaining personal autonomy and for clean cognitive processes to support personal goals. The Nobel Prize winner D. Kahneman, recommends using a binary cognitive indicator. "Cognitive ease" is the indicator signifying that things are going well with little need for mobilizing resources; metabolic costs can be saved and as a result, a person is likely to be in good mood. The indicator "cognitive strain" is the opposite; it signals problems and the need to activate resources, spending metabolic costs, or spending energy. "Cognitive strain" can originate,

---

3 "Aaron (Tim) Beck passed away last night. He was one hundred years old. He was the greatest of the 20th century psychiatrists and the founder Cognitive Therapy. My heart is Heavy." Mail received on the 1 of November 2021 from Marty Seligman.

for example, from thoughts that are ill-aligned with the other BETA components or thoughts that create inconsistencies and contradictions in the brain's generative models. The use of the two indicators helps people to move closer to the principal MBSAT indicator of general well-being: reducing the average number of decision mistakes, or the minimization of Free Energy formulated as the minimization of prediction errors.

Claude Shannon, the father of information theory, wrote: "Information is reduction of uncertainty." (Shannon, 1948). Uncertainty is the source of stress (Peters et al., 2017). Uncertainty about the external environment, not understanding how to cope with it, and in what way uncertainty will affect the individual's future is at the center of MBSAT's model of Stress, Anxiety and Worry – SAW, discussed in detail in Session 5 below (Figure 9.2), The model is built as a system fueled by two causal loops in which worrying thoughts and mental proliferations create a dynamic that increases Free Energy and thus exacerbates stressful states and the ensuing imbalance of BETA. It integrates ideas from Buddhist psychology, in particular the two-arrows simile in which the first arrow corresponds to the real pain of an adverse situation (losing one's job, getting divorced or having a negative health diagnosis), whereas the second arrow corresponds to self-generated suffering created by mental proliferations, that is aggravating thoughts about the real pain reinforcing feelings of discomfort and fear, sensations of anxiety and eventually unskillful decisions and actions.

Learning to keep truthful, cool thoughts in a troubling situation is the purpose of this session. In their article "A Wandering Mind is an Unhappy Mind" (Killingsworth & Gilbert, 2010), the authors present the results from their research in psychology at Harvard University. According to their research, they found that people spend on average 46% of awake time in mind wandering, a condition that leads to unhappiness. As mentioned in Young (2017, page 112) and in Chapter 3 of this book, T. Metzinger equates mind wandering with loss of attention and cognitive agency, that is the ability to control the direction of deliberate thinking. In other words, it can lead to loss of precision in people's active inferential processes, adversely affecting their prediction capability and increasing the frequency of prediction errors and decision mistakes.

In MBSAT minding thoughts is about developing the capacity to observe one's own thoughts. It is a challenging activity, because thoughts are hard to notice spontaneously compared to the other elements of BETA. Body sensations for example are usually noticeable at once. If you sleep on the right side the whole night, you probably notice spontaneously a sensation of numbness in that side of the body the next morning and might even realize its cause. It is similar to action impulses; if you have a mosquito bite for example, the impulse to scratch is obvious, or if you are thirsty, you have a clear impulse to drink. Emotions, too, are normally easy to notice, for example, the feelings of warmness and satisfaction, when something has worked out well.

Observing thoughts as such without specific triggers is different. It requires a capacity of impartial self-observation; it implies simultaneously being inside and outside of yourself as you watch your mind and its thoughts. Cognitive psychologists and mindfulness teachers call this metacognition. It is a state where you become twofold: one is the first "you" doing the thinking (generating thoughts); the other "you" is the observer who watches the thoughts of the first you.

7.4
Practices

7.4.1 Practice 1 - Minding the Silver Screen of your Thoughts

This is a minding meditation intended to help us observe our thoughts. It is inspired by cherished childhood memories and represents an homage to the pioneering movie screenings of my uncle Tony and my dad. When I was growing up, my dad was a country representative of "Charlie Chaplin United Artists" and "Allied Artists", two film companies that provided him with film copies. Using a large portable projector and heavy film reels considered high-tech at the time, my father played the movies for the kids in our neighborhood. Uncle Tony then had the idea of bringing the projector twice a month to a small rural town 2 hours away from the city, to show the films to people who hadn't access to movies otherwise. For us kids this was always fun, even the long breaks that were necessary to change the movie reels, as the movies came in several reels. During the breaks my friends used to go behind the screen "to play actors", and pretend to be the artists in the movie.

Minding the silver screen of your thoughts involves several steps:

Step 1:

Begin by finding a quiet place to practice and settle into a posture that is relaxed and attentive at the same time. Start the practice by checking your body sensations and emotions, following the instructions presented in the two previous sessions.

After a quick check of your body sensation and emotions, begin by shifting your attention to your breath, just following your natural breath, remembering that there is no need to establish a special way of breathing, simply staying with your normal respiration rate of inhaling and exhaling. And when your awareness drifts away from your breath, this is not a reason for concern as you may remember from the previous sessions. It happens to all of us. In this case, just recognize that it has happened and slowly return to your breath.

Step 2:

As you have already checked into the first two elements of your BETA, the body sensations and emotions, we now turn to the third, our thoughts. The invitation is to shift your awareness to the workbench of your mind, an imaginary place in your mind where you are ready to do some mind work. In this practice the virtual workbench is transformed into a silver screen. Your mind is the invisible projector that keeps projecting thoughts like scenes in a motion picture that keeps running continuously with yourself as permanent leading actor on the Silver Screen of your mind. Having mentally created your personal space in the imaginary cinema, you can now picture yourself taking a seat in one of the rows from where you have the best view (Figure 7.1). When you are ready, start watching your thoughts as if they were actors on the silver screen, while remaining seated, with your eyes gently closed. Becoming fully aware of your thoughts will require training. While some thoughts/actors are easily recognizable, many are masters of disguise, deception and the art of disappearing, almost like Japanese Ninjas, the secret agents operating in feudal Japan. Often it is these secretive thoughts that create difficulties in our lives. You will need to be patient and build experience in recognizing these concealed thoughts/actors.

Figure 7.1 Minding the Silver Screen of Your Thoughts

Step 3:

Installed comfortably in the seat of your private mental cinema, you can watch your thoughts/actors on the silver screen with the attitude of a movie-goer, who reflects on the characters and the roles of the actors in the movie. Some actors are villains, others are heroes, and still other victims; some show up once, and others are recurrent. See if you can classify the actors/thoughts using a rudimentary scale, remembering that there are essentially a few categories at play: good actors that create cognitive ease, bad actors that cause cognitive strain, and so-so actors in between, in line with Kahneman's indicators mentioned above.

Here is an example of classification. Imagine that as you are watching your personal life unfolding on the silver screen in front of you, when a thought pops up: "I knew she wasn't up to the task; she shouldn't have been promoted". You catch the thought as it displays. Now the task is to uncover the true culprit like a detective, as if you were Colombo, Poirot, or Maigret. You move behind the screen and see that the actor named envy was there in secret, hidden behind the thought: "I knew she wasn't up to the task."

A useful strategy in this practice is to classify the thoughts according to three cognitive tonalities: aversive thoughts, greedy thoughts, and neutral thoughts. Once you have roughly assigned the thoughts to these broad categories, keep inquiring about the more specific nature of the thoughts as in the example above about the colleague's promotion: the primary thought is aversive in nature with a more specific tonality of envy.

You can use this technique to uncover the actors behind your thoughts. Keep practicing for a few minutes. When you decide to conclude the practice, gently leave the personal silver screen by transiting to your breath, staying with your breathing for a few more moments, before externalizing your awareness and coming back to the present moment. With time and with practice you will learn to recognize the thoughts/actors in a continuous-time manner on the silver screen of your mind.

7.4.2 Practice 2 - Mindfully walking while minding your thoughts/actors on your silver screen

While the previous practice is of the formal kind requiring specifically dedicated time at an undisturbed place, the present practice is of informal nature, meaning it can be practiced simultaneously with a routine activity that doesn't require much attention. Many people like these types of practices; in today's hectic environment with its shortage of time and overloaded agendas, they are considered as efficient and time-saving. However, it is not without challenges to execute them properly and reap the expected benefits. The main drawback is splitting attention between the activities that can foil the intended effects. Informal practices do indeed require some practice to be really effective. It means training to attain a capability that F. Scott Fitzgerald, the great American novelist circumscribed in these words: "The test of a first-rate intelligence is the ability to hold opposed ideas in the mind at the same time, and still retain the ability to function." In the case of this practice, participants must hold two activities in their minds: walking safely a certain stretch and simultaneously observing the quality of their thoughts. These activities are not actually opposed; yet minding the quality of your thoughts while also minding your movements as you walk can be challenging, and conversely the intention of minding your thoughts undoubtedly adds complexity to the experience of walking. Therefore, it is best to do this practice in an environment, where you are not disturbed and the path ahead of you is clear. Trying to do this practice on your way to the office for example, or another destination, just to save time may not be beneficial.

The practice consists of two parts.

Part 1: Walking mindfully

Although the activity appears to be quite simple, mindful walking is actually a complex meditation comprising four principal movements that involve multiple minute moves of muscles, joints, and tendons, which need to be executed with clear awareness and intention. The four key movements are the following:

- First movement: lifting the foot and sensing the upward movement.
- Second movement: moving the foot forward.
- Third movement: lowering the foot and sensing the heaviness as the foot moves towards the ground.
- Fourth movement: sensing the foot touching the ground, either hard (wood, concrete, etc.) or soft (lawn, sand, carpet), then bending the sole of the foot in preparation for the next step.

Start to make a few steps by executing mindfully each of the four walking movements. Once you feel confident of the sequence of movements, check the path you intend to walk, making sure it is without hindrances, and then start walking, slowly at first and then gradually going faster but still moving mindfully until you reach your natural rhythm of walking.

Part 2: Minding your thoughts/actors while walking

After having found a mindful, yet natural way of walking, you can begin to implement the steps of the formal practice "Minding the silver screen of your thoughts", only that this time you are watching your internal film while walking (Figure 7.2). If you are one of the many people who are used to reading your emails on your phone while walking, maybe even answering them, you may be an expert in walking and multitasking. The difference in this practice is the intention: it is more than a cognitive task; the objective is meta-cognition.

Figure 7.2 Walking mindfully with Nun Viên Thê'

7.5
Exercises

7.5.1 Exercise 1 - The Thought Swap Exercise (TSE)

Introduction:

One of the principal sources of stress, tension, and lack of well-being is the nature of the automatic patterns of our thought process. The father of Cognitive Behavioral Therapy, Dr. A. Beck, found in his research that people often have automatic thoughts and unhelpful ways of thinking. Typical examples are the following:

- Overgeneralizing (I failed this test; I will also fail my studies).
- Magnifying (I didn't sleep well; I'm going to have a bad day).
- Operating with should/ought (he should have known that this is unacceptable).
- Jumping to conclusions (I don't see the point of talking as I will not change my opinion).
- Mind-reading (he said he likes me and my work, but I know he actually doesn't).

Such unhelpful, ingrained patterns of thinking are called Automatic Negative Thoughts – ANTs, making life difficult for us and others around us.

In Beck's cognitive model (illustrated in Figure 2.6 in Chapter 2) a situation triggers an automatic thought, that can often be an ANT, which then creates a reaction affecting the other elements of our BETA (body sensations, emotions, and action impulses). In reality, ANTs or any other type of thoughts are triggered by core beliefs that are formed as the result of previous experiences. We will learn more about beliefs in the next chapters. For now, what is of interest to us is developing a tool to swap unhelpful ANTs for more skillful thoughts.

Guidelines:

Positive psychologists have discovered that an effective strategy to increase well-being is the generation of brief, but frequent experiences of positive emotions, sensations, and thoughts in daily life. The Thoughts Swap Exercise (TSE) seeks to assist individuals by multiplying such moments of positivity. It aims at providing a tool to reframe negative automatic thoughts that are often unconscious. As mentioned, negative automatic thoughts can reflect the patterns of our early conditioning and dominate and shape our BETA, often producing unskillful reactions.

This exercise can also be applied to patterns of exaggerated or unrealistic positive thinking. Although maybe less frequent, a person might have habitual, overly benevolent thoughts, irrespective of context, that may be maladaptive as they hinder a clear perception of reality. This would be the case for example of an overindulgent supervisor who accepts, again and again, the excuses of an employee for sub-optimal yields, just to find out much later that the employee consistently lined his own pockets and misappropriated part of the production.

The exercise consists of two steps:

Step 1: Recalling an event

As objectively as you can, describe a situation that has generated a negative reaction from you. Now try to remember what negative automatic thoughts sprang up in your mind. Then describe the feelings and sensations generated by the experience and possibly your impulse to act resulting from your thoughts, feelings and sensations. Try to remember as vividly as you can as if the event was happening right now.

Step 2: Swapping thoughts

Reimagine the situation as it originally occurred.

Then, constructively and positively see if it is possible to re-engineer your thoughts, finding possible alternative explanations and interpretations and imaging yourself being in good mood.

Describe what your emotions are now and what impulses to act you feel. If you find it difficult to fathom your feelings based on the re-engineered thoughts, you might describe the expected BETA: Body sensations, Emotions/feelings, Thoughts and Action impulses that would be likely to result from swapping your thoughts with respect to the same situation.

Learning points of this exercise:

- The power of automatic thinking and how it shapes the experience, most often in a negative, defensive way.
- Thoughts have a malleable characteristic.
- How automatic thoughts shape our feelings and vice versa: feelings can also shape our cognition and thoughts.
- The bidirectional connection between thoughts and feelings provides two gates to reframing an experience from negative to positive (starting from thoughts or starting from feelings).
- A third gate is context: given the contextual influences on thoughts, mood and feelings one can auto re-engineer cognition and mood and bend them towards appreciation by intentionally creating more positive contexts, thus amplifying the well-being zone.
- Learning new forms of taking care of oneself.

7.6
Learnings from Session 3

In addition to the learning from the Thought Swap Exercise mentioned above, there are many more conclusions to be drawn.

What we can learn from Session 3:

- How the quality of thoughts shapes our experience.

- The hidden, unconscious nature of cognition and how it influences our BETA.

- How to start recognizing the patterns of our mind and being aware of thoughts.

- Learning to relate thoughts to other elements of the BETA.

- Relating to thoughts as thoughts, not facts. Seeing thoughts as elaborations of our mind that may or may not be related to your internal life or our surroundings.

- Registering experiences with an open and receptive mind, avoiding automatic thoughts, labeling or creating stories.

- Developing a spaciousness of the mind by observing how thoughts arise and pass.

- Observing the personal silver screen in the mind with the thoughts acting and not being affected by them.

7.7
Action Plan (AP)
for the Week of Session 3

The main principle of effective training is to practice briefly but regularly.

- Practice every day, limiting the practices to a maximum of 15 to 20 minutes.

- The first day begin with Practice 1 "Minding the silver screen of your thoughts", concentrating on catching the villain actors. Make brief notes on your observations in your diary and continue to do so in the following days.

- The next day do the same for heroic actor thoughts.

- On the third day do the practice without a specific focus, seeing what type of actor thoughts appear more frequently on the silver screen and making a note of it.

- On day 4 do Practice 2, minding your thoughts actors while walking.

- On the following days you may alternate as you wish. For example, using half of the time (7-10 minutes) for villains and the other half for heroic actor thoughts or using the open approach and seeing what actor thoughts show up.

- Remember to jot down some comments and reflections in your diary every day after practicing.

- Throughout the week practice the Thought Swap Exercise - TSE (Section 7.5) as frequently as possible during the day. You can exercise with simple, spontaneous thoughts swapping or reframing them and observing the difference it makes.

- **Keep track of your feedback requests for your Free Energy Minimizer Self (FEMS).** If you haven't heard back from your contacts, ask them whether they intend to respond.

7.8
Personal Notes and Insights
The Writing Space for Your Experiences and Observations

Examples:

This morning during my thoughts observation practice, I simply wave at Johnny Envy, my envy actor thought. I noticed him behind the thoughts: "Now because they have a new car, they think they are better than the rest." (example of a desirable entry)

Today, I observed and recognized Johnny Envy's thoughts; it made me upset, and my pulse started to accelerate as I watched him. I feel I made good progress in awareness and meta-cognition (judgment). (example of an entry with unnecessary judgment)

MINDING BETA IV - ACTION IMPULSES

Actions as Source of Proprioceptive Signals and Experiences

Mindfulness-based Strategic Awareness Training Comprehensive Workbook:
New approach Based on Free Energy and Active inference for Skillful Decision-making,
First Edition. Juan Humberto Young.
Companion website: www.wiley.com/go/young/mbsatworkbook

8.1
Getting Started
Task of Session 4, Investment and Benefits

Task of Session 4:

Training the learning rate[1] of the recognizing models for proprioceptive[2] signals as encoding vital information for decision making. Proprioception refers to the fourth component of BETA: Actions and Action impulses.

Minding skill trained in Session 4:

Increasing the precision in observing and describing action impulses and actions.

Learning to recognize how actions and action impulses influence our decisions in daily life and in crucial situations.

Minding the difference between action impulse and action.

Minding the interconnection of action and impulses to act with the other BETA components.

Expected benefits of this session and corresponding practices are:

· Increase understanding of own action impulses and actions.

· Increase understanding of other's action impulses and actions.

· Increasing the ability to interpret actions and actions impulses as information signals for decision-making.

· Ability to better regulate action impulses and actions thus reducing prediction errors

Investment required to reap the benefits of this session:

The time required for reading and practicing is unchanged. It is kept to a minimum with the intention to help you integrate your MBSAT mind training into your daily schedule, allowing for consistent practicing without creating stress.

● Time to read this chapter: about 30 minutes, depending on your reading skills.

● Time for explicit practicing: on average approximately 15 minutes per day.

● Time for implicit practicing during the day: As you go through your day pay attention to your action impulses and actions and the relation between them. This requires awareness and minding but no extra time.

● Time to analyze feedback responses (Box 8.1): at your discretion.

---

1 The learning rate refers to increasing the speed and accuracy of recognizing the elements of BETA; this in turn allows for more precision in decision-making and facilitates updating of beliefs.

2 Proprioception is related to the body in movement, to action and location (see Chapter 4, Section 4.3.2).

"With home office, I found myself going to pantry all the time to grab snacks and later felt bad about it. My brain seemed exhausted from Zoom meetings and lack of outside contacts... A few times I could catch the action impulse in time and divert the attention to an alternative (a power nap, moving around, etc.). Now I want to continue learning to control my action impulses. It has to do with autonomy... The impulse comes before the action. After all, we call ourselves "human beings", not "human doings."

8.2
Quiz
Session 3: Minding BETA III – Thoughts

This is a voluntary quiz to review Session 3. It could be fun to see for yourself what you have retained. At the same time, the review can help you shift your learnings from the short-term to the long-term memory and store them there safely.

1) How does MBSAT conceive thoughts? Explain in a few words of your own.

_____

_____

_____

_____

_____

2) In your own words, briefly explain the notions of cognitive ease and cognitive strain.

_____

_____

_____

_____

_____

3) What is the main role of the information processing function of the brain?

_____

_____

_____

_____

_____

4) Cognitive Behavioral Therapy and MBSAT have a key element in common that helps people reduce Free Energy (prediction and decision mistakes). Explain in a few words.

_____

_____

_____

_____

_____

5) What thoughts help people reduce Free Energy? Choose one of the following:

☐ Positive thoughts

☐ Negative thoughts

☐ Both

If you choose c, explain why.

_____

_____

_____

_____

6) Please describe as succinctly as possible the concepts of mind wandering and metacognition.

    a) Mind wandering means...

_____

_____

    b) Metacognition means...

_____

_____

7) What would you say could be the value of minding thoughts in people's lives?

_____

_____

_____

_____

_____

8) Which of the three of types of prediction and inference are activated by thoughts? Choose one or two of the following:

☐ Interoceptive

☐ Exteroceptive

☐ Proprioceptive

Recommended solutions of the quiz can be found on the companion website: www.wiley.com/go/Young/mbsatworkbook

8.3
Introduction and Concepts

PREDICTION TYPE: PROPRIOCEPTION

Mindfulness and meditation are often associated with sitting still for long hours and a reclusive way of life. In contrast, MBSAT stands for being mindful in action and synchronizing mindfulness with an active way of life. Instead of withdrawing from VUCA world, MBSAT seeks to be a calming, constructive force in today's turmoil. An active interpretation of mindfulness is not entirely new. A case in point are the Kung Fu nuns of the Drukpa Buddhist order of Nepal. For them actions are an integral part of their spiritual and religious practice. Rather than spending long hours in meditation, the nuns are involved in community service, promoting gender equality, education and environmental protection amongst other initiatives. After the devastating earthquake in Nepal in 2015 they became first responders for search and rescue, going to remote places where no other help arrived, not even the Red Cross.

> *"We believe that helping others is our true religion and we believe that sitting still in one place doing meditation is not that effective these days."*
>
> A nun from the Nepalese Kung Fu Drukpa order

Note: These committed, selfless nuns practice active meditation in the form of Kung Fu self-defense and therefore are often called "Kung Fu nuns". When they travel to remote regions to help people, their Kung Fu training is a way of enabling aid.

An anecdote that made a lasting impression on me stems from Humberto Maturana, the Chilean, Harvard-trained biologist and author of the widely recognized autopoiesis theory that he developed together with his student Francisco Varela, who is the person responsible for bringing a scientific approach to mindfulness to the West. In this anecdote, Maturana tells about a walk in the woods with his young child. As they walked he cleared the path by cutting the tall, hard grass that made it difficult to advance. Suddenly his son asked him: "Dad, why don't you like grass?" "Why are you asking me?" Maturana replied. His son answered that he saw him cut the grass, so he assumed he must loathe it. This is a wonderful example of how our actions create information signals that reflect intentions, values, and emotions, whether truthful or misinterpreted.

Action is one of the mechanisms to test and, if necessary, revise predictions. This is captured by the term Active Inference, amply analyzed and discussed in Part 1 of this book. Another way of revising predictions consists of updating the brain's generative models to allow for more precise predictions.

With skillful actions people are able to materialize their predictions. For example, the prediction that some needed items are available in a store nearby may prompt us to set our bodies in motion and trigger the action of walking to the store. With each step forward the person is coming closer to the store and theoretically reducing prediction error, assuming the store is open as predicted. We can call this a continuous-time Active Inference process.

If the store is open, Free Energy has been successfully minimized. In case the store is closed, the need to find another supplier, and perhaps a certain frustration, impede Free Energy minimization and may call for some correction. At the level of the brain's generative model, the person might incorporate the belief that in the future it is best to check the internet or call the store for opening hours before undertaking the action of walking to the store.

Figure 8.1 below visualizes this continuous-time Active Inference process and the possible outcomes.

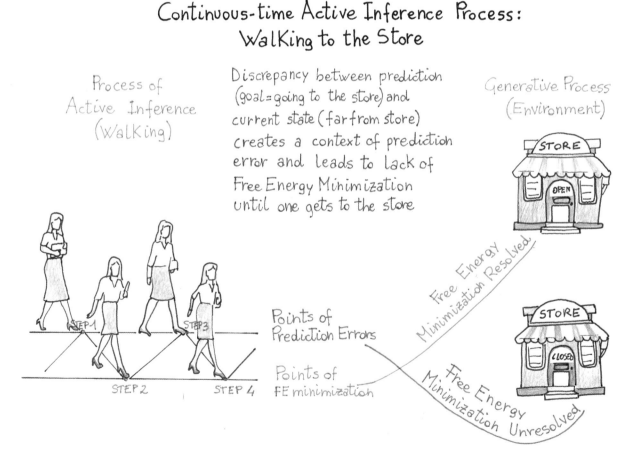

Figure 8.1 Continuous-time Active Inference Process: Walking to the Store

Actions and predictions are closely interconnected. It is an issue that is also of utmost importance in business. One of the most difficult challenges in management is deciding what areas, activities, and actions to fund in order to maintain the viability of a business. It is a subject that occupies businesspeople as well as academics at business schools. Large resources are dedicated to improving the quality of business planning and predictions of business conditions. Several years ago, a novel approach emerged (McGrath & Macmillan, 1995) that was contrary to the general approach based on predicting revenues and then working down to the expected profits. The novel approach reversed the sequence by beginning with a target of predicted profits, forcing decision makers to think hard about the assumptions, then moving up to the predicted required revenues and allowable costs for achieving a predetermined desirable profit. Planning under this approach is conceived as learning about opportunities by incorporating emerging information and implementing actions to achieve the goals.

At the level of individuals, actions are also taken for achieving goals, with the ultimate objective of increasing people's survival chances, which bears similarities to the planning model above. The two principal functions of actions are the following:

a) Actions have an epistemic value, meaning they are taken in order to generate information that helps reduce VUCA (volatility, uncertainty, complexity and ambiguity).

b) Actions also have a utilitarian value as they help people achieve desired states and goals. (Hohwy, 2020).

The two functions are intertwined. The brain decides on strategies that reduce VUCA of future outcomes by minimizing the expected Free Energy (reducing decisional errors) and devises actions (Bottemanne & Friston, 2021), for example, the action to get vaccinated against COVID-19, expecting to avoid getting sick and stay healthy (the desired state).

Besides the importance for individuals to be able to act skillfully for their personal benefit, it is also crucial to be able to understand other people's actions. Skillfully understanding and anticipating the actions of others is only possible, if an individual is able to skillfully anticipate own actions in the first place. In other words, the generative models of people's actions act as a mirror of other people's actions. Neurologically this is enabled via mirror neuron circuitry, whereby the actions of others are matched with the person's neurological, motoric system used to perform the same actions. This works, because understanding actions happens at different levels:
a) The intention.
b) The goals of the action.
c) A signal that triggers the movement of the body to realize the action.
d) The execution of the action in time and space.

For example, imagine that someone is crossing the street and suddenly accelerates the pace to get to the other side. The action will be clear for an observer who understands that:
a) The intention or goal is to cross the street.

b) For achieving this goal it is necessary to move.

c) A car is approaching, so accelerating the pace is required to avoid getting hit by the car (Kilner & Frith, 2008).

The mirror circuitry works well for recognizable and familiar actions, but not so well for unfamiliar and unrecognizable actions. In such cases Active Inference predictive models are necessary. Imagine for example, in the example above, that the person sees the car approaching and instead of accelerating the pace does the opposite and slows down. How to understand this action? As the observer will not have a neural mirror circuit for this case, understanding the action requires Active Inference in the context of what is happening. The car is coming fast and the person slowing down her walking pace. What is required is inverse planning, observing the action in time and space (what neuroscientists call the kinematic level) and infer the goals and intention of the action. In this case the conclusion is that the person apparently wants to commit suicide. (Brass, et al., 2007; Patel et al., 2012; Baker, Saxe and Tenenbaum, 2009). This suggests the need to understand own actions in order to be able to understand others' actions.

Actions define us.

We are not just what we think, we are also what we do. When a politician engages in corrupt acts, we say that she is corrupt. Her actions define, who she is.

With this session and its focus on actions and action impulses, we conclude the cycle of the four BETA components and complete Part 1 of the training program. (For a comprehensive view of the program structure, please, see Figure 4.7 Structural Design of the MBSAT Program in Chapter 4, Box 4.2).

For reasons of clarity it may be important to emphasize that balancing BETA and in the process minimizing Free Energy (i.e. incoherent, potentially destructive energy) doesn't mean to be smiling all the time, as this would amount to a state of Pollyanna, nor does it mean to be so accepting as to put up with everything which would entail resignation. Balancing BETA that is conducive to genuine flourishing is a state of high-intensity, fully-lived BETA that might comprehend disagreeing and even forcefully resisting situations or conditions that are harmful.

Figure 8.2 illustrates these connections. Amongst other things, it shows that high minimization of Free Energy has different modalities. Resignation in the lower right corner is depicted as a non-adaptive state despite its capacity to minimize Free Energy. Resigning is very different from consciously allowing averse situations to be without resisting them, trusting that options and possibilities can be generated at the right moment and circumstances. An equanimous attitude of allowing has the potential to kindle new energy and renew flourishing eventually.

Figures 8.4 and 8.5 also help clarify the connections between different states of BETA and the likelihood of being able to minimize Free Energy which is the ultimate goal of what we are trying to achieve by aligning and evening out BETA components.

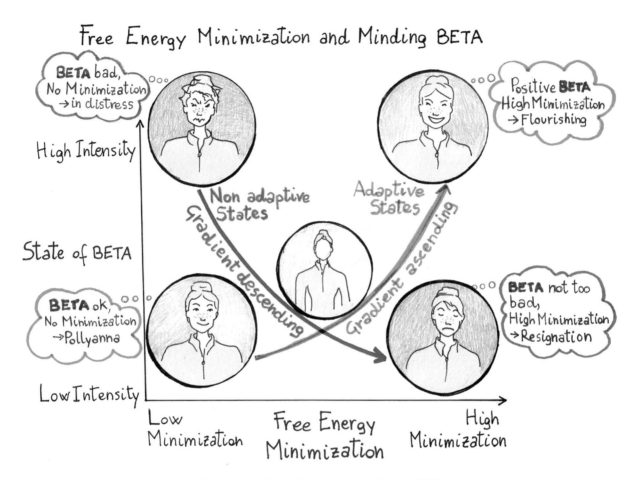

Figure 8.2 Free Energy Minimization and Minding BETA

8.4
Practices

8.4.1 Practice 1 - Minding Action Impulses

We often act impulsively and in automatic-pilot mode, without realizing what drives us. The objective of this practice is to become aware of our actions, and more critically of our action impulses, and train the ability to observe them. This helps us regain autonomy and the freedom to choose the course of action. We might even choose not to act at all or to act later, after reflecting on the consequences.

There are basically four options to respond to an action impulse: drop the action, reduce it, increase it, or create a new action. In this practice, we swiftly classify the action impulses we observe according to these four criteria.

Step 1: Preparing

As usual, we begin by finding a place, where we can practice without being distracted and adjust our posture so that we can stay relaxed and attentive at the same time.

Start the practice by checking your body sensations, emotions and thoughts in line with what you have learned in the previous sessions. Then shift your awareness to your breath, breathing naturally. While you are focusing on your breath, your mind might start to wander; if it happens it is no reason for concern. It happens to everyone, simply recognize where your mind has gone and gently bring your attention back to your breath.

When you are ready, you may go to the imaginary workbench of your mind, the virtual space you created in the previous sessions, and where you can do some mind work. On the workbench of this practice are the Free-Energy-Minimizing Actions Quadrants. For now, simply keep them in the background of your mind.

Step 2: Recognizing action impulses

As you are in an attentive, calm position with your eyes gently closed, you may start observing what action impulses emerge. It may take a few moments; usually, after a while some urge starts to manifest itself, and as you keep concentrating and ignoring it or refusing to act on it might get stronger. Recognizing and observing action impulses requires some training. While some action impulses are easy to notice (for example itching or the urge to change the position), many are more difficult to spot. Often these are the ones that create difficulties in our lives. You will need to be patient and build experience in recognizing action impulses.

Step 3: Using the action quadrants as tool

Once you have recognized an action impulse, you can use the basic four options (dropping/reducing, increasing/creating) as rudimentary but practical classification. The four options are illustrated in Figure 8.6 as a matrix with four action quadrants (Section 8.5.1). You can use it as an easy tool to determine your response to action impulses. Don't spend time analyzing the action, just spontaneously classify the impulse according to the four categories of the quadrants. For example, if you catch the impulse to scratch yourself, simply categorize it without much thinking; then, see if you can identify another impulse to act and reiterate the process.

You can apply this technique for several minutes until you decide to conclude the practice. At that point begin to transit your awareness to your breath, staying with your breathing for some more minutes, before externalizing your awareness and coming back to the present moment. With time and with practice you will learn to recognize your action impulses with ease and classify them with precision.

With this practice that focuses on the "A" of BETA the training cycle of "Minding BETA" gets completed. One by one we have learned to observe each element of our BETA: Body sensations, Emotions, Thoughts and Action and action impulses. We trained in a systematic manner after each session, following each week one element of the acronym BETA, starting with body sensations and now this week ending with action impulses. In everyday life BETA is driven either by external events or self-generated triggers such as anticipating future occurrences or remembering past events. All these events impact people's lives with different intensity, velocity and duration, hence the need for "Minding BETA" to countervail the vagaries and ensure a balanced BETA that can support skillful decision making.

Going forward, it is important to learn to practice dynamically and continuously, not only in difficult times when the need for coping mechanisms is acutely felt. To practice dynamically start with the elements of the BETA that are more obvious and therefore easy to catch. For example, if one can catch a thought this can be the starting point for a practice and then moving to the other elements of the BETA. The audio files accompanying this book can assist with a comprehensive and integrative BETA practice.

8.4.2 Practice 2 - Mindful Salsa

a) Introduction:

When I designed this practice several years ago, I based it on studies showing that dancing could be useful for treating mental distress (Pinniger et al., 2012). However, as I was not sure about the introduction of the intervention, I consulted colleagues, specialists in Mindfulness-Based Cognitive Therapy (MBCT). They thought it was an unusual intervention, given their orientation towards cognitive interventions, whereas dancing is a kinematic activity (movement in space and time). Currently, several years later, Mindful Salsa is a well-established key signature practice of the MBSAT program and very popular with participants. In Zurich, it is interesting to watch bankers in MBSAT courses loosening up with Mindful Salsa, moving their bodies at the beat of music. In Japan, Singapore and Korea, MBSAT teachers tell me that their participants love the intervention as it opens up new experiential dimensions. And there is positive feedback from many other countries.

As I expanded my research for this workbook, I discovered that Mindful Salsa is much more than an unusual idea based on my trivial, personal intuition; it carries enormous mental and emotional value and is indeed a powerful intervention. The initial insights were triggered by people with a different kind of experience an experience related to the senses. A first eye-opener was a conversation with music teacher Wendell Hanna, the wife of my friend, bestseller author Ron Purser, and daughter of Professor Thomas Hanna, the pioneer founder of somatics, a field concerned with movement, flexibility, and health. Wendell explained to me how music activates multiple regions of the brain and stimulates positive moods. Another eye-opener regarding music and dance came from Tina Mantel, one of my neighbors in Zurich, Switzerland, one of the few Swiss who graduated from the Julliard School of Music and Dance in New York. She explained to me how dance, too, has the capacity to activate various brain regions and how body movements get stimulated, when persons interact with music.

When I immersed myself in computational neuroscience, the enormous potential of music and movement became clear to me from a scientific viewpoint. Not surprisingly it is all about prediction, here in relation to melody and rhythm. "The special case of music perception thus entails an active engagement with the sensorium, both in terms of proprioception (i.e., wanting to move) and interoception (feeling pleasure)", (Koelsch et al., 2019; Pearce et al., 2006). Thus, computational neuroscience leads to the conclusion that Mindful Salsa is a practice for increasing the learning rate and precision of people's proprioceptive and interoceptive predictions simultaneously.

Here are the steps to follow.

b) Guidelines:

Your first decision is about the type of music you would like to dance to. The choice is yours; it might be soft or fast and lively. This may depend on your mood at the moment or on the mood you want to create. Then choose the music piece you feel like moving to. It can be a spontaneous process, simply turning on your music system, mobile or any other equipment and start dancing as you listen to the music.

See, if it is possible to move freely and improvise the movements as you listen to the music. When your awareness is concentrated on the music, movements will follow more smoothly. As you get absorbed by the music, it becomes easier to anticipate the rhythm and gradually you will experience more precise coordination of your movements with the music.

You can experiment with letting go of a judging stance, just being playful, dropping any worries, if your dancing is out of synchronization with the music, reminding yourself that it is not about learning to dance, but simply anticipating the rhythm and going with the flow.

If you like, you can concentrate on the sound of a single instrument that particularly attracts you, seeing if it is possible to follow how this instrument interacts with the others in the music piece.

Below you find some suggestions for music. The selection is the same as in the MBSAT book manual (Young, 2017) and reiterated here as the participants liked the repertoire.

Hopefully you will enjoy the experience.

Music Band	Title of piece
A Million Flavours	The Last Wave
Dziha Kamien	Homebase (live), Live in Vienna
Fattburger	Spice
Gabin	La Maison
Green Empathy	Airport
High End	After Traffic (soft)
Jazeboo Havana Moon	Acapulco
Jens Buchert	Mélange Eclectique (soft)
Joe McBride	Oi Gata (soft)
Johann Asmundsson	So low (fast)

8.4.3 Practice 3 - Continuous-time practice: CEO of BETA

a) Introduction:

As this session forms the completion of the first part of the program dedicated to minding the BETA, the intention is to conclude with a practice that facilitates minding BETA continuously as an integral part of everyday life.

> As everything around us changes continuously
> we also need to mind ourselves and our BETA continuously.

The program would be incomplete and of limited practical impact if minding BETA would require you to interrupt your activities at any time and withdraw to meditate in a formal, prolonged way. It must be possible to mind BETA in a continuous mode as you go about your daily chores and must take care of your responsibilities. So MBSAT includes the practice of CEO of BETA, one of the most liked and widely implemented signature practices of the MBSAT program that you can use on the spot any time.

CEO of BETA is also an integrative practice, because it includes all elements of BETA and therefore is the brace that holds Sessions 1-4 together, forming Part 1 of the 8-week MBSAT program.

CEO stands for catching, evening-out and opening BETA. It is a practice that over the last 8 years since the launch of MBSAT has become, for many, the most valuable skill they have learned in the program and the tool they rely on to improve the quality of their decision-making. It assists MBSAT practitioners to balance and synchronize their body sensations, emotions, thoughts, and action impulses and consequently ensures more skillful decision-making. The practice has its inspiration in the millennia-old tradition of mantra repetition and in the 3-Minutes-Breathing Space found in other popular mindfulness-based interventions (Young, 2017, p. 140-141).

CEO of BETA is a short practice designed to help you switch the mode of your mind from an agitated state to a calmer state and to open up to the possibilities of new options. The focus of the practice is your BETA, comprising your Body sensations, your Emotions, Thoughts and Actions impulses or urges, that is the integral human experience. When you are agitated, it is because one or several components of your BETA are agitated. This practice intends to help you identify those agitated elements of your BETA and gently shift your mindset towards a calmer and more balanced state. This allows you to tackle the challenges ahead of you with more strategic awareness.

It is a very useful practice and easy to do. You can do it more systematically and formally, meaning you can practice it two or three times a day, or informally whenever you feel the need to change the state of your mind. As mentioned it is one of the signature practices of MBSAT that has proven to be extremely popular with the people who have participated in a MBSAT course. They use it in daily life, for example, when they commute to work on the bus or train. Many use it before they need to engage in a particular activity, for example before an important meeting with their boss, a client or business partner, or before having a difficult conversation with a spouse, son, or daughter, etc. If you are in the office you might find a quiet corner, and if this is difficult you can actually do a CEO of BETA anywhere, also with your eyes open, if you are in a place where closing your eyes would be awkward.

So, let's begin.

b) Guidelines:

The practice is composed of three steps. **It is useful to mentally repeat to yourself the beginning of each step as this helps you to transition to the next phase.** Its duration can vary from a minimum of three minutes, one minute per step, to several more minutes, possibly 10 minutes, depending on the situation.

Step 1: Catching our BETA

In this step, we shift our awareness from one component of the BETA to the next. We begin by focusing our awareness on the sensations in our body. It can be any physical sensation we are able to catch, maybe sensations of warmth where our bottom touches the chair, sensations of contact at our feet touching the floor, or possibly sensations of tension or discomfort in some part of our body. Perhaps we want to do a very quick body sweep from our toes to the crown of our head.

Moving away from our body sensations, we begin catching any emotions that are present at this moment, for example, catching feelings of anxiety, anger, frustration or disappointment. Depending on the situation you might also catch jealousy or envy or simply nervousness and excitement - just catching any emotion we might be able to identify without any judgment, more with an attitude of curiosity.

Leaving behind our emotions, we now move towards our thoughts, catching whatever thoughts we might be able to observe. It might be thoughts such as: How do I tell my boss about this problem? How can I tell my wife that I am losing my job? How can I tell my girls and boys that we are not going for vacation this year?, etc. Again, just catching our thoughts without any judgment attached.

And finally moving to catch our action impulses: I feel like punching my boss, I would rather stand up and leave this boring meeting, etc. Staying a few moments here, just noticing any impulses that emerge.

The duration of this step will depend on the particular state of your BETA. If it is very agitated, you might want to explore the components of your BETA a bit longer.

Step 2: Evening out your BETA

Having recollected our BETA we start focusing on our breath, moving our awareness to the region around our belly, if that feels comfortable, or our nose or chest and beginning to follow our in-breaths and out-breaths. There is no need to create a special breathing rhythm. We simply follow the natural process and rhythm of inhaling and exhaling, staying here for a few moments, feeling our breathing. And if we notice our mind going back to thoughts around our BETA, we just acknowledge it and gently bring our awareness back to our breath.

We stay with our breath for a few moments until we feel calmer and refreshed.

Step 3: Opening our BETA

From a state of calmness and with the potent ally of an integrated, balanced BETA we begin facing whatever situation we might encounter or need to confront, for example a difficult conversation, a complex decision, etc. An easy way to start opening is by bending our thoughts towards a mindful, positive response to the current challenges. This will help us respond also emotionally with more openness and positivity. Our senses and action impulses will then follow this positive, open-minded orientation. The openness builds confidence that things will be ok or work out eventually. Even if there are no immediate solutions, our open BETA will provide the necessary conditions for positive options in the future.

Figure 8.3 below recapitulates the three steps from wide (recollecting our dispersed BETA) to narrow (focusing on the breath to even out our BETA to wide once more (opening our BETA to welcome what life offers us), all embodied in a MBSAT buddy in the form of a sand glass to express that it is a practice that requires just a few minutes and makes such a great difference.

When presenting this practice I often mention the general desire of many people to become CEO of an organization; however, we can and should first become a good CEO of our BETA. It is hard to be an effective CEO of anything if you can't be a good CEO of your BETA.

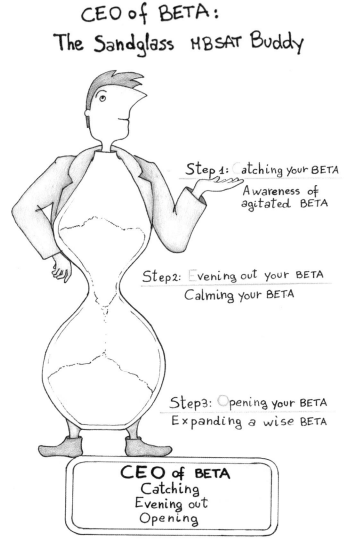

Figure 8.3 CEO of BETA: The Sandglass MBSAT Buddy

Keeping one's BETA in balance has become more and more difficult as we are saturated by an overflow of information and impulses in our digital age (Gergen 1991). The following scene in Figure 8.4 below has become all too familiar. Therefore, keeping our BETA in balance is a constant challenge in daily life.

BETA Saturation

Figure 8.4 BETA Saturation in our digital times

How difficult it can be to maintain BETA in balance in everyday life can best be exemplified by a recurrent experience such as looking at some article on display and deciding to buy it. Figure 8.6 illustrates the complexity of BETA's involvement in the seemingly banal occurrence, from the initial glance at an article – in this example a luscious, soft sweater -, to sensing pleasure at its sight and touch, feeling the craving to have it and then struggling with conflicting feelings and thoughts about the pros and cons of the purchase.

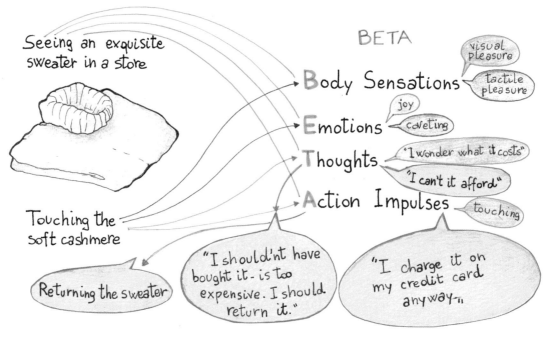

Figure 8.5 The challenge of keeping BETA in balance

8.5
Tools and Models

8.5.1 The Free Energy Minimizing Action Quadrants

The action quadrants depicted in Figure 8.6 below offer a tool to help us observe and classify the usefulness of action impulses within the context of what we are experiencing at the moment. We already made use of it in Practice 1 of this session "Minding Action Impulses". The idea here is to invite you to use it any time you notice an urge to act, as often as you become aware of an action impulse during the day, even when you are not formally engaged in practice. It is another step to becoming more autonomous in your life instead of being driven by ingrained patterns of behavior.

The quadrants are an adaptation of a schema of the business strategy formulation model created by Kim & Mauborgne (2005) to guide companies in their decision on what actions should be eliminated, reduced, increased, or newly generated in order to realize their strategies. The figure transposes the logic from an organizational process to individual behaviors. It is a practical, easy-to-apply classification aide to orient your actions. The tool can be used in two ways: ad hoc in the here or in a longer-term dimension, when you think about your objectives and more broadly about your goals in life.

In fact, we will use the quadrants as a long-term tool later in the program to help you establish your personal strategic plan that you started to put in motion in Session 2 above by requiring feedback on your decision-making. MBSAT aspires to generate concrete value for participants by improving their quality of life in a sustainable way. Therefore, we will return to the action quadrants tool in Session 8 as we are going to tackle the exercise called SOPA (Skillful BETAs and Beliefs, Opportunities and Positive Action) with the goal to realize your Free Energy Minimizing Self (FEMS).

The Free-Energy Minimizing Action Quadrants

Figure 8.6 The Free-Energy Minimizing Action Quadrants

8.6
Learnings from Session 4

We often learn from actions after they have already occurred. If an action worked well, we tend to repeat the behavior; if the outcome wasn't so good, we often have regrets and tend to refrain from it in the future. Here in Session 4, we train to become aware of the precursor of action, the action impulse. Being aware of an impulse before taking action opens up an array of new options.

Here are some of the benefits we can gain from Session 4.

• Learning to observe and reflect on the effects of actions and their impulses in your life.

• Learning to see your actions/action impulses as a corollary of the patterns of your mind and a way to know yourself better.

• Being aware of your own actions may also help you infer other people's actions.

• Developing a spaciousness of the mind by registering behavioral experiences (actions) with an open and receptive mind without labeling or creating stories.

• Ability to relate actions and action impulses to other elements of the BETA and continuously coordinate and synchronize them with the entire BETA.

• Seeing actions as means to implement predictions.

• Developing the ability to be more aware of your body in movement as one of the multiple expressions of action.

• Developing the ability to anticipate and coordinate movements in interaction with music.

• Experiencing letting go of inhibitions and appreciate the joy of movement as a way of relating to actions generated by your body.

8.7
Action Plan (AP)
for the Week of Session 4

The strategy to make the most of Session 4 is to practice daily for the minimum of 15-20 minutes. The cumulative effect of the daily practice compensates for the short duration.

- On the first day begin with Practice 1, Minding Action Impulses.

- Next day do Practice 1 again, **making sure to write down your observations in your diary**.

- On days 3 and 4 you can enjoy Practice 2, Mindful Salsa.

- On days 5 and 6, in addition to a practice you can freely choose, incorporate the CEO of BETA in your daily routines, doing it preferably 2-3 times during the day or more, if you like.

- On the last day, take 15 minutes to make a list of activities you do routinely and classify them with the help of the Action Quadrants tool. Then note your insights in your diary.

- **Check, if you have received all the responses for your Free Energy Minimizer Self (FEMS) and start to sift through the material**. If the material is too scant to create a meaningful self-portrait, take the necessary steps (reminding respondents, sending a few more feedback requests to other contacts, etc.).

- Remember to jot down some brief comments and reflections every day after finishing your home practice.

8.8
Personal Notes and Insights

The Writing Space for Your Experiences and Observations

Example:

After sitting down for Practice 1 I felt dryness in my throat and noticed an urge to get a

glass of water, but I resisted. As I continued with the practice I remembered a phone call

I had forgotten to return. For a moment I resisted again, then I gave up and called my

friend.

Box 8.1

<u>Analysis of the Responses to Your FEMS Feedback Requests</u>

In Session 2 you have started to request feedback from family, friends, work relations, and other contacts on moments when you were at your best and on situations that required a decision from you.

By now you will have a small portfolio of responses that serve as a basis for your Free Energy Minimizer Self (FEMS). It allows you to envision yourself when your strengths are evident and helps you recognize decision-making patterns.

In Session 8 you will work intensively on defining and designing an action-oriented vision of your FEMS. Your feedback portfolio will serve as valuable input at that point. For now, the task is to systematize and evaluate the responses to gain insights.

Read again the introduction to the FEMS exercise in Session 2 above (paragraph 6.5.3), where you find valuable information on the process of building your FEMS strategic plan. Here are some additional suggestions on how to proceed to analyze the feedback responses.

Read all the answers you got and take notes on what calls your attention in connection with your decision-making and personal strengths. Look for commonalities or for topics that stick out. Then create a table or Excel sheet with the name of the respondents on the left and salient topics as titles of columns. The first draft will provide an overview that enables you to go deeper, refine your overview, and create more precise columns.

A preliminary overview could take the form of a generic table similar to the following:

Respondents	Strengths apparent	Decisions with great outcomes		Decisions that did not work out as expected	
		Event and result	Strength applied	Event and result	Hindrances
Sibling					
Colleague					
Friend					
Supervisor					
etc.					

The more responses you got the richer your picture will become, the finer the details you can carve out, and the more accurate the conclusions you can draw.

When your analysis is complete you can draw conclusions in form of a brief essay, where you formulate insights in your own words. It is another step towards greater self-knowledge and more skillful decision-making.

MINDING THE PORTFOLIO OF BELIEFS I

Minding Adversity - Irimi

Mindfulness-based Strategic Awareness Training Comprehensive Workbook:
New approach Based on Free Energy and Active inference for Skillful Decision-making,
First Edition. Juan Humberto Young.
Companion website: www.wiley.com/go/young/mbsatworkbook

9.1
Getting Started
Task of Session 5, Investment and Benefits

Task of Session 5:

Training the learning rate[1] of the generative models to accelerate the process of updating unskillful beliefs.

Cultivating a strategically aware, Free-Energy minimizing mind to facilitate Mindful Real Options - MROs for skillful decision making.

Minding skill trained in Session 5:

Minding our beliefs; becoming conscious and aware of implicit beliefs.

Minding adversity: how we respond to adversity and cope with it.

Expected benefits of this session and corresponding practices are:

· Understanding how beliefs shape our lives by driving our behavior.

· Increasing our ability to update beliefs; maintaining a context-relevant portfolio of beliefs to elevate the precision of predictions, reduce prediction errors and improve the quality of decision-making.

· Increasing the ability to interpret beliefs as information signals for decision-making.

· Learning techniques of beliefs management to better cope with anxiety and stress.

· Increasing our ability to generate Mindful Real Options (MROs), thereby broadening the range of choices and solutions to cope with adversity.

· Developing an intrinsic decision-making mindset more aligned with the recent evidence and developments of the Bayesian view of the brain and computational neuroscience.

Investment required to reap the benefits of this session:

As we start the second segment of the training program with Session 5 (see Figure 4.7 Structural Design of the MBSAT Program in Chapter 4 above), it is good to remind ourselves of the most effective way to learn: short but regular daily training. The demand on your daily schedule is modest: 15-20 minutes a day are sufficient. What is essential, however, is the discipline to practice every day.

The regularity of your practice also facilitates your awareness and capacity to observe throughout the day, when you are engaged in your activities. This way you learn and benefit continuously without additional investment in time.

1 The learning rate refers to increasing the speed and accuracy of recognizing the elements of BETA; this in turn allows for more precision in decision-making and facilitates updating of beliefs.

"With MBSAT I discovered patterns and beliefs that developed in my childhood and solidified later in my life. I became aware that I imposed these beliefs on myself. To deepen my understanding I had a conversation with my mother about my perception of situations in my childhood. It turned out that I remembered some situations much worse than they were in reality. As I can look now at these childhood experiences/memories with the knowledge of today, I have been able to update these patterns/beliefs and this has had an incredibly positive impact on my life in a very short lapse of time."

"We believe that helping others is our true religion and we believe that sitting still in one place doing meditation is not that effective these days."

A nun from the Nepalese Kung Fu Drukpa order

As beliefs drive our actions the credo of the Kung Fu nuns of the Nepalese Drukpa order quoted above in Session 4 is relevant here as well. It is repeated here because it beautifully illustrates the interconnection between beliefs and actions. As mentioned, the engagement of these nuns is a lifeline for many destitute and isolated communities in the Himalayas as they teach, assist patients and help in every possible way.

9.2
Quiz

Session 4: Minding BETA IV – Action Impulses

This voluntary quiz helps you test what you have retained from Session 4 and consolidates your learnings. It also presents you with a synopsis of the essential topics.

1) How does MBSAT conceive actions and action impulses? In a few of your own words, summarize your understanding.

_____

_____

_____

_____

_____

2) What actions help people reduce Free Energy? Choose one of the following:

☐ Positive actions

☐ Negative actions

☐ both

If you choose c, explain why.

_____

_____

_____

_____

_____

3) In Session 4 the Free-Energy Minimizing Actions Quadrants were introduced as a tool. Briefly explain the model and your understanding of the concept.

_____

_____

_____

_____

_____

4) In your view, what is the value of minding actions in people's lives?

_____

_____

_____

_____

5) Which one of the three types of predictions and inference are mainly activated by actions?

- [ ] Interoceptive
- [ ] Exteroceptive
- [ ] Proprioceptive

6) Explain the intention of the CEO of BETA practice and comment shortly on its three steps.

7) Is Mindful Salsa just a fun practice? Write down your own thoughts about this question.

Recommended solutions of the quiz can be found on the companion website: www.wiley.com/go/Young/mbsatworkbook

9.3
Introduction and Concepts

Howard Raiffa (Raiffa, 1993, 2007) was a giant and a pioneer of Decision and Negotiation Analysis, a field he created at the Harvard Business School and at Harvard Kennedy School. As a student, I was fortunate enough to be able to take two graduate-level courses on decision and negotiation analysis with him shortly before he retired. He was also the founding director of the International Institute for Applied Systems Analysis (IIASA) in Vienna. His classes were about helping students develop a probabilistic decision-making mindset; a pioneer Bayesian statistician, he believed that people's beliefs are what shapes their decisions, maintaining that skillful decision-makers should keep sampling the environment until they have enough relevant information within their cost limitation to enable them to update their beliefs and to come up with higher probabilities for good decision outcomes.

From Howard I learned that bad decisions result more often from the decision maker's beliefs and mindset than from the decision-making techniques and processes. For example, in general people prefer the status quo and tend to avoid change because of its challenges. When they are unable to control this bias, their decisions will perpetuate the status quo even when change is needed. In this situation, no decision-making technique can help them.

The fact that Howard's approach and his models of decision analysis had a Bayesian focus facilitated my understanding of the Bayesian Cognitive Neuroscience models that build the theoretical base at the core of MBSAT's practical interventions.

In the first part of the program, the intention has been to train in each session one of the elements of BETA, learning to synchronize all four components and minding their interdependence and joint effects. This is essential to keep the level of Free Energy low and for having a calm and balanced state as a necessary condition to continue the training and advance to the next stage. In this chapter, we begin the second part of the MBSAT protocol. As participants are now able to leverage their trained BETA, they start to develop a strategic mindset that facilitates the renewal and refinement of their recognition and generative models. The combined skills of keeping an equanimous BETA and more precise brain models allow Strategic Awareness to emerge as an advanced capacity that aligns individuals' private and professional experiences optimally with the dynamically changing VUCA environment. Participants learn to optimize their decision-making in pursuit of their worthy goals, enabling desirable outcomes while minimizing Free Energy (decision errors).

Minding BETA is about keeping body sensations, emotions, thoughts, and actions impulses in a relaxed and synchronized state. This is the first and foremost focus of the MBSAT training. Any component of BETA can disturb the interaction of the whole. It is not hard to see how unhelpful thoughts can affect the whole BETA and lead to unnecessary agitation, for example misinterpreting a body sensation such as a headache or stomachache by thinking it must be the symptom of a serious condition. Likewise strong positive feelings of relaxation while drinking wine can produce a range of unwelcome effects from losing control of one's actions to alcohol addiction. Or a few seconds of impulsive action, like shouting at a spouse, an employee or one's children, can cause major tensions in one's family or at work that affect everything and impede minimizing Free Energy.

The second important focus of MBSAT is the training of minding the Portfolio of Beliefs (POB). With the explosion of social media and the proliferation of unreliable data (fake news), the need for well-founded beliefs based on trustworthy facts is greater than ever. Everything that people do in life, every decision is driven by these tiny, invisible engines: beliefs. Burgeoning multidisciplinary interest in understanding the central role of beliefs in people's lives is fast growing, to the point of the emergence of a distinct, multidisciplinary research field called "The science of beliefs".

There is a trend towards polarization in the world as people adopt opposing beliefs and increasingly tend to defend them in acerbic debates, even forming antagonistic camps to the detriment of not only individuals but society as a whole. The academic interest of the scientific community is driven by the understanding that solutions to many personal and societal issues will require a science about how beliefs form and develop as well as how they change or persist.

One of the individuals who participated in the January 2020 storm on the capitol in Washington, USA, and whose pictures wearing a furry headdress and a bullhorn went around the world, was sentenced to 3 years in prison; during the trial, he said: "I admit to the world I was wrong. I have no excuses. My behavior was indefensible... I am truly repentant." It is sad to see a young man jeopardizing his personal future in this way. Certainly, underlying his BETA was a series of beliefs driving his decision and triggering the behavior that he now laments. The reality is that these kinds of misguided behaviors are common; they happen to us all, luckily most of the time in a less dramatic way than in the young man's case. But who has not followed some aberrant belief and later disapproved of it, sometimes too late. One of the goals of the MBSAT training is to help people experience the least possible number of decisions or actions they will regret or must apologize for later. This is why keeping and maintaining an adequate, well-contextualized portfolio of beliefs is so crucial for well-being.

What are beliefs actually, you might ask? Many definitions of beliefs exist. In MBSAT we circumscribe beliefs as they are defined in neuroscience and economic science, namely as subjective probabilities of expectations regarding outcomes or states of the world (Molnar & Loewenstein, 2021). This means that everything we believe might be true or it might not, it depends. One needs to first find evidence for the beliefs. The late Argentine physician and philosopher Jose Ingenieros wrote in his most important work, *The Mediocre Man*, (2004), that beliefs without evidence are prejudices awaiting observations. For him, prejudices are the mark of the mediocre and routinized man afraid of new ideas, lacking tolerance, and being vulgar, not able to conceive excellence for himself and the society. The mediocre man always wants more instead of enough and is unable to recognize the best from the worse.

The following story highlights the subjective nature of beliefs.

Good Thing, Bad thing, Who knows? A Sufi Tale

There was once a farmer who owned a horse and had a son.

One day his horse ran away. The neighbors came to express their concern:

"Oh, that's too bad. How are you going to work the fields now?" The farmer replied: "Good thing, bad thing – who knows?"

In a few days, his horse came back and brought another horse with her. Now, the neighbors were glad: "Oh, how lucky! Now you can do twice as much work as before!" The farmer replied: "Good thing, bad thing – who knows?"

The next day, the farmer's son fell off the new horse and broke his leg. The neighbors were concerned again: "Now that he is incapacitated, he can't help you around the farm, that's too bad." The farmer replied: "Good thing, bad thing – who knows?"

Soon, the news came that a war broke out, and all the young men were required to join the army. The villagers were sad because they knew that many of the young men would not come back. The farmer's son could not be drafted because of his broken leg. His neighbors were envious: "How lucky! You get to keep your only son." The farmer replied: "Good thing, bad thing – who knows?"

Anonymous Sufi Tale

The farmer's story illustrates the circumstantial value of beliefs and adversity; it all depends on the circumstances. When the farmer's horse disappears, everyone believes it is adversity for the farmer; however, the stoic farmer relativizes the bad situation, "Good thing, bad thing, who knows," to later find himself with two horses. The farmer's circumstantial view is one of the elements we seek to cultivate in MBSAT: suspending beliefs, a way of deferring similar to what the Greeks of the Pyrrhonism school called Epoché, which means suspending judgment. For pyrrhonists it is people's dogmas (fixed beliefs) that interfere with finding satisfaction in life.

Once we have learned to be comfortable within states of Epoché (beliefs suspension), the next move is entering in Maieutical questioning, using a method of asking yourself seemingly insignificant questions, in reference to the Maieutikos techniques used in ancient Greece by midwifes to deliver babies (Socrates' mother was a midwife). In analogy, Socrates called his method of asking successively plain, probing maieutic questions, a method he used with his students to uncover unsupported beliefs. It is actually quite similar to the Bayesian approach for updating beliefs which starts from an experience-based hypothesis in the form of a prior belief, then questions the likelihood of that belief with respect to an event, to finally come up with a posterior belief that is a more authentic and factual rendering of the event.

Maintaining an updated portfolio of beliefs plays a key role in our lives to preserve the low levels of Free Energy that support our desire for higher levels of mental and physical fitness.

Above the thread of cognition, affect, motivation, and behavior, is metacognition, the ability to reflect on one's thoughts. Metacognition helps guide people and fosters adaptive behaviors. For example, imagine the following, not uncommon experience: You are late for work and driving under time pressure. In front of you is a dilettante driver, preventing you from accelerating. You sense agitation in your body, feelings of frustration, and drastically negative thoughts toward this person. Nevertheless, you refrain from acting, avoiding the danger of passing the car and abstaining from insulting the person in any way. You are capable of observing your angry thoughts as you mobilize your metacognitive ability to self-regulate your BETA and say to yourself: "It is best to avoid anything that could put this person, me or others in the morning traffic in danger." Despite intensive thoughts and feelings of retaliation, it is possible to exercise agency by activating meta-cognitive abilities.

> Metacognition (Dobson, 2013) is essential for moving from cognitive
> content to cognitive process, that is how one's relates to the experiences.
> It is a core argument to consciously train Active Inference processes.

Active Inference processes combine sensorial, cognitive and behavioral elements and are the mechanism that facilitates maintaining low levels of Free Energy (decision mistakes, surprise, entropy).

9.4
Tools and Models

The following tools and models are essential for Part 2 of the MBSAT training and at the same time of great value for many situations throughout life. It is good to remember to have them handy, when you confront challenges. They are all accompanied by illustrations to support sensorial understanding and visual memory.

9.4.1 Tool 1 - Minding the triad of perception, beliefs and predictions

Have a look at the graphic below, and compare the two scary MBSAT buddies. Which one is larger?

Figure 9.1 Minding our Recognition Models

Before continuing to read please see the answer on page 380.

The graphic presents the classic challenge that all human beings confront: connecting perceptions (whatever is being recognized by the senses) to generative models in the brain that activate beliefs about what could be the causes of the sensations to guide predictions in support of skillful decisions.

In fact, the two scary MBSAT buddies are of exactly identical size, as you can easily convince yourself by looking at the two red lines on page 380. It is the context and the distance that lead to a different perception and make believe that one is large than the other.

The example illustrates the challenge of connecting the triad of perception, belief, and prediction as they are interrelated and influence each other. Wrong perceptions build wrong beliefs leading to wrong predictions. In the same way, faulty beliefs lead to faulty perceptions and to faulty predictions. For example, individuals who believe in male supremacy will perceive women as less talented or less intelligent, which leads to predictions such as "Company XYZ will not make it; the CEO is a woman." It is therefore crucial to mind the triad of perception, belief, and prediction and keeps it well aligned, to support skillful decision-making.

9.4.2 Tool 2 - The MBSAT Stress, Anxiety and Worry (SAW) Model

Stress, anxiety, and worry are typical of today's work and lifestyles. They are a pervasive force in our daily experience and create disturbances in our BETA. One of the most harmful effects is that they also narrow our perception, thus impeding the strategic awareness that we so urgently need in times of VUCA.

The SAW model is a counteracting tool that liberates us from being helpless victims and gives us back autonomy. It has two loops, visualized in Figure 9.2.

The first loop corresponds to the dynamics of the BETA in relation to an actual, difficult situation, for example, marital problems, financial worries, losing a job, health difficulties, or any other problematic situation that comes our way. The loop is set in motion, when we confront a real difficulty and don't know how it could possibly be resolved, a state that generates uncertainty/VUCA leading to worried thoughts and feelings of powerlessness. Buddhists call the impact of the painful situation the first arrow.

The second loop begins when the worried thoughts start to proliferate. The worrying then turns into feelings of fear and increased discomfort, prompting sensations of anxiety. This second loop can be conceived of as a meta loop generated by "worries over worries". At this point, the BETA is out of control and the two loops are now connected in an endless spiral of worry, anxiety and stress. Buddhists will call this phase of "worry over worries" the second arrow.

The training of MBSAT is to concentrate mental and physical efforts on the second, self-generated meta-loop. This is where we have some personal control, whereas in the first loop we have little influence, at least in the short term. If one gets a bad job report for example, there is not much that can be

MBSAT Stress, Anxiety and Worry (SAW) Model

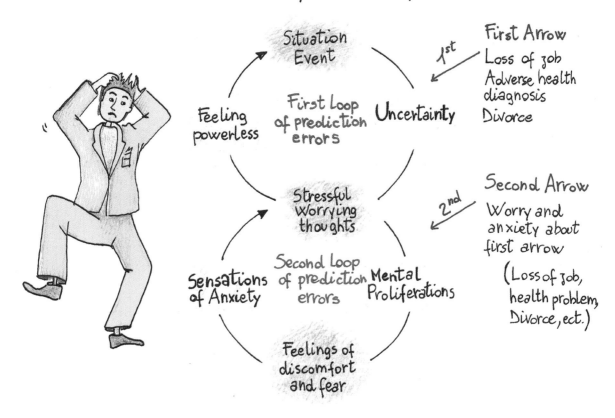

Figure 9.2 MBSAT Stress, Anxiety and Worry (SAW) Model

done other than increasing the performance to get a better evaluation next year. What we can do in the meantime is to mind our BETA with respect to the bad outcome, in order to maintain our vitality and prevent us from falling into the second loop that could affect our mental health, erode our capacity to rebound and worsen the original problem.

The SAW model helps us become aware of avoidable, detrimental worrying and focus our efforts on the primary issue in a more constructive way.

> *"I was climbing a difficult route in the Alps with a friend.*
> *As I'm not as fit as I used to be, I was worried and noticed how my*
> *worries and fears were blocking me. My grip and movements were*
> *insecure. A short CEO-BETA exercise was able to calm me and*
> *I became aware of the Second Arrow. The obvious dangers of the route,*
> *the First Arrow, were clear and given. For the Second Arrow, it was*
> *I who was responsible. Its paralyzing effect could have fatal*
> *consequences. I experienced once again how important it is to deal*
> *with my worries and fears. Which is the First Arrow,*
> *which is the Second? What blocks me?*
> *These are essential questions."*

9.4.3 Tool 3 - Bayesian Questioning and Reframing (BQR)

In my last job some of my colleagues tried to undermine our profit center with the argument that not being Swiss I couldn't possibly represent the bank with the clients. "The clients come to our bank expecting to find Swiss bankers, not foreign bankers," they argued. Yet after a while, I started to get invitations from some of the same colleagues to join them in meetings with their clients. "Strange," I thought, "what is happening?" As I later learned the clients themselves requested my colleagues to include me. Intrigued, I asked some of them why they insisted on my participation. They told me they were surprised to see a person who was not Swiss running an important department. They thought this was unusual at the time and concluded that I had to be exceptionally competent, unknowingly adopting a kind of reasoning advocated by Taleb (2018).

This is a sort of light Bayesian thinking, finding the evidence for a surprising event. I explained to the clients that it had nothing to do with exceptional intelligence, but with lots of hard work to deliver exceptional performance. It was the simple realization that outsiders in a group must double their efforts to succeed. The first female President of the European Commission, Ursula von der Leyen, was also very conscious of this reality. When asked in a recent interview, what it took her to succeed, she answered that as a woman she knew she would have many barriers to overcome and therefore needed to work harder than everybody else and deliver above-average performance.

Bayesian Questioning and Reframing (BQR) is essentially about developing a mindset that interprets perceptions as hypotheses, learning to ask common sense yet rational and relevant questions. Most importantly, it is about finding novel interpretations of events in accordance with fresh evidence. This allows us to update beliefs about the causes of events, thus increasing the precision level of one's triad of perception, beliefs, and predictions. It is not about explicit Bayesian calculations but about the ability to minimize long-term prediction errors. (Hohwy, 2018).

In Chapter 3, there is a section dedicated to the concept of transparency and opacity. The essence of the concept is that transparent phenomena are invisible to us, as we see through them and therefore are unable to become aware of them. This is the case with most phenomena in our daily life, meaning that we are conscious of what our BETA is experiencing, but not of the process of how the experience is constructed. For example, we might experience feeling, thoughts, and actions of bigotry; however not the process of how these experiences are constructed. Paradoxically, understanding the construction process of experiences requires adding opacity to our conditioned, transparent BETA. The tool of Bayesian Questioning and Reframing (BQR) is designed as a cognitive method facilitating the opacity creation process by using questioning to make opaque the otherwise transparent conditioned beliefs and biases we have, thus in effect opening the possibility for updating the beliefs. Clearly, beliefs cannot be updated unless we become aware of how they were formed in the past and came about.

A precondition for BQR is a calm, well-synchronized BETA that facilitates entering and staying in a state of suspending opinions, prejudgments, prejudices, and any form of ex-ante fix beliefs. In certain

Eastern philosophical and spiritual traditions this state is called "Choiceless Awareness". In Greek phi-losophy, the term used is Epoché Awareness States (EAS). From the basis of EAS, the next step is to engage in an Active Inference process using BQR to gather evidence for what could be possible causes of the situation. The process is similar to what the clients did when they were surprised to see a non-Swiss person managing a large department at UBS's head office in Zurich, Switzerland, suspending judgment while investigating what the causes could be. In this phase, an efficient way to enhance the opacity, and thus awareness, is to use abductive thinking by formulating simple, ingenuous questions without expecting definitive answers. This stimulates an ongoing inquiry process that gets closer to the possible causes of events.

You may want to check Chapter 1 Section 1.3 at this point for a more detailed discussion of a Bayes-ian Questioning mindset. The figure presented in Section 1.3 is repeated here for ease of reference as Figure 9.3.

Figure 9.3 Bayesian Questioning Mindset in MBSAT

9.4.4 Tool 4 - Minding Real Options in MBSAT

The essence of minding options in MBSAT is twofold. Building options implies keeping reactivity in check and abstaining from following blindly our conditioned patterns; at the same time, it is also a practical and valuable tool to reduce anxiety and proliferating worries. Creating options prevents feelings of helplessness and facilitates solutions.

It is about building choices. In finance, the concept of real options has the meaning of investing resources in stages in order to gain more information over time and make better-informed decisions on whether to keep investing or to disinvest, if the conditions are not propitious for a full commitment. Firms in businesses with high uncertainty have been using this approach for years, for example in mineral exploration activities.

In MBSAT, the training is designed to assist people to build more choices in their life. As Figure 9.4 suggests, a strategically aware mind is able to minimize Free Energy with the help of an equanimous, allowing attitude that enables building fresh choices, even the choice to refrain from responding at all instead of reacting impulsively.

Here the term "real" has the meaning of "genuine" or "practical": Minding Real Options in MBSAT is about creating actual possibilities in real life for more flourishing and well-being.

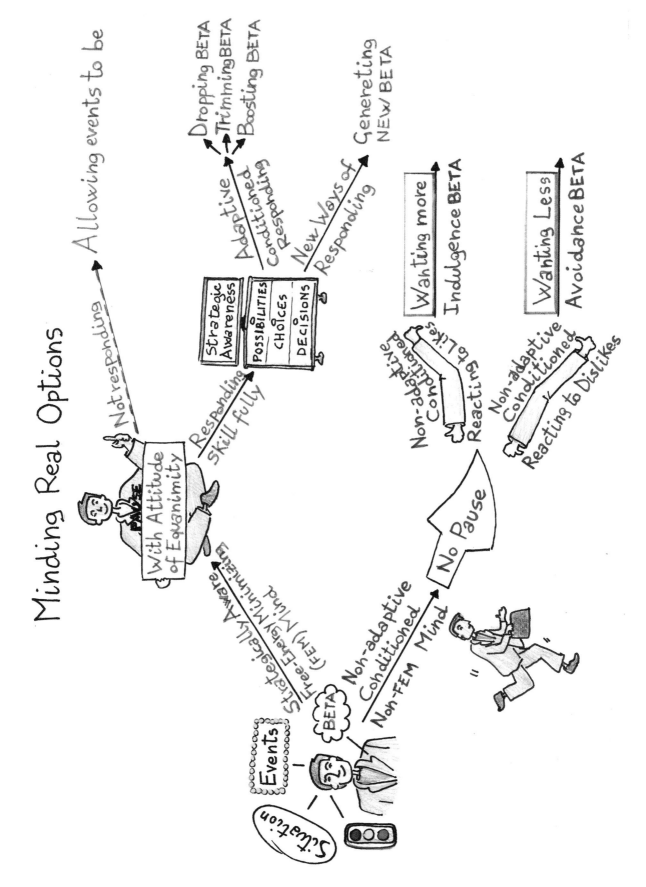

Figure 9.4 Minding Real Options

9.5
Practices

9.5.1 Practice 1 - Minding Adversity - Irimi

This practice is inspired by a technique called Irimi in Aikido, a traditional Japanese martial art focusing on minimizing violence by blocking and disabling an aggressive attacker using the attacker's own momentum. The intention is not to inflict harm but to stop the adversary. Aikido is a defensive system that allows a practitioner to manage an aggressive situation and let things cool down.

The principle is straightforward. In an attack there is energy. It is adversarial, negative energy. The point is to turn this energy around and convert it into a neutral force. By focusing on keeping your balance, being centered, and understanding other people's moves, Aikido is a study of wisdom based on commonsense and mastery of the body.

Ursula Sensei, my Aikido teacher, used to say that the value and practicality of Irimi are easy to see. "After all," she would explain, "most people apply it intuitively when walking in the street. When someone comes toward you on the sidewalk, you don't back off. You continue walking in the direction of the other person and just before you bump into each other, one of you or both move aside to avoid a collision. Then you both continue your path. Well, that is a form of Irimi."

The Irimi meditation practice is built around the Aikido principle of moving into the realm of adversity instead of away from it when you are confronted with an objectively difficult situation, the so-called first arrow, and with the self-generated emotional and mental difficulties of the second arrow (Figure 9.2 above). In the framework of MBSAT both are considered to be bundles of free energy (negative). Participants are invited to blend their positive energy with these difficulties to create a generative, unifying force by remaining open-minded and balanced, maintaining an attitude of equanimity and epistemic curiosity towards the difficulties, and being ready to learn and build real options for solutions.

There are two steps for Irimi meditation. In the first step, we recollect ourselves to find a state of openness that we called above in Tool 3 "Choiceless Awareness" or state of Epoché. With this regained poise, we then move into considering the situation with equanimity and start developing options.

Step 1: Moving to Epoché Awareness States (EAS)

We begin by finding a posture that is composed and relaxed at the same time. If you are seated align the head and neck, with the chin slightly inclined towards the chest. Place the hands where it feels comfortable, in your lap or on your knees. Feeling the contact with the chair or the support of the floor or bed, where you might be resting.

Now, begin to focus on your breath, with no need to create a particular breathing rhythm. Simply following the experience of inhaling and exhaling, maybe choosing a place where it is easy for you to focus on the breathing process, whether it is the nostrils, the throat, the chest, or the belly.

After a few moments of breathing quietly, we begin to observe the BETA, starting where it is most convenient for you at this moment. It could be an impulse, an emotion or a thought. Then continue to complete the cycle of the four components of the BETA.

At this point, we reverse the sequence of the practice, starting now to observe from the last BETA component and proceeding sequentially toward the element with which you started the practice.

Staying here for a few moments following the breath before moving to the second part of the practice.

Step 2: Practicing Bayesian Questioning and Reframing (BQR)

Now we recall an event or situation that is creating some difficulty, it could be for instance a relational issue at the office, in your family or in social life (with friends, extended family, etc.). As an example let us imagine that you are the female manager of a known business in your town. After work, you like to go to a restaurant that serves your favorite pizza, but there is this male waiter who treats you in an unfriendly way.

Next, we focus on **uncovering beliefs and hypotheses about the causes of the event**, seeing if it is possible to go behind the event as if going backstage in a theater and finding out what beliefs may be driving the dynamics of the situation. In the fictitious example, you might believe that the man is chauvinist and dislikes women in power positions.

Then we try to **find evidence for your hypothesis**; in the example case, you could ask yourself, whether the waiter is rude only to you or to all female guests. You could also try to observe, whether he is particularly attentive to men; if that were the case, there could be another explanation for this behavior. **Build also additional hypotheses**. Could it be perhaps that the waiter actually likes serving men, because in his experience they tip more generously than women?

Moving now into counterfactual thinking, we search for **evidence of the opposite** of our original belief and hypothesis. In the example of the waiter, the argument and counterargument could unfold as follows. Let's say you have observed that the waiter is indeed nice to most patrons, women and men. So, you have concluded that the issue must be with you; indeed your belief is that he doesn't like you. Now, imagine the opposite, namely that he likes you and feels attracted to you. However, he is aware that he is serving you and that you are the executive of a reputable business in town. This makes him feel uneasy and frustrated as he views it as unrealistic to establish a relationship with you. So, he expresses his disillusionment and frustration by annoying you every time you come to the restaurant, somehow hoping that eventually, you might give up and not return, sparing him the frustration.

Still absorbed in meditation you decide whether **you want to test the new belief and hypothesis** or refrain from it. A test could be that on your next visit to the restaurant you make a gentle, genuine remark to the waiter, for example on any pleasant characteristic you can spot (every person has nice attributes). Maybe you notice his stylish haircut and comment on it or involve him in some friendly small talk. A small gesture or gentle remark could then be the opener for finding more realistic evidence for beliefs about a difficult relationship and clear the way for a more agreeable working relationship.

The Irimi practice doesn't need to be long; about 15 minutes is a good rule of thumb. What is most effective and rewarding is repeated practice on the same difficulty, to keep refining the causes. Although it is possible in principle to gain enough data in a single sitting to be able to update and reframe a hypothesis and belief, a more likely scenario is a gradual updating of beliefs as searching for evidence and making sense of the findings often requires time.

The main benefit of this practice is training the ability to self-questioning our beliefs and hypotheses. It is a powerful tool for increased flourishing. Cognitive behavioral therapists use this type of approach to help individuals with depression and psychosis to update and reframe their aberrant core beliefs (beliefs such as I am useless, I will never find love in my life, everyone is against me, etc.). But this practice is just as important in normal life. In Eastern psychology and in Positive Psychology techniques similar approaches are used to help people improve conditions in their lives and foster well-being. In this context, the practice of self-questioning is called analytical meditation or, more traditionally, Vipassana meditation.

Figure 9.6 illustrates the concept of Irimi. The Aikidoka master enters the room full of problems courageously, grabs the issues, and flips them over, transforming them effectively into new possibilities. This is a form of Minding Real Options (Figure 9.5 above) by creating fresh perspectives. It is also an excellent strategy to minimize Free Energy.

9.5.2 Practice 2 - Reframing and recalibrating for belief updating

The belief-reframing practice seeks to assist individuals to recalibrate and update their beliefs. This practice can also be implemented as a structured tool whenever you need to reframe non-adaptive automatic beliefs that are often unconscious. Negative Automatic Beliefs (NAB), reflect the patterns of our conditioning, and dominate and shape our BETA, often producing unskillful reactions and decisions.

The process of reframing beliefs about adversity is illustrated in Figure 9.5.

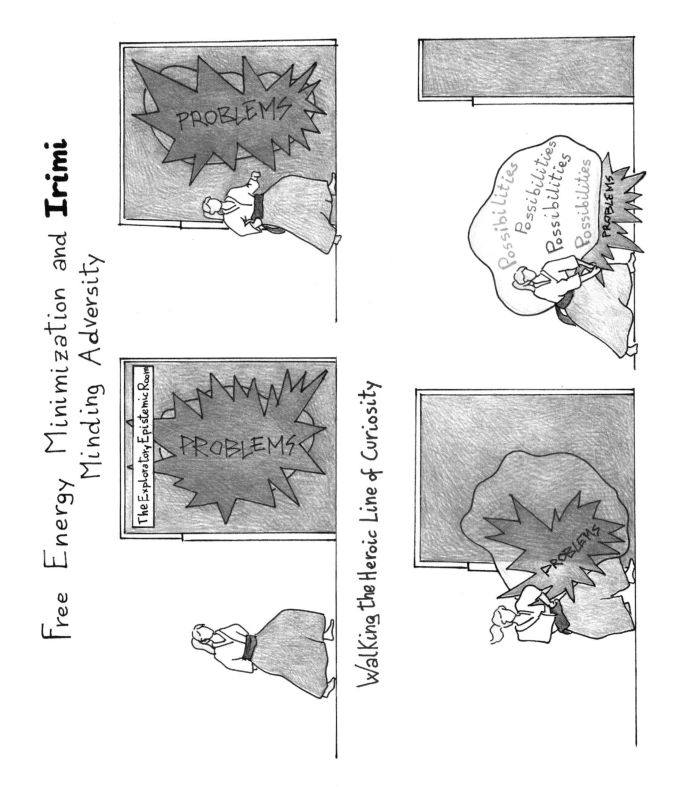

Figure 9.5 Free Energy Minimization and Irimi: Minding Adversity

The practice consists of several steps:

Step 1: Identifying an event

As objectively as you can, describe an event that has generated an undesirable BETA for you.

Once the situation is clearly present in your mind, catch the state of the BETA generated by the situation. You can begin with any element of the BETA you are able to easily observe; it could be an emotion, a body sensation, a thought, or an impulse for action. Then move to the following components of BETA until you vividly sense the state of all four elements.

Step 2: Identifying the underlying belief

Next, go deeper into the causes of your experience and start to uncover the beliefs driving your BETA during the event as originally occurred.

Begin by observing more in detail each component of BETA, asking yourself questions about the origin of the sensations, emotions, thoughts or actions, and impulses. For example, suppose you are upset at your older daughter because you have discovered that she is in secret actively messaging with someone. You suspect it is a boyfriend and feel hurt, as you believe it shows that your daughter has not sufficient trust in you to talk about a relationship obviously so important to her.

Step 3: Probing the validity of the belief

Now start asking simple, seemingly obvious questions to check the validity of your belief. You can begin by asking questions about the circumstances or the objectivity of your observations.

Remember to use an abductive inquiry approach (formulating a new hypothesis without necessary evidence, you are just probing. Thinking like an artist: "What would my belief be if…".) In the situation mentioned above, you as a parent could ask yourself: Is our daughter always messaging in secret or only with prospective boyfriends? When I was her age, did I tell my beloved parents everything? Is secretive messaging an unmistakable sign of lack of trust?

Step 4: Reframing the event: swapping beliefs

Now reframe the event with a **"belief swap"**[2], replacing your belief with a new one based on a more adaptive interpretation, and observe the consequences of the swap on the quality of your BETA. Following the same example, you as a parent might come to the conclusion that the need for some privacy is a natural phase of growing up. So you could swap your prior belief: "Secretive messaging is a sign of lack of trust" with the new belief: "Secretive messaging at this age is a sign of healthy psychological development."

---

2   Session 3 above introduced the Thought Swap Exercise (TSE). The same approach is applied here to beliefs.

Step 5: Optional follow-up

This step is about acting from a more calm and relaxed BETA, supported by more flexible beliefs able to generate real options for responding. In the example above, the parent will find an appropriate moment to say to the daughter: "I noticed that for the last two weeks you have been texting more actively than normal. Maybe there is something I can help with if one of your friends has an issue or you have some difficulty yourself. Remember, I am here for you, ok?"

9.5.3 Practice 3 - Continuous-time practice: CEO of BETA for Minding Adversity and Worry (MAW)

This short, informal practice is designed to help you switch from a worrying mode to a calmer mode and get out of a worry automatic pilot. Like the basic CEO of BETA, you can apply it anywhere on the go, when you feel an urgent need. You can also repeat it during the day, when you are in a situation that causes you persistent worries.

Like the basic CEO of BETA, the CEO of Minding Adversity and Worry has three steps. The difference from the generic CEO of BETA is that the first step introduces a concrete worry as a focal point by suggesting that practitioners identify and label what is worrying them, for example, saying to themselves: "I worry about my job" or "I worry about my relationship with X." This contains the problem by shifting from an overwhelming feeling of worry to a specific issue.

In the second step awareness is shifted to the breath as in the regular CEO of BETA, but with a slight variation. The idea is to start counting in- and out-breaths or alternatively to silently repeat the words: "Exhaling, inhaling, exhaling." This is a strategy to focus the attention on the counting, away from worrying thoughts. The mind has a hard time to count breaths and worry about issues at the same time, especially if your intention is to create a respite from worries.

Step 3 is similar to the basic form of CEO of BETA. What is important in the last step of this version is to create a sense of new possibilities, the antidote to the feeling of helplessness created by the worries.

Here are some practical guidelines for the practice:

Step 1: Catching the BETA

Start directing your attention to your present inner experiences, becoming aware of your BETA. Just notice and acknowledge you find. Whatever you observe is already there. Then try to identify what you worry about. You might ask yourself: What bleak scenarios are bothering me? What gloomy predictions bog me down? Then put your worry into words, for example: "I worry about my job" or "I worry about my relationship with X," "I worry about being late," and so on. Try to be as specific as you can. If it is something about your job that worries you, try to define it precisely: Maybe an upcoming review? Or the latest changes in the organization? This process is called labeling. Giving your worry a name facilitates decentering and helps you calm the mind.

Step 2: Evening out the BETA

Now shifting your awareness to the breath and moving into Epoché, suspending all beliefs about the worry, simply following the natural rhythm of breathing. (For an explanation of Epoché, see Section 9.3 Introduction and Concepts). Maybe counting silently each breath: in 1, out 1— in 2, out 2, and so on. When you reach 5 restart again: in 1, out 1, etc. If you find the counting annoying or distracting, you may silently repeat the words: inhaling, exhaling, inhaling, etc.

Step 3: Expanding the BETA

When you are ready, expand your awareness to your whole body, noticing your sensations, your posture, and facial expression. Then imaging yourself going into a room of possibilities, maybe bringing the image of the aikidoka expert lady of Figure 9.6 above to your mind, moving like her into a room of fresh possibilities as you resume your daily activities.

The benefits of the CEO of BETA for Minding Adversity and Worry are manifold:

- The practice helps to switch from a worrying mode to a calmer mode and allows the practitioner to get out of a worry automatic pilot.

- It helps to step back from the moment and to look at worry as an external phenomenon.

- Perceiving worry thoughts as mental events leads to a sense of relief.

- The practice also changes the time orientation of our thoughts and shifts them from worrying about the future to dealing with them in the present.

- The CEO of BETA on Worry helps to momentarily recalibrate and rebalance the agitated BETA.

- The reframed BETA after the practice brings a sense of possibilities and options.

9.6
Learnings from Session 5

In this session, we learn to use a generic Active Inference model for updating beliefs using Bayesian Questioning and Reframing.

Based on the MBSAT Stress, Anxiety and Worry Model we learned to separate the objective element, the real reason for a worry (loss of job, divorce, bad health diagnosis, etc.) from mental proliferations at a metacognitive level, that is the worry about the worry.

The practices of the session are not designed to eliminate difficulties, but to learn how to relate with an open mindset to whatever difficulty we may experience and how to reduce vulnerability to worries and anxiety. By containing worries and rebalancing BETA, space for new possibilities is created and fresh perspectives can emerge.

- The practices of the session enable one to approach difficulties with a sense of allowing and curiosity instead of aversion and judgment.

- We come to understand that worries are patterns of the mind. Looking at worry as another mental pattern helps develop a spacious quality of the mind.

- Focusing on the body allows us to disengage from complex worrying thoughts.

- Irimi reinforces the way we relate emotions and thoughts to body sensations.

9.7
Action Plan (AP)
for the Week of Session 5

The home practice for the fifth week should not take more than 15-20 minutes as in the previous sessions. The most important objective is that you practice every day.

- On the first day begin with Practice 1, Minding Adversity – Irimi.

- The following day do the same. Irimi is an important and very valuable practice in our difficult times. Remember to write down your observations.

- On the third day and fourth day do Practice 2, Reframing and recalibrating for belief updating.

- On day 5, incorporate the CEO of BETA on Minding Adversity and Worry during the day in addition to either Practice 1 or 2 (your choice).

- Keep following up on the requests for your Free Energy Minimizer Self (FEMS) that you initiated in Session 2. If you haven't yet received responses from your contacts, it is time to politely insist, so you are prepared for formulating your strategic plan in Session 8.

- Every day after finishing the practices, jot down a few comments and reflections in your diary or use the space provided below.

9.8
Personal Notes and Insights
The Writing Space for Your Experiences and Observations

Example:

While practicing Irimi I got agitated on the first day. On the second day I used the same

issue for the practice and this time I finished in good spirits, confident that eventually,

I will find a good solution.

Box 9.1

<u>Two Essential Lifelines: Inner Equilibrium and Attunement to the Outer World</u>

In the first part of the training program (Sessions 1-4), the primary focus has been on realizing a basic inner equilibrium: increased calmness and higher levels of coherence between body sensations, emotions, thoughts and actions impulses - BETA. A well-equilibrated, harmonic BETA is a prerequisite for a flourishing life.

To realize the required synchronization of BETA, we have been working on refining our recognition models and honing the precision of our internal perceptual processes, recognizing more accurately the meaning and significance of signals in our internal milieu. The implicit question driving this part of the training has been: "How can I mind my BETA?" Applying the corresponding practices persistently and within their context is the answer. For example, using the CEO of BETA before a critical event reduces stress, restores calmness and ensures better outcomes.

Here in Session 5, we have initiated the second part of the training program (Sessions 5-8). In this part, the focus is on realizing equilibrium in synchronization with the external environment. This means expanding the focus of the training to incorporate the environment in all its manifestations: family, social relationships, work, leisure, and any other conceivable aspect of our interactions with the external environment.

The focus here is on learning to update the generative models of our brains to capture the surrounding reality more precisely, as accurate information processing is the essence of skillful decision-making. The question driving this part of the training is: "How can I increase the precision of my beliefs that drive my generative models of reality?" The beliefs driving our generative models may be reliable or on the contrary misleading concerning our perceived reality.

Applying the practices of the second part of the training program will assist you in developing a mindset firmly rooted in abductive inquiry and Bayesian information processing, two capabilities that allow you to update beliefs even in the face of incomplete information. The practices are designed based on insights from two main sources: Karl Friston's active inference process and the Bayesian approach to decision-making by Howard Raiffa, the eminent scientist of decision theory. They form the base for the practices in this second part. Amongst others, they enable forming subjective probabilities to come up with some kind of measurement of uncertainty ("I think the chances of getting this job is 70%"), thus allowing to better handle difficult situations. They also help plan personal preferences concerning desirable utility outcomes. ("It would be wonderful to get this job; if not, I think I can live with the one I have. Then, I will try to reduce my work load and have more free time for other activities that interest me.")

At Harvard, after reading a case, the instructor routinely asked: "What should the manager do in this situation?" and the students always launched many different, often contradicting answers. Ending the debate, the instructor used to say: "In fact there is no right or wrong answer."

There are no easy, clear-cut answers in life. The main goal is to develop a questioning mind-set to explore different possibilities and develop options. In his Bayesian style, Howard Raiffa sometimes said: "Think about what additional information you need to increase your confidence level regarding what you are deciding."

With the practices of MBSAT's second part of training (provided they are executed with a balanced BETA) your mindset becomes fitter for the challenges of our VUCA world. As a consequence, decisions in life will become more skillful and Free Energy in the form of adverse side effects of poor decisions will decrease. Stress will diminish and satisfaction in life rise.

MINDING THE PORTFOLIO OF BELIEFS II

Minding Beliefs About Money

10.1
Getting Started
Task of Session 6, Investment and Benefits

Task of Session 6:

Training to recognize and update economically and financially driven beliefs for sustainable mental health and well-being.

Training to become aware of the influence of economically and financially driven beliefs on decision-making and training to regulate the impact.

Increasing the precision of predictions in order to reduce the incidence of prediction errors of financially and economically motivated decisions.

Training the learning rate[1] of the economically and financially based generative models and updating of beliefs for skillful decision making.

Expected benefits of this session and corresponding practices are:

- Understanding the effects of money on people's BETA based on research and evidence-based information.
- Learning to debias unhelpful priors (beliefs and biases) about Powerful Money (POMO).
- Learning to build posterior beliefs (after checking evidence) and new priors (updated beliefs) about Mindful Money (MIMO).
- Improving the ability to formulate predictions about money issues that enable minimizing Free Energy and making skillful decisions that generate BETAs for sustainable well-being.

Investment required to reap the benefits of this session:

- Time required for reading the material: less than 3% of your awake time on a normal day, equivalent to approximately 30 minutes (depending on you reading skills).

- Time required for home practice: On average about 1.5% of your awake time or 15 minutes per day.

---

1 The learning rate refers to improving the speed, precision and accuracy for updating beliefs.

"I have grown up in a modest family and my parents were struggling to make ends meet. Being able to go to school and buying the school materials was quite an effort. Anything extra was out of reach. It is still hard for me to remember those times. It just dawned on me during this practice that this is why I'm now so generous with my own kids and give them all they want."

"My childhood was similar. My parents had to be very thrifty to keep our family afloat. I think I learned many valuable lessons from living with modest means. Therefore, I'm actually quite strict with my own kids, although I could afford to spoil them. I want them to be aware that our current comfortable lifestyle is by no means granted."

10.2
Quiz

Session 5: Minding the Portfolio of Beliefs I - Minding Adversity

The quiz is optional and should be entertaining, a kind of fitness for your mind, it is simply an invitation to reflect on your learning from Session 5.

1) What is MBSAT's approach to dealing with adversity and can you describe what is somewhat counterintuitive about it?

_____

_____

_____

_____

_____

2) What is the MBSAT signature practice to tackle adversity?

_____

_____

_____

_____

_____

3) What are beliefs and what is their function according to the MBSAT protocol?

_____

_____

_____

_____

_____

4) In MBSAT we use the Bayesian Maieutic Questioning and Reframing (BMQR) method to find alternative explanations to our beliefs. Explain this approach.

_____

_____

_____

_____

_____

5) Briefly describe what we call the challenging triad in MBSAT.

6) Explain the MBSAT SAW model (Stress, Anxiety and Worry Model).

7) What do we mean in MBSAT by "Mindful Real Options"?

10.3
Introduction and Concepts

In this chapter, we tackle a challenging issue: people's relationship with money. It is a contentious theme because every person has privately held beliefs about money. Money is at the source of many predicaments in contemporary societies; either the lack of it or its abundance. For some individuals, money is the reason for their existence and their overriding motivation in their lives, which is the manifestation of Powerful Money (POMO), the dominance of economic and financial incentives. Within the MBSAT protocol, money takes on an important significance, because without having a reliable understanding of the role money plays in our lives it is hard to improve the quality of our decisions. Unprecise economic and financial beliefs will drive generative models, thus creating flawed related predictions that cannot help people achieve higher levels of authentic well-being.

Manfred Kets de Vries, a business school professor at INSEAD and one of the world's foremost authorities on the psychology of top executives, who has spent decades studying and researching the minds of executives and leaders at the top of the compensation pyramid writes about his findings:

> *"Having met many very wealthy individuals, I have come to realize that being wealthy has its own problems. Far too often, money comes to possess the person as opposed to the person possessing the money. Ironically, instead of gaining greater satisfaction through wealth, many people find that the acquisition and possession of money creates an even greater state of dissatisfaction. (Kets de Vries, 2007, p. 232)"*

Having spent most of my professional life around very wealthy individuals, I also have observed the behaviors Professor Kets de Vries alludes to. It is paradoxical, as one could assume that having reached higher levels of material wealth, people would be free to pursue what really makes them happy. But instead, money becomes the dominant core in many people's lives. Money becomes POMO: powerful Money, a reinforcer that elicits and drives their BETA. Under POMO money loses its unconditioned quality as a means to sustain one's life that drives most people's natural BETAs. On the contrary, under POMO, money becomes a conditioned reinforcer that leads people to increase the behaviors of their

BETA for the ultimate goal of money and wealth acquisition, very similar to the behaviors that are observed in people with addictions to substances. However, on the other hand, having also worked and lived in very poor countries I have seen people with very scarce resources still being able to fully enjoy their lives within their material limitations.

The model in Figure 10.1 seeks to explain the dynamics of money accumulation: how we can easily get into a spiral of wanting more and more, craving for always greater wealth, but also how we can liberate ourselves from these driving forces by simply being content and experiencing satiation.

The dynamics of the model start with **Loop 1**, where a person at a young age experiences scarcity in the BETA due to lack of money, which invariably leads to comparing with others (peers, neighbors, etc.), exacerbating the state of unhappiness.

The unhappy BETA leads to increased attachment to money and a drive to accumulate wealth in order to prevent states of lacking, creating **Loop 2**.

At some point one can possibly experience a satiated BETA, allowing one to exit from the spiral with a content BETA (an attitude inspired by MIMO – Mindful Money), thus landing in **Loop 3** with feelings, thoughts, and sensations of contentment.

However, many get sucked into the vortex of accumulation or succumb to the treadmill effect, never quite pleased with what they have no matter how much they already possess (Figure 10.3). As Arthur Schopenhauer (2016) wrote: "Wealth is like water, the more we drink the thirster we become." This unquenchable aspiration leads to the addictive **Loop 4**, where individuals are so dominated by their money beliefs that they become prisoners to the master of powerful money (POMO).

> "There is a paradox at the heart of our lives. Most people want income and strive for it. Yet as Western societies have got richer, their people have become no happier."
>
> Richard Layard (2005, p.3)

Before we move to the practical training of this session, here is a synopsis of money from the perspective of behavioral economics and the economics of happiness, followed by some insights from computational neuroscience.

R. Easterlin (Easterlin et al., 2010) was one of the first social scientists to study the effects of money on happiness. His study revealed that despite the increased level of income of the past decades, people in general were not happier. This suggested that the link between money and happiness is at least to some degree paradoxical, given that the general consensus is that more money will increase the level of happiness. This phenomenon is called the Easterlin happiness-income paradox. In a more recent study, two Nobel prize winners, D. Kahneman and A. Deaton (2010), found that an increase in income actually does increase life satisfaction; however, it doesn't improve emotional well-being. This suggests a more

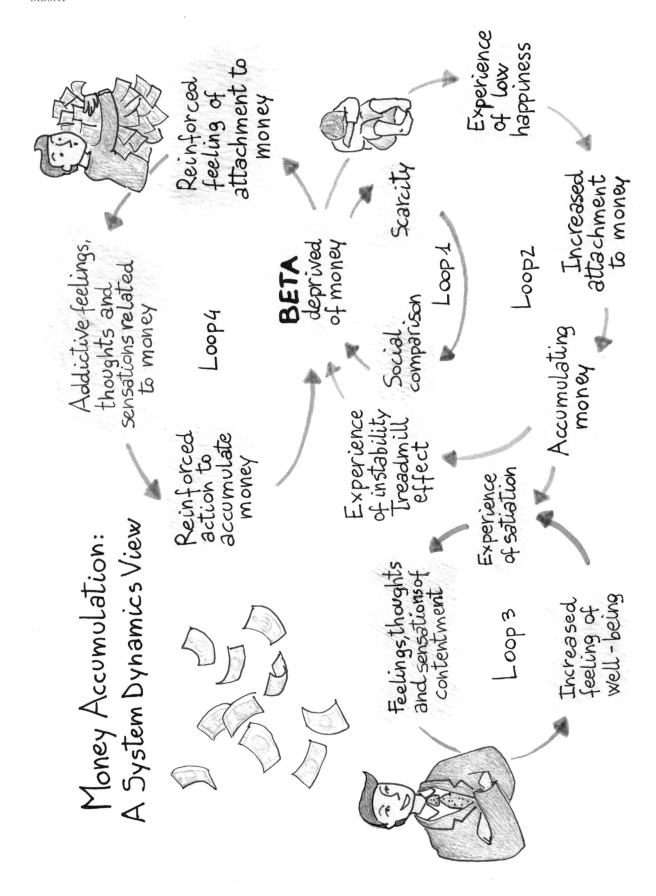

Figure 10.1 Money Accumulation: A System Dynamics View

complex happiness construct. According to this more differentiated notion of happiness a person can be satisfied with her life, when she reasons about it and accepts that her material life is secure, while living in a highly competitive society. In comparison, another person living in a more congenial society might feel subjectively happier despite lacking material goods.

For positive psychologists higher levels of well-being or happiness are achievable when finding a balance between the two mentioned interpretations of well-being: a material- based, evaluative, cognitive view and an emotional-based interpretation driven by sensations and feelings of well-being, what the Eastern philosophies, and especially Buddhist Psychology, define as Vedana or feeling tone. In MBSAT the approach suggested is for finding a balance between a material, rationally based orientation and an emotional, feeling-based approach and integrating these two aspects of well-being into a robust and sustainable view of well-being.

The latest findings in neuroscience offer additional insights into the intricate effects of money on feelings.

"When I reflect on my professional career, I realize that it has been a race to capture the same feelings of happiness I had many years ago, when you granted me my first compensation bonus of 3,000 CHF. Today as Managing Director of one of the largest banks in the world, I am still waiting to have the same feelings despite the fact that my bonuses today are in the higher 6 digits and occasionally in the lower 7 digits." This comment stems from a participant in a MBSAT course who was a collaborator in my department at UBS. He still vividly remembers his experience upon receiving the bonus I offered him as a younger man at end of his first year working with us. In his own words, he still has not been able to recapture the deep feelings of happiness he felt back then upon receiving a fraction of what he now earns, despite the large amount of money he currently makes.

What is happening here? Actually, with his first bonus, my ex-collaborator received a stimulus in the form of an unexpected reward and experienced an intensive gratification that is equivalent to strong feelings of liking. This condition activates the brain liking circuit in the brain, which are small hotspots that react to opioid-like stimulations. In contrast, with his later bonuses, what has been activated in the brain is the circuit of "wanting" that drives the motivation to get a reward (the bonuses) involving neurochemical agents such as dopamine.

The activation of these two different systems offers a plausible explanation of the prediction error that striving for higher bonuses will result in higher levels of well-being.

> *"Wanting to understand is wisdom,*
> *wanting a result is greed."*
> Sayadaw Tejania (2016)

10.4
Exercises

10.4.1 Exercise 1 - The work vs. recreation exercise

Introduction:

This exercise involves decisions about how people invest their personal energy. For didactical purposes, the exercise design contains some over-simplifications; however, its main purpose is to highlight essential choices people make about how to allocate the most important resource they have: their time, and to reflect on how they experience their BETAs as a result of these choices.

Simplifications:

- The exercise assumes that participants have only two choices about how to allocate their time: either for making money or for non-working activities (family, sports, hobbies, music, learning a new skill or expanding personal knowledge in other ways, going to classes after work or getting a degree in a subject of special interest, unrelated to work or career, maybe the history of arts, culture, ethnology, etc. The time required for sleeping, eating and the like is included in non-economic activities, i.e. the choices concern allocating the time and resources remaining after accommodating physiological necessities.

- The exercise assumes a direct link between the two variables: thus, investing more time and energy to earn money reduces the time and energy available for non-working activities.

- The model assumes an aspiration line/budget constraint that limits the activities and time choices; the aspiration line could be moved but with some psychological costs (worries, anxieties, etc.) and repercussions on physical health.

Experimenting with opportunity costs and trade-offs

Step 1: Defining aspirations

On Figure 10.1, "Work and Money: Opportunity Costs and Trade-offs", the vertical axis represents non-working activities and time, which also stands for subjective well-being, the horizontal axis money earning activities. The slanting line represents your aspiration line, which operates similar to a budget constraint, meaning there are limits to time and activities. In the example, a person starts with a salary of W/M1. Given the current slope of the aspiration/budget line, this allows non-monetary activities (spending time with family, vacation, sports, etc.) at the level of SW1, also representing a certain level of well-being. If the person dedicates more time and activities to making money, the level of income, salary, or profit (whatever the measure is) increases from W/M1 to W/M2. However, the time and activities available for other activities, hence the subjective well-being, represented on the vertical axis drops from SW1 to SW2 as the person naturally will have fewer resources for non-money earning time and activities.

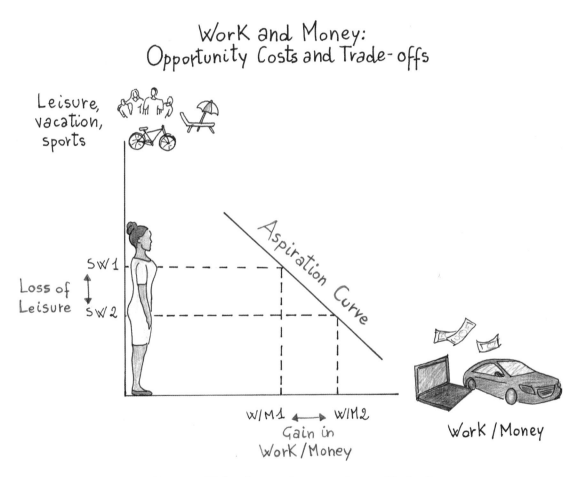

Figure 10.2 Work and Money: Opportunity Costs and Trade-offs

Now, take a blank piece of paper and draw a similar graphic, just marking the vertical and horizontal lines.

To facilitate the exercise you can add some values, for example, you can assign an annual income to the horizontal line, starting with a value you find relatively high. Then, maybe closing your eyes, reflect on the energy, time, and effort you need to invest to earn this amount of money and imagine the time left that you could dedicate to non-money earning activities. Next, see if you can draw your actual aspiration line, remembering that the more energy and time is used for money-producing activities the less time you have for non-monetary activities. To simplify the task you can find the point where the vertical and the horizontal points meet and then draw a slanting line approximately at a 45-degree angle.

Step 2: Reflecting on implications

Now, finding a quiet place, maybe again closing your eyes, bring to your awareness the graphic you just drew, and see if you can predict the position of new points that would reflect your ideal, desired spot on the aspiration line. Bear in mind that if you choose to increase the money earning time (moving the points on the horizontal axis to the right), a decrease will follow the vertical line of non-money earning activities.

Now ask yourself how you can I increase time spent on my non-economic activities? As you know, high-quality time for non-economic activities tends to increase sustainable well-being. You look at your drawing and ask yourself what if you moved the aspiration further line up to the right? In that case, you can keep the same amount of money-earning time and activities and simultaneously enjoy more non-economic activities.

Unfortunately, as soon as you reflect on moving the aspiration line upward, the satisfaction, in reality, goes down. This is because your intention to move the line upwards means that you are not satisfied with the status quo anymore; you would like to have more, hence with the same amount of income you now have less subjective well-being. The components of your BETA are not synchronized anymore. This imbalance creates stress, anxiety, greed and possibly other negative BETAs. For example, you feel that you should spend more time with your family; at the same time, your thoughts are telling you to keep working to advance your career, thus creating conflictive BETAs. The aspiration line is in reality a composite of beliefs and biases constantly shifting up and down.

Now, closing your eyes, reflect for a few moments on what you have learned, simply noticing and allowing whatever aspects of your BETA to become prominent. Before you end the exercise, you are invited to conclude with a CEO of BETA beginning with any element you are keenly aware of right now that attracts your attention. It is important to remember that this is purely a learning exercise (epistemic), not a task to solve a problem. The purpose of this exercise is to raise awareness and enhance clarity regarding a crucial dilemma in our lives.

10.4.2 Exercise 2: Having vs. experiencing

This is an exercise that requires some imagination, especially in Steps 2 and 3. The idea is to stimulate insights by imagining events and becoming aware of the effect on one's BETA. The exercise design has a scientific foundation in view of recent findings in neuroscience providing evidence that our brains make little distinction between what we imagine and what we actually experience.

Step 1: I wish I had…

Find a quiet place and settle into a comfortable position. Beginning by catching your BETA without rushing, taking your time, then passing to the second step of CEO, evening out, and bringing your awareness to the breath, following the experience of breathing from moment to moment for a couple of minutes.

Once you are ready, bringing to your attention an item you really would like to have, something you strongly feel would make you happy but you cannot afford. It could be an exquisite piece of clothing, maybe a cashmere overcoat, or a special bicycle, a high brand watch, the most advanced audio video system, or an even larger item: an electric car or a new apartment. Keep this item as the focus of your awareness and see if you can recognize the state of the BETA, knowing that the item is out of reach financially and you are not able to fulfill your fervent desire. After spending some time recognizing the state of your BETA, you are invited to move your awareness back to your breathing.

Staying with your breath for a while. Now imagining that through an act of magic, you are able to acquire what you wanted: the new car, the brand watch, the cashmere overcoat. Noticing now the state of your BETA; what body sensations, emotions, thoughts and action impulses do you experience now? Staying with your now most probably joyful BETA for some more moments, before returning your attention to your breath, simply breathing in and out and staying a few moments with the experience of breathing before ending the exercise.

Step 2: I wish I could…

Having completed Step 1 of the exercise, you have the choice of moving to the second step continuously or doing it later.

If you decide to continue, from the awareness of your breath, begin by bringing to your awareness a non-material desire, for example knowing how to play a musical instrument, speaking a new language, mastering applied mathematics, spending time in a desirable place, maybe El Prado museum or visiting the temples of South East Asia. Keep this desire as the focus of your awareness, and see if you can recognize the state of your BETA as you realize that you are not able to fulfill this desire and intensive wish. After spending some time recognizing the state of your BETA, you are invited to move your awareness back to your breathing and keep breathing a few moments.

Again staying with the breath, imaging that by an act of magic, you are able to acquire what you desire: you now can play the piano like a concert pianist, you can speak the language you always wanted to speak, you can go visit the museums of the world, are totally versed in applied math, etc. Imagining the state of your BETA now; what body sensations, emotions, thoughts and actions do you experience now? Staying with your most probably joyful BETA for some moments, experiencing and noticing before returning your attention to your breath, passing on to following your breath quietly and staying with it for a few moments before ending the exercise.

Step 3: Reflecting on having vs. experiencing

This is the last step. It can be useful to do it a day after you have accomplished the two previous steps. It is a meditation on a virtual event. The suggestion is that you follow the narrative as it is presented below. Later, during your home practice, you may modify the story line slightly to be closer to your personal context while maintaining the essence.

As usual, find a quiet place and an adequate posture, comfortable yet alert, perhaps sitting with your eyes closed. Now imagine some time has already passed, maybe a couple of years. You are having a wonderful dinner with one of your dearest friends whom you haven't seen in years, mostly due to the COVID-19 pandemic restrictions. Your friend notices your watch and says: "Wow, what a nice watch, this is one of the really expensive brands." "Yes," you reply, "I got it a couple of years ago." Then you ask your friend: "But tell me, what have you been doing all these years?" Your friend tells you it's actually mostly the same: "The same routines only that now I work 60% from home," she says. "And you," asks your friend, "what is going on with you?" Well, like you, mostly the same as usual, only that during the pandemic I started to learn piano and now I kind of play it well enough to enjoy myself and play for my family." Wow, says your friend, "that is really impressive. I imagine it has required stamina, concentration and dedication, hasn't it?" "Yes," you reply, "but it is such as joy. Imagine, me playing the piano, who would have thought of that?" "Is it difficult?" your friend wants to know. "Actually like most things in life it is simply a question of discipline and practice. If I could do it, anyone can, really," you tell your friend. Then your friend asks: "How long did it take until you could start to play some easy pieces?" "Only about three months. And I didn't practice long hours, I just practiced at least 15 minutes every day and I'm still doing so. Apparently this is the key; I read that for anything you try to learn it is much more effective to practice every day at least 15 minutes instead of doing practice marathons on weekends. It did work for me," you tell your friend. "Again," says your friend, "I am profoundly impressed. I bow to you in full respect."

Now imagine you are back at your home, and sitting on your preferred sofa, reflecting about the nice evening with your friend. Going through the night's experience, you realize that most of the dinner time was spent talking about your experience of learning to play the piano. There was very little conversation about other things and certainly not about your beautiful watch. You wonder, why? You now remember that at the beginning of the MBSAT book there was an explanation of Self-Determination Theory (SDT), a motivational theory. You remember that sustainable motivation and happiness can be achieved at the intersection of three conditions: mastery, autonomy and relationships. You then get the insight that the evening with your friend was in fact a celebration of these conditions: your sense of mastery being able to play the piano, your sense of autonomy as you were able to self-generate positive BETAS with music and sharing these experiences in relation with your friend. And with these thoughts in your mind you go to bed and fall into a pleasant, restorative sleep.

As you arrive at this point of the meditation, you may let go of the narrative, checking in to your BETA and returning to the awareness of your breathing. Stay a few moments with your breath until you feel ready to conclude the exercise and return to your own world.

10.5
Practices

10.5.1 Practice 1 - From POMO to MIMO meditation:
Detecting our financial and economic beliefs and biases

As pervading the force of money is in our lives, as blatant is the general lack of awareness with regard to the beliefs and biases that drive us. Our convictions related to money are mostly implicit; we also tend to avoid speaking openly about our attitudes towards money. The MBSAT practice from POMO to MIMO, from Powerful Money to Mindful Money, aims at uncovering the priors driving our behavior. It is an analytical meditation designed to help us regain autonomy over the effects of money in their lives and update our beliefs, if we choose to do so.

Often our beliefs and biases date back to experiences early in our lives that are so deeply buried in our memories that we seem to have forgotten them. Yet these early experiences usually have a decisive influence, because they impact us at a time when we are forming our view of the world. The meditation below helps us refresh these memories and catch the origin of our beliefs and biases.

Phase 1: Catching the past[2]

We begin this practice as usual by finding a quiet place and settling into a comfortable position that allows us to stay attentive and focused.

As the next step we catch our BETA, becoming aware of our body sensations, emotions, thoughts, and action impulses, and after a few moments pass on to focusing on our breath, following the natural rhythm of our breathing.

All of us have had situations in our childhood or adolescence when we had an intense desire for something that we wanted to have, and our parents denied it to us. In this meditation, we want to learn from those experiences.

See if it is possible to recall an incident where you really wanted something, perhaps a toy or a bicycle,

---

2   The next practice in Section 10.5.2 below is about catching the present. These practices complement each other.

a motorcycle, etc., or perhaps you had a craving for skiing, traveling or similar, but your parents could not afford what you wanted or said categorically no for some other reason.

With that experience in your mind, remember the circumstances surrounding the incident as vividly as you can. Staying with this situation in your mind as vividly as you can, see if you can recognize the states of your BETA at the time when the incident happened. Can you identify the different parts of your BETA? For example, how does the experience manifest itself in your body? Were there perhaps any sensations of tightness in different parts of the body? Were your shoulders raised or hunched? Was your jaw clenched? What else can you notice? What emotions and impulses for action can you discover?

Remember that there is no intention to change what you are feeling, sensing, or thinking. The idea is to become aware of your experience and to recognize that it is part of you. These thoughts, feelings, and sensations have been with you for most of your life, unconsciously or semi-consciously. The body sensations emotions, thoughts, and action impulses, that came up with the experience at that time in your childhood are the raw material to begin discovering the relation between you, money and the significance of money in your life.

Now see if it is possible to catch some specific elements of the BETA at the time. For example, you might have been really upset, feeling angry and slamming the door of your room in frustration. See if you can recall some of the thoughts going on in your head at the time. For example, you might have said to yourself that you were going to do everything to make money so no one could stop you from having what you wanted.

Give this process enough time so that you can immerse yourself in the experience, explore it and stay with it, and then slowly and gently come back to the surface of your awareness. When you feel ready, slowly disengage your attention from your discoveries and move your attention toward your breath. Once again feel your breath flowing in and out of your body and stay with this soothing movement for the last few moments before opening your eyes.

10.5.2 Practice 2 - Training for skillful decisions
Updating the priors to create MROs

This practice is about updating priors (existing beliefs) to create Mindful Real Options – MROs as a way out of an impasse, the approach we discussed above in Session 5. Here we practice with an example to update beliefs (posteriors in computational neuroscience) about money.

Phase 2: Catching the present

You can let a couple of days pass after practice 1 and then repeat the same meditation but this time using an experience of a desire you have in the present moment: a new car, going for the ideal trip, buying a home, getting the jacket you always dreamt of, a new watch, etc.

Once you have identified the states of the BETA originating from the experience of the desired object at this moment, see if it is possible to find commonalities in the states of the BETA now and the states of the BETA you recalled when doing the meditation about the experience of denial (a toy, a bicycle, etc.) in your youth (Practice 1 above, Catching the past). Take your time to observe for example, if the same sensations of frustration manifest in both experiences. What thoughts are coming to your mind? Are there any similarities? Can you recognize manifestations of this experience in your body sensations? Maybe pulsing in the temples or the heart? Any pressure in the head? What feelings and thoughts emerge?

As you calmly and patiently observe you may notice a connection between the BETAs of Practice 1 above (catching the past) and this practice (catching the present), particularly when you observe the thoughts you are experiencing at this moment as you think of your current desire, something you strongly yearn for at present.

Now, given that your belief about the desirable item is that it will bring you a high level of well-being, ask yourself the following question: Can I find evidence that I am able to achieve a high level of well-being without the desired item? Most probably you will find that it is still possible. Compelling evidence you could look for is, whether there are happy people who don't possess your object of desire either. Almost certainly this is the case; this could suggest that it is also possible for you to find happiness without the object you long for.

At this point you might choose to update your prior, that is the belief that you can't be happy without the object of your desire, and create a posterior belief along the line of: Actually I can be happy without the object of my desire; many are, so why not me? And now on the basis of the new belief, aka your posterior, explore alternative options (Mindful Real Options (MROs)) to satisfy your desires, wishes and aspirations to enable more skillful decisions.

As you ponder these fresh perspectives, you probably start to feel more relaxed and cool. From this calmer state, you can begin to end the practice by staying a few more moments with your breath.

What you have applied in this practice is the art of abductive reasoning without complete information, for example, without being sure, whether the object makes people truly happy and without knowing how many happy people there are without possessing the object of desire, etc.). Then you have used active inferential processes to search for evidence, if possessing an object of desire that you a priori value, is the only way to increase happiness.

Let us briefly recapitulate the process. First, you build a hypothesis: "having the object of desire (a new car, a large house, a larger bonus, the best cashmere overcoat, etc.) is the best and only path to full happiness". Next you seek evidence that actually does not support your hypothesis or casts doubts on it. For example, you ask yourself: "What would be the likelihood of finding happy people who don't have the object I so much desire?" Probably you will find that the likelihood is high. Then, you can formulate a new hypothesis. "Although I still value that object of desire, possessing or having it is not the only way to authentic happiness". By doing so you just updated your belief about money by moving from a POMO belief where the object of desire rules your BETA, to a MIMO belief, where you are in control of your BETA.

You can view this process from a computational neuroscience approach for updating beliefs or from an analytical philosophical view following the classic procedure of building a thesis, followed by formulating an antithesis and concluding with a synthesis deriving from both, the thesis and antithesis.

10.5.3 Practice 3 - Continuous-time practice: CEO of BETA from POMO to MIMO

This CEO of BETA is similar to last session's CEO of BETA for Minding Adversity and Worry (MAW) (Section 9.5.3 in Session 5 above). What is special here is the specific focus on a money-related worry. Instead of calling this CEO of BETA "on money worry" we also call it "CEO of BETA from POMO to MIMO" as it helps shift our mindset from being overwhelmed by the power of money to managing money mindfully. You can use this brief practice anytime you feel your money worries surge. In times of heightened concerns, you can apply it repeatedly during the day which is why MBSAT categorizes it as a continuous-time practice.

Like all versions of the CEO of BETA, the CEO of money worry has three steps. The difference from the other CEO's is that the first step introduces the money worry as a focal point by suggesting that practitioners identify and label what exactly is worrying them, for example, saying to themselves: "I worry about having enough money to pay for my degree" or "I worry about being able to pay for school for my kids." This creates focused awareness and allows the practitioners to get out of a worry automatic pilot fast.

In the second step awareness is shifted to the breath as in the regular CEO with the slight variation that was already introduced in the CEO of BETA on worry. As in the previous sessions the suggestion is to count in- and out-breaths or alternatively to silently repeat the words: "exhaling, inhaling, exhaling."

Step 3 is identical to the basic form of CEO and consists of awareness of the body (expanding awareness) and nurturing an open BETA to convey a sense of possibilities that is crucial in this version of the CEO's series.

Here are some additional guidelines for the practice:

Step 1: Catching the BETA

Start directing your attention to your present inner experiences: becoming aware of your BETA, just noticing and acknowledging what you detect. Whatever you observe is already there. You might ask yourself: What thoughts, what bleak scenarios or negative predictions are worrying me right now? Then put your money worry into words, for example: "I worry about not having enough to pay my rent" or "I worry about not being able to change my car", or "I worry about not having the money to pay for my kids' education," and so on. Try to be as specific as you can.

Step 2: Evening out the BETA

Shifting your awareness to your breath and moving into Epoché, suspending all beliefs about the worry, simply following the breath. Maybe counting each breath, start counting silently: in 1, out 1—in 2, out 2—and so on. When you reach 5 start afresh with: in 1, out 1, etc. If you find the counting annoying or distracting, you may silently repeat the words: inhaling, exhaling, inhaling, etc.

Step 3: Expanding the BETA

When you are ready, expand your awareness to your whole body, noticing your sensations, your posture, and your facial expression. Although the issue might still be around, by now you have regained some control insofar that the worries cannot highjack your whole BETA anymore; the awareness you recovered restores your agency. Slowly but surely you begin to see possibilities and options that were previously obscured by worries.

The benefits from the CEO of BETA from POMO to MIMO mirror the benefits of the CEO of BETA on worries in general that we reflected on in Session 5 above. They are so important that they merit a recap:

- Switching from a money-worrying frenzy to a calmer mode.

- Getting out of a worry automatic pilot.

- Stepping back from the moment and looking at money worries as an external. phenomenon unnecessarily aggravated by our agitated BETA.

- Finding relief by perceiving money worry thoughts as mental events.

- Changing the time orientation by shifting them from worrying about the future to dealing with the issues in the present.

- Recalibrating and rebalancing the agitated money-worry BETA.

10.6
Reflections

In understanding the relationship with money we can certainly learn something from people who have made money and have reflected on its value.

To help us, we can look at the testimony of Steve Jobs, who is probably the individual that has shaped and influenced modern and post-modern society more than anyone else. His ideas, products, and his company Apple are ubiquitous in every aspect of people's lives: how we work, how we entertain ourselves, how we communicate, and how we get the exact time are some of the areas of life in which Steve's influence is felt.

In a world where there is an abundance of dubious stories of rag-to-riches, Steve represents a genuine example of free market forces, from the anonymity and simplicity of his garage to building one of the world's largest and most valuable companies. With his energy, talent, ingenuity, and dynamism he represents the epitome of good capitalism. Sadly, he left this world too early. Below is a quote of one of his last thoughts that could serve as a reflective pause in our life.

"I reached the pinnacle of success in the business world. In others' eyes, my life is an epitome of success. However, aside from work, I have little joy. In the end, wealth is only a fact of life that I am accustomed to.

At this moment, lying on the sick bed and recalling my whole life, I realize that all the recognition and wealth that I took so much pride in, have paled and become meaningless in the face of impending death. In the darkness, I look at the green lights from the life-supporting machines and hear the humming mechanical sounds, I can feel the breath of God and of death drawing closer...

Now I know, when we have accumulated sufficient wealth to last our lifetime, we should pursue other matters that are unrelated to wealth... Should be something that is more important: Perhaps relationships, perhaps art, perhaps a dream from younger days ... Non-stop pursuing wealth will only turn a person into a twisted being, just like me.

God gave us the senses to let us feel the love in everyone's heart, not the illusions brought about by wealth. The wealth I have won in my life I cannot bring with me. What I can bring is only the memories precipitated by love. That's the true riches that will follow you, accompany you, giving you strength and light to go on. Love can travel a thousand miles.

You can employ someone to drive the car for you and make money for you but you cannot have someone to bear the sickness for you.

Material things lost can be found. But there is one thing that can never be found when it is lost – "Life". Whichever stage in life we are at right now, with time, we will face the day when the curtain comes down.

Treasure love for your family, love for your spouse, love for your friends... Treat yourself well. Cherish others."

Steve Jobs

10.7
Learnings from Session 6

There are three essential lessons from this session.

10.7.1 Lesson 1 - The need to pay attention to opportunity costs and limited resources

There is no free lunch: the essence of decision-making as committing to a course of action excludes by definition other possibilities. In this session we have refined the understanding that the choices we make about allocating time to earn money can significantly affect the time and resources available for non-economic activities: time with family, reading a book or learning new stuff (a language, playing a musical instrument, etc.) and other self-fulfilling activities that can contribute to our well-being.

"I simply don't understand, why my wife filed for divorce. I have worked so hard to be able to offer her all this comfort," a participant in an MBSAT course at a bank in Zurich moaned. He explained that his wife told him in their final break-up that she didn't want all this luxury, the large house, the many cars; what she wanted most was a husband to share her life with. "You chose to use your life for making more money than we need, giving up the time for us and the kids to be together. This is not the kind of life I want. I made my choice," she told him.

Exercise 1 and Figure 10.2 above shed light on the conundrum. The banker intended to minimize Free Energy in his workplace; he tried to reduce the expected uncertainty inherent in today's working environments by striving to perform well and so secure his job. On the other hand pockets of Free Energy (dissatisfaction, family stress, disillusion, etc.) were building up in his family life that eventually resulted in the dissolution of his marriage.

Clearly, there are no easy answers to these dilemmas. Each person needs to find her/his own resolution. In this session we have highlighted the challenges and the need to face these dilemmas with an IRIMI mindset, moving towards the challenges instead of ignoring them which might only aggravate the situation in the longer run.

10.7.2 Lesson 2 - Strategic awareness of what you want is key for skillful decisions

The second lesson of this session is the realization of the hedonic treadmill phenomena, first discussed by Brickman and Campbell (1971) and subsequently studied by various other behavioral scientists and economists. In its most condensed, simplistic form its message is that material goods are not a basis for sustainable well-being. The pleasure material goods provide abates quickly as people get used to them, thus creating a constant need for new material stimuli to compensate for the waning satisfaction. This generates a never-ending race of hedonic gratification, like being caught on a treadmill, running perpetually to fulfill an insatiable craving.

The illustration below in Figure 10.3 presents a person who first owns a lead egg, but soon craves a silver egg, then a gold egg, and finally a platinum egg. After reaching the top of the precious metal hierarchy the insatiable person goes for larger sizes of platinum eggs. This is not a trivial phantasy but an occurrence that can be observed in real life again and again. Just witness the trends in the car industry, where SUVs have crowded out smaller models even in urban traffic, despite pleas from environmentalists. Or take the watch industry as an example. Before the 1990s the average size of wrist watches was around 38mm in diameter. Then in the early 2000s a wave of purchasing power from newly rich elites in Eastern Europe and Asia led to voracious demand for more conspicuous goods and the watch manufacturers responded by using more precious metals and increasing the size of the watches; today the standard size of many luxury watch brands is over 40 mm in diameter, even reaching sizes of up to 46mm.

Figure 10.3 Minding POMO – Powerful Money, The Hedonic Treadmill

What can be done to rein in our proneness to chase always more? The conversation of the two friends in Exercise 2 points to a possible answer. Back at home after dinner the friend with the nice watch who learned to play piano, realizes that the night's conversation revolved around her experience of learning to play and how playing piano has positively influenced her life. She notices that her beautiful watch got just a few seconds of her friend's attention and herself wasn't keen on talking about her watch either.

She remembers a passage in the MBSAT explaining how material goods are susceptible to hedonic adaptation, meaning once the novelty of owing an item (car, watch, etch) wears off, the owner's excitement abates, and normalcy moves the person back to the level of satisfaction before the purchase. In contrast, with experiences such as learning to play the piano, learning a language, learning physics, etc. there is always something new to learn - new words, new hand combinations, new theorems, keeping the individual engaged with the learning process and creating motivational energy and emotions.

Active involvement provides experiences compared to possessions a higher level of immunity against adaptation, thus building the case that generating experiences can be a good base for sustainable happiness. Hence the second lesson is to invest our BETA's resources in experiences as they are less susceptible to the hedonic treadmill phenomenon and more supportive of sustainable well-being.

10.7.3 Lesson 3 - The importance of updating financial and economic legacy beliefs

In this workbook, the process of Active Inference occupies a central role as the mechanism that helps individuals update their brain models, particularly the beliefs driving both their generative and recognition models,[3] and throughout the workbook we emphasize the importance to maintain the generative and recognition models fine-tuned and updated to formulate precise predictions, reduce prediction errors and make skillful decisions as the basis for personal and social sustainable well-being.

With the POMO to MIMO meditation, MBSAT practitioners are invited to engage in a brain/mind practice that is conducive to deliberately updating personal economic and financial beliefs and becoming aware of the importance to keep these beliefs up to date within the circumstances of the environment. This is all the more important as money is pervasive in our lives and has characteristics that further intensify its influence, amongst them the following:

• Money as an extrinsic stimulus and motivator is a potent reinforcer for our BETA.

• Money issues are linked with worrying and anxiety. More skillful beliefs about money can reduce worrying and anxiety and enhance the precision of people's predictions about financial and economic issues, thus helping to normalize the relation to money.

• Money issues tend to seep into relationships. Becoming aware of the BETA patterns in relation to money can help improve vital human relations on an individual as well as a societal level.

---

3 Especially Chapters 1-4 provide ample scientific information and detailed yet easy to understand explanations on the subject of active Inference.

MBSAT practices are helpful in several ways even as money issues remain constants in our lives. Some of the benefits have already been mentioned, amongst others gains from the continuous-time practice CEO of BETA from POMO to MIMO (see above Section 10.5.3.).

- The POMO to MIMO meditations in Practice 1 and 2 above will not eliminate money issues but people can learn to relate to them with awareness, in other words with an attitude of MIMO (Mindful Money).

- The POMO to MIMO meditation creates spaciousness for new possibilities as it facilitates taking a step back and considering the situation more calmly.

- With the CEO POMO to MIMO micro-meditation, people can disengage from sticky money thoughts.

- Decreasing the importance of money as an extrinsic motivator allows to increase the potential for creativity at work and in many other areas.

It is important to note that updating financial and economic beliefs is in principle identical to belief updating in other areas.

The logic of the meditation from POMO to MIMO detailed in the instructions of
Practice 1 and 2 of this session can be used for updating beliefs in any area, when you feel
the need to revise them to ensure alignment with the changing environment.

Beliefs that are fine-tuned and up-to-date make your predictions more precise
and keep the average of your predictions errors low, thus enable skillful
decision-making not only with respect to money but in any other aspect of your life.

The generic sequence of the metacognitive (mindfulness) Active Inference model of belief updating comprises three steps:

Step 1: Recognizing your existing belief or prior:

Ask yourself what beliefs might be driving your BETA with respect to an issue at hand and formulate a prior hypothesis based on these beliefs (for example: buying the latest, brand-new smartphone Pro Max is my most fervent desire; with it I will be part of a selective group of super happy phone owners).Then enter Epoché Awareness States (EAS) of belief suspension:

Step 2: Temporarily suspending a belief

Put your beliefs on hold and search for evidence that disconfirms your priors (existing beliefs) using Bayesian Questioning and Reframing, that is probing the accuracy of your hypothesis by asking yourself simply, innocuous questions, for example: are there super happy phone owners without possessing the latest smartphone Pro Max? Will being part of an anonymous, dispersed group of owners of a certain phone model change my life in any way?)

Step 3: Building an updated posterior belief:

Based on new information gained from the previous step formulate an updated belief, for example: "There are many super happy phone owners who don't have a new device Pro Max, so I too can still be super happy without having one."

Once you have established an updated posterior belief, it then will function as your next prior.

In this way, you can continuously update your beliefs as new information becomes available or emerges from your Bayesian Questioning and Reframing stimulated by changes in the environment.

This morning as I was writing these lines I received a notice from Apple: "An update is available for your Mac". Downloading the newest versions is how I keep my computer updated with the latest software to optimize the operation of my external artificial information processing system: my computer. Similarly, with practices like "From POMO to MIMO" applied to different aspects of my life I try to keep my internal information processing system updated: my brain/mind interface.

Keep reminding yourself that the ultimate goal is to minimize Free Energy (entropy, disorder, prediction errors, decision mistakes) and not the maximization of a particular goal. Minimizing Free Energy is your best bet for sustainable well-being and flourishing.

10.8
Action Plan (AP)
for the Week of Session 6

The action plan for your home practice is straightforward and follows a familiar pattern.:

• Practice every day, limiting the homework to a maximum of 15 to 20 minutes.

• On the first day, do Exercise 1, Work vs. recreation, with the help of your own sketches, experimenting with different personal aspirations lines, and reflecting on opportunity costs, trade-offs, and choices you might have.

• On the second day, practice with Exercise 2, Having vs. experiencing, using the guidelines you find in the exercise.

• On day 3 start doing the POMO to MIMO meditation with the guidelines of Practice 1, Catching the past.

• On day 4 continue with the second part of the "POMO to MIMO" meditation, that is Practice 2, Catching the present.

• On day 5, repeat Exercises 1 and 2 for 6-10 minutes each, focusing your attention on possible changes that you might observe in comparison to day 1 and 2.

• On day 6, redo the "Pomo to MIMO" meditation, distributing the standard 20 minutes of home practice between Practice 1, Catching the past, and Practice 2, Catching the present.

• Throughout the week, whenever you are confronted with a money issue that represents a challenge, or when you feel money worries arising, do the continuous time practice CEO of BETA from POMO to MIMO. You can do this brief practice several times a day, if you feel a need for it.

• Every day after finishing the practices, jot down some comments and reflections in your diary or in the space provided below about your practice experience, without evaluating or judging yourself, just logging your personal path as you establish a regular personal practice.

10.9
Personal Notes and Insights

The Writing Space for Your Experiences and Observations

Example:

This morning during my home practice, I noticed how issues in my office affect my

non-professional activities, not just by limiting the time available, but by changing the

BETA, especially my emotional state.

_____

_____

_____

_____

_____

_____

_____

_____

_____

_____

_____

_____

MINDING THE PORTFOLIO OF BELIEFS III

Minding our Social Experience - SoE

Friendliness

11.1
Getting Started
Task of Session 7, Investment and Benefits

Task of Session 7:

Training both our recognition and generative models in social interactions.

Training to become aware of the beliefs driving our social interactions and how they influence our relationships and attitudes and opinions.

Increasing the precision of our predictions in social interactions for mutually beneficial relationships.

Training the learning rate of the recognition and generative models and their beliefs updating capacity to improve skillful decision-making in social interaction that facilitates cooperation and social life.

Minding skill trained in Session 7:

Increasing the precision in observing, interpreting and anticipating social interactions.

Training the capacity to probe, revise and update fixed, non-adaptive beliefs and pre-conceptions.

Expected benefits of this session and corresponding practices are:

A richer, more satisfying social life and fulfilling relationships via:

· Increasing the ability to recognize the dynamic of own and others' BETAs in social interactions, what social neuroscientists and psychologists call "theory of mind."

· Improving the capacity to reinterpret and update existing beliefs of our social-based generative models.

· Enhancing the ability to better regulate our social BETA, thus reducing prediction errors and decision mistakes.

Investment required to reap the benefits of this session:

- Time to read the material: less than 3% of the time you spend awake per day, equivalent to 30 minutes maximum (depending on your reading skills)

- Time for practicing: on average, 1.5% of your waking time or approximately 15 minutes per day.

- Given that we are continuously relating to others, continuous-time practicing every day all day what you learn in this session is your most important and also your most rewarding investment.

"Mike is not from Scandinavia; he isn't the type,"
Mo said during a break. *"No, he is from Israel,"* I replied.
"That is what I thought," Mo said, an Arab student
from a Middle Eastern country.
At that moment, my colleague Mike who lives
in Scandinavia, approached me, asking about having
dinner together: *"Juan, are we ok for dinner tonight?"*
"Oh, so sorry, Mike, tonight I can't," I declined.
"Ok, I will accompany you, Mike," Mo said.
The next day, I asked them how it was. *"Excellent,"*
they both replied and off they went to a karaoke bar,
where they stayed until late, talking and singing.

11.2
Quiz

Session 6: Minding POMO – From Powerful Money to Mindful Money

This is a voluntary quiz to review Session 6. It could be an important step forward to see for yourself what you have retained. Being aware of one's relationship to money and being able to regulate it mindfully is crucially important for skillful decision-making and sustainable well-being.

1) Explain Prof. De Vries's view of money and its effect on people.

_____

_____

_____

_____

_____

2) What is the Easterlin money/happiness paradox?

_____

_____

_____

_____

_____

3) What is the meaning of "Hedonic Treadmill"?

_____

_____

_____

_____

_____

4) What is the essential factor that the "POMO to MIMO" minding practice seeks to change?

_____

_____

_____

_____

_____

5) Explain in your own words the dynamics of opportunity costs and trade-offs between work activities and family and pleasure activities.

_____

_____

_____

_____

_____

6) Explain your understanding of the MBSAT model of money accumulation in your own words.

_____

_____

_____

_____

_____

7) What is the quality we are cultivating in MBSAT concerning money?

_____

_____

_____

_____

_____

8) What kind of predictions and inferences are activated by money-focused BETAs? Indicate yes or no in the options below and see if you can explain.

   a) Interoceptive   b) Exteroceptive   c) Proprioceptive

_____   _____   _____

_____   _____   _____

_____   _____   _____

_____   _____   _____

_____   _____   _____

Recommended solutions of the quiz can be found on the companion website: www.wiley.com/go/Young/mbsatworkbook

11.3
Introduction and Concepts

The friendship offered insistently is opportunistic.
One that sings its deeds is short-lived; a written one is just literary.
Only the friendship that is muted and inconspicuous,
but can be felt by the unselfish reality of its facts is genuine friendship.

Verses dedicated to my mother, Eva Maria, by her literature teacher, Arsenio Blanco,

In nature, many species display friendly cooperative behavior. For example, an elaborate form of cooperation was discovered amongst small vampire bats in Panama and Costa Rica. They need to feed on blood every two or three days; otherwise, they die. Each evening, they go hunting for food, and not all are lucky. So to survive, they have developed a system of mutual support: those who hunted successfully regurgitate food and give it to the unlucky ones so they can survive. It is how bats can reduce Free Energy and stay in states that reduce uncertainty (not being hungry), assuring their survival. However, the little bats keep a record of the less cooperative members. When these selfish bats cannot find food, the group refuses to share with them in retaliation for their self-serving behavior. This type of reciprocal cooperation is known in game theory as "tit for tat". It is a natural way of flushing uncooperative members out of the group, and in biology, it is considered a most successful natural selection strategy.

One goal of this session is to assist individuals in developing a more precise and postmodern theory of mind that facilitates openness, friendliness, and respect towards other people and their BETAs. In today's global and cultural changing environment, the ability to genuinely interact with individuals beyond our reference circle is a requirement for successful social cooperation and advancement. It is a precondition to reduce the corrosive effects of social Free Energy (prejudices, inadequate, biased beliefs).

The practices and exercises of this session work in tandem, complementing and reinforcing each other to in become aware of beliefs driving our social interactions and update them, if they are a hindrance for flourishing relationships.

The sequence begins with three exercises that we call Behavioral Social Experiments (BSE): Noticing the Others, Celebrating the Others, and Respecting the Others, that we call the NCR experiments, mimicking the acronym of the global information technology corporation NCR. Schoeller et al. (2021) suggest that good social relations aim to reduce epistemic vulnerability from an information theory perspective, which happens when people understand what other people are doing, and why they are doing it; additionally, this builds trust as an enabler of cooperation and good communication.

These experimental exercises are followed by a belief-updating practice and other practices and exercises conducive to effective communication, collaboration and skillful decision-making in social interaction.

The Parable of the long spoons

Once upon a time, a person searching for truth prayed and asked: "Lord, what is the difference between heaven and hell?" And the Lord answered: "It is quite simple. Let me show you." Two doors appeared in front of the seeker. "Let's go through the first door," the Almighty said.

They stepped into a room with a large round table, and on top of the table was a large dish of delicious food. Sitting around the table were emaciated and feeble-looking people. They had very long spoons, so long in fact that it was almost impossible to handle them and put food in their mouths, so they were all on the point of starving (Figure 11.1).
"Now," said the Lord, "let's go to the other room.

Figure 11.1 Parable of the long spoons (Room 1)

They walked through the second door, an identical table with the same delicious food. The people seated around the table had the same overly long spoons, but they looked happy and healthy and talked and laughed.

"What does this mean?" the seeker asked, and God answered: "Wait, you will understand in a moment when they eat their meal." The people picked up the spoons by their long handles, dipped them in the dish, and fed the person across the table, quickly reaching the other's mouth from a distance. Then they took turns and kept feeding each other in this way until the enormous dish was empty (Figure 11.2).

Parable of the long spoons (Room 2)

Figure 11.2 Parable of the long spoons (Room 2)

"In the first room, you witnessed hell; here you are experiencing heaven," said God to the seeker. "In the first room, people are greedy, only thinking about themselves and thus creating their hell. Here they are friends, they love each other, they cooperate and care for one another, creating heaven."

This tale by an anonymous author is known as the parable of the long spoons.

11.4
Behavioral Social Experiments

11.4.1 Behavioral social experiment-BSE 1: Noticing others

In BSE 1, we are training the awareness of the quotidian to observe and highlight the unnoticed people in our environments.

We all have people that we often encounter during our daily routines without having any actual contact, when going to or coming from work, going to our favorite shops, people at our offices, fitness clubs, or restaurants, people in our neighborhood (postmen or women, garbage collectors, and so forth) and in other places we frequently visit. We encounter these people all the time, but never pay attention to them; we don't notice them as they are taken for granted as part of our daily landscape. The goal of BSE 1 is training our awareness for remarking the unremarked individuals in our lives. And as we train to notice them, we cultivate a more attentive attitude towards all human beings around us.

Unlike most practices this experimental practice comprises an active phase where you called to enact a change. It consists of 3 steps: a short preparatory reflection, a concrete action (the actual experiment) and a reflection on the outcome.

Step 1: Preparatory reflection

a) Begin by finding a quiet place to be for a few minutes, settling in and performing a CEO of BETA.

b) After you have done the CEO, see if you can bring to your attention persons you encounter daily, but with whom you don't have any actual contact. This could be people you meet during your trip to the office, in your neighborhood, at your fitness center, or at any place you routinely visit. Perhaps there are also people at your office you hardly ever notice unless you have something to complain about (administrative employees, cleaning staff, etc.).

c) Then select one or two individuals from the persons you have identified as present but unnoticed in your daily routines. Take a moment to resolve experimenting with a change and conclude this brief preparatory reflection with another CEO of BETA by focusing in the third step on opening up to the person or persons you identified.

Step 2: Action

a) Decide to pay attention to the persons you identified in the previous step. Here are some suggestions of how you could do this:

Light Noticing:

- A head-nod.
- A light smile.
- A simple "Hi" or any other salutation (good morning, evening, etc.).
- Thank-you recognitions.

b) If you already do all of these things or some of them, practice with these alternatives:

Deeper Noticing:

- Asking "How are you" and seeing how the interaction develops depending on the other person's response.
- You could say that you are pleased to see this person again and that he or she looks well.
- Saying goodbye with good wishes to the person and their family.
- Under all circumstances avoiding polarizing themes.

Step 3: Reflection on outcomes

At the end of the day, after a few minutes of CEO of BETA, simply sit and use 5 to 10 minutes to review your thoughts and feelings from the behavioral experiment. How did the experience feel to you, now that you have conveyed your attention to this person? What are your impressions? Simply recognizing your BETA, and as you return to your normal life making a point of noticing people who tend to be overlooked.

11.4.2 Behavioral social experiment-BSE 2: Celebrating others

In our lives there are people whom we like and are fond of. Affectionate relationships are essential in our lives; they enable us to live with joy, find meaning and all other positive attributes necessary for a happy life. The people dear to us can be members of our family, colleagues at work or people who are part of our extended social network. They could be classified as special friends in a broad sense of the term as there is mounting evidence suggesting that friendship is "the most important factor influencing our happiness, mental well-being, physical health, and even mortality risk... Friends provide moral and emotional support, as well as protection from external threats and the stresses of living in groups, not to mention practical and economic aid when the need arises." (Dunbar, 2018, p. 32)

BSE 2 is about celebrating these people in our lives and ensuring that we don't take them for granted and forget to mind our relations with them.

As in BSE1 this experimental practice also includes an active phase where you actually try out a social interaction that is slightly different from your habitual behavior. In contrast to BSE1 the BSE 2 experiment is likely to involve more time. Depending on the action you choose it may take several days.

Step 1: Preparatory reflection

a) Like in the previous experiment, begin by finding a quiet place for the next few minutes and practice a CEO of BETA.

b) Then, see if you can bring to your attention persons dear to you. Group these individuals in three virtual circles of friends in your mind: a family circle, a work circle and a circle related to your social network. Begin with the family circle: it could consist of your husband, wife, children, mother, father, siblings, or any other member of your family like your favorite auntie or cousin, for example. Next, move to the work circle: colleagues, superiors, staff members you are responsible for, clients, and any person with whom you have a deep relationship in your work environment. Now start moving your awareness to people who are part of your social circle; these could include friends from your youth, leisure, study activities, or any person who is not family or work.

c) After having identified three groups of friends, choose a person from each group whom you particularly appreciate and whose existence in your life you would therefore like to celebrate. Here are some examples of why you might want to celebrate a person:
  - A friend you haven't seen and heard from in a while (perhaps someone from your social network).
  - A friend you see all the time, but whom you usually take for granted so that you would like to catch up by expressing your gratitude (perhaps someone you jog or play tennis with).
  - A friend you had some disagreements with (perhaps at work).
  - A friend separated from you by physical distance (perhaps a family member).
  - Any friend especially important to you.

d) When you have made up your mind about whom you would like to celebrate, imagine a concrete action you could experiment with.

Here are some suggestions of celebration modalities:

Light celebration:
  - Send an email note.
  - Call your friend to say you miss him/her.
  - Send an e-postcard.
  - Send a regular mail postcard.

If you already do all this occasionally or some of it, practice with other, more engaging alternatives.

Deeper celebration:

  - Write a nice letter to the persons you celebrate telling how much you appreciate your friendship and how valuable it is for you. You could send the letter or put it where the person finds it. You could also read the letter aloud to the person you celebrate, or you might simply tell the person your appreciation by using the letter as a basis.

- Send or bring chocolates, flowers, or something else you know your friend appreciates, perhaps a book or something ornamental, with a note celebrating your friendship.

- Go out for dinner, watch a movie, a play or going to a concert or on a tour, visit an exhibition, etc.; let your friend choose the film, play, or the restaurant or whatever you are going to do together.

- You can think of any other way of celebrating your friendship, for example, organizing a gathering or party to celebrate your friendship.

d) When you have made your plan, conclude the preparatory reflection with another CEO of BETA, taking your time, without rushing and savoring the opening of your whole being in the last step.

Step 2: Action

Now it is time to realize what you have imagined. As you do so, remind yourself from time to time that you are doing this voluntarily, so it should also be enjoyable for you.

Step 3: Reflection on outcomes

After you celebrated the persons you selected (if possible one of each of the three circles of family, work and social network), choose a quiet moment for a deeper reflection on the outcomes. Begin with a CEO of BETA and review your thoughts and feelings from the behavioral experiments. How was the experience for you? What are your impressions, now that you have celebrated your friends? Simply noticing and recognizing your BETA. To conclude the experimental practice, shift your attention to your breath and stay with your breath until you feel in sync with your BETA and ready to return to your surroundings.

11.4.3 Behavioral social experiment-BSE 3: Respecting others

There are people we hardly notice, because they are mostly indifferent to us (BSE 1), others we truly like (BSE 2), and then there are also those we try to avoid, to put it mildly. Aversion towards others may originate from mild irritations but, in many extreme cases, is the result of outright hate towards other people. In mild forms it can arise from temporal irritations even in relation to a friend, but it can also be the consequence of intense hatred of people only because of what they are or just because they exist.

Aversion can stem from unconscious beliefs about how one perceives the disliked other, but it can also be generated from ingrained, conscious beliefs. One of the key questions each person should ask him-/herself is this: Can I accept all other people's humanity, even if they are diverse from me?

Minding and updating beliefs about the other are probably amongst the biggest challenges for people in our increasingly globalized world. The intention of this experiment is not to bring people to love each other, although this would be an excellent outcome of course, not only for society but for everybody as we would probably all be happier. The aspiration is less ambitious, but still demanding in its realization:

The realistic goal we train for in MBSAT is learning to respect each other.

This means respecting even those whom we don't like or for whom we might even feel some degree of aversion. Cultivating respect of others irrespectively of who they are will undoubtedly increase the levels of personal well-being for the respectful person as well as the respected person - a classical win-win situation.

Respect has been characterized from different angles. John Rawls (1999), the famous Harvard philosopher, viewed respect as respecting the needs of others under unequal conditions. Thus, if you belong to a majority with regard to a certain criteria, this means respecting the needs of the minorities; or if you are a straight person, respecting those with more unconventional needs, and so forth. Jürgen Habermas (2003), the well-known German philosopher, highlighted another aspect; he viewed respect as respecting the beliefs of those whose interests and life conditions push them to disagreements with us.

A critical psychological and philosophical dimension in MBSAT exercises and practices is the notion that aversion towards others is a significant hurdle to conquer. At the same time, the goal is not to convert people into loving saints; instead, the goal is to train participants to respect the naturally given humanity of all mankind and other sentient beings. It is also understood that as long as there are unjustifiable thorns of aversion in people's BETAs, there will be no real possibility for growing and flourishing.

Like BSE 2 the Behavioral Social Experiment 3 - BSE 3 consists of several steps, including an active phase that may take more than a day to prepare and realize.

Step 1: Preparatory reflection:

a) As before, begin by finding a quiet place for the next 15 minutes and first take a moment to do a CEO of BETA.

b) After the CEO of BETA, see if you can bring your attention to persons who generate antipathy and aversion in you. This time build four virtual circles of persons in your mind. The family circle: here, you could include members of your family you don't particularly like or with whom you have often unpleasant encounters. Do the same for your work circle and your social circle. Additionally, build a virtual group you might call the anonymous circle. These are people that you have never met and don't know in person but that arouse some kind of animosity in you, for example, because of their customs or habits, culture, religion, opinion, role in society, etc., in brief, any group of people evoking an antagonistic BETA.

c) When you have the four virtual groups in your mind, identify two individuals in the family, work and social circles and two types or groups of people in the anonymous circle. For each of these pairs chose one individual or type towards whom you have light feelings of aversion and one that provokes more intense antipathy. The following list helps you to reflect and keep track:
  ● Two members of your family with whom you don't have a good relation, one causing mild feelings of aversion and the other more intense ones.

- Do the same with two individuals from your work environment. One could be a person you have a disagreement with and another you feel you simply can't stand.
- Go through the same process for people in your social circle. Pick one individual that generates light feelings of distaste and another that provokes stronger aversion.
- Lastly, identify two types of people you dislike in general without knowing them personally, one type or group you find relatively unpleasant and another you totally dislike.

d) The next step aims at cultivating and training a respectful attitude by taking a concrete action to show your respect. An act of paying respect is a very effective approach for getting in touch with one's beliefs and softening ingrained, fixed patterns, as acting engages our whole BETA.

Here are some suggestions how you could train your capacity for being respectful in social interactions. The suggestions below are divided in easily implementable deeds and actions that require more commitment.

Enacting social respect in light cases of aversion:
- Invite your less favorite family member for a coffee.
- Maybe joining a work colleague you dislike for a coffee break.
- Do the same here with a person you kind of dislike in your social circle.
- Make a short appreciative comment to an individual belonging to a group you feel antagonistic about by finding an aspect of the person that you genuinely like. If you prefer not to comment on the person's physical attributes (which would be understandable, although I believe it is always possible to find something that you can find admirable and beautiful in any person), then maybe you can find something nice to say about what the person wears or about a task the person performs well, any positive element that you genuinely find attractive in the person. This experiment only works if your comments are genuine, because besides uplifting the other person it should have a positive feedback effect on you. This is only possible, if the accompanying feelings are authentic.

Enacting social respect with deeper engagement:
- Invite the family member of more profound animosity for lunch, dinner, or any other gathering, letting the person choose the place to meet. See if it is possible to tell this person about the states of your BETA. Prepare yourself to keep minding and regulating your BETA for the entire duration of the interaction.
- Regarding your relationship at work, see if it is possible to find an opportunity to engage in a more meaningful interaction with the person that evokes higher levels of animosity in you. It could be a working lunch. Go patiently and gently about finding out what creates the aversion towards this person.
- Try the same experiment with the individual in your social sphere towards whom you feel more pronounced animosity.
- With regard to your anonymous circle your aversion is more generalized, therefore it might be helpful if you find out more about the group. You could ask a group member to recommend you

literature to broaden your knowledge about these people, or get involved in their arts, music, or philosophy; any information that could help expand your perception and beliefs regarding this group of people and foster possibly emerging feelings of respect. These activities might bring you naturally in contact with representatives of this group, providing you with opportunities to show your respect also in concrete interactions.

e) When you have made a plan in your mind, sit for a few more moments, focusing on your breath. Then conclude the preparatory reflection with a CEO of BETA, concentrating on Step 3, opening up to new possibilities in your social interactions

Step 2: Action

After your preparatory reflection it is time to put your resolutions in practice. Take your time to do it in a way that is satisfactory for all, including yourself.

All the experiments of BSE 3 should be undertaken without any expectations, just with the sole purpose of learning and building trainable data for your BETA in social interactions with people for whom you feel light or more profound animosity. This is especially important with regard to your experiments with the anonymous circle. It would be truly regrettable if you ended up making an isolated negative experience and generalize it in a way that would compound your existing animosity towards all members of the group.

Step 3: Reflection on outcomes

After each experiment with any of the circles take a moment at the end of the day to sit, do a CEO of BETA and digest your experience, remembering that you set out to train your capacity of social respect. How did it go? What have you learned or gained? How does the experiment feel in hindsight? Keep observing your BETA for answers, the four doors through which we experience life.

If you can, make some brief notes in your diary, so that you can later reconstruct how your personal journey has evolved.

11.4.4 Behavioral social experiments: Reflection

After you have done the entire series of behavioral social experiments (BSE 1-3), sit quietly and reflect on the whole experience. The focus is on your NCRs (Noticing, Celebrating, Respecting others) since we train our capacity to recognize information in social interactions and to review and update our beliefs if they are inaccurate. Making notes on your observations in your diary is very helpful. Writing helps clarifying observations and learnings from experiences.

The practices in this session specifically address beliefs and judgments and the task of detecting possible causes of beliefs and the consequences for decision-making. For now, the goal is to train the sensitivity of your BETA in social interactions with people you like, dislike, and towards those you are indifferent. Thus, in your concluding meditative reflection you are invited to focus your attention on whether your BETA has undergone changes, and if so in what way – just noticing without evaluating or judging.

Figure 11.3 summarizes visually the effects of our attitudes on society. Ingrained, fixed stereotypes can lead to social fragmentation. The inclusive path requires us to mind our social experience and cultivate NCR.

Figure 11.3 Free Energy Minimization and Friendliness –
Minding the Social Experience (SoE)

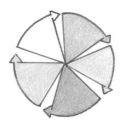

11.5
Aspects of Minding
the Social Experience with Others

Social experiences have many dimensions. Four salient areas of observation that require our attention in interactions with fellow human beings are detailed below. The first two concern our perception of others, the third the dynamics of interaction and the fourth focuses on observing our evolving BETAs.

Salient areas of observation in Minding SoE:

a) **The mental models of other people:**

Recognizing other people's ideas, beliefs, thoughts, mental models is key in social interactions. Some denote this ability as the theory of mind. Our own mental models have to be optimally fine-tuned to enable skillful relating.

b) **The physical phenotype of the other:**

The physical appearance is what strikes us first in social interactions. It comprises all physical characteristics of a person, for example, the color of the eyes, hair type and color, skin tonality, height, body shape and any other physical aspects, even physical deformations. Often these aspects trigger spontaneous reactions in our BETAs that call for careful minding, if we care for openness vs. repeating pre-existing patterns of behavior.

c) **The cultural dimension in social interaction:**

This area of observation comprises cultural elements, for example, differences in rules of civility. What is normal in one culture might not be welcome in another. This concerns the way we speak, dressing styles, eating habits and many any other cultural differences between people. Noticing these differences tactfully is a precondition for cultivating sensitivity towards others and enacting social respect – the R of NCR.

d) **The rate of change of your BETA in social interaction:**

All the variables of social experiences are subject to change; they are vectorized as data scientists call any magnitude that is subject to change. The changes can be pretty intense, but as one keeps observing them, their intensity may decline or alter in some other way. At times these changes are slow, and at other times they are faster. Being aware of these changes helps us improve our social experiences. Minding SoE is the foundation of good relationships.

11.6
Practices

11.6.1 Practice 1 - Minding SoE for updating social beliefs I:
Finding the origin of our social priors (beliefs and biases)

In this minding meditation, the purpose is to identify one's social priors.

Imagine yourself as one of the most famous detectives: Olivia Benson or Hercule Poirot on the mission of catching your non-adaptive beliefs about individuals different from you. These are beliefs that are socially and humanly inacceptable, because they routinely hamper human development and a person's ability to flourish. Here are some examples: beliefs about the inferiority of women if you are a man; about the superiority of some ethnic groups with respect to others; about the superiority of one culture or religion over another, etc. The mission is challenging as the culprits "non-adaptive beliefs about others" is a clever adversary; it knows how to disguise itself, lie, dissimulate; it has many tricks to deceive you. You need to be patient but determined. Most probably, you will not find it in your first round of investigations; you might need to go through different iterations before you can catch it.

The guidelines for this uncovering practice are as follows:

After going through the usual preparations of settling into an appropriate posture in a quiet place, we begin the meditation with a CEO of BETA of 3-5 minutes and then return our attention on the breath.

Now at your own pace start by bringing to your mind the time when you were growing up. See if it is possible to summon lively memories of that period; maybe beginning with early images of you as a kid with your family, likely a specific image of all of you at the dinner table; your parents, your siblings, and any other person part of the familiar scene. See if you can remember some conversations from that time, maybe a comment along these lines: "Jenny, you should not study engineering, these are male professions;" or "Jack, I don't understand why you want to become a nurse? The profession is for girls." Another theme could have been who you play with: "I don't want you to play with Ali, you hear?" "But why not?" you probably protested, and the answer was something like: "Just do as we tell you. He and his family are different from us." You can then move on to your time at school. A teacher explaining math may have responded to a girl's difficulties to understand with the remark: "Don't worry, math is easier for men." Conversely, the French teacher may have been telling a boy in the class that languages are easier for women.

With these experiences in your mind, remember the circumstances surrounding the incident as vividly as you can. Staying with the experience, whatever it is, and seeing if it is possible to catch some specific elements of the BETA at the time. For example, can you retrace how the experience manifested itself in your body? Were you perhaps upset and angry, slamming the door of your room in frustration? Can you recall the thoughts going on in your head at the time? Remember that there is no intention to change what you feel, sense, or think. The idea is to become aware of your experience and recognize that it is part of you. These thoughts, feelings, and sensations have been with you for most of your life, unconsciously or semi-consciously.

Sometimes we have a memory blank and cannot come up with any incidents; it is not that we didn't have these sorts of experiences in the past; we all have. It is simply that those incidents are so deeply buried in our long-term memory consciousness that they are not so easy to recall. In cases of problematic recollection, merely bring your awareness to the present. For example, you can scrutinize your current views to find out, whether you attribute certain qualities (talents or weaknesses) to certain groups of people. Perhaps you notice that you have firm opinions about one or the other type of persons. These are opportunities to identify the underlying social beliefs.

Give this process enough time so that you can immerse yourself in the experience, explore it and stay with it, and then slowly and gently come back to the surface of your awareness. When you feel ready, gradually disengage your attention from your discoveries and shift your attention back to your breath. Once again, feel your breath flowing in and out of your body and stay with this pulsing movement for the last few moments before opening your eyes.

The body sensations, emotions, thoughts, and action impulses that came up with the experience at that time in your childhood are the raw material to begin discovering the relation between you and your beliefs about others, especially beliefs that limit the scope and warmth of your social interaction and may have become over time a hindrance for personal growth. As you conclude the practice, you could make a resolution to keep meditating and investigating the source of non-adaptive beliefs or priors.

Practical concerns

Ensure that the practice room is neither noisy nor too bright or too dark (avoiding drowsiness, enabling calmness) and that it is comfortably warm in winter and fresh in summer. In other words, the place should be conducive to the practice. The duration of the practice can vary from 10-15 minutes to as long as half an hour or more, depending on your needs and your situation.

These guidelines are applicable to all practices involving a sitting meditation and to most exercises that include a sitting reflection.

11.6.2 Practice 2 - Minding SoE for updating social beliefs II: Training for skillful decision: Building adaptive social posteriors

Once you have identified your non-adaptive social beliefs or priors in the terminology of neuroscience, the next step is to recognize what authentic desires and practical reasons are prompting you to update your beliefs. You might find that holding strong beliefs against other people is not beneficial for your well-being. You might also recognize that it can limit your advancement possibilities. For example, imagine having negative beliefs about women in power. Then a woman gets promoted to the top position in your company, and the HR department asks you to become her deputy. What would you do? Be loyal to your belief, or be opportunistic and take the position? And would you be able to perform at your best in this conflicting situation? Probably not on a long-term basis. This could be an understandable, self-serving reason for updating your beliefs.

Instead of taking a "wait-and-see" stance until a real-life situation pushes you to review your priors as in the example above, you can be foresightful and build social posteriors for skillful decision-making by implementing MBSAT's "Minding SoE" practices.

Let us assume that you have identified non-adaptive social beliefs in Practice 1 above and decided to update them. In this case settle into a sitting meditation and begin with a short CEO of BETA as you did in Practice 1. Then return your attention to your breath. After a short while, when you feel calm but attentive, begin by identifying a non-adaptive belief you would like to work on. For example, you might hold the belief that women, in general, are not good at sciences. As you keep breathing quietly, ask yourself why you would like to review this belief. There could be many reasons. Maybe you have a daughter who would like to study natural sciences, or you had a discussion with a close friend who called you prejudiced. Whatever it is, the intention is to recognize one's motives without judging, just in search for knowing yourself. It could even be that there is no detectable, clear-cut reason. In that case let the matter rest for now.

After another round of breathing, you may begin to search for evidence to question your belief. Can you think of examples that contradict it? Could it be that the contrary is closer to reality than your belief?

At this point, you might not have enough evidence off the cuff based on solid data or actual examples of women active in scientific positions. If that is the case, set yourself the task of further investigating and finding more evidence that could contradict your priors (beliefs). Conclude your meditation with awareness of the breath and gradually returning to the reality around you as you did in Practice 1. Deep rooted beliefs seldomly can be overturned in one sitting. You must be prepared to engage in an iterative process that takes some time.

For didactical purposes let us assume that your investigation takes you to Iceland, where women outperform men in mathematical abilities. On your trip you also discover that Iceland is the country with the highest level of equality between men and women in international rankings. Thus, instead of finding a confirmation of your biologically-based prior you found a cultural explanation of existing differences.

Now, you can update your prior (women are less good at science than men) to an adaptive posterior belief (women and men are equally good at science, if the society they grow up in provides equal opportunities for men and women).

11.6.3 Practice 3 - Continuous-time practice: CEO of BETA on minding fellow human beings

The CEO of BETA is a kind of companion that is always at hand whenever we feel the need for centering ourselves or muster some extra energy. This is why we call it a continuous-time practice – a helpful practice that accompanies us in everyday life and can be done wherever we are, as many times as we like.

It is also a very versatile practice, as we can alter the focus as we go along, and our immediate concerns change. After becoming familiar with the universal version of the CEO of BETA in Session 4 we have already practiced the CEO of BETA for Minding Adversity and Worry in Session 5 and the CEO of BETA from POMO to MIMO (from Powerful Money to Mindful Money) in Session 6. Now we continue the CEO-of-BETA series with the CEO of BETA on minding fellow human beings.

You could use this special CEO of BETA for example, when you implement your behavioral social experiments along the lines of Section 11.4 above and seek ways to make them a truly enriching experience. Or you can do the CEO of BETA on minding fellow human beings, whenever you would like to cultivate your relationships with others. What is important in all circumstances is a clear subdivision in three steps, repeating to yourself silently: Step 1..., Step 2..., Step 3. This is what allows you to halt the vortex of inner events and pass on to evening out your BETA and then open up to new possibilities.

In the following guidelines, we follow the 3-step format as always.

Step 1:

Gather all four components of your BETA, noticing your body sensations, emotions, thoughts, and action impulses, without judging or evaluating, simply observing what is there at this moment. In doing so, bring to your attention the concern that has prompted you to practice a CEO of BETA: a relationship you would like to improve, a conflict with another person you would like to resolve, ambivalent feelings towards another person that you would like to sort out, or any other relational concern you might have. Become aware of how this concern impacts your BETA.

Step 2:

Shift your attention to your breath and keep breathing, following the natural rhythm of the inflow and outflow of air without trying to control or alter it, maybe concentrating on the breathing in your abdomen as it slightly expands and retracts, or in your breast as it lifts and gives way in intervals, or perhaps in your nose. Enjoy the soothing effect of the gentle, regular movement.

Step 3:

When you feel that your BETA has become more even, open your mind and heart to the person(s) you have been considering in Step 1 by enhancing comprehension and kindness. Putting oneself in others' shoes can ease a great deal of tension and clear the way for relating constructively. Let a feeling of confidence arise in you that there is a good way forward. Then return to your surroundings, taking the empathy and the open and appreciative attitude with you to your current tasks.

It could well be that it is you who is in need of kindness and support, because you feel exhausted and under pressure. In that case, you can dedicate a CEO of BETA to yourself, offering yourself the comfort of acknowledging your state and allowing things to be as they are for the time being. Under these circumstances, the CEO of BETA is like a comforting treat. Amongst other things, this equanimous attitude makes it easier to undertake constructive changes when the time is propitious.

11.7
Exercises

11.7.1 Exercise 1 - Minimizing Free Energy in relation to others: Decision-making in social interactions/Cooperation and trust

Cooperation and trust are inseparably interlinked. Without trust, there is no cooperation. This is exemplified by the well-known "Prisoner's Dilemma", a classic case in game theory, in which the outcomes for each player are interdependent, and the outcomes are consequences of decisions. The dilemma is the following:

> Two thugs commit a crime together. Soon afterwards he police catch them, arrest them and put them in two separate rooms for interrogation. They offer each of the two the same deal. The one who confesses and testifies against the accomplice is acquitted and free to go, while the other will be sentenced to five years in jail. However, if both testify against each other, each of them gets three years in jail, two years less than convicted individually. The third option is that neither of the two criminals testifies; in this case each of them gets only one year due to lack of solid evidence.

This is a practice that offers the opportunity to practice collaborative skills and reflect on individual gain vs. collective advantage. If they are loyal to each other because they fully trust each other, their combined jail time is two years (one year for each). If they betray each other, their combined jail time is 6 years (3 years for each). There is of course the temptation to walk free by testifying, hoping the accomplice is loyal, but the risk is high.

This famous case involves issues of cooperation, trust and loyalty. Ultimately cooperation is also an issue of decision-making. Whether you cooperate or not requires a decision as is evident in the prisoners' dilemma.

Often cooperation also involves truthfulness, as trust encourages people to speak the truth and sincerity is a key enabler of cooperation. Deceit and truthfulness is an issue in the following exercise. It allows us to train collaborative skills by reflecting on requirements, implications and decisional outcomes of cooperation versus lack thereof. The practice is based on an opera by the famous Italian composer Puccini, entitled *Tosca*, after one of the central characters, a beautiful singer.

The practice comprises the following steps:

Step 1:

To do the exercise you need to be familiar with the plot. Listening to Puccini's opera Tosca is naturally your best option. If this is not possible, read a summary of the plot (many versions available on the internet).

Here is a very condensed synopsis:

The story takes place in Rome shortly after the French revolution. French troops ("republicans", the revolutionaries of this epoch) have attempted to conquer Rome, but the King of Naples and his "royalists" regained control of the city. Scarpia is head of the king's secret police and orders to jail and torture a sympathizer of the republicans. He sees a chance to obtain the favors of Tosca, a famous and beautiful singer, because he knows that Tosca is in love with his prisoner. He offers her a deal: if she grants him a night with her, he will let the prisoner free. Tosca agrees in disgust and demands from Scarpia a pass for herself and her lover so that they can leave Rome together. Scarpia issues the pass, but tells Tosca that for appearances, and to save his face, he must stage a fake execution of the prisoner, shooting him with blanks.

Step 2:

This step requires you to consider probable outcomes.

In principle, the story has four possible outcomes, purely hypothetically:

Outcome 1:
Tosca gives Scarpia what he wants; Scarpia keeps his promise and Tosca escapes with her lover. **Both Tosca and Scarpia live.**

Outcome 2:
Tosca is disgusted; she lies and stabs Scarpia to death; Scarpia has been truthful, the prisoner survives, and Tosca lives on. **Tosca lives, Scarpia dies.**

Outcome 3:
Tosca is truthful and gives Scarpia what he wants. Scarpia cheats and has the prisoner executed. Tosca takes her own life in desperation. **Tosca dies, Scarpia lives.**

Outcome 4:
Scarpia cheats, he orders a real execution of the prisoner. Tosca also lies, stabs Scarpia to death and takes her own life as she realizes her lover is dead. **Both Tosca and Scarpia die.**

All four possible outcomes are depicted in Figure 11.4 in the following order, quadrant by quadrant

Outcome 1: upper left   Outcome 2: upper right

Outcome 3: bottom left   Outcome 4: bottom right

Figure 11.4 Decisional Outcomes: Tosca and Scarpia in Puccini's Opera

Step 3:

a) After familiarizing yourself with the plot and possible outcomes, find a quiet place to sit, settle in by adjusting your posture as usual and begin with the CEO of BETA. Then bring your attention to the opera and its two main characters, Tosca and Scarpia. Choose one of them for a virtual role play. If you choose to play Tosca's part, ask yourself, how far you are prepared to go to save your lover, whose life hangs in the balance. If you choose Scarpia's part, reflect on what Tosca might do in your view to save her lover.

b) Make a choice and decide what you are going to do in your role as Tosca or as Scarpia.

c) Now reflect alone on your choice. You might discuss it with a trusted friend or partner. However, avoid discussing your choice in public as you might risk being misunderstood or misinterpreted.

Conclusion:

In the plot of Puccini's opera both Tosca and Scarpia die. One of the challenges of this exercise is to see, if it is possible to find a better outcome for both.

The practice is an example of decision-making and outcome interdependence. Minding our Social Experience (SoE) involves choices and decisions. Depending on the skillfulness of our decisions, our relationships enable us to minimize Free Energy or on the contrary generate more Free Energy in the form of conflicts and uncertainty.

The case of Tosca and Scarpia also illustrates how complex cooperation can be, when strong emotions are at play and trust and truthfulness are uncertain. Minding SoE is a pre-requirement to achieve reliable cooperation.

11.7.2 Exercise 2 - The Ultimatum Game: Cooperation and decision-making

In this exercise we continue to train our decision-making skills in the context of cooperation and minding our Social Experience (SoE).

Ultimatum games typically require decisions of the type take-it-or-leave-it. They force us to confront our desires and make choices.

Imagine the following:

Your wealthy auntie passed away recently. One day, you get an email from a lawyer's office inviting you for a meeting to hear your auntie's will. The message also mentions that you are one of the beneficiaries.

Step 1:

a) We begin as usual, finding a place to sit, performing a CEO of BETA, then staying with our breath for a few moments.

b) Now imagine your auntie as vividly as you can before she passed away. Everyone in your family always referred to her as the rich auntie. She had married a wealthy businessman but never had children of her own, just three nephews, including yourself. When her husband passed away, she inherited all his fortune.

c) Next bring your awareness to the following scene. You are now at the lawyer's office and quite excited, thinking about what you are going to do with the inheritance. You are directed to a meeting room where you find your two other cousins and the lawyer. There is a lot of expectation in the air.

The lawyer solemnly opens the will. He announces that the auntie's estate of 10 million after taxes is divided into three parts corresponding to her three nephews.

Moreover, the lawyer says, there are rules for accepting the inheritance.

d) According to the rules you are the only one who can accept the inheritance for the three; if you refuse, all the estate will be used for social initiatives.

e) The lawyer now reads the will: she left 4.998 million to one of your cousins and the exact same amount to the other cousin. You inherit the remaining 4,000 (four thousand). You have 20 seconds to decide, whether you accept the inheritance or not.

f) Try to envision the situation as realistically as you can.

Do you accept or refuse? Why?

What about your BETA and each of its components?

Step 2:

Now imagine that before going to the lawyer's office, you decide to sit down and do some of the practices you learned in the MBSAT course. You know that there is the possibility that your auntie might have prepared a trick for you; you were not always nice to her. So you prepare yourself for any outcome from the will reading. On the way to the lawyer you do another CEO of BETA. Then you join the meeting with the lawyer and your cousins with a more equanimous BETA.

Again you are asked to decide whether you accept the in heritance for the three of you or whether you refuse.

Is your decision different from the first time? Why?

What thoughts accompany your decision? What emotions and body sensations?

Imagine that your best friend asks you what happened. What would you tell him?

Step 3:

Take your time to reflect deeply on your decisions in both cases as you continue to sit. When you have gained some understanding of what happened and the reasons behind it, shift your attention to the breath and stay focused on your breathing for a while, following the soothing rhythm of inhaling and exhaling, noticing the ebb and flow of fresh air coming in and going out.

When you feel ready, gradually shift your attention to the world around you and conclude the exercise, perhaps noting some of your observations and insights in your diary.

11.8
Tools and Models

11.8.1 The Free-Energy Minimazing Tool for Communication

As amply explained in this book, as individuals, we are confronted with the imperative of reducing Free Energy (that is decision errors in the metric used in MBSAT) to survive and thrive. As social beings, we also recruit other brains or generative models to respond jointly to the challenge of survival. Sometimes these alliances work, at other times they don't; however, when they work, one can think of a collaborative process of two or more individuals sharing a brain and their generative recognition and generative models to build a shared brain, helping members reduce their Free Energy; like in a "duet for one" (Friston & Frith, 2015).

An easy to understand and effective communication approach to enhance BETA synchronization between individuals is the model of Positive psychologist Shelley Gable (Gable et al., 2006). It is based on her research that identifies communication along two dimensions. One dimension is the intensity of action, going from active to passive forms of communicating. The other dimension refers to communication content that can be either destructive or constructive. This results in the four permutations illustrated in Figure 11.5:

a. The active/constructive quadrant refers to communication that is unmistakably supportive and accompanied by a BETA that clearly expresses a "duet for one."

b. Active/destructive implies negative utterances that are further reinforced by disparaging BETA.

c. Passive/constructive refers to utterances that are positive on the surface but put forward so that the overall impression is close to neutral. It is an indifferent way of communicating that shows little constructive BETA involvement.

d. Passive/destructive communication expresses indifference but with a negative undertone. In this quadrant, a person experiencing joy or even sorrow would probably feel let down by the other party's passive/destructive BETA response.

Mindful, Free-Energy Minimizing Communication

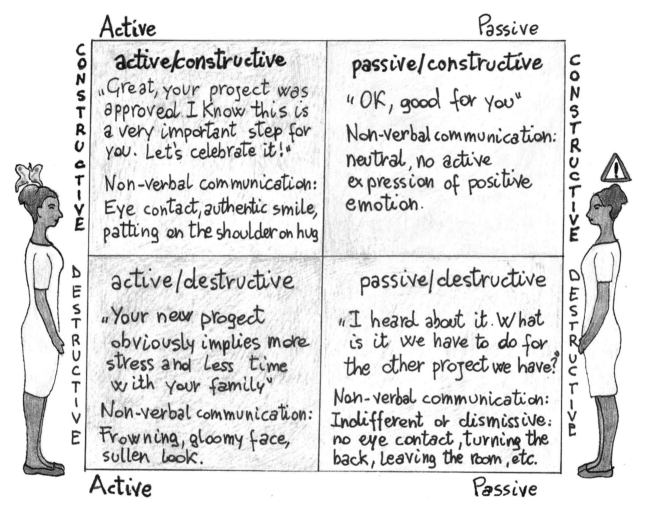

Figure 11.5 Mindful, Free-Energy Minimazing Communication

You can use this model as a tool to make your personal communication more effective and more rewarding through improved relationships. To implement it and train with it just keep asking yourself repeatedly during your daily routines::

- In what mode was I right now?
- Was this mode appropriate?
- Did it produce the results I expected?

You could even present the model to people close to you (a partner or a team you are working with). You will see that people soon start playing games with it and making jokes, when a response falls in the wrong quadrant.

> *Since I have been using this tool and paying attention to how I communicate,*
> *I no longer speak in the active/destructive way. The change in my team was quick*
> *and noticeable. For example, my employees come to me more openly and motivated*
> *with questions or ideas. In my relationship with my partner, the pattern*
> *of active/destructive communication happens from both sides. After our last quarrel*
> *we were able to reflect on this together and we could recognize what*
> *unfulfilled needs are at the origin. I am motivated to continue learning and training.*

Based on this model, you can also train your collaborative abilities deliberately by engaging in a more structured exercise.

Here are some guidelines how you can train with the tool in an exercise style:

Step 1:

a) As in the previous exercises, find a place to sit and start by doing a CEO of BETA, then stay with your breath for a few minutes.

b) Now see if it is possible to bring to your awareness an incident or an experience with a person that, in your opinion, resulted in a failed communication. It could be a discussion with someone in your family, at work, or in any other setting. The other person could be someone you know or someone you met by chance.

c) Next, see if it is possible to identify the mode of communication you applied in the exchange using the following three types of communication:
- active/destructive
- passive/ destructive
- passive/ constructive

You might discover that it was not only one but several of the three ways that you used in talking to the person.

Step 2:

a) Now, see if it is possible to bring to your mind the active/constructive mode of communication in the same context and replay the exchange under this mode, focusing your attention on the verbal and bodily interaction with the person.

b) Finally, imagine the outcomes of the interaction using this active/constructive mode of communication. What would have changed?

c) After quietly pondering the consequences of the different styles of communication, conclude the exercise by focusing a while on your breath, simply following your natural breathing, in and out, again and again. Then slowly and gently return to your normal environment.

11.9
Reflections

11.9.1 Reflection 1:
Albert Einstein's question: Is the universe friendly?

Minding our Social Experience (SoE) encompasses all of the themes we have touched upon above: our brain models with their priors (biases, patterns) and the need for reviewing and updating, the way we actively relate to others (Noticing, Celebrating, Respecting (NCR)), cooperation, trust and truthfulness, active/constructive communication. If we continuously hone these capabilities the world around us will be a pleasant and friendly place to live in.

The following invitation to reflect on how we shape our world stems from one of the most influential physicists of the past century, Albert Einstein. From the perspective of MBSAT, Einstein implies that the world we live in is shaped by our priors and the orientation of our BETAs. If we believe that the universe is friendly (the prior), we will use our ingenuity and energy (the E, T and A of our BETA) in constructive ways to advance humanity. However, if we believe that the universe is unfriendly (the opposite prior), we will create defensive systems and invest in arms.

Albert Einstein: Is the universe friendly?

I think the most important question facing humanity is: "Is the universe a friendly place?" This is the first and most basic question all people must answer for themselves.

For if we decide that the universe is an unfriendly place, then we will use our technology, our scientific discoveries and our natural resources to achieve safety and power by creating bigger walls to keep out the unfriendliness and bigger weapons to destroy all that which is unfriendly, and I believe that we are getting to a place where technology is powerful enough that we may either completely isolate or destroy ourselves as well in this process.

If we decide that the universe is neither friendly nor unfriendly and that God is essentially "playing dice with the universe," then we are simply victims to the random toss of the dice and our lives have no real purpose or meaning.

> But suppose we decide that the universe is a friendly place. In that case, we will use our technology, scientific discoveries, and natural resources to create tools and models for understanding that universe because power and safety will come through understanding its workings and its motives.
>
> God does not play dice with the universe.
>
> *Albert Einstein, physicist, and humanist*

If you would like to reflect on this fundamental choice more deeply, you can turn the quote into a meditative exercise. The hope is that meditating on Einstein's words can bring clarity and coherence to our BETA and help us find a personal, unambiguous answer.

Guidelines for the meditative reflection:

Step 1:

a) Find a place to sit quietly and start with a CEO of BETA, then read the quote several times.

b) Now slowly close your eyes and repeat the quote to yourself. You might need to alternate between repeating the quote from memory and opening your eyes to read any passage you might have forgotten. It might take several attempts until you can repeat the whole text to yourself without reading.

Step 2:

a) When you have memorized the quote, focus your awareness on the content and explore your beliefs concerning the three choices Einstein confronts us with. Is the world unfriendly, friendly or random? See if you can define your personal standpoint.

b) Finish the practice by going back to the breath, resting your awareness on your breathing for a while before ending the practice.

11.9.2 Reflection 2:
Friendliness as a necessity in functional management

Friendliness is often seen in management as a "nice to have" feature that is only possible to cultivate in good times, when there is some slack and no pressing struggle for financial viability. Quite to the contrary, MBSAT argues that friendliness is a must for business in many respects, be it in the form of empathy towards clients, as a way of collaborating that brings out the best in people, by creating an atmosphere that stimulates creativity, or in many other ways.

This is actually very old wisdom. In the 16th century tale from Japan (an epoch of fierce Samurai culture) below, friendliness and outright love towards people is extolled as a natural way to attract talented people, in other words for recruiting the crucial talent so necessary to ensure a successful future for any company.

How to Acquire Talented People: A 16th Century Samurai Tale

Before Lord Katsushige passed on his position as lord to his son, he gave him a note consisting of twenty items. All of the items were recommendations from Lord Katsushige's own father, Naoshige, the revered founder of the clan. Now his advice was being handed down to the third generation.

Amongst the items was the recounting of a father-to-son talk between Naoshige, the then Lord and clan leader, and Katsushige when he was a young man.

Lord Naoshige: "In order to rule the nation, you should have able men."

Son Katsushige: "Do you mean I have to pray to Buddha and the gods for the appearance of these men?"

Lord Naoshige: "You pray to God for things beyond human power and endeavor. Yet it is within your power to get talented people to appear."

Son Katsushige: "How is this possible?"

Lord Naoshige: "Irrespective of any matter, things gather around him who loves them. If he loves flowers, every variety of flower will begin to gather around him, even though he has not had a single seed until that time. And, in due course, there will grow a flower of the rarest kind. Likewise, if you love people, the result will be the same. Make a point of loving and respecting."

Source: Yamamoto, edited by Stone (2002) p. 40-41

11.9.3 Reflection 3:
God values every person the same

Below is a statement by a contemporary Anglo-Saxon journalist that could be useful for reflecting on the value of every human being. The statement was made during a TV discussion on politics and the state of Western society and is quoted verbatim, reflecting spoken language.

"People of faith, people who know for a fact that God exists, but even more critically, who know they are not God - let me repeat, people who know they are not God - are the only reason this is still a decent society. Because when you know you are not God, it puts everything in perspective, and you know there are things you can't do... I mean which human being hasn't thought, especially in traffic: 'I'd like to kill that person...' <Scattered laughter from the audience> No, I'm serious... You don't have the right to do that because you are not God. There are all kinds of limits, but also once you realize you are not God, someone else is, there is the fundamental recognition that every human being, from the president to some homeless guy, from people you know to some person in India or Africa, every human being on the planet is equal. Not in ability or experience, but in value, the thing that matters most: in value. God values every person exactly the same."

11.10
Learnings from Session 7

In this session we have gained new knowledge at several levels.

In essence we have

- learned new, behavioral approaches to social change.
- learned to relate more friendly to people around us.
- trained our skills to update our mental models.
- honed our decision-making abilities.
- learned about the many facets of cooperation and inclusiveness.
- learned about the power of priors/beliefs in shaping the entire universe.

More in detail this session provides the following learnings and training benefits.

a) Learning s from the cycle of Behavioral Social Experiments BSE 1-3:

- We gained hands-on, practical experience regarding the power of action to generate social change.
- We have trained our social awareness and honed our ability to notice. A trained BETA notices human fullness even in those indifferent to us. Noticing is a precondition for MBSAT's objective of Strategic Awareness.
- We honed our ability to mind and not take relationships for granted by training to duly celebrate persons close to us.
- A trained BETA respects those different from us even if we don't like them. This is one of the most challenging benefits to achieve. It requires rewiring our socially driven neurological infrastructure to reduce biases and stereotypes. Lack of respect to others different from us, who are indeed members of the universal humanity, is ultimately a lack of self-respect, a lack of our own humanity. However, without self-respect, it is almost impossible to achieve higher levels of flourishing, the ultimate goal.

b) Learnings from Practices 1-2:

- We learned to uncover priors/beliefs we are unaware of by approaching them in analytical meditation. By doing so we have continued our learning process of Session 6, where we trained to uncover our financial and economic priors.

- We learned to build more adaptive and skillful posteriors by exposing our beliefs to questioning and searching for evidence that challenges them.
- We enhanced the dynamics of our generative and recognition models in the brain/mind by learning to update beliefs about social relations.
- Our skills in updating our social generative and recognition models will help us reduce Free Energy by reducing prediction and decision errors.
- We have become more prepared for the social interaction in an increasingly more diverse and culturally fluid world.

c) Learning s from Exercises 1-2:

- We learned that decision-making in social contexts is especially challenging as one outcomes also depend on other players' decisions.
- We learned that short-term personal gain is not always congruent with collective, combined gains, raising the question of sustainability of decisions solely based on personal interest.
- The story of Tosca, the fable of the long spoons and other passages in this session taught us what we might lose, if we forgo cooperation. At the same time we learned more about the conditions that enable cooperation.

d) Learnings from tools and quotes:

- We trained to establish "duet for one" communication with active constructive interactions that improve our individual as well as our social Free Energy minimization capabilities (reduction of decision and prediction errors).
- By reflecting on Einstein's view of the universe we learned how powerful a belief can be to the point of shaping the entire world.
- Throughout the session we have enhanced our ability to cultivate authentic friendliness, an essential social skill that helps us reduce VUCA.
- We have enhanced your social-based exteroceptive, interoceptive, and proprioceptive predictions capacities by training our social awareness and improving our verbal and non-verbal communication.

11.11
Action Plan (AP)
for the Week of Session 7

It is important to keep up your discipline to practice daily, but all you need is 15-20 minutes a day. You may remind yourself that short but regular practice is much more effective than longer practices in bigger intervals.

- On the first and second day concentrate on the Behavioral Social Experiments. As BSE 1 can be combined with your daily routines and doesn't require extra time, do it on both days or longer. It is actually a continuous time practice that you hopefully continue to do for a long time until noticing it becomes a part of you, a personal trait. On day 1 and 2 also do the lighter versions of BSE 2 and 3 and start preparing the actions that require more commitment.

- On day 3 implement Practice 1 to start uncovering your social priors/beliefs. You can use this practice over and over to detect unconscious or semi-conscious beliefs.

- On the day 4, practice updating your social beliefs with Practice 2.

- On day 5, practice decision-making in social interactions with *Tosca* and the ultimatum game (Exercise 1 and 2).

- On day 6 dedicate yourself to memorizing the communication tool and to reflecting on Einstein's quote. Continue using the active-constructive communication tool in the following days as it doesn't take time off your other activities. Turn it into a continuous-time practice that accompanies you wherever you are. Moreover, continue reflecting on the Einstein quote.

Short Journaling:

Every day after finishing the practice, jot down a few comments and reflections in your diary or alternatively in the space provided below. You already have the habit of writing short notes by now. Just continue by recording your observations as straightforwardly as possible, without evaluating. It's all about learning, not grading ourselves.

11.12
Personal Notes and Insights

The Writing Space for Your Experiences and Observations

Example:

Today I exchanged a few words with the courier who often brings me parcels. I was

astonished how warm his reaction was, as if he had waited for me to say something.

The short exchange cheered me up.

I finally came around to send a thank you note to the assistant who is always so helpful.

She is absent unfortunately, so I got an automated reply. I'll contact her again later.

MINDING THE STRATEGIC ADAPTATION IN LIFE (SAL)

Decisions as the Basis of Well-being

Mindfulness-based Strategic Awareness Training Comprehensive Workbook:
New approach Based on Free Energy and Active inference for Skillful Decision-making,
First Edition. Juan Humberto Young.
Companion website: www.wiley.com/go/young/mbsatworkbook

12.1
Getting Started
Task of Session 8, Investment and Benefits

Task of Session 8:

Reviewing the vital learning points of the program.

Developing a plan for the Free Energy Minimization Self – the FEMS plan.

Training to make balanced, skillful decisions towards sustainable, personal flourishing.

Connecting balanced, skillful decisions with an action plan.

Minding skill trained in Session 8:

Strengthening the ability to make strategically aware, skillful and balanced decisions.

Preparing to put the resulting decisions into action.

Expected benefits of this session and corresponding practices are:

· Increased understanding of the goals of the program and its transformative power for one's life path.

· Practical understanding of Strategic Awareness (SA) in active life: Applied SA for personal flourishing.

· Hands-on experience with learning to formulate, implement and update the personal strategic plan FEMS (Free-Energy Minimizer Self) for achieving increased well-being and flourishing.

Investment required to reap the benefits of this session:

◉ Time to read the material: less than 3% of the time you spend awake per day, equivalent to 30 minutes maximum (depending on your reading skills).

◉ Time for developing the Plan for the Free Energy Minimizing Self – the FEMS plan.

The plan can be worked on in several steps and continuously perfected after the program. Life-long updating is an optimal way to sustainable flourishing and a fulfilled life. As this activity is very personal and without a pre-defined endpoint, the investment in time depends entirely on your personal engagement. Clearly, the time invested is compensated generously time and again by avoiding decision errors and benefiting from a clear-minded orientation in life.

"Good things take time, as the saying goes.
One of the life lessons I learned on the MBSAT journey
is accepting my own pace and stepping forward.
Three years after my MBSAT course I am still optimizing
my SOPA list every month; it helps me not to forget
who I am and advance my business in a way that
is congruent with my values and goals in life, including
what I would like to achieve for my family and kids."

12.2
Quiz

Session 7: Minding our Social Experience (SoE)

This is the last voluntary quiz to reaffirm your understanding of MBSAT's foundations and the core social elements that are essential in human life. Taking a few moments and seeing for yourself, what you have retained from Session 7 can make a lot of difference in your life. Constructive relationships are a truly crucial component of well-being. Besides it is an entertaining way of reviewing your learnings.

1) What does the parable of the long spoons teach us? Comment its meaning in a few words of your own.

_____

_____

_____

_____

_____

3) List the NCR behavioral experiments in MBSAT?

a. _____

b. _____

c. _____

3) What is the purpose of behavioral social experiments in MBSAT?

_____

_____

_____

_____

_____

4) Give some examples of NCR behavioral experiments you have implemented yourself.

_____

_____

_____

_____

_____

5) Name and briefly describe the four main aspects of observation relevant for minding our social experience.

Aspect 1: _____

_____

Aspect 2: _____

_____

Aspect 3: _____

_____

Aspect 4: _____

_____

6) In your opinion what is the role of Minding in updating social beliefs? What is your key insight regarding Minding in general?

_____

_____

_____

_____

_____

7) What are the insights you have drawn from the prisoner dilemma exercise in MBSAT?

_____

_____

_____

_____

_____

8) Discuss the decisional outcomes of the opera *Tosca*.

_____

_____

_____

_____

_____

9) Discuss the Ultimatum game and your personal conclusions from the game.

_____

_____

_____

_____

_____

10) Comment on your views regarding the Mindful Free Energy Minimizing Communication Model.

_____

_____

_____

_____

_____

11) Write a few lines about your thoughts on:

a) Einstein's fundamental question on the nature of the universe.

b) The Samurai advice on hiring valuable collaborators.

c) The implications for human relations of the American journalist's comment that we are not God.

a) Is the universe friendly?

_____

_____

_____

_____

_____

b) How to hire valuable collaborators:

_____

_____

_____

_____

_____

c) What does the comment of the American journalist suggest for universal human relationships?

_____

_____

_____

_____

_____

Recommended solutions of the quiz can be found on the companion website: www.wiley.com/go/Young/mbsatworkbook

12.3
Introduction and Concepts/Consolidation

We are approaching the end of the program. Hopefully, you have gained practical and conceptual knowledge for improving the value of your decisions, which is the crucial mediator of the quality of people's lives. Valuable, skillful decisions are what lead to higher levels of mental health, well-being, and flourishing. Conversely, it is unskillful decisions that create mental malaise such as stress, anxiety, and other undesirable states.

> *"Life is the sum of all choices."*
> Albert Camus

In practical terms, as you finish the program, the real work of application is about to begin as far as implementing the training during these past weeks and integrating the learnings in your everyday life are concerned. It is with this goal in view that this session concentrates on developing and formulating your Mindful Free Energy Minimizer Self with a plan to guide you and help you to keep scores of how well you are doing in minding the strategic awareness of your BETA and beliefs, the drivers of your decisions and actions. The plan is also an easy-to-use tool that allows you to continuously update your skillful beliefs, opportunities and positive actions (SOPA) after completing the 8-session course. SOPA is a tool that can accompany you everywhere all the time.

Figures 12.1 – 12.4 below provide a recap in graphical form of what you have learned and trained.

The first invitation is for reducing four states:
- Agitation that creates anxiety.
- Reactivity that creates regrets.
- Self-centeredness that builds egotistic BETAs.
- Lack of flexibility that impedes creativity and learning.

Figure 12.1: The Four States We Need to Reduce

The second invitation is to activate four desirable states starting with the letter "C" (the four "Cs"):

- Calmness that reduces agitation.

- Clarity that helps reduce reactivity.

- Caring that reduces self-centeredness.

- Consciousness that reduces lack of flexibility.

Figure 12.2: The Four States We Need to Activate

The third invitation is to train with and practice the MBSAT protocol for learning to mind the four crucial dimensions of our life: our BETA, our Portfolio of Beliefs, our Social Experience, and our Strategic Adaptation in Life.

Figure 12.3: The Four Skills We Need to Train

The table below summarizes the states we need to reduce and the four Cs we need to activate, and then relates all of them to the four dimensions of the MBSAT training in the 3rd column on the right. It is a complete overview of what the MBSAT training seeks to achieve.

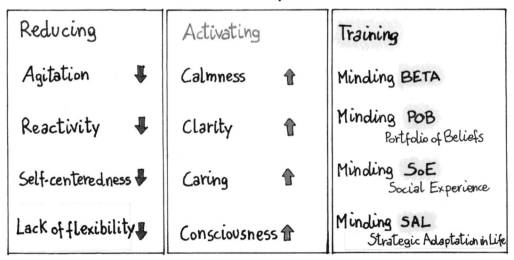

Figure 12.4: Summary: The Four Dimensions of MBSAT Training

MBSAT views the external environment as a generative process[1] of potential experiences for survival but also for distress. We discussed that the nature of the environment is VUCA, an acronym originally created by military scientists to describe the evolving dynamics of war as becoming more volatile, uncertain, complex and ambiguous. The acronym has rapidly been adopted in civil life, first in the business world and by now it has become an uncontroversial, widely used word in daily vernacular, reflecting that life in general is becoming more VUCA.

Volatility means erratic events one can't predict well, even if there is information about their causes. Uncertainty refers to events where there is little or no information on one or more variables: the probability of occurrence, timing, magnitude, potential effects and side effects, etc. Complexity entails interdependent events, often characterized by interconnected causes that make it difficult to point out what could be the critical elements driving changes. Finally, events become increasingly ambiguous, meaning that parameters are unclear (good or bad? friend or foe? helpful or harmful? etc.).

Based on information theory and computational neuroscience it has been proposed that humans, in their quest for well-being and survival, have encoded models of the environment in the neurological circuits of their brains. This suggests that the brain/mind is an information processing organ that requires to keep sensorial abilities in optimal states to be able to perceive and register data that is useful, truthful, and relevant for survival and doing well. This is by no means an easy task for people in an information-driven environment that is increasingly unstable. It is well documented and recognized that the information and data swirling around in the environment are often of dubious quality, either unintentionally or by purposeful design (noisy fake news, biased information with polarizing tendencies, etc.) thus making it hard for people to find factual, objective data upon which to base their daily decisions.

In earlier sessions we have also learned that our brains embody generative models. Some models of the environment are naturally protogenetic, meaning that we are born with them. For example, babies just know that crying will catch their parents attention and that smiling will bring joy to people around them. These are the models that inform our natural beliefs; for example, that we need to drink water, eat food, require sleep, and so on. We also all know that we can't jump from a balcony believing that we can fly or that we can't stay underwater for more than a short while without artificial support (diving equipment) or else we perish. These beliefs help us maintain our natural, biological integrity.

But as soon as we start growing up and engaging with human-made, created environments, another set of generative models begins to form based on the experiences we make. These models are representations of the world around us in the form of encoded beliefs or priors that help us interact with the surroundings we are engaged in and help us survive and lead a good life. However, when the information passing back and forth between people's generative models (beliefs) and the VUCA generative process (the environment) is out of synchronization, it creates adverse states, conflicts and unhappiness in people's lives. This is why

---

1 More information on the notion of the generative process can be found above in Chapter 2 (Figure 2.1 and Section 2.3.3), Chapter 3 (Section 3.3), and Chapter 4 (Section 4.7.2).

human-created, artificial, i.e. non-protogenetic, beliefs are centerstage in MBSAT training: sustainable well-being depends on updating our beliefs and actions to skillfully adapt ourselves to the environment, or, if it is possible to change or accommodate the environment to our beliefs, predictions and decisions, as long it doesn't harm others and the natural ecosystem. These strategies will hopefully result in reducing Free Energy (decision errors), thus sustaining higher levels of well-being and our desire for flourishing.

In a post modern society like ours, it is information and its interpretation (Lyotard, 1994) that builds the strategic advantage for optimal efficacy (doing well) and efficiency (low costs) in utilizing our natural intelligence (NI) and extended artificial intelligence (AI): computers, mobile phones, tablets, amongst others. For this reason, MBSAT 2.0 as presented in this workbook is at its root an applied, computational, neuroscience-based mind learning protocol, comparable to a machine learning protocol for artificial intelligence. The intention of MBSAT is to help participants process information more efficiently and effectively in order to improve their chances of survival and prosperity in interaction with the external environment and assist them in minding their personal, internal milieu (their BETAs: body sensations, emotions, thoughts and action impulses). This is the ultimate purpose you have trained for over these past weeks, or, in machine learning language, you have been "fed training data" using behavioral experiments, meditation practices, and exercises in order to increase your abilities to accurately process information and ensure agile skillful decision making.

However, training human, natural intelligence (NI) is quite different from training machine learning (AI). Kissinger et al. (2021) characterize the difference as follows: "Although AI can draw conclusions, make predictions, and make decisions, it does not possess self-awareness, in other words the ability to reflect on its role in the world. It does not have intention, motivation, morality, or emotions..." (p. 26). This is why it is necessary to first train the BETA or the doors of perception to ensure appropriate aperture and calmness as foundation for transformative work. This corresponds to the first part of the MBSAT training program. Then follows the required transformation to learn to live better on the hard, bumpy road of the world and contribute towards becoming a digitalized, more inclusive, peaceful and universal society. For the individual this requires the ability to transform own generative models and beliefs about reality in a VUCA world. This corresponds to the second leg of the training MBSAT program: learning to update and minding our beliefs to support skillful decisions and actions for reducing Free Energy and maintain our viability in a dynamically changing society.

The critical difference between training NI and AI is the natural ability of human beings as autonomous agents to run a virtual theater in their brains/mind, building simulations and counterfactual scenarios, anticipating themselves acting or abstaining from action and pondering possible consequences. This metacognitive ability is unique in human beings; it casts the brain/mind as a biological, predictive organ, and this is precisely where appropriate, active and continuous mindfulness practices are useful. As we have learned mindfulness in MBSAT means training to observe and mind ourselves to increase agency and autonomy to lead a life with less conflicts, internally and externally with others and society.

In light of the above, it is easy to realize that it makes sense to use the brain as a prediction organ instead of as a reactive biological device, since reacting ex-post facto to our needs or messages from the environment may be too late to be optimal. Mother nature (adaptive evolution) has evolved our brain to anticipate our needs. It is not hard to see that a brain emitting wrong predictions would not be active in the game of life for a very long time; eventually such a brain would succumb to its own failures and cease to exist. Therefore, it is imperative for survival that our brains are capable of generating skillful predictions.

In MBSAT 2.0 we have learned that it is important to keep track of a computational quantity: Free Energy. At the computational level keeping track of Variational and Expected Free Energy is the goal of the program. It is how we monitor the quality of our predictions, prediction errors and decisions. Minimizing Free Energy means that we are right on track with our predictions and with the quality of our decisions. We also learned to maintain an open, equanimous BETA to help us maintain well calibrated, generative models, in the form of adaptive beliefs and to vectorize and orient them in the most appropriate directions to sustain our needs. Algorithmically this corresponds to a continuous process of minimizing Free Energy using Active Inference.

Up to now we have looked at how the brain minimizes Free Energy from a predominantly cognitive angle. Another question is how changes in the brain are implemented biologically. The fact is that currently it is not known for sure how this happens. The human brain is incredibly complex. On average it has between 85 to 100 billion cells/neurons; each neuron has a capacity of about 30,000 inputs, where one input can transmit around 5,000 measuring units (quanta) of neurotransmitter signals in five milliseconds and in addition receive millions of data also in milliseconds. Thus, one can imagine the difficulty of understanding the precise functioning of such an organ. In other words, we simply don't have enough knowledge about this natural marvel, its capacity and how this carbon-based electrochemical system works. We only have some rough ideas about how neurons pass on information, for example that networks of neurological circuits are activated by electrical impulses and facilitated by biochemical substances (hormones), passing information top-down and bottom-up in a hierarchical order.

From a practical, computational neuroscience point of view (Rolls, 2014; Solms, 2018), the best mechanism for tracking and minimizing the computational quantity of Free Energy is by minding our basic innate BETA (sensations, emotions, impulses thoughts) and keeping it under control by using available mental resources from our consciousness in the working memory (Baddeley, 1992). Emotions, impulses and sensations represent natural, instinctive, expressive behaviors, reactions and physiological responses resulting from coordinated neuronal events to help us survive. These cellular events arise as responses to events happening in our lives encoded as rewards or punishments. Therefore, happiness or unhappiness are reactions of our BETA to the felt sense of rewards or punishments. Thus, when avoiding punishment, there are feelings of relief, while on the other hand not getting rewards creates anger and frustration. Positive valences (happiness, enjoyment) facilitate moving towards rewards as they help us reduce Free Energy; negative valences such as aversion and fear on the other hand do the opposite: they increase Free Energy; sometimes just momentarily to later redirect the BETA to sustainable FEM states.

Innate BETA needs are regulated unconsciously, and the reaction is instinctive, thus with little energetic costs, for example, feeling thirsty and drinking a glass of water without further thinking, or feeling an itch and scratching unconsciously. However, if you start to think about when to drink (now or later) and what (water, beer, juice, etc.) or whether to scratch yourself with your hand or use a scraper, conscious content to the short-term working memory is added to fulfill your needs and yes, you just instigated a small extra effort created a demand for more work for in the form of deciding "the best way to fulfill your needs", as this requires energy; in other words, you just created Free Energy. From the viewpoint of information theory you just created more uncertainty or disorder in your decisional space, which can be good as now there is more information on how to go about fulfilling your thirst, yet it also engendered certain metabolic costs for running your generative models: predicting in this form is no longer automatic, but involves alternative beliefs and the policies about what choice (water, beer or juice) or decision will reduce Free Energy more efficiently by giving you more satisfaction (evidencing your generative model) and producing less regrets (prediction errors).

Culturally learned needs, though in principle consciously driven, are sometimes fulfilled automatically as habits to save metabolic costs. For example, let us consider the cultural belief that brushing your teeth is a good health practice. To avoid filling our short-term working memory with thoughts about how to satisfy the need for dental hygiene, we build teeth-brushing habits that routinize the fulfillment and avoid cumbersome, energetically expensive conscious processes. They work like the cache in computing by storing information for faster access in future use; for example, in the case of brushing the teeth the sight of the toothbrush automatically provides effortless access to the full dental cleaning habit/routine (Maisto et al., 2019).

In connection with beliefs in Chapters 9-10, Sessions 5-6 and Chapter 3 of Part 1 we noted that people's needs and lives are mostly driven by unconscious, hence transparent (i.e. invisible to the mind) processes to avoid the high metabolic costs of keeping cognitive content. While this strategy is effective and efficient for our daily low-risk routines, it is insufficient for adopting new cultural beliefs, updating beliefs, or getting rid of legacy beliefs. These tasks require activating long-term memory and bringing the change requirements to our conscious short-term working memory, which has limited capacity. Changing beliefs necessitates additional work and metabolic resources in the form of experiments and interventions to support building new neurological connections in the brain and consolidating them in the form of new beliefs and behaviors.

You may recall the case of a MBSAT student mentioned earlier (indicate the session), a talented man who grew up in a country with extremely polarized views on ethnic relations and how conflictive he felt regarding one of his team members from a different ethnic group. Following a MBSAT course, he was able to recognize his personal issues of prejudice and bias with respect to this person. This made him really sad, given that his aspiration as a leader was to be fair to all members of his team. After additional MBSAT training, he realized that it was not his fault to harbor those beliefs given that they were generalized in the environment where he grew up. He also recognized the actual changes in the environment, and was aware that his beliefs were no longer adaptive and that he needed to change them to live a normal life under the new circumstances. Obviously, it was not sufficient to merely recognize his biases; he realized that he also needed to update his beliefs on human relations in the context of a more diverse and integrated world and adjust his BETA and behavior. This new reality compelled him to double down on learning and training at a deeper level, bringing to his conscious memory experiences from the past that shaped his beliefs and making these beliefs opaque (visible). Despite his desire to engage in transformative work, he gave up after all, presumably because it was too hard and painful for him or perhaps his motivation was not strong enough. Unable to enact the necessary changes to his portfolio of beliefs and confronted with the prospect of living with permanent conflicts he quit his high-level position and moved out of his country of birth.

This case illustrates the essence of MBSAT training, learning to become aware and vectorize our BETA (orienting it in an appropriate direction) and bringing to our attention (our short-term working memory) mental representations from the long-term memory in the form of failed decisions, prediction errors and beliefs we want to dissolve and recalibrate, building more adequate posteriors (new beliefs) that will effectively support our Free-Energy Minimizing Self-FEMS.

In MBSAT this is called minding our Decision Acuity. For Moutoussis et al. (2021) decision acuity represents learning speed, a cognitive ability to consider the effects of outcomes in the future, and a low level of decision variability. In MBSAT's terminology it means honing the precision of strategically aware BETAs and Beliefs to extract valuable knowledge from the environment that enables decisions moving us into the zone of Free Energy minimization and away from the zone of high Free Energy. Figure 12.5 illustrates this dynamic and summarizes it in an easy to interpret, yet comprehensive visual.

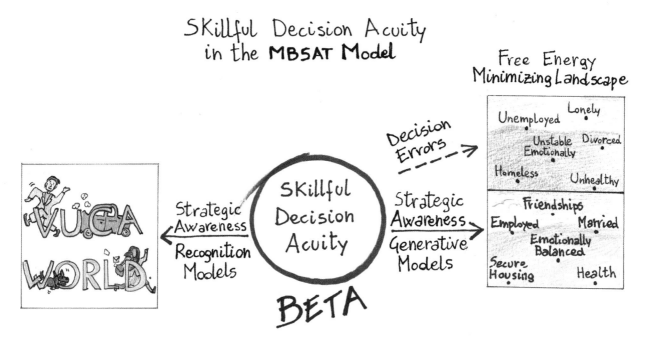

Figure 12.5 Skillful Decision Acuity

12.4
Practices

12.4.1 Exercise/Practice 1 - SOPA: Skillful BETAs, Opportunities, and Positive Actions

SOPA stands for **S**killful betas and beliefs; **O**pportunities and **P**ositive **A**ctions. In this session, the last of the 8-session training program, SOPA is presented as an exercise. Its true purpose is, however, that you turn it into an ongoing practice by using the SOPA plan as a tool that accompanies you for a long time and that you keep updating as your life evolves. (Regarding the distinction between practice and exercise, please, see the preliminary note in Section 5.4.1, Chapter 5 Session 1 above.)

SOPA is MBSAT's tool for personal strategic planning to become a Mindful Free Energy Minimizer Self, able to minimize decision and prediction errors. In principle, it works in the same way as corporate strategic planning. Companies program their business activities and calibrate their portfolio of products and offerings, including new products and eliminating old ones, to stay in the profit zone, remain viable as entities and prosper as much as possible. In a similar vein individuals are well advised to plan ahead in order to stay in zones of Free Energy minimization (equivalent to zones of higher profits) and away of zones of Free Energy proliferation (zones of losses). This means staying in states of personal well-being, away from incurring excessive metabolic costs resulting from making prediction and decision errors. SOPA is the personal strategic planning tool for recalibrating people's beliefs, activate Strategic Awareness to perceive opportunities and plan positive actions to realize their aspirations. Beliefs are at the source of what we do in life. They inform our goals and prompt our actions. SOPA helps individuals to keep their beliefs and generative models in shape so they can generate value in the form of skillful predictions and decisions and to plan skillful actions to achieve their desires and valuable goals. In Spanish SOPA means soup. So you can think of SOPA as a nourishing soup that gives you the necessary strength and vitality on the way to your future life path.

SOPA builds the conditions for micro neurological states to coincide with desired macro states of perceivable well-being. It is nice to want to live in states of Free Energy minimization given how critical it is to be in these states for our authentic well-being. However, if our neurological networks don't build micro-states of minimized Free Energy, our desire remains just elusive aspirations without true positive effects on our daily lives. For example, a desire to be equanimous and not treating people rudely to will not materialize unless at the micro level of the generative models in the brain there are certain structural changes that only can happen with repeated practice of responding with kindness instead of treating other people rudely.

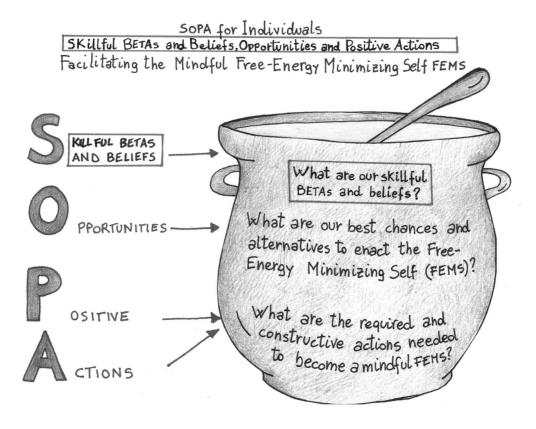

Figure 12.6 SOPA for Individuals – Skillful BETAs and Beliefs, Opportunities and Positive Actions;
Facilitating the Free-Energy Minimizing Self (FEMS)

Only consistent practicing can build the required new neurological connections in the brain for being nice to people, while simultaneously diminishing the activation of the neuro-cellular networks of rudeness toward people. Otherwise it would hardly be possible to be nice to others in an authentic, natural way. In fact, we would increase the internal conflicts between our desires to be nice and our habits of being rude. Hence, any serious training to improve the quality of our BETAs and decision-making which are the mechanisms for reducing Free Energy must include practice to improve the generative models of our brains at a micro-neurological level, to build innate and natural reactions and responses that are congruent with our aspired macro states of how we interact with the environment. This means working not only at a conceptual level, but more importantly to model and practice new forms of the BETA, as it is the only way to build the required new neurological network at the cellular level of the brain and align it with the desirable macro states of well-being and flourishing. It is the old struggle between a desired conscious behavior (wanting to be nice) and the unconscious actual behavior (being rude). This conundrum is similar to what Argyris and Schön (1978) called espoused theories (wanting to be nice) vs. theories-in-use (being rude), discussed above in Chapter 3 (Section 3.4.2).

Behavioral experiments to initiate the required transformative process can be short and inexpensive. For example, one of my past clients, the CEO of a large, strictly patriarchal multibillion investment company, had friction with his staff. He reported with amazement the positive outcomes of simple NCR behavioral experiments: greeting formerly unnoticed people (a simple good morning), celebrating his closer collaborators (a token gift for good work: a bunch of flowers, a chocolate bar, etc.) and respecting those he believed were against him (letting them voice their objections and ideas). "Wow, Juan, it is amazing, such small changes from my part, and my people seem to be so much happier. It was unbelievable."

SOPA helps identify the beliefs that either support or interfere with people's well-being and helps them design a strategic plan to update unhelpful beliefs and ensure an adaptable and useful portfolio of beliefs. As illustrated in Figure 12.6, the acronym SOPA relates to three concrete processes of inquiry and renewal, happening in part sequentially and in part simultaneously as one component feeds into the others and back-and-forth reiterations may be needed.

The first phase of the practice invites participants to investigate their BETA and Beliefs in the context of an experience that prevented them from minimizing Free Energy (creating prediction and decision errors).

In the second phase participants seek to find answers to the question what opportunities are at hand for reframing BETAs and updating Beliefs to achieve a more favorable Free Energy outcome, either dealing with the consequences of the earlier experience or preparing for future challenges.

The final inquiry consists in identifying what could be personal positive actions, policies and strategies to get closer to becoming a Free Energy Minimizer Self (FEMS): a state where our own decisions continuously create value and well-being for ourselves, others and the environment.

The goal of this practice and exercise is to design a realistic and concrete strategic Free Energy minimization plan to facilitate skillful decision making around four key dimensions of life: family, work, leisure/self-related and social activities. In the hassle of everyday life very few people take the time to make a deeply reflected, comprehensive plan for their future that also includes concrete actions, and yet the importance of such a plan for sustainable well-being and self-efficacy is obvious. With their personal SOPA plan MBSAT participants are in a better position to master the challenges of VUCA world.

The practice consists of three main steps each of which relates to a separate worksheet:

Structure of the SOPA practice:

STEP 1: Identifying Skillful Betas and Beliefs	**SOPA WORKSHEET 1:** Observing and Identifying Beliefs
STEP 2: Updating Beliefs and Generative Models	**SOPA WORKSHEET 2:** Updating Beliefs
STEP 3: Opportunities and Positive Actions	**SOPA WORKSHEET 3:** Opportunities and Positive Actions for Free-Energy Minimization

Each of the steps above consists of a sequence of actions detailed below. As it will take some time to work each worksheet through thoroughly you could spread the practice over several days. In any case the idea is that your personal strategic plan that results from the combination of the three worksheets will accompany you from now on, that is you will keep the worksheets updated and consult them whenever you need orientation or must take important decisions.

> "One of the life lessons I learned on the MBSAT journey is accepting my pace and keep moving forward. I am still optimizing my SOPA list every month. I have been doing so several years, ever since my first MBSAT course. It helps me organize my priorities and gives me a sense of identity, who I am."

Let's begin with the guidelines for Step 1.

Step 1: Identifying Skillful Betas and Beliefs

This step will challenge you to shift your awareness between present moment short-term working memory using worksheets and past experiences stored in your long-term memory, activating metacognitive abilities to investigate past events in a kind of inner virtual theatre.

We begin by finding a comfortable posture in a quiet place where it is also possible for you to read and write. Then desaturating the BETA by calming down and recollecting yourself. Depending on the state you might be in, you could start with a CEO of BETA (Chapter 8, Session 4 above).

With a desaturated and calm BETA we now open the SOPA Worksheet 1: Observing and Identifying Beliefs (Figure 12.7 below), either on an electronic device (laptop, iPad, phone, etc.) or in a pen-and-paper format.

When you are ready, identify one of the four belief dimensions: work, family, leisure/self-related or social life. Gently closing your eyes at this point might be a useful strategy as you will cut stimuli from the external environment, making it easier to concentrate on your internal world.

Take your time to bring to your awareness a recent experience related to the dimension you selected that spontaneously comes to your mind. For example, if you have chosen the work dimension, it could be that you are upset and resentful because your recent year-end bonus was not what you expected.

See, if you can catch your belief driving your generative model about year-end bonuses. For example, it could be that you believe that working harder should get you a higher bonus. If this is the case, this belief is your prior. This is the example you find below in the SOPA Worksheet 1 in the first row on work related generative models.

Assuming that you settle on this belief (hard work equals large bonuses), see if you can rate how difficult it has been to uncover and observe this belief on a scale from easy to hard.

Still holding your eyes gently closed, see if you can rate your precision level of holding this belief, from low, medium and high, where high precision means a very strong, firm belief and low precision a belief that you feel is of lesser importance to you.

Finally, rate the effort that you expect would be required to update this belief.

Before ending the practice, move your awareness to the breath and simply follow the breath naturally for a few minutes before ending the practice and opening the eyes.

Now opening the eyes, you may look again at the worksheet. The example regarding bonuses has been rated in the worksheet as easy to observe (left side of first 3 columns), held with high precision (right side of next 3 columns) and requiring medium effort to update (center of last 3 columns).

After you have familiarized yourself with the columns, fill in the worksheet with your own topic, starting by writing down on the left the belief that you discovered as driver behind the selected experience. Then check the three corresponding areas: difficulty of observing the belief (first 3 columns on the left); precision of holding the belief (next 3 columns in the center) and finally indicate the estimated effort that may be required to update it.

Then staying with the awareness of your BETA for a few more moments, simply letting your impressions of the practice sink in.

Depending on how you feel, you are now free to repeat the process and add one or more beliefs/priors in any of the domains (family, leisure/self-related and social life).

Alternatively, you might either close the practice, or you can decide to proceed to Step 2 of the practice. However, if you need to figure out first how to implement this practice and the insights you have won in your daily life, it may be advisable to rest for a day before moving to Step 2.

Step 2: Updating Beliefs and Generative Models

After Step 1, possibly a day ago, you may be keen to continue and tackle the second part of the SOPA exercise and practice, exploring with curiosity the causes of the prediction failure, either in the example above or an example of your own, based on your personal experience. With Step 2 you begin the process of reviewing and updating your generative models. When events don't go according to existing beliefs and end in disappointment, it is time to ponder updating.

We start with recollecting and aligning our BETA, either with a CEO of BETA or, for more active people, with a Mindful Salsa, an easy and pleasant way to synchronize interoceptive predictions (emotions and feelings), proprioceptive predictions (movements of the body) and exteroceptive predictions (the rhythm of the music). Having a well synchronized BETA is a wonderful start for this important practice.

 SOPA Worksheet 1: Observing and Identifying Beliefs

Mindfulness-Based
Strategic Awareness Training

Identified Beliefs / Priors	Beliefs Liquification and Precisification								
Beliefs driving the related generative models	Difficulty of observing belief			Precision of holding beliefs			Belief updating effort		
	EASY	MEDIUM	HARD	LOW	MEDIUM	HIGH	EASY	MEDIUM	HARD
Work related generative models									
Hard work leads to high bonuses.	✓					✓		✓	
Family related generative models									
Family should provide a safe space for personal growth.		✓				✓			✓
Leisure and self related* generative models									
Leisure should be purely recreational / restorative.	✓					✓			✓
*self-related refers to activities for personal growth and/or well-being									
Social life related generative models									
Social contacts should support aspirations in work area.	✓				✓			✓	
Being outspoken and straightforward is best even when truth is upsetting.		✓				✓	✓		

Figure 12.7 SOPA Worksheet 1: Observing and Identifying Beliefs

Now, finding a quiet place and settling into a comfortable posture from where you can also access the SOPA worksheets. For this practice we use the SOPA Worksheet 2 "Updating Beliefs", the second form of the SOPA worksheet set (Figure 12.9).

The intention is to further develop the work on the beliefs identified in Worksheet 1. Therefore, report the same belief(s) in the left column and enter in words your earlier findings regarding the status of the belief(s), recapitulating Step 1. For the example we have used earlier, it would look as follows:

Generative Models: Observed Beliefs (Priors)	Status of Belief (Recap of Worksheet 1)		
Beliefs driving the related generative models	Difficulty of observing belief	Precision of holding beliefs	Belief updating effort
Work related generative models			
Hard work leads to high bonuses.	easy	high	medium

Figure 12.8 Section a) of SOPA Worksheet 2

Next, we start entering training data for supporting the process of belief updating. First, identify a practice to assist you with the updating process. In the example of a disappointing bonus, it is the POMO practice, From Powerful Money to Mindful Money (Session 6). Then enter your estimation of how often you will need to practice for a transformative result. In this case, a daily POMO meditation of about 20 minutes daily for one week is suggested.

Continue by meditating on what the causes could be for your negative experience that triggered so much anger, frustration, anxiety, and disappointment (preventing you from reducing Free Energy). Take your time to close your eyes and delve into your inner world of thoughts and emotions. For example, you might be thinking you worked very hard this year and therefore believe that you truly deserved a higher bonus, but your boss doesn't appreciate how hard you worked. Or perhaps you find that although you did well, the company didn't, prompting them to save on bonuses. Eventually, as you keep practicing you will start moving to deeper layers of your long-term memory and consciousness and maybe find deeper causes for your "hard work = higher bonus" belief and generative model. You might recall a formative experience of your parents telling you: "If you get good grades, we get you the new bike you want so much." You may also remember other instances when your parents told you, if you did as they suggested, they were going to reward you, for example you didn't particularly like vegetables, they would offer you a perk if you emptied your plate. And your memory may wander off to a particular experience of you as an adolescent eating all the vegetables, because your parents promised you the money to buy the ticket to see Star Wars II. Such insights suggest that you might be conditioned from an early age to expect a reward every time you make an effort.

SOPA Worksheet 2: Updating Beliefs

Generative Models: Observed Beliefs (Priors)	Status of Belief (Recap of Worksheet 1)			Belief Updating Process			Estimated Free-Energy Effect of Causal Hypotheses			
Beliefs driving the related generative models	Difficulty of observing belief	Precision of holding beliefs	Belief updating effort	With what Practice	Frequency of Practice	Preliminary Causal Hypotheses of Prediction Error	An appreciative precisification (Subjective Estimation)			
							weak	medium	strong	Weight in %
Work related generative models										
Hard work leads to high bonuses.	easy	high	medium	POMO	weekly					
						I didn't work hard enough.			✓	50%
						The company didn't do well this year; they are saving on bonus payouts.		✓		30%
						I always expect a reward when I go the extra mile.	✓			15%
						Random causes				5%
Family related generative models										
Family should provide a safe space for personal growth.				Irimi	twice per week				✓	
Leisure and self related* generative models										
Leisure should be purely recreational / restorative.				Mindful walking	daily			✓		
* related to personal growth and/or well-being										
Social life related generative models										
Social contacts should support aspirations in work area.				Meditation on Friendliness	every other day			✓		
Being outspoken and straightforward is best even when truth is upsetting.				Full emotion observation meditation; Thought swap Exercise	after each event					

Figure 12.9 SOPA Worksheet 2: Updating Beliefs

Equipped with this data (events and insights), you can open your eyes and take up the worksheet again to fill in the column "Preliminary Causal Hypotheses of Prediction Error" (the erroneous anticipation of getting a high bonus this year). The column is entitled "preliminary" because as you keep practicing POMO, you might modify your current findings. The worksheet is quite literally meant as a tool you keep working with for some time, amending and complementing your entries as your practice progresses. In doing so, limit the hypotheses to no more than 3-4.

Your worksheet could look like the example in Figure 12.10:

Belief Updating Process			Estimated Free-Energy Effect of Causal Hypotheses			
With what Practice	Frequency of Practice	Preliminary Causal Hypotheses of Prediction Error	An appreciative precisification (Subjective Estimation)			
			weak	medium	strong	Weight in %
POMO	weekly					
		I didn't work hard enough.			✓	50%
		The company didn't do well this year; they are saving on bonus payouts.		✓		30%
		I always expect a reward when I go the extra mile.	✓			15%
		Random causes				5%

Figure 12.10 Section b) of SOPA Worksheet 2

Now moving to the next column: Estimated Free-Energy Effect of Causal Hypotheses. This is probably the most critical aspect of the updating beliefs process, as the precision attached to the hypotheses provides direction and confidence to successfully update beliefs and choose the relevant actions for reducing Free Energy and increasing our well-being. The task here is to estimate how much each hypothesis contributed to the undesired outcome, hence it is about attributing scores and weights. It is your relative subjective level of confidence or the precision of your hypotheses, which by the way are also predictions about what could be the causes of failing to get the bonus. You can also sample the environment about these causes to build more accurate precision. For example, you can talk with colleagues to find out if they are also disappointed with their bonus. If the answer is yes, it supports the hypothesis that the company's bonus payout was very restrictive this year, in other words it has less to do with your performance.

We start by estimating the level of influence: weak, moderate or strong, checking the respective boxes. For example, you might reckon that your generative model "hard work leads to higher bonuses" failed because you didn't work hard enough this year and this is to a large extent the cause of the Free Energy (anger, frustration, disappointment, etc.) that ensued, so you check the box "strong".

You can continue and evaluate another cause such as the causal hypothesis "The company didn't do well this year." If you reckon that the company had indeed mediocre results, you might score the effect on the outcome as medium, still feeling frustrated, but less so because you know the limitation of the company's finances.

After adding the check marks in the respective columns for all the causal hypothesis you wrote down, you proceed by assigning an approximate numerical value in the last column. These scorings are of course subjective appreciations or subjective estimations. For example, you can decide that not having worked hard enough is 50% of the cause why did you did not got the bonus. You could estimate that the finances of the company may have contributed another 30% to the undesired outcome. Then, following the examples used in Worksheet 2, let's say you give a score of 15% for your conditioning that prompts you to always expect a reward when you go the extra mile. The remaining 5% you might think could be random causes. As mentioned above, for this practice it is best to limit the preliminary causal hypotheses to 3-4 items with their respective level of precision (weight) and use random causes as a joker to round the precision to a total 100%.

Having rated the causes driving your belief/generative model of "hard work = higher bonus" with different precision weights, you can now begin to play with different weights, seeking to find out how this could help you minimize Free Energy, that reducing frustration, disappointment, and regrets and decreasing prediction errors and decision mistakes.

At this point you may be ready to engage in updating your prior/belief "hard work = higher bonuses" as the evidence (not getting the expected bonus) suggests that your current generative model failed in helping you to minimize Free Energy. This is the focus of Step 3 below based on the SOPA Worksheet 3.

Box 12.1
Using Data Collected from Friends and Acquaintances

During this program, you have collected data by asking friends, family, colleagues, and other acquaintances to provide feedback on instances where they have observed you making decisions and taking actions resulting in good outcomes. These are instances of your Free-Energy Minimization Self (FEMS) in action. The collected data is a source of rich information about you operating at your best.

Based on your initial analysis of the responses following the guidelines in Box 8.1 above (Chapter 8 Session 4), you can now do mining of this data from different perspectives: for observing and identifying beliefs (SOPA Worksheet 1), updating your beliefs (SOPA Worksheet 2), and supporting your spontaneous hypotheses about what positive actions will lead you to minimize Free Energy in your BETA and achieve your goals (SOPA Worksheet 3).

For example, imagine that you discovered there is a new opening in another department in your company that interests you, but you are insecure about what action to take: either go ahead and try to get the position or just drop the opportunity, believing that maybe later something else will show up. You remembered in one of the vignettes in the databank you have collected; a friend wrote that one of your skills is to move swiftly in the face of opportunities; she gave you the example of buying your apartment in a seller's market with little supply of apartments. She remembers how you made an offer without all the details, which got you the apartment.

With this additional information, you might decide to take action to get the job and initiate the necessary steps or policies (internal lobbying, interviewing, etc.) to secure the job, expecting to increase your BETA satisfaction and achieve your goal.

Step 3: Opportunities and Positive Actions

Now we come to SOPA Worksheet 3, the third table "Opportunities and Positive Actions" (Figure 12.12 below). You might need to let some days pass after SOPA Worksheet 2: Updating Beliefs before starting Worksheet 3. Again the best strategy to begin this step is to do a CEO of BETA or a Mindful Salsa. Find a quiet place, maybe with the eyes closed, and start to formulate new beliefs (posteriors). For example "To get a higher bonus I need not only to work hard but also to generate above average results." "If I want higher bonuses, I need to find another company with stronger financial results." Or "I should change my expectations, and not always expect a reward for above average work; maybe the satisfaction of having performed well is a sufficient intrinsic reward."

Now move to the following column "Opportunities and Actions". For example, you know there is a new opening in another company, that is in better financial shape than yours. Or as you are doing well in the company, your boss is willing to give you more leeway to make your own decisions about the direction of your department.

Move now to positive actions that will facilitate Free Energy minimization, for example changing your employer, negotiating more autonomy, etc. You can use as reference the Free-Energy Minimizing Action Quadrants we discussed in Session 4. The matrix is repeated here for ease of reference (Figure 12.11).

- **Drop**: This means cutting and eliminating entirely an existing activity when the action of cutting would considerably increase the person's well-being, for example, smoking.

- **Trim**: This means reducing existing activities. It means that by reducing their frequency, intensity, or duration it would significantly improve well-being, for example, decoupling personal conditioning from performance, that is trimming the rewards expectations and disengaging them from the level of performance.

- **Boost**: This means increasing activities, resulting in a boost to the quality of life, for example, using your expanded autonomy to make more decisions that increase your satisfaction at work.

- **Generate**: These are activities that are not part of a participant's present activity inventory, but they have been recognized as a way to improve the quality of life, for example, developing the habit of going to concerts, museums, and other cultural activities, or intellectual activities such as taking courses on subjects of interest. For example you can generate a new action by applying for an opening at a competing company. Another positive action you can take if you are a team leader is to boost the level of autonomy you are giving to your collaborators at work.

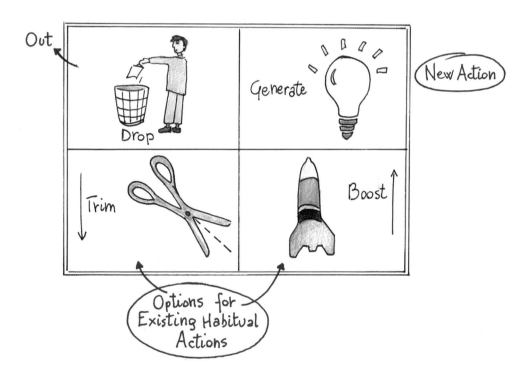

Figure 12.11 The Free-Energy Minimizing Action Quadrants

Once you have classified the positive actions, you can then give a personal likelihood about the expectation of the actions reducing Free Energy, in other words what your personal expectations are.

Begin by assigning a value to the expected Free Energy minimization effect of the BETA for each action (Worksheet 3, column "Opportunities and Actions"). In the first example you decide to take a course, which may increase your workload, but also provide you satisfaction. So, for now you rank it medium. In the second example you plan to change your employer. You might be happier after changing or, on

SOPA Worksheet 3: Opportunities and Positive Actions for Free Energy Minimization

Updated Beliefs / Posteriors	Opportunities and Actions	Positive Actions: Options				Expected Free-Energy Minimization					
						BETA			Valuable Goal		
		Drop	Gener-ate	Trim	Boost	low	medi-um	high	low	medi-um	high
Work dimension											
To get a higher bonus I need not only to work hard but also to generate above average results.	Take a course in time management for improving efficiency.				✓		✓			✓	
If I want higher bonuses, I need to work for another company with stronger financial results.	Take advantage of an opening in another company.	✓					✓				✓
I should change my expectations, and not always expect a reward for above average work; maybe the satisfaction of having performed well is a sufficient intrinsic reward.	Be happy with more leeway to take decisions in your department granted by your boss.			✓				✓			✓
Family dimension											
Leisure dimension											
Social life and self related dimension											

Figure 12.12 SOPA Worksheet 3: Opportunities and Positive Actions

the contrary, regret the move; it can go either way. So, you give it also a medium. In the third example of having more freedom, your BETA is likely to benefit, and you rank it high.

Then you reflect on how the planned action will affect the goal implied in your updated belief and the effect on Free-Energy minimization. If you take a course, it will improve your chances of getting a bonus, but as it is still uncertain, you check medium. In the case of a new company, you are likely to get a higher bonus, because this is how you select the new employer. Therefore, you check high. Regarding bonus expectations, you realize that the meaning of work is a valuable goal and the likelihood that it helps minimizing Free Energy irrespective of income is high. So, you rank it high.

Now you have practice with SOPA, you can continue and complete it with information for the other dimensions of life: family, social and self-related life and leisure. This becomes your personal blueprint guiding your decisions and direction towards flourishing.

In formulating SOPA, my years of experience as a senior manager at one of the largest American accounting and management consulting firms, designing and supervising information systems and strategic projects was useful.

12.4.2 Practice 2 - Continous-time pratice: CEO of BETA "Strategic Awareness"

Strategic awareness, as trained in MBSAT, has a practical and discerning quality to it. It makes us lucid and alert to the implications of our decisions for both others and ourselves, and conveys a subtle distinction between what is constructive and beneficial in the long run and what is detrimental, even if it is only latently so.

This makes the CEO of BETA on strategic awareness an invaluable mini practice for all kinds of situations. It is easy to integrate at work and in your private life.

As all the others CEO of BETA the practice has three steps:

In **Step 1** we gather our scattered minds, catching the present state of our BETA.

In **Step 2** we focus on breathing, becoming aware of the in-flow and out-flow of air and the contraction and expansion of the abdomen.

In **Step 3** we expand the awareness to whatever issue of strategic significance we may be confronting, with an attitude of strategic openness, and patience. We are not looking for solutions, but holding the situation in mind with gentle curiosity, without judging, simply in awareness for a few moments and breathing with it. When we feel ready, we slowly open our eyes, calm and refreshed and ready for whatever the generative process shows us.

12.5
Learnings from Session 8

Here are some expected benefits resulting from this session:

- You have learned the SOPA process, to design and formulate a strategic plan that can guide your Free Energy Minimizing Self (FEMS) to navigate a life that allows you to keep higher levels of well-being and flourishing.

- You have learned to integrate all the knowledge of the past eight weeks into a way of life to improve the quality of your decision.

- You know the importance of synchronizing the micro-neuronal states of your established beliefs (like being rude) with your macro desirable states (wanting to be nice). In other words, if you have always been rude, then your brain has a default rudeness network, that gets automatically activated; in spite of your conscious desire to be nice. You will need to practice being nice to build an alternative niceness neurological network to compete with your habitual rudeness network. This requires time and practice.

- You are open and willing to revise your established beliefs (priors).

- You are becoming self-conscious of your own biases, for example, moving away from self-motivated reasoning (self-justification) and confirmation bias by not seeking only information that supports our beliefs, but establishing a commitment to finding facts and avoiding fake news, even if they seem contrary to our self-motivating interests.

- You are avoiding oversimplification of reality, move into the richness of life and dive into its complexity with joy and curiosity.

- You are committed to establishing relations with people who you can help you as you advance in your path towards a Free Energy Minimizer Self.

12.6
Action Plan (AP)
for the Time after the Program

The action plan for the future as an MBSAT graduate is straightforward.

● Practice every day. Limit the practices to a maximum of 15 to 20 minutes.

● Vary the practices.

● Use different practices for specific issues: POMO for issues concerning money, Irimi for difficult situations in life, and the practices of Session 7 (Minding your Social Experience (SoE)) for issues concerning relationships.

● Use the CEO of BETA in its different versions as a continuous practice to change your mood in various circumstances.

● Keep minding your BETA and your beliefs.

● Help others improve their living conditions by recommending programs for personal growth, not only MBSAT but also other programs, for example, MBSR or MBCT for people with deeper psychological and mental issues.

● Use every opportunity for practicing; for example when you happen to walk, take a break, commute, or travel, before you close your eyes and fall asleep at night, etc.

● Every day after finishing the practice, jot down a few comments and reflections in your diary. If you have been using the space provided in the workbook and don't yet have your own diary, it is time to create one now – a personal diary that is appealing to you and makes it enjoyable to write down a few comments on your practice.

● And always keep practicing. Hans-Georg Gadamer, one of my doctoral advisers' favorite philosophers, wrote that understanding is more than conceptual interpretation, it is also application (Praxis in German). In his important book *Truth and Method* (2004), Gadamer collapses the traditional division of understanding, interpretation, and application and explains that they are not independent activities, but all interrelated. Thus, our Free-Energy Minimizer action plan should include understanding, interpretation, and application (practicing). As a practical example, you may think of a man who understands that women are an integral part of humanity and equally important as men for the survival of the human race. He interprets this understanding as signifying that both women and men have equal rights. However, he realizes that in daily life he doesn't think and behave as if they were equals and becomes aware that he needs to practice to become a more equal-minded person.

12.7
Personal Notes and Insights
The Writing Space for Your Experiences and Observations

In this session you have worked with the SOPA Worksheets 1-3; you have become familiar with the CEO of BETA "Strategic Awareness" and reviewed what you have learned in the course of the training in a consolidating summary as the program draws to a close. There is a lot to comment on! It is a good moment to stay committed to the practice of making some brief notes on your salient experiences and insights.

Examples:

In this last session, I started to completely grasp the applicability and the practical value of the training for my life! The program has ended by helping me to define concrete, positive actions. I'm definitely committed to continuing my personal practice and implementing what I have learned.

The SOPA Worksheets have really struck home the message of how my beliefs shape my decisions and actions. I also gained a deeper understanding of the practical value of Strategic Awareness and how minding Strategic Awareness can help me in VUCA world!

Epilogue: Accompanying Thoughts for Your Continuous Practice

A prominent argument throughout this workbook is that the human brain is an adaptive biological organ that is actively seeking to reduce prediction and decision errors to minimize Free Energy and adapt efficiently and effectively to the environment. The evolutionary goal of this ingrained function is to increase our chances for survival, well-being and flourishing (Badcock et al., 2019a). In a dynamically changing environment, accurate predicting gets increasingly difficult as changes lead us to misperceptions or inaccurate readings of information generated by the environment.

But here is the paradox:

> Prediction errors are also a valuable source of information to update our beliefs and to construct more accurate generative models of the world.
>
> While minimizing Free Energy is equivalent to minimizing prediction errors, surprise and decision mistakes, this doesn't mean that being unable to minimize Free Energy is necessarily a bad outcome. Prediction and decision errors surely increase Free Energy, meaning more entropy and disorder in the external and internal environment. However, from an information-theoretical viewpoint, this also signifies that there is more information in states of entropy, thus maybe more available material for learning, which could improve people's survival opportunities. This apparent paradox makes it necessary to be strategically aware and have the wisdom to know when and what valuable data can be extracted from predictions and decision errors, especially when operating in unfamiliar VUCA environments.

Mental health and Strategic Adaptation in Life (SAL)

In a dynamic VUCA world it is not possible to live free of predicaments and worries which underlie decision and prediction errors. Every human being desires a trouble-less life; it is a worthwhile and attainable goal and a precondition for higher levels of well-being and flourishing. Sadly, it is hard to achieve and often obstructed by faulty decision-making processes that lead to unwise decisions. It begins with the limited perception capacity of an agitated BETA, further restrained by fixed, non-adaptive beliefs out of context for the situation at hand. This faulty process generates aversive energy (Free Energy in other words), impeding strategic awareness and triggering unskillful decisions that compromise well-being.

I take a point from computational psychiatry postulates, affirming that healthy organisms, take optimal decisions within the framework of their possibilities, while unhealthy minds are unable to optimize decision-making (Moutoussis, et al, 2015). For example, a healthy-minded farmer in the hills of Panama will be able to optimize his decisions with respect to his coffee farm, despite living in a space with scarce resources and weak, underfunded institutions (lack of government support, etc.). On the other hand, an unhealthy-minded farmer in Switzerland will struggle to optimize his decisions with respect to his farm despite living in an environment of rich resources (government subsidies, etc.). Therefore, mental health turns out to be a critical success factor for skillful decision-making.

One of the goals of MBSAT is to improve people's mental health as the necessary substrate for decision-making skills, thus generating fewer decision errors and fewer regrets as a good pathway to higher quality of life. MBSAT posits that Strategic Awareness (SA) does the heavy lifting as the enabler of skillful decision-making. It allows people to amplify the perception capacities of their BETAs and promotes more flexible and less preconceived, non-adaptive beliefs. SA supports more contextualized information processing abilities that generate more accurate predictions, more skillful decisions and actions and reduce the average of prediction and decision errors.

Strategic Adaption in Life (SAL) as a skill subdivides the process of decision-making into two phases:

a) An evaluative phase, with SA and Active Inference processes working interactively and adjusting people's precision/attention to find acceptable, less risky options.

b) An implementation phase that entails a policy or strategy to allocate resources, either for updating the beliefs of the generative models, or for the actions needed to adapt the environment to predictions and decisions.

And that is precisely what the SOPA plan supports. It is a template that facilitates the creation of a personal Free-Energy minimizing strategic plan by first identifying the areas of personal development, and then building a Free Energy minimization budget of actions and activities required to sustain people's well-being and flourishing. It is an appreciative system based on predictions about relevant and innovative ways for minimizing Free Energy (Vickers, 1995).

As we are moving into an epoch whose culture is increasingly dominated by Artificial Intelligence (AI) and Machine Learning (ML) it is useful to remind ourselves that we still are a society consisting of and shaped by human beings. This evolving reality suggests that we need to develop new ways of human mind learning in order to focus on the aspects of life that AI and ML cannot address such as intuition, emotionality, morality (the esthetics of the good), and other qualities fundamentally different from the characteristics of AI and ML that in MBSAT are captured as Strategic Awareness.

The Living Zone of Free-Energy Minimization

Today's fast-moving and changing world generate new challenges, amongst others the need to recognize the volatility of the environment and the perceptual uncertainty that comes with it, meaning that what we infer might not be real. The statistical structure of the world is changing and with it the data that we take in; therefore, we need generative models that are able to process information with a high level of precision and validation to counterbalance the propensity to decision and prediction errors.

MBSAT differentiates three essential zones in which a person's life unfolds, depicted in Epilogue Figure 1:

- The Zone of Free-Energy *Maximization* driven by aversion:
  This zone is on the left of Epilogue Figure 1. Whenever dislike arises in us, we are in the zone of aversion. We try to stay away from what we dislike or ban it altogether from our lives. Aversion produces ample Free Energy; therefore, we call this the zone of Free-Energy Maximization.

- The Zone of Free-Energy *Maximization* driven by attachment:
  We enter the zone of attachment (far right in the illustration below), when we like something, and wish to keep it and preserve the pleasurable feeling that comes with it. Just like aversion, the feelings of craving also produce a lot of Free Energy. It is the zone of Free-Energy maximization of attachment.

- The Zone of Free-Energy *Minimization* driven by equanimity:
  This is the zone of balance and serenity in the center of the illustration where ideally the lives of mindful, Free Energy minimizing individuals unfold. MBSAT expands this zone by two zones of adaptive transition toward aversion and attachment by defining a zone of Free-Energy Minimization driven by strategic awareness. For MBSAT living in this extended zone of strategic awareness may help most people to maintain enduring well-being.

Life in the first two zones, aversion and attachment, is characterized by reactive behavior, a doing mode in automatic pilot, characterized by impulsiveness and compulsive patterns with little awareness. It is a life of reactivity. Entering and staying in these zones is generating Free Energy and results in imbalances between the different elements of BETA that produce additional entropic, useless, and potentially harmful energy.

The overflow of undesirable energy is comparable to the concept of externalities in economic science which refers to the side effects of productive energy used in production processes. The concept always brings to my mind a childhood memory of a tile factory that was built on the banks of a pristine river in a beautiful region of my country, which converted the once crystal-clear water into a mud current in just one year of operation as part of the energy used in the tile production was transformed into useless detrimental energy polluting the river.

You might also think of a house lacking maintenance. Eventually, the house will create Free Energy as it gradually deteriorates and its rotten and rusty state transforms it into an uninhabitable place. An analogous process occurs in our brain under the influence of uncontrolled, compulsive, and reactive states that generate Free Energy and conflictive BETAs. In these states we are unable to achieve neuronal homolog self-regulation that would be necessary to synchronize body sensations, emotions, thoughts, and action impulses, thus reducing Free Energy.

In the zone of equanimity, individuals live their lives more consciously and calmly. It is a zone of balance, tolerance, and serenity even when facing provoking events. Equanimity is the ability to regulate our cognitive and emotional state and adapt the intensity and quality of our responses, based on strategic awareness that allows for lucidity, a wider perspective, and greater objectivity. Thus, individuals in the zone of equanimity are aware of their actions and capable of responding mindfully to life's events instead of being driven by impulses. When they respond to events around them, their equanimous BETAs are congruent and measured and able to minimize Free Energy, even when there is a strong motive to feel anger or attraction.

The art of living most of the time in the zone of equanimity implies that you are able to respond adaptively when the inevitable happens and life's events carry us into the zones of aversion or attachment. The general tendency is to get caught in negativity or mired in different degrees of addiction. The artistic element of equanimity is to realize that aversion and attachment can vary considerably in significance and intensity and to adapt responses accordingly, avoiding overreactions. Such moderate responses are indicated as adaptive aversion and adaptive attachment in Epilogue Figure 1. These areas imply responsive behavior as opposed to a knee-jerk reaction.

The two areas of transition of adaptive aversion and adaptive attachment, when combined with the zone of equanimity, form the broad domain of strategic awareness and the realm of Mindful Real Options (MROs), which we discussed in Session 5. If it is not possible to stay permanently in the zone of equanimity, we can strive to maintain ourselves in the realm of strategic awareness, responding skillfully and mindfully to situations of aversion and attachment.

Let us look at an example. Imagine that an employee or team member provokes an adverse situation by handing in a much-needed report late or, even worse, losing an important client. As supervisor or colleague you could let yourself drift completely into the negativity zone, go red with anger, shout, or even insult the failing person, which could make the situation worse (the employee walking out, a drop in morale, or many other negative consequences). Alternatively you could reprimand him or her with fairness, albeit firmly, pointing out the damage, and taking measures to prevent similar situations happening in the future (e.g., regular checks before the deadline or additional personnel training). With these responses you remain clearly in the zone of strategic awareness and correct the situation with wisdom and friendliness.

The same applies to situations in the zone of attachment, for example, going out for dinner with friends and having more than usual of a very fine wine in the animated ambience of the group, yet without losing your composure or doing something foolish.

Obviously, the aim is to stay in the zone of strategic awareness that coincides with the zone of responding behavior. As our BETAs are operating within a dynamic VUCA environment, the Free-Energy minimizing individual needs to train attention and precision to respond skillfully on demand with rapid and intuitive command of strategic awareness, thus operating with wisdom, equanimity, compassion and open awareness (WECO), the opposite of VUCA.

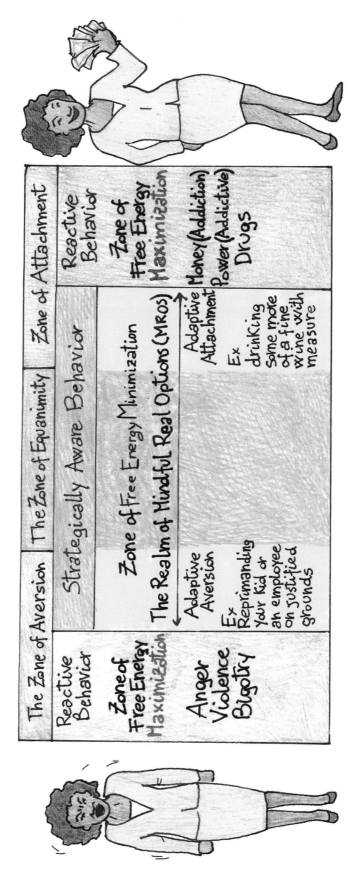

Epilogue Figure 1 The Living Zone of Free-Energy Minimization

From VUCA TO WECO: Paddling with MBSAT

Epilogue Figure 2 visualizes symbolically how we have to navigate turbulent and dangerous waters marred with difficulties. Luckily we have a paddle with two blades to guide us through the rapids of the VUCA environment: Minding BETA and Updating Beliefs.

When you learn to paddle in the Free-Energy maximization zones of the institutionalized VUCA world, which is a generative process rich in data, you also learn to extract useful information from it. This **experience dependent learning** can support you to stay in a personalized world of Free Energy Minimization characterized by Wisdom, Equanimity, Compassion and Open Awareness (WECO).

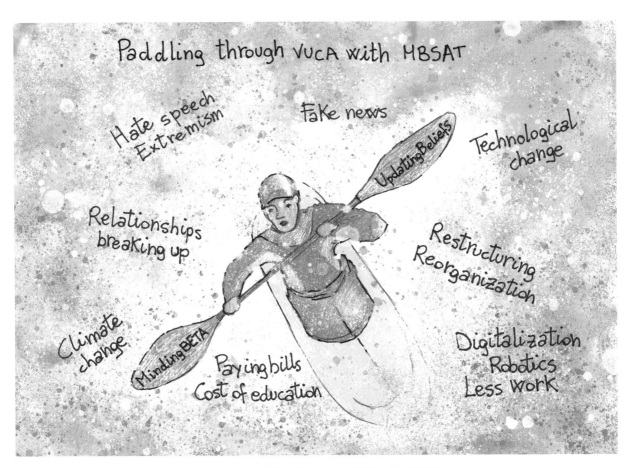

Epilogue Figure 2 Paddling through VUCA with MBSAT

The hope is that with this MBSAT training you are able to establish your personal world of WECO. The states of WECO allow people to have a good life as defined by Nishida (1992), a life that allows people to attain their ideals and internal aspirations beautifully, without harming others (Epilogue Figure 3).

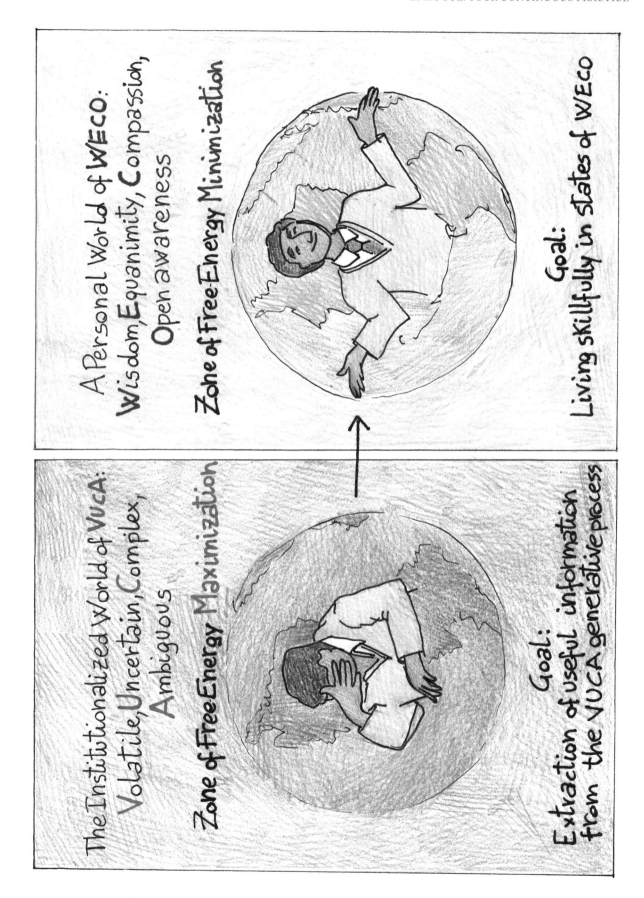

Epilogue Figure 3 From the Institutionalized World of VUCA to the Personalized World of WECO

Minding the Triad of Perception, Beliefs and Predictions

The question in Session 5 was: which of the two scary MBSAT buddies in the graphic is larger?

The answer is: they are equally tall!

Our perception is being fooled by the perspective of the tunnel. The experiment serves as a reminder to not take our perceptions for granted, but question them. Our recognition models require minding in order to keep our perception in fine-tuned condition.

Legend:
Equal length
Different impression

References

Abelson, R. P. (1986). Beliefs Are Like Possessions. *Journal for the Theory of Social Behaviour, 16*(3). https://doi.org/10.1111/j.1468-5914.1986.tb00078.x

Argyris, C. and Schön, D. (1978). Organizational Learning: A theory of Action perspective. Addison-Wesley.

Amabile, T. M. (1998). How to kill creativity. *Harvard Business Review, 76*(5).

Apps, M. A. J., & Tsakiris, M. (2014). The free-energy self: A predictive coding account of self-recognition. *Neuroscience and Biobehavioral Reviews* (Vol. 41). https://doi.org/10.1016/j.neubiorev.2013.01.029

Badcock, P. B., Davey, C. G., Whittle, S., Allen, N. B., & Friston, K. J. (2017). The Depressed Brain: An Evolutionary Systems Theory. *Trends in Cognitive Sciences* (Vol. 21, Issue 3). https://doi.org/10.1016/j.tics.2017.01.005

Badcock, P. B., Friston, K. J., & Ramstead, M. J. D. (2019a). The hierarchically mechanistic mind: A free-energy formulation of the human psyche. *Physics of Life Reviews* (Vol. 31). https://doi.org/10.1016/j.plrev.2018.10.002

Badcock, P. B., Friston, K. J., Ramstead, M. J. D., Ploeger, A., & Hohwy, J. (2019b). The hierarchically mechanistic mind: an evolutionary systems theory of the human brain, cognition, and behavior. *Cognitive, Affective, & Behavioral Neuroscience, 19*(6), 1319–1351. https://doi.org/10.3758/s13415-019-00721-3

Baddeley, A. (1992). Working Memory. *Science, 255*(5044), 556–559. https://doi.org/10.1126/science.1736359

Baker, C. L., Saxe, R., & Tenenbaum, J. B. (2009). Action understanding as inverse planning. *Cognition, 113*(3), 329–349. https://doi.org/10.1016/j.cognition.2009.07.005

Barrett, L. F. (2017). The theory of constructed emotion: an active inference account of interoception and categorization. *Social Cognitive and Affective Neuroscience, 12*(1). https://doi.org/10.1093/scan/nsw154

Bastos, A. M., Usrey, W. M., Adams, R. A., Mangun, G. R., Fries, P., & Friston, K. J. (2012). Canonical Microcircuits for Predictive Coding. *Neuron, 76*(4), 695–711. https://doi.org/10.1016/j.neuron.2012.10.038

Bénabou, R., & Tirole, J. (2002). Self-confidence and personal motivation. *Quarterly Journal of Economics* (Vol. 117, Issue 3). https://doi.org/10.1162/003355302760193913

Bénabou, R., & Tirole, J. (2016). Mindful Economics: The Production, Consumption, and Value of Beliefs. *Journal of Economic Perspectives, 30*(3), 141–164. https://doi.org/10.1257/jep.30.3.141

Boland, R.J, and Collopy, F. (2004). *Managing as Designing*. Stanford Business Books

Bottemanne, H., & Friston, K. J. (2021). An active inference account of protective behaviours during the COVID-19 pandemic. *Cognitive, Affective and Behavioral Neuroscience* (Vol. 21, Issue 6). https://doi.org/10.3758/s13415-021-00947-0

Bouizegarene, N., Ramstead, M., Constant, A., Friston, K., & Kirmayer, L. (2020). *Narrative as Active Inference.* https://doi.org/10.31234/osf.io/47ub6.

Brass, M., Schmitt, R. M., Spengler, S., & Gergely, G. (2007). Investigating Action Understanding: Inferential Processes versus Action Simulation. *Current Biology, 17*(24). https://doi.org/10.1016/j.cub.2007.11.057

Brickman, P. &, & Campbell, D. T. (1971). *Hedonic relativism and planning the good society in Adaptation-level theory* (M.H. Appley, Ed.). Academic Press.

Bruineberg, J., & Rietveld, E. (2014). Self-organization, free energy minimization, and optimal grip on a field of affordances. *Frontiers in Human Neuroscience, 8*(AUG). https://doi.org/10.3389/fnhum.2014.00599

Brunner, J (1990) *Acts of meaning.* Harvard University Press.

Carhart-Harris, R. L., & Friston, K. J. (2019). REBUS and the anarchic brain: Toward a unified model of the brain action of psychedelics. *Pharmacological Reviews, 71*(3).

Case, A & Deaton, A. (2020). *Deaths of Despair and the Future of Capitalism.* Princeton University Press.

Christensen, C., Kaufman, S., & Shih, W. (2008). Innovation killers. *Harvard Business Review, January.*

Clark, A. (2016). *Surfing Uncertainty.* Oxford University Press.

Clark, A. (2017). Predictions, precision, and agentive attention. *Consciousness and Cognition* (Vol. 56). https://doi.org/10.1016/j.concog.2017.06.013

Clark, A. (2020). Beyond Desire? Agency, Choice, and the Predictive Mind. *Australasian Journal of Philosophy, 98*(1), 1–15. https://doi.org/10.1080/00048402.2019.1602661

Clark, J. E., Watson, S., & Friston, K. J. (2018). What is mood? A computational perspective. *Psychological Medicine, 48*(14), 2277–2284. https://doi.org/10.1017/S0033291718000430

Conant, R. C., & Ross Ashby, W. (1970). Every good regulator of a system must be a model of that system. *International Journal of Systems Science, 1*(2). https://doi.org/10.1080/00207727008920220

Connors, M. H., & Halligan, P. W. (2015). A cognitive account of belief: a tentative road map. *Frontiers in Psychology, 5.* https://doi.org/10.3389/fpsyg.2014.01588

Constant, A., Clark, A., Kirchhoff, M., & Friston, K. J. (2022). Extended active inference: Constructing predictive cognition beyond skulls. *Mind and Language, 37*(3). https://doi.org/10.1111/mila.12330

Csikszentmihalyi, M. (1991). Flow: The psychology of optimal experience: Steps toward enhancing the quality of life. *Design Issues, 8*(1).

de Vries, M. K. (2007). Money, Money, Money. *Organizational Dynamics, 36*(3). https://doi.org/10.1016/j.orgdyn.2007.04.001

Demekas, D., Parr, T., & Friston, K. J. (2020). An Investigation of the Free Energy Principle for Emotion Recognition. *Frontiers in Computational Neuroscience* (Vol. 14). https://doi.org/10.3389/fncom.2020.00030

den Ouden, H. E. M., Kok, P., & de Lange, F. P. (2012). How Prediction Errors Shape Perception, Attention, and Motivation. *Frontiers in Psychology, 3*. https://doi.org/10.3389/fpsyg.2012.00548

Dobson, K. S. (2013). The Science of CBT: Toward a Metacognitive Model of Change? In *Behavior Therapy* (Vol. 44, Issue 2). https://doi.org/10.1016/j.beth.2009.08.003

Dunbar, R. I. M. (2018). The Anatomy of Friendship. *Trends in Cognitive Sciences, 22*(1), 32–51. https://doi.org/10.1016/j.tics.2017.10.004

Easterlin, R. A., McVey, L. A., Switek, M., Sawangfa, O., & Zweig, J. S. (2010). The happiness–income paradox revisited. *Proceedings of the National Academy of Sciences, 107*(52), 22463–22468. https://doi.org/10.1073/pnas.1015962107

Easwaran, E. (1985). *Dhammapada*. The Blue Mountain Centre of Meditation.

Easwaran, E. (2007). *Bhagavad Gita* (Second Edition). Nilgiri Press.

Fazekas, P., & Nanay, B. (2021). Attention is amplification, not selection. *British Journal for the Philosophy of Science, 72*(1). https://doi.org/10.1093/bjps/axy065

Feldman Barrett, L. (2017). How emotions are made: The secret life of the brain. In *How emotions are made: The secret life of the brain.*. Macmillan.

Feldman Barrett,L. (2020), *Seven and a half lessons about the brain*. Mariner Books.

Fiol, C. M., & O'Connor, E. J. (2003). Waking Up! Mindfulness in the Face of Bandwagons. *Academy of Management Review, 28*(1), 54–70. https://doi.org/10.5465/amr.2003.8925227

Forrester, J. W. (1993). System Dynamics and the Lessons of 35 Years. *A Systems-Based Approach to Policymaking.* https://doi.org/10.1007/978-1-4615-3226-2_7

Foucault, M. (1988). *The Care of the Self.* Vintage, USA.

Friedman, M. (1970). A Friedman doctrine - The Social Responsibility of Business Is to Increase Its Profits. *New York Times Magazine, 6*(Newspaper Article).

Friston, K. (2009). The free-energy principle: a rough guide to the brain? *Trends in Cognitive Sciences, 13*(7), 293–301. https://doi.org/10.1016/j.tics.2009.04.005

Friston, K. (2010). The free-energy principle: a unified brain theory? *Nature Reviews Neuroscience, 11*(2), 127–138. https://doi.org/10.1038/nrn2787

Friston, K. (2012a). Prediction, perception and agency. *International Journal of Psychophysiology, 83*(2), 248–252. https://doi.org/10.1016/j.ijpsycho.2011.11.014

Friston, K. (2012b). The history of the future of the Bayesian brain. *NeuroImage, 62*(2), 1230–1233.

Friston, K. (2018). Does predictive coding have a future? *Nature Neuroscience, 21*(8), 1019–1021. https://doi.org/10.1038/s41593-018-0200-7

Friston, K. J., & Stephan, K. E. (2007). Free-energy and the brain. *Synthese, 159*(3). https://doi.org/10.1007/s11229-007-9237-y

Friston, K. J., Lin, M., Frith, C. D., Pezzulo, G., Hobson, J. A., & Ondobaka, S. (2017). Active inference, curiosity and insight. *Neural Computation, 29*(10). https://doi.org/10.1162/NECO_a_00999

Friston, K., & Frith, C. (2015). A Duet for one. *Consciousness and Cognition, 36*, 390–405. https://doi.org/10.1016/j.concog.2014.12.003

Friston, K., da Costa, L., Hafner, D., Hesp, C., & Parr, T. (2021). Sophisticated inference. *Neural Computation* (Vol. 33, Issue 3). https://doi.org/10.1162/neco_a_01351

Friston, K., Kilner, J., & Harrison, L. (2006). A free energy principle for the brain. *Journal of Physiology-Paris, 100*(1–3), 70–87. https://doi.org/10.1016/j.jphysparis.2006.10.001

Friston, K., Thornton, C., & Clark, A. (2012). Free-energy minimization and the dark-room problem. *Frontiers in Psychology, 3*(MAY). https://doi.org/10.3389/fpsyg.2012.00130

Gable, S. L., Gonzaga, G. C., & Strachman, A. (2006). Will you be there for me when things go right? Supportive responses to positive event disclosures. *Journal of Personality and Social Psychology, 91*(5), 904–917. https://doi.org/10.1037/0022-3514.91.5.904

Gadamer, H.-G. (2004). *Truth and Method* (2nd Revised edition). Continuum.

Gergen, Kenneth, J. (1991). *The Saturated Self.* Basic Books.

Gigerenzer G., Reb J. and Luan S. (2022) Smart Heuristics for Individuals, Teams, and Organizations. *Annual Review of Organizational Psychology and Organizational Behavior* p. 171-198

Goldin, P. R., Moodie, C. A., & Gross, J. J. (2019). Acceptance versus reappraisal: Behavioral, autonomic, and neural effects. *Cognitive, Affective, & Behavioral Neuroscience, 19*(4), 927–944. https://doi.org/10.3758/s13415-019-00690-7

Gregory, R. L. (1980). Perceptions as hypotheses. *Philosophical Transactions of the Royal Society of London. Series B, Biological Sciences, 290*(1038). https://doi.org/10.1098/rstb.1980.0090

Gunaratana, V. H. (2011). Mindfulness In Plain English. *East* (Issue April). Wisdom Publications.

Hadot, P. (1995). *Philosophy as a way of life: Spiritual exercises from Socrates to Foucault.* Wiley-Blackwell.

Habermas, J. (2003). Intolerance and discrimination. *International Journal of Constitutional Law*, 1(1), 2–12.

Hammond, J. S., Keeney, R. L., & Raiffa, H. (2002). *Smart choices: a practical guide to making better life decisions*. Harvard Business Review Press..

Hickman, S. D. (2016). This Is The Hour: A Call for Reflection and Introspection in the Field of Mindfulness. *Mindfulness* (Vol. 7, Issue 2). https://doi.org/10.1007/s12671-015-0445-0

Hirsh, J. B., Mar, R. A., & Peterson, J. B. (2013). Personal narratives as the highest level of cognitive integration. *Behavioral and Brain Sciences, 36*(3), 216–217. https://doi.org/10.1017/S0140525X12002269

Hobson, J. A., & Friston, K. (2014). Consciousness, Dreams, and Inference. *Journal of Consciousness Studies, 21*(1–2), 6–32.

Hohwy, J. (2013). *The Predictive Mind*. Oxford University Press.

Hohwy, J. (2018). *The Predictive ProcessingHypothesis in The Oxford Handbook of 4E Cognition, Chapter 7: Vol. Chapter 7* (A. , Newen, L. and de Bruin, & S. Gallagher, Eds.). Oxford University Press.

Hohwy, J. (2020). New directions in predictive processing. *Mind & Language, 35*(2), 209–223. https://doi.org/10.1111/mila.12281

Hohwy, J. (2021). Self-supervision, normativity and the free energy principle. *Synthese, 199*(1–2). https://doi.org/10.1007/s11229-020-02622-2

Holmes, J. (2022). Friston's free energy principle: new life for psychoanalysis? *BJPsych Bulletin, 46*(3). https://doi.org/10.1192/bjb.2021.6

Ingenieros, J. (2004). *The Mediocre Man*. Longseller.

Isen, A. M. (2000). Some perspectives on positive affect and self-regulation. *Psychological Inquiry, 11*(November 2014).

Isen, A. M. (2004). Positive affect facilitates thinking and problem solving. *Feelings and Emotions: The Amsterdam Symposium*.

Isen, A. M. (2015). Positive Affect and Decision Processes. In *Handbook of Consumer Psychology*. https://doi.org/10.4324/9780203809570.ch10

Jensen, M. C. (2000). Value maximization and the Corporate Objective Function. *Harvard Business School, 12*(2).

Joffily, M., & Coricelli, G. (2013). Emotional Valence and the Free-Energy Principle. *PLoS Computational Biology, 9*(6). https://doi.org/10.1371/journal.pcbi.1003094

Kabat-Zinn, J. (2013). Mindfulness-based interventions in medicine and psychiatry: What does it mean to be "mindfulness-based"? In *The healing power of meditation: Leading experts on Buddhism, psychology, and medicine explore the health benefits of contemplative practice*. Shambhala Publications Inc.

Kahneman, D. (2012). Thinking, fast and slow: Daniel Kahneman. In *Thinking, fast and slow*. Penguin.

Kahneman, D., & Deaton, A. (2010). High income improves evaluation of life but not emotional well-being. *Proceedings of the National Academy of Sciences, 107*(38), 16489–16493. https://doi.org/10.1073/pnas.1011492107

Kahneman, D., & Tversky, A. (1979). Prospect theory: An analysis of decision under risk. *Choices, Values, and Frames*. https://doi.org/10.1017/CBO9780511803475.003

Karnani, A. (2008). Controversy: The essence of strategy. *Business Strategy Review, 19*(4). https://doi.org/10.1111/j.1467-8616.2008.00560.x

Keller, G. B., & Mrsic-Flogel, T. D. (2018). Predictive Processing: A Canonical Cortical Computation. *Neuron, 100*(2), 424–435. https://doi.org/10.1016/j.neuron.2018.10.003

Killingsworth, M. A., & Gilbert, D. T. (2010). A wandering mind is an unhappy mind. *Science* (Vol. 330, Issue 6006). https://doi.org/10.1126/science.1192439

Kilner, J. M., & Frith, C. D. (2008). Action Observation: Inferring Intentions without Mirror Neurons. *Current Biology, 18*(1), R32–R33. https://doi.org/10.1016/j.cub.2007.11.008

Kim, J., Esteves, J. E., Cerritelli, F., & Friston, K. (2022). An Active Inference Account of Touch and Verbal Communication in Therapy. *Frontiers in Psychology, 13*. https://doi.org/10.3389/fpsyg.2022.828952

Kim, W. C., & Mauborgne, R. (2005). Value innovation: A leap into the blue ocean. *Journal of Business Strategy* (Vol. 26, Issue 4). https://doi.org/10.1108/02756660510608521

Kim, J., Esteves, J. E., Cerritelli, F., & Friston, K. (2022). An Active Inference Account of Touch and Verbal Communication in Therapy. *Frontiers in Psychology, 13*. https://doi.org/10.3389/fpsyg.2022.828952

Kirchhoff, M., Parr, T., Palacios, E., Friston, K., & Kiverstein, J. (2018). The Markov blankets of life: autonomy, active inference and the free energy principle. *Journal of The Royal Society Interface, 15*(138), 20170792. https://doi.org/10.1098/rsif.2017.0792

Kissinger, H., Schmidt, E., & Huttenlocher, D. (2021). *The Age Of AI: And our Future*. Little, Brown and Company.

Kiverstein, J. (2020). Free Energy and the Self: An Ecological–Enactive Interpretation. *Topoi, 39*(3). https://doi.org/10.1007/s11245-018-9561-5

Kiverstein, J., Miller, M., & Rietveld, E. (2020). How mood tunes prediction: a neurophenomenological account of mood and its disturbance in major depression. *Neuroscience of Consciousness, 2020*(1). https://doi.org/10.1093/nc/niaa003

Knill, D. C., & Pouget, A. (2004). The Bayesian brain: The role of uncertainty in neural coding and computation. *Trends in Neurosciences, 27*(12). https://doi.org/10.1016/j.tins.2004.10.007

Koelsch, S., Vuust, P., & Friston, K. (2019). Predictive Processes and the Peculiar Case of Music. *Trends in Cognitive Sciences, 23*(1), 63–77. https://doi.org/10.1016/j.tics.2018.10.006

Krieger, J. L. (2005). Shared Mindfulness in Cockpit Crisis Situations: An Exploratory Analysis. *Journal of Business Communication, 42*(2), 135–167. https://doi.org/10.1177/0021943605274726

Kwisthout, J., Bekkering, H., & van Rooij, I. (2017). To be precise, the details don't matter: On predictive processing, precision, and level of detail of predictions. *Brain and Cognition, 112.* https://doi.org/10.1016/j.bandc.2016.02.008

Langer, E. J. (2005). On *Becoming an Artist.* Ballantine Books.

Layard, R. (2011). *Happiness: Lessons from a New Science.* Penguin.

Levinthal, D., & Rerup, C. (2006). Crossing an Apparent Chasm: Bridging Mindful and Less-Mindful Perspectives on Organizational Learning. *Organization Science, 17*(4), 502–513. https://doi.org/10.1287/orsc.1060.0197

Limanowski, J., & Friston, K. (2018). 'Seeing the Dark': Grounding Phenomenal Transparency and Opacity in Precision Estimation for Active Inference. *Frontiers in Psychology, 9.* https://doi.org/10.3389/fpsyg.2018.00643

Loewenstein, G., & Molnar, A. (2018). The renaissance of belief-based utility in economics. In *Nature Human Behaviour* (Vol. 2, Issue 3). https://doi.org/10.1038/s41562-018-0301-z

Lucas, R. (1981). *Optimal investment with Rational Expectations* (NED-New Edition, Vol. Vol1). University of Minnesota Press.

Lutz, A., Mattout, J., & Pagnoni, G. (2019). The epistemic and pragmatic value of non-action: a predictive coding perspective on meditation. *Current Opinion in Psychology* (Vol. 28). https://doi.org/10.1016/j.copsyc.2018.12.019

Lyotard, J. F. (1984). *The postmodern Condition.* University of Minnesota Press.

Maisto, D., Friston, K., & Pezzulo, G. (2019). Caching mechanisms for habit formation in Active Inference. *Neurocomputing*, 359, 298–314. https://doi.org/10.1016/j.neucom.2019.05.083

March, J. G. (1994). *A primer on Decision Making: How Decisions Happen.* Free Press.

Marr, D. (1982). *Vision A Computational Investigation into the Human Representation and Processing of Visual Information.* W.H. Freeman.

Maturana, H. R., Verden-Zoller, G., & Bunnell, P. (2009). *Origin of Humannness in the Biology of Love.* Imprint Academic.

McCann, B. T. (2020). Using Bayesian Updating to Improve Decisions under Uncertainty. *California Management Review, 63*(1). https://doi.org/10.1177/0008125620948264

McGrah, R., & McMillan, I. (1995). Discovery-driven planning: McGrath, R. G. and MacMillan, I. C. Harvard Business Review 73 (4), 44–54 (July–Aug 1995). *HBR, 73*(4).

Metzinger, T. (2003). Phenomenal transparency and cognitive self-reference. *Phenomenology and the Cognitive Sciences, 2*(4). https://doi.org/10.1023/b:phen.0000007366.42918.eb

Molapour, T., Hagan, C. C., Silston, B., Wu, H., Ramstead, M., Friston, K., & Mobbs, D. (2021). Seven computations of the social brain. *Social Cognitive and Affective Neuroscience, 16*(8). https://doi.org/10.1093/scan/nsab024

Molnar, A., & Loewenstein, G. F. (2021). Thoughts and Players: An Introduction to Old and New Economic Perspectives on Beliefs. *SSRN Electronic Journal.* https://doi.org/10.2139/ssrn.3806135

Moutoussis, M., Fearon, P., El-Deredy, W., Dolan, R. J., & Friston, K. J. (2014). Bayesian inferences about the self (and others): A review. *Consciousness and Cognition* (Vol. 25, Issue 1).

Moutoussis, M., Story, G. W., & Dolan, R. J. (2015). The computational psychiatry of reward: broken brains or misguided minds? *Frontiers in Psychology* (Vol. 6). https://doi.org/10.3389/fpsyg.2015.01445

Moutoussis, M., Garzón, B., Neufeld, S., Bach, D. R., Rigoli, F., Goodyer, I., Bullmore, E., NSPN Consortium, Guitart-Masip, M., Dolan, R. J. (2021). Decision-making ability, psychopathology, and brain connectivity. *Neuron*, 109(12). https://doi.org/10.1016/j.neuron.2021.04.019

Nishida, K. (1992). *An Inquiry into the Good.* Yale University Press.

North, D. C. (2010). *Understanding the Process of Economic Change.* Princeton University Press.

Ocasio, W. (2011). Attention to Attention. *Organization Science, 22*(5). https://doi.org/10.1287/orsc.1100.0602

Pagnoni, G. (2019). The contemplative exercise through the lenses of predictive processing: A promising approach. In *Progress in Brain Research* (Vol. 244). https://doi.org/10.1016/bs.pbr.2018.10.022

Pagnoni, G., & Guareschi, F. T. (2017). Remembrance of things to come: a conversation between Zen and neuroscience on the predictive nature of the mind. *Mindfulness, 8*(1). https://doi.org/10.1007/s12671-015-0438-z

Parr, T., Corcoran, A. W., Friston, K. J., & Hohwy, J. (2019). Perceptual awareness and active inference. *Neuroscience of Consciousness, 2019*(1). https://doi.org/10.1093/nc/niz012

Patel, D., Fleming, S. M., & Kilner, J. M. (2012). Inferring subjective states through the observation of actions. *Proceedings of the Royal Society B: Biological Sciences, 279*(1748). https://doi.org/10.1098/rspb.2012.1847

Pearce, M. T., & Wiggins, G. A. (2006). Expectation in Melody: The Influence of Context and Learning. *Music Perception*, 23(5), 377–405.

Peters, A., McEwen, B. S., & Friston, K. (2017). Uncertainty and stress: Why it causes diseases and how it is mastered by the brain. *Progress in Neurobiology* (Vol. 156, pp. 164–188). Elsevier Ltd. https://doi.org/10.1016/j.pneurobio.2017.05.004

Pezzulo, G., Rigoli, F., & Friston, K. (2015). Active Inference, homeostatic regulation and adaptive behavioural control. *Progress in Neurobiology, 134*, 17–35. https://doi.org/10.1016/j.pneurobio.2015.09.001

Pinniger, R., Brown, R. F., Thorsteinsson, E. B., & McKinley, P. (2012). Argentine tango dance compared to mindfulness meditation and a waiting-list control: A randomised trial for treating depression. *Complementary Therapies in Medicine* (Vol. 20, Issue 6). https://doi.org/10.1016/j.ctim.2012.07.003

Purser, R. (2019). *McMindfulness*. Repeater Books.

Raiffa, H. (1993). Decision analysis: introductory lectures on choices under uncertainty. 1968. *M.D. Computing : Computers in Medical Practice, 10*(5). https://doi.org/10.2307/2987280

Raiffa, H. (2007). Decision analysis: A personal account of how it got started and evolved. In *Advances in Decision Analysis: From Foundations to Applications*. https://doi.org/10.1017/CBO9780511611308.005

Ramstead, M. J. D., Constant, A., Badcock, P. B., & Friston, K. J. (2019). Variational ecology and the physics of sentient systems. *Physics of Life Reviews, 31*, 188–205. https://doi.org/10.1016/j.plrev.2018.12.002

Ramstead, M. J. D., Kirchhoff, M. D., & Friston, K. J. (2020). A tale of two densities: active inference is enactive inference. *Adaptive Behavior, 28*(4). https://doi.org/10.1177/1059712319862774

Ramstead, M. J. D., Kirchhoff, M. D., Constant, A., & Friston, K. J. (2021). Multiscale integration: beyond internalism and externalism. *Synthese*, 198(S1), 41–70. https://doi.org/10.1007/s11229-019-02115-x

Rao, R. P. N., & Ballard, D. H. (1999). Predictive coding in the visual cortex: a functional interpretation of some extra-classical receptive-field effects. *Nature Neuroscience, 2*(1), 79–87. https://doi.org/10.1038/4580

Rapport, F., Clay-Williams, R., Churruca, K., Shih, P., Hogden, A., & Braithwaite, J. (2018). The struggle of translating science into action: Foundational concepts of implementation science. *Journal of Evaluation in Clinical Practice, 24*(1). https://doi.org/10.1111/jep.12741

Rolls, E. T. (2014). Emotion and decision-making explained: A précis. *Cortex*, 59, 185–193.

Ryan, R. M., & Deci, E. L. (2018). *Self-Determination Theory Basic Psychological Needs in Motivation, Development, and Wellness*. Guilford Publications.

Sachs, J. (2012). *The price of Civilization; Chapter 9*. Random House Trade.

Sajid, N., Ball, P. J., Parr, T., & Friston, K. J. (2021). Active inference: demystified and compared. *Neural Computation* (Vol. 33, Issue 3). https://doi.org/10.1162/neco_a_01357

Sampson, E. E. (2019). Celebrating the other: A dialogic account of human nature. *Celebrating the other: A dialogic account of human nature.* https://doi.org/10.4324/9780429038846

Sandved-Smith, L., Hesp, C., Mattout, J., Friston, K., Lutz, A., & Ramstead, M. J. D. (2021). Towards a computational phenomenology of mental action: modelling meta-awareness and attentional control with deep parametric active inference. *Neuroscience of Consciousness, 2021*(1). https://doi.org/10.1093/nc/niab018

Schoeller, F., Miller, M., Salomon, R., & Friston, K. J. (2021). Trust as Extended Control: Human-Machine Interactions as Active Inference. *Frontiers in Systems Neuroscience*, 15. https://doi.org/10.3389/fnsys.2021.669810

Schopenhauer, A. (2016). *101 Facts of Life*. Publishdrive.

Schrödinger, E. (1992) *What is Life?* Cambridge University Press.

Schwartenbeck, P., Fitzgerald, T. H. B., Mathys, C., Dolan, R., Kronbichler, M., & Friston, K. (2015). Evidence for surprise minimization over value maximization in choice behavior. *Scientific Reports, 5.* https://doi.org/10.1038/srep16575

Searle, J. R. (2004). *Mind: A Brief Introduction*. Oxford University Press.

Seitz, R. J., & Angel, H.-F. (2020). Belief formation – A driving force for brain evolution. *Brain and Cognition, 140*, 105548. https://doi.org/10.1016/j.bandc.2020.105548

Seligman, M. E. P. (2012). "Flourishing - a new understanding of wellbeing" at Happiness & Its Causes 2012. *Flourishing - a New Understanding of Wellbeing.*

Sellars, J. (n.d.). *Roman Stoic Mindfulness: An Ancient Technology of the Self.*

Seth, A. K. (2015). Presence, objecthood, and the phenomenology of predictive perception. *Cognitive Neuroscience, 6*(2–3), 111–117. https://doi.org/10.1080/17588928.2015.1026888

Seth, A. K., & Friston, K. J. (2016). Active interoceptive inference and the emotional brain. *Philosophical Transactions of the Royal Society B: Biological Sciences* (Vol. 371, Issue 1708). https://doi.org/10.1098/rstb.2016.0007

Shannon, C. E. (1948). A Mathematical Theory of Communication. *Bell System Technical Journal, 27*(3). https://doi.org/10.1002/j.1538-7305.1948.tb01338.x

Simon, H. A. (1982). Models of Bounded Rationality: Economic Analysis and Public Policy. *Models of Bounded Rationality* (Vol. 1).

Simon, H. A. (1991). Bounded Rationality and Organizational Learning. *Organization Science, 2*(1), 125–134. https://doi.org/10.1287/orsc.2.1.125

Smith, R., Badcock, P., & Friston, K. J. (2020). Recent advances in the application of predictive coding and active inference models within clinical neuroscience *PCN Psychiatry and Clinical Neurosciences.* https://doi.org/10.1111/pcn.13138

Smith, R., Moutoussis, M., & Bilek, E. (2021). Simulating the computational mechanisms of cognitive and behavioral psychotherapeutic interventions: insights from active inference. *Scientific Reports, 11*(1). https://doi.org/10.1038/s41598-021-89047-0

Sloterdijk, P. (2013). *You must change your life.* Polity Press.

Solms, M. (2019). The Hard Problem of Consciousness and the Free Energy Principle. *Frontiers in Psychology, 9.* https://doi.org/10.3389/fpsyg.2018.02714

Solms, M. L. (2018). The Neurobiological Underpinnings of Psychoanalytic Theory and Therapy. *Frontiers in Behavioral Neuroscience*, 12. https://doi.org/10.3389/fnbeh.2018.00294

Spratling, M. W. (2017). A review of predictive coding algorithms. *Brain and Cognition* (Vol. 112). https://doi.org/10.1016/j.bandc.2015.11.003

Sterling, P. (2012). Allostasis: A model of predictive regulation. *Physiology and Behavior, 106* (1). https://doi.org/10.1016/j.physbeh.2011.06.004

Stewart, I. (2019). *Do dice play god?* Profile Books Ltd.

Stone, J.F. (2002) *The Joy of Meditation.* SquareOnePublishers.

Taleb, N. N. (2018) *Skin in the Game.* Penguin Random House.

Tejaniya, S. U. (2016). *When Awareness Becomes Natural.* Shambala Publishers.

Tirole, J. (2017). *Economics for the Common Good.* Princeton University Press.

van de Cruys, S., Friston, K. J., & Clark, A. (2020). Controlled Optimism: Reply to Sun and Firestone on the Dark Room Problem. *Trends in Cognitive Sciences* (Vol. 24, Issue 9). https://doi.org/10.1016/j.tics.2020.05.012

Vasil, J., Badcock, P. B., Constant, A., Friston, K., & Ramstead, M. J. D. (2020). A World Unto Itself: Human Communication as Active Inference. *Frontiers in Psychology, 11.* https://doi.org/10.3389/fpsyg.2020.00417

Vosgerau, G., & Synofzik, M. (2010). A cognitive theory of thoughts. *American Philosophical Quarterly* (Vol. 47, Issue 3).

Vickers, G. (1995). *The Art of Judgment.* Sage Publications

Wack, P. (1985). Scenarios : shooting the rapids. *Harvard Business Review, 85617.*

Weick, K., & Sutcliffe, K. (2001). *Managing the unexpected: Assuring high performance in the age of complexity.* John Wiley & Sons Inc.

Wiese, W., & Metzinger, T. (2017). Vanilla PP for Philosophers: A Primer on Predictive Processing. *Philosophy and Predictive Processing.*

Young, J. H. (2017). *Mindfulness-based Strategic Awareness Training*. Wiley Blackwell.

Zeki, S., & Chén, O. Y. (2020). The Bayesian-Laplacian brain. *European Journal of Neuroscience* (Vol. 51, Issue 6). https://doi.org/10.1111/ejn.14540

Zull, J. E. (2002). *The Art of Changing the Brain*. Stylus Publishing.

Further Reading[1]

Adams, R. A., Stephan, K. E., Brown, H. R., Frith, C. D., & Friston, K. J. (2013). The computational anatomy of psychosis. *Frontiers in Psychiatry* (Vol. 4). https://doi.org/10.3389/fpsyt.2013.00047

Agrawal, A., Gans, J., & Goldfarb, A. (2018). *Prediction Machines: The Simple Economics of Artificial Intelligence.* Harvard Business Review Press.

Ahmadi, A. (2017). Peter Sloterdijk's General Ascetology. *Critical Horizons, 18*(4). https://doi.org/10.1080/14409917.2017.1374914

Ainley, V., Maister, L., Brokfeld, J., Farmer, H., & Tsakiris, M. (2013). More of myself: Manipulating interoceptive awareness by heightened attention to bodily and narrative aspects of the self. *Consciousness and Cognition, 22*(4). https://doi.org/10.1016/j.concog.2013.08.004

Alexander, R., Aragón, O. R., Bookwala, J., Cherbuin, N., Gatt, J. M., Kahrilas, I. J., Kästner, N., Lawrence, A., Lowe, L., Morrison, R. G., Mueller, S. C., Nusslock, R., Papadelis, C., Polnaszek, K. L., Richter, S. H., Silton, R. L., & Styliadis, C. (2021). The neuroscience of positive emotions and affect: Implications for cultivating happiness and wellbeing. *Neuroscience and Biobehavioral Reviews* (Vol. 121). https://doi.org/10.1016/j.neubiorev.2020.12.002

Allen, M., & Friston, K. J. (2018). From cognitivism to autopoiesis: towards a computational framework for the embodied mind. *Synthese, 195*(6). https://doi.org/10.1007/s11229-016-1288-5

Aram, J. (1992). *Presumed Superior: Individualism and American Business.* Pearson College Div.

Argyris, C. (2011). Reasons and Rationalizations: The Limits to Organizational Knowledge. *Reasons and Rationalizations: The Limits to Organizational Knowledge.* https://doi.org/10.1093/acprof:oso/9780199268078.001.0001

Atzil, S., Gao, W., Fradkin, I., & Barrett, L. F. (2018). Growing a social brain. *Nature Human Behaviour* (Vol. 2, Issue 9). https://doi.org/10.1038/s41562-018-0384-6

Azari, B., Westlin, C., Satpute, A. B., Hutchinson, J. B., Kragel, P. A., Hoemann, K., Khan, Z., Wormwood, J. B., Quigley, K. S., Erdogmus, D., Dy, J., Brooks, D. H., & Barrett, L. F. (2020). Comparing supervised and unsupervised approaches to emotion categorization in the human brain, body, and subjective experience. *Scientific Reports, 10*(1). https://doi.org/10.1038/s41598-020-77117-8

---

[1] This fairly long list of further readings is partly due to the comprehensive nature of this workbook. It has also to do with the COVID-19 pandemic that unexpectedly created extra time for a thorough review of research literature. I have read all the publications listed here in full or in sufficient detail to highlight all relevant passages. For those interested in diving deeper into these themes, it may serve as a valuable source.

Bach, D. R., & Dayan, P. (2017). Algorithms for survival: A comparative perspective on emotions. *Nature Reviews Neuroscience* (Vol. 18, Issue 5). https://doi.org/10.1038/nrn.2017.35

Baeza Flores, M. (2022). *Humberto Maturana: Biología del Conocer*. Ediciones Sylvia y Marcelo.

Baker, C. L., Jara-Ettinger, J., Saxe, R., & Tenenbaum, J. B. (2017). Rational quantitative attribution of beliefs, desires and percepts in human mentalizing. *Nature Human Behaviour*, *1*(4). https://doi.org/10.1038/s41562-017-0064

Barrett, L. F. (2020). *71/2 Lessons about the Brain*. Houghton, Mifflin Harcout.

Barrett, L. F. (2006). Solving the emotion paradox: Categorization and the experience of emotion. *Personality and Social Psychology Review* (Vol. 10, Issue 1). https://doi.org/10.1207/s15327957pspr1001_2

Bayne, T. (2004). Closing the gap? Some questions for neurophenomenology. *Phenomenology and the Cognitive Sciences*, *3*(4). https://doi.org/10.1023/b:phen.0000048934.34397.ca

Beach, L. R. (1997). *The Psychology of Decision Making*. Sage Publications.

Beck, A. T. (1970). Cognitive therapy: Nature and relation to behavior therapy. *Behavior Therapy*, *1*(2). https://doi.org/10.1016/S0005-7894(70)80030-2

Beck, A. T., & Haigh, E. A. P. (2014). Advances in cognitive theory and therapy: The generic cognitive model. *Annual Review of Clinical Psychology* (Vol. 10). https://doi.org/10.1146/annurev-clinpsy- 032813-153734

Beck, A. T. (2019). A 60-Year Evolution of Cognitive Theory and Therapy. *Perspectives on Psychological Science*, *14*(1). https://doi.org/10.1177/1745691618804187

Beck, A. T., Finkel, M. R., & Beck, J. S. (2021). The Theory of Modes: Applications to Schizophrenia and Other Psychological Conditions. *Cognitive Therapy and Research* (Vol. 45, Issue 3). https://doi.org/10.1007/s10608-020-10098-0

Berthon, P. R., & Pitt, L. F. (2019). Types of mindfulness in an age of digital distraction. *Business Horizons* (Vol. 62, Issue 2). https://doi.org/10.1016/j.bushor.2018.10.003

Boonstra, E. A., & Slagter, H. A. (2019). The Dialectics of Free Energy Minimization. *Frontiers in Systems Neuroscience*, *13*. https://doi.org/10.3389/fnsys.2019.00042

Botvinick, M., & Toussaint, M. (2012). Planning as inference. *Trends in Cognitive Sciences* (Vol. 16, Issue 10). https://doi.org/10.1016/j.tics.2012.08.006

Boutang, J., & de Lara, M. (2016). *The Biased Mind: How Evolution Shaped our Psychology*. Springer International.

Brewer, J. (2019). Mindfulness training for addictions: has neuroscience revealed a brain hack by which awareness subverts the addictive process? *Current Opinion in Psychology* (Vol. 28). https://doi.org/10.1016/j.copsyc.2019.01.014

Brewer, J. A., Davis, J. H., & Goldstein, J. (2013). Why Is It So Hard to Pay Attention, or Is It? Mindfulness, the Factors of Awakening and Reward-Based Learning. *Mindfulness, 4*(1). https://doi.org/10.1007/s12671-012-0164-8

Brouwer, A., & Carhart-Harris, R. L. (2021). Pivotal mental states. *Journal of Psychopharmacology* (Vol. 35, Issue 4). https://doi.org/10.1177/0269881120959637

Brown, R. (2006). What is a brain state? *Philosophical Psychology* (Vol. 19, Issue 6). https://doi.org/10.1080/09515080600923271

Buchanan, L., & O'Connell, A. (2005). *A Brief History of Decision Making.* www.hbr.org

Burr, C. (2017). Embodied decisions and the predictive brain. *Philosophy and Predictive Processing.* https://doi.org/10.15502/9783958573086

Burr, C., & Jones, M. (2016). The body as laboratory: Prediction-error minimization, embodiment, and representation. *Philosophical Psychology, 29*(4). https://doi.org/10.1080/09515089.2015.1135238

Bzdok, D., & Meyer-Lindenberg, A. (2018). Machine Learning for Precision Psychiatry: Opportunities and Challenges. *Biological Psychiatry: Cognitive Neuroscience and Neuroimaging* (Vol. 3, Issue 3). https://doi.org/10.1016/j.bpsc.2017.11.007

Campbell, C., Sands, S., Ferraro, C., Tsao, H. Y. (Jody), & Mavrommatis, A. (2020). From data to action: How marketers can leverage AI. *Business Horizons, 63*(2). https://doi.org/10.1016/j.bushor.2019.12.002

Carhart-Harris, R. L., & Friston, K. J. (2010). The default-mode, ego-functions and free-energy: a neurobiological account of Freudian ideas. *Brain, 133*(4), 1265–1283. https://doi.org/10.1093/brain/awq010

Chalmers, D. J. (2022). *REALITY+: Virtual Worlds and the Problems of Philosophy.* Allen Lane.

Chekroud, A. M. (2015). Unifying treatments for depression: An application of the Free Energy Principle. *Frontiers in Psychology, 6*(FEB). https://doi.org/10.3389/fpsyg.2015.00153

Chen, J. (2011). Understanding Social Systems: A Free Energy Perspective. *SSRN Electronic Journal.* https://doi.org/10.2139/ssrn.1269035

Cho, Y. S., & Linderman, K. (2019). Metacognition-based process improvement practices. *International Journal of Production Economics, 211.* https://doi.org/10.1016/j.ijpe.2019.01.030

Christensen, C. M. (2010). How will you measure your life? *Harvard Business Review* (Vol. 88, Issues 7–8).

Churchman, C. W. (1971). *The Design of Inquiry Systems: Basic Concepts of Systems and organization.* Basic Books.

Churchman, W. C. (1979). *The System Approach and Its Enemies.* Basic Books.

Cieri, F., & Esposito, R. (2019). Psychoanalysis and Neuroscience: The Bridge Between Mind and Brain. *Frontiers in Psychology*, *10*. https://doi.org/10.3389/fpsyg.2019.01983

Clark, A. (2017). How to Knit Your Own Markov Blanket: Resisting the Second Law with Metamorphic Minds. *Philosophy and Predictive Coding, Rupert 2009*.

Clark, A. (2018). A nice surprise? Predictive processing and the active pursuit of novelty. *Phenomenology and the Cognitive Sciences*, *17*(3). https://doi.org/10.1007/s11097-017-9525-z

Coltheart, M., & Davies, M. (2021). How unexpected observations lead to new beliefs: A Peircean pathway. *Consciousness and Cognition*, *87*. https://doi.org/10.1016/j.concog.2020.103037

Coltheart, M., & Langdon, R. (2019). Somatic delusions as motivated beliefs? *Australian and New Zealand Journal of Psychiatry* (Vol. 53, Issue 1). https://doi.org/10.1177/0004867418815981

Coltheart, M., Menzies, P., & Sutton, J. (2010). Abductive inference and delusional belief. *Cognitive Neuropsychiatry* (Vol. 15, Issues 1–3). https://doi.org/10.1080/13546800903439120

Connolly, P. (2018). Expected free energy formalizes conflict underlying defense in Freudian psychoanalysis. *Frontiers in Psychology*, *9*(JUL). https://doi.org/10.3389/fpsyg.2018.01264

Connolly, P. (2019). The Gravity of Objects: How Affectively Organized Generative Models Influence Perception and Social Behavior. *Frontiers in Psychology*, *10*. https://doi.org/10.3389/fpsyg.2019.02599

Connolly, P. (2022). Instability and Uncertainty Are Critical for Psychotherapy: How the Therapeutic Alliance Opens Us Up. *Frontiers in Psychology*, *12*. https://doi.org/10.3389/fpsyg.2021.784295

Connors, M. H., & Halligan, P. W. (2017). Belief and Belief Formation: Insights from Delusions. *New Approaches to the Scientific Study of Religion* (Vol. 1). https://doi.org/10.1007/978-3-319-50924-2_11

Connors, M. H., & Halligan, P. W. (2020). Delusions and theories of belief. *Consciousness and Cognition* (Vol. 81). https://doi.org/10.1016/j.concog.2020.102935

Constant, A. (2021). The free energy principle: it's not about what it takes, it's about what took you there. *Biology and Philosophy*, *36*(2). https://doi.org/10.1007/s10539-021-09787-1

Constant, A., Hesp, C., Davey, C. G., Friston, K. J., & Badcock, P. B. (2021). Why Depressed Mood is Adaptive: A Numerical Proof of Principle for an Evolutionary Systems Theory of Depression. *Computational Psychiatry*, *5*(1). https://doi.org/10.5334/cpsy.70

Corcoran, A. W., Pezzulo, G., & Hohwy, J. (2020). From allostatic agents to counterfactual cognisers: active inference, biological regulation, and the origins of cognition. *Biology and Philosophy*, *35*(3). https://doi.org/10.1007/s10539-020-09746-2

Coricelli, G., Joffily, M., Montmarquette, C., & Villeval, M. C. (2021). Tax Evasion: Cheating Rationally or Deciding Emotionally? *SSRN Electronic Journal*. https://doi.org/10.2139/ssrn.1028476

Corlett, P. R., Mohanty, A., & MacDonald, A. W. (2020). What we think about when we think about predictive processing. *Journal of Abnormal Psychology* (Vol. 129, Issue 6). https://doi.org/10.1037/abn0000632

Cuijpers, P., & Cristea, I. A. (2016). How to prove that your therapy is effective, even when it is not: A guideline. *Epidemiology and Psychiatric Sciences*, *25*(5). https://doi.org/10.1017/S2045796015000864

Damasio, A., & Damasio, H. (2016). Exploring the concept of homeostasis and considering its implications for economics. *Journal of Economic Behavior and Organization*, *126*. https://doi.org/10.1016/j.jebo.2015.12.003

de Berker, A. O., Rutledge, R. B., Mathys, C., Marshall, L., Cross, G. F., Dolan, R. J., & Bestmann, S. (2016). Computations of uncertainty mediate acute stress responses in humans. *Nature Communications*, *7*. https://doi.org/10.1038/ncomms10996

Deane, G. (2020). Dissolving the self. *Philosophy and the Mind Sciences*, *1*(I). https://doi.org/10.33735/phimisci.2020.i.39

Deane, G., Miller, M., & Wilkinson, S. (2020). Losing Ourselves: Active Inference, Depersonalization, and Meditation. *Frontiers in Psychology*, *11*. https://doi.org/10.3389/fpsyg.2020.539726

Déli, E., & Kisvárday, Z. (2020). The thermodynamic brain and the evolution of intellect: the role of mental energy. *Cognitive Neurodynamics* (Vol. 14, Issue 6). https://doi.org/10.1007/s11571-020-09637-y

Depraz, N. (2019). Epoché in light of samatha-vipassanā meditation: Chögyam trungpa's buddhist teaching facing Husserl's phenomenology. *Journal of Consciousness Studies*, *26*(7–8).

Depraz, N. (2014). *Attention et vigilance: À la croisé de la phénoménologie et des sciences cognitives*. PUF.

Diaconescu, A. O., Wellstein, K. v., Kasper, L., Mathys, C., & Stephan, K. E. (2020). Hierarchical bayesian models of social inference for probing persecutory delusional ideation. *Journal of Abnormal Psychology*, *129*(6). https://doi.org/10.1037/abn0000500

Dixit, A. K., & Nalebuff, B. (1991). *Thinking Strategically: The Competitive Edge in Business, Politics, and Everyday Life*. W. W. Norton Company, Inc.

Dixon, M. L., & Gross, J. J. (2021). Dynamic network organization of the self: implications for affective experience. *Current Opinion in Behavioral Sciences* (Vol. 39). https://doi.org/10.1016/j.cobeha.2020.11.004

Dreeben, S. J., Mamberg, M. H., & Salmon, P. (2013). The MBSR Body Scan in Clinical Practice. *Mindfulness*, *4*(4). https://doi.org/10.1007/s12671-013-0212-z

Dryden, W. (2020). Awfulizing: Some Conceptual and Therapeutic Considerations. *Journal of Rational-Emotive and Cognitive-Behavior Therapy*, *38*(3). https://doi.org/10.1007/s10942-020-00358-z

Easwaran, E. (2007). *The Upanishads* (Second Edition). Nigiri Press.

Edelson, M. G., Polania, R., Ruff, C. C., Fehr, E., & Hare, T. A. (2018). Computational and neurobiological foundations of leadership decisions. *Science*, *361*(6401). https://doi.org/10.1126/science.aat0036

Eldar, E., Rutledge, R. B., Dolan, R. J., & Niv, Y. (2016). Mood as Representation of Momentum. *Trends in Cognitive Sciences* (Vol. 20, Issue 1). https://doi.org/10.1016/j.tics.2015.07.010

Emanuel, A. S., Updegraff, J. A., Kalmbach, D. A., & Ciesla, J. A. (2010). The role of mindfulness facets in affective forecasting. *Personality and Individual Differences*, *49*(7). https://doi.org/10.1016/j.paid.2010.06.012

Engel, A. K.; Friston, K. J. and Kragic, D. (2015). *The Pragmatic Turn: Towards Action-Oriented Views in Cognitive Science.* The MIT Press.

Epley, N., & Gilovich, T. (2016). The mechanics of motivated reasoning. *Journal of Economic Perspectives*, *30*(3). https://doi.org/10.1257/jep.30.3.133

Fabry, R. E. (2017). Predictive processing and cognitive development. *Philosophy and Predictive Processing*.

Farashahi, S., Donahue, C. H., Khorsand, P., Seo, H., Lee, D., & Soltani, A. (2017). Metaplasticity as a Neural Substrate for Adaptive Learning and Choice under Uncertainty. *Neuron*, *94*(2). https://doi.org/10.1016/j.neuron.2017.03.044

Fehr, E., & Gächter, S. (2000). Fairness and retaliation: The economics of reciprocity. *Journal of Economic Perspectives*, *14*(3). https://doi.org/10.1257/jep.14.3.159

Fields, C., Friston, K., Glazebrook, J. F., & Levin, M. (2022). A free energy principle for generic quantum systems. *Progress in Biophysics and Molecular Biology*, *173*, 36–59. https://doi.org/10.1016/j.pbiomolbio.2022.05.006

Figdor, C. (2021). Shannon + Friston = Content: Intentionality in predictive signaling systems. *Synthese*, *199*(1–2). https://doi.org/10.1007/s11229-020-02912-9

Fine, D., Manyika, J., Spatial, P. E., Tacke, T., Tadjeddine, K., & Desmond, M. (2019). *Inequality: A persisting challenge and its implications.* A McKinsey Special Report.

Fleming, S. M. (2020). Awareness as inference in a higher-order state space. *Neuroscience of Consciousness*, *2020*(1). https://doi.org/10.1093/nc/niz020

Fleming, S. M., & Daw, N. D. (2017). Self-Evaluation of Decision-Making: A General Bayesian Framework for Metacognitive Computation. *Psychological Review*, *124*(1). https://doi.org/10.1037/rev0000045

Fleming, S. M., & Dolan, R. J. (2012). The neural basis of metacognitive ability. *Philosophical Transactions of the Royal Society B: Biological Sciences* (Vol. 367, Issue 1594). https://doi.org/10.1098/rstb.2011.0417

Fleming, S. M., Dolan, R. J., & Frith, C. D. (2012). Metacognition: Computation, biology and function. *Philosophical Transactions of the Royal Society B: Biological Sciences* (Vol. 367, Issue 1594). https://doi.org/10.1098/rstb.2012.0021

Flores, F. (2012). *Conversations for Action*. CreateSpace Independent Publishing Platform.

Frijda, N. H., Manstead, A. S. R., & Bem, S. (2010). The influence of emotions on beliefs. In *Emotions and Beliefs*. https://doi.org/10.1017/cbo9780511659904.001

Friston, K. (2011). Embodied Inference: or "I think therefore I am, if I am what I think ." *The Implications of Embodiment (Cognition and Communication)*. Andrews UK Limited.

Friston, K. (2013). Life as we know it. *Journal of the Royal Society Interface*, *10*(86). https://doi.org/10.1098/rsif.2013.0475

Friston, K. (2018). Am I self-conscious? (or does self-organization entail self-consciousness?). *Frontiers in Psychology*, *9*(APR). https://doi.org/10.3389/fpsyg.2018.00579

Friston, K. J. (2019). Waves of prediction. *PLoS Biology*, *17*(10). https://doi.org/10.1371/journal.pbio.3000426

Friston, K. J., Parr, T., Yufik, Y., Sajid, N., Price, C. J., & Holmes, E. (2020). Generative models, linguistic communication and active inference. *Neuroscience and Biobehavioral Reviews* (Vol. 118). https://doi.org/10.1016/j.neubiorev.2020.07.005

Friston, K. J., Stephan, K. E., Montague, R., & Dolan, R. J. (2014). Computational psychiatry: The brain as a phantastic organ. *The Lancet Psychiatry* (Vol. 1, Issue 2). https://doi.org/10.1016/S2215-0366(14)70275-5

Friston, K., FitzGerald, T., Rigoli, F., Schwartenbeck, P., O'Doherty, J., & Pezzulo, G. (2016). Active inference and learning. *Neuroscience and Biobehavioral Reviews* (Vol. 68). https://doi.org/10.1016/j.neubiorev.2016.06.022

Friston, K., Schwartenbeck, P., FitzGerald, T., Moutoussis, M., Behrens, T., & Dolan, R. J. (2013). The anatomy of choice: Active inference and agency. *Frontiers in Human Neuroscience*, *SEP*. https://doi.org/10.3389/fnhum.2013.00598

Friston, K., Schwartenbeck, P., FitzGerald, T., Moutoussis, M., Behrens, T., Friston, K., & Dolan, R. J. (2013). The anatomy of choice: dopamine and decision-making. *Philosophical Transactions of the Royal Society B: Biological Sciences*, September.

Frith, C., & Friston, K. (2013). False perceptions and false beliefs: understanding schizophrenia. *Neuroscience and the Human Person: New Perspectives on Human Activities*.

Gallagher, S., & Allen, M. (2018). Active inference, enactivism and the hermeneutics of social cognition. *Synthese*, *195*(6), 2627–2648. https://doi.org/10.1007/s11229-016-1269-8

Gallistel, C. R. (2020). Where meanings arise and how: Building on Shannon's foundations. *Mind and Language*, *35*(3). https://doi.org/10.1111/mila.12289

Gelfand, M. J., Jackson, J. C., Pan, X., Nau, D., Pieper, D., Denison, E., Dagher, M., van Lange, P. A. M., Chiu, C. Y., & Wang, M. (2021). The relationship between cultural tightness–looseness and COVID-19 cases and deaths: a global analysis. *The Lancet Planetary Health, 5*(3). https://doi.org/10.1016/S2542-5196(20)30301-6

Gergen, K. J. (1994). *Realities and Relationships: Soundings in Social Construction.* Harvard University Press.

Gergen, K. J. (2009). *Relational Being: Beyond Self and Community.* Oxford University Press.

Gilbert, D. T., & Wilson, T. D. (2009). Why the brain talks to itself: Sources of error in emotional prediction. *Philosophical Transactions of the Royal Society B: Biological Sciences, 364*(1521). https://doi.org/10.1098/rstb.2008.0305

Goldman, M. S., & Fee, M. S. (2017). Computational training for the next generation of neuroscientists. *Current Opinion in Neurobiology* (Vol. 46). https://doi.org/10.1016/j.conb.2017.06.007

Gorban, A. N., Tyukina, T. A., Pokidysheva, L. I., & Smirnova, E. v. (2021). Dynamic and thermodynamic models of adaptation. *Physics of Life Reviews* (Vol. 37). https://doi.org/10.1016/j.plrev.2021.03.001

Gordon, M. A. (2019). Introduction: Practice as Transformative Wholeness. In *Aikido as Transformative and Embodied Pedagogy* (pp. 3–56). Springer International Publishing. https://doi.org/10.1007/978-3-030-23953-4_1

Greifeneder, R., Jaffé, M. E., Newman, E. J., & Schwarz, N. (2020). The psychology of fake news: Accepting, sharing, and correcting misinformation. In *The Psychology of Fake News: Accepting, Sharing, and Correcting Misinformation.* https://doi.org/10.4324/9780429295379

Gries, T., Müller, V., & Jost, J. T. (2022). The Market for Belief Systems: A Formal Model of Ideological Choice. *Psychological Inquiry, 33*(2), 65–83.

Grudin, R. (2006). *The Politics of Manipulation versus the Culture of Awareness.* Shoemaker Hoard.

Gu, X. (2018). Incubation of craving: a Bayesian account. *Neuropsychopharmacology, 43*(12). https://doi.org/10.1038/s41386-018-0108-7

Gu, X., FitzGerald, T. H. B., & Friston, K. J. (2019). Modeling subjective belief states in computational psychiatry: interoceptive inference as a candidate framework. *Psychopharmacology, 236*(8). https://doi.org/10.1007/s00213-019-05300-5

Haggarty, S. J., Karmacharya, R., & Perlis, R. H. (2021). Advances toward precision medicine for bipolar disorder: mechanisms & molecules. *Molecular Psychiatry, 26*(1), 168–185. https://doi.org/10.1038/s41380-020-0831-4

Hanley, A. W., & Garland, E. L. (2019). Mindfulness training disrupts Pavlovian conditioning. *Physiology and Behavior, 204.* https://doi.org/10.1016/j.physbeh.2019.02.028

Hardin, G. (1985). *Filters Against Folly.* Penguin Books USA, Inc.

Harkness, D. L., & Keshava, A. (2017). Moving from the What to the How and Where – Bayesian Models and Predictive Processing. *Philosophy and Predictive Processing*.

Hart, O., & Zingales, L. (2017). Companies should maximize shareholder welfare not market value. *Journal of Law, Finance, and Accounting*, *2*(2). https://doi.org/10.1561/108.00000022

Hartwig, M., & Peters, A. (2021). Cooperation and Social Rules Emerging From the Principle of Surprise Minimization. *Frontiers in Psychology*, *11*. https://doi.org/10.3389/fpsyg.2020.606174

Hartwig, M., Bhat, A., & Peters, A. (2022). How Stress Can Change Our Deepest Preferences: Stress Habituation Explained Using the Free Energy Principle. *Frontiers in Psychology*, *13*. https://doi.org/10.3389/fpsyg.2022.865203

Haskins, L. A. B., & vanDellen, M. R. (2019). Self-regulation as relating to one's ideal possible self. *Social and Personality Psychology Compass*, *13*(10). https://doi.org/10.1111/spc3.12499

HBR Guide. (2018). *Data Analytics Basics for Managers*. Harvard Business School Publishing Corporation.

HBR'S 10 Must Reads. (2019). *On AI, Analytics, and the New Machine Age*. Harvard Business Publishing Corporation.

Heersmink, R. (2020). Varieties of the extended self. *Consciousness and Cognition* (Vol. 85). https://doi.org/10.1016/j.concog.2020.103001

Heininga, V. E., & Kuppens, P. (2021). Psychopathology and positive emotions in daily life. *Current Opinion in Behavioral Sciences* (Vol. 39). https://doi.org/10.1016/j.cobeha.2020.11.005

Henrich, J., & Muthukrishna, M. (2021). The Origins and Psychology of Human Cooperation. *Annual Review of Psychology* (Vol. 72). https://doi.org/10.1146/annurev-psych-081920-042106

Hesp, C., Tschantz, A., Millidge, B., Ramstead, M., Friston, K., & Smith, R. (2020). Sophisticated affective inference: Simulating anticipatory affective dynamics of imagining future events. *Communications in Computer and Information Science*, *1326*. https://doi.org/10.1007/978-3-030-64919-7_18

Heyes, C., Bang, D., Shea, N., Frith, C. D., & Fleming, S. M. (2020). Knowing Ourselves Together: The Cultural Origins of Metacognition. *Trends in Cognitive Sciences* (Vol. 24, Issue 5). https://doi.org/10.1016/j.tics.2020.02.007

Hohwy, J., & Seth, A. (2020). Predictive processing as a systematic basis for identifying the neural correlates of consciousness. *Philosophy and the Mind Sciences*, *1*(II). https://doi.org/10.33735/phimisci.2020.ii.64

Holmes, J. (2020). *The Brain has a Mind of its Own*. Confer Books.

Holmes, J. A. (2016). Biological v. Psychotherapeutic: Friston and psychodynamic therapy. *British Journal of Psychiatry* (Vol. 209, Issue 2). https://doi.org/10.1192/bjp.209.2.171

Holmes, J., & Nolte, T. (2019). "Surprise" and the Bayesian brain: Implications for psychotherapy theory and practice. *Frontiers in Psychology, 10*(MAR). https://doi.org/10.3389/fpsyg.2019.00592

Huang, M. H., Rust, R., & Maksimovic, V. (2019). The Feeling Economy: Managing in the Next Generation of Artificial Intelligence (AI). *California Management Review.* https://doi.org/10.1177/0008125619863436

Hutchinson, J. B., & Barrett, L. F. (2019). The Power of Predictions: An Emerging Paradigm for Psychological Research. *Current Directions in Psychological Science, 28*(3). https://doi.org/10.1177/0963721419831992

Huys, Q. J. M., & Petzschner, F. H. (2015). Failure modes of the will: From goals to habits to compulsions? *American Journal of Psychiatry* (Vol. 172, Issue 3). https://doi.org/10.1176/appi.ajp.2014.14121502

Huys, Q. J. M., & Renz, D. (2017). A Formal Valuation Framework for Emotions and Their Control. *Biological Psychiatry* (Vol. 82, Issue 6). https://doi.org/10.1016/j.biopsych.2017.07.003

Huys, Q. J. M., Daw, N. D., & Dayan, P. (2015). Depression: A Decision-Theoretic Analysis. *Annual Review of Neuroscience, 38*, 1–23. https://doi.org/10.1146/annurev-neuro-071714-033928

Huys, Q. J. M., Maia, T. v., & Frank, M. J. (2016). Computational psychiatry as a bridge from neuroscience to clinical applications. *Nature Neuroscience* (Vol. 19, Issue 3). https://doi.org/10.1038/nn.4238

Ivanov, I., & Schwartz, J. (2018). Computational Psychiatry of Emotions and the Promise of it: Where it May Lead us. *Acta Psychopathologica, 04*(06). https://doi.org/10.4172/2469-6676.100180

Jean, A. (2020). A brief history of artificial intelligence. *Medecine/Sciences* (Vol. 36, Issue 11). https://doi.org/10.1051/medsci/2020189

Jiang, Y. v., & Sisk, C. A. (2019). Habit-like attention. *Current Opinion in Psychology* (Vol. 29). https://doi.org/10.1016/j.copsyc.2018.11.014

Kaaronen, R. O. (2018). A theory of predictive dissonance: Predictive processing presents a new take on cognitive dissonance. *Frontiers in Psychology, 9*(NOV). https://doi.org/10.3389/fpsyg.2018.02218

Kahneman, D., & Tversky, A. (1972). Subjective probability: A judgment of representativeness. *Cognitive Psychology, 3*(3). https://doi.org/10.1016/0010-0285(72)90016-3

Kelly, M. P., Kriznik, N. M., Kinmonth, A. L., & Fletcher, P. C. (2019). The brain, self and society: a social-neuroscience model of predictive processing. *Social Neuroscience, 14*(3), 266–276. https://doi.org/10.1080/17470919.2018.1471003

Khalsa, S. S., Adolphs, R., Cameron, O. G., Critchley, H. D., Davenport, P. W., Feinstein, J. S., Feusner, J. D., Garfinkel, S. N., Lane, R. D., Mehling, W. E., Meuret, A. E., Nemeroff, C. B., Oppenheimer, S., Petzschner, F. H., Pollatos, O., Rhudy, J. L., Schramm, L. P., Simmons, W. K., Stein, M. B., ... Zucker, N. (2018). Interoception and Mental Health: A Roadmap. *Biological Psychiatry: Cognitive Neuroscience and Neuroimaging* (Vol. 3, Issue 6). https://doi.org/10.1016/j.bpsc.2017.12.004

Kiefer, A., & Hohwy, J. (2018). Content and misrepresentation in hierarchical generative models. *Synthese*, *195*(6). https://doi.org/10.1007/s11229-017-1435-7

Kim, D. J. (2022). Understanding the History, Theoretical Perspectives, and Influence of Mindfulness: Building Sustainability Through Mindfulness in Education. *International Journal of Educational Reform*. 105678792211067. https://doi.org/10.1177/10567879221106715

King, A., Gravina, N., & Sleiman, A. (2018). Observing the Observer. *Journal of Organizational Behavior Management*, *38*(4). https://doi.org/10.1080/01608061.2018.1514346

Kirchhoff, M. (2018). Predictive brains and embodied, enactive cognition: an introduction to the special issue. *Synthese* (Vol. 195, Issue 6). https://doi.org/10.1007/s11229-017-1534-5

Kirchhoff, M. D. (2019). *Extended Consciousness and Predictive Processing: A Third-Wave* . Routledge.

Kirk, U., Downar, J., & Montague, P. R. (2011). Interoception drives increased rational decision-making in meditators playing the ultimatum game. *Frontiers in Neuroscience*, *APR*. https://doi.org/10.3389/fnins.2011.00049

Kirk, U., Pagnoni, G., Hétu, S., & Montague, R. (2019). Short-term mindfulness practice attenuates reward prediction errors signals in the brain. *Scientific Reports*, *9*(1). https://doi.org/10.1038/s41598-019-43474-2

Kraut, R. (2007). *What is Good and Why: The Ethics of Well-Being*. Harvard University Press.

Kringelbach, M. L. (2005). The human orbitofrontal cortex: Linking reward to hedonic experience. *Nature Reviews Neuroscience* (Vol. 6, Issue 9). https://doi.org/10.1038/nrn1747

Kross, E., Verduyn, P., Sheppes, G., Costello, C. K., Jonides, J., & Ybarra, O. (2021). Social Media and Well-Being: Pitfalls, Progress, and Next Steps. *Trends in Cognitive Sciences* (Vol. 25, Issue 1). https://doi.org/10.1016/j.tics.2020.10.005

Kruger, J., & Dunning, D. (1999). Unskilled and unaware of it: How difficulties in recognizing one's own incompetence lead to inflated self-assessments. *Journal of Personality and Social Psychology*, *77*(6). https://doi.org/10.1037/0022-3514.77.6.1121

Kube, T., & Rozenkrantz, L. (2021). When Beliefs Face Reality: An Integrative Review of Belief Updating in Mental Health and Illness. *Perspectives on Psychological Science*, *16*(2). https://doi.org/10.1177/1745691620931496

Kwisthout, J., & van Rooij, I. (2020). Computational Resource Demands of a Predictive Bayesian Brain. *Computational Brain and Behavior*, *3*(2). https://doi.org/10.1007/s42113-019-00032-3

Kyselo, M. (2014). The body social: An enactive approach to the self. *Frontiers in Psychology*, *5*(SEP). https://doi.org/10.3389/fpsyg.2014.00986

Latour, B. (2018). *Down to Earth*. Polity Press.

Laukkonen, R. E., & Slagter, H. A. (2021). From many to (n)one: Meditation and the plasticity of the predictive mind. *Neuroscience and Biobehavioral Reviews* (Vol. 128). https://doi.org/10.1016/j.neubiorev.2021.06.021

Leonardi, P., & Neeley, T. (2022). *The Digital Mindset: What it Really Takes to Thrive in the Age of Data, Algorithms, and AI*. Harvard Business Review Press.

Lima Portugal, L. C., Alves, R. de C. S., Junior, O. F., Sanchez, T. A., Mocaiber, I., Volchan, E., Smith Erthal, F., David, I. A., Kim, J., Oliveira, L., Padmala, S., Chen, G., Pessoa, L., & Pereira, M. G. (2020). Interactions between emotion and action in the brain. *NeuroImage, 214*. https://doi.org/10.1016/j.neuroimage.2020.116728

Limanowski, J., & Blankenburg, F. (2013). Minimal self-models and the free energy principle. *Frontiers in Human Neuroscience* (Issue SEP). https://doi.org/10.3389/fnhum.2013.00547

Limanowski, J., & Friston, K. (2020). Attenuating oneself. *Philosophy and the Mind Sciences, 1*(I). https://doi.org/10.33735/phimisci.2020.i.35

Linson, A., Clark, A., Ramamoorthy, S., & Friston, K. (2018). The active inference approach to ecological perception: General information dynamics for natural and artificial embodied cognition. *Frontiers Robotics AI, 5*(MAR). https://doi.org/10.3389/frobt.2018.00021

Loewenstein, G. F., Hsee, C. K., Weber, E. U., & Welch, N. (2001). Risk as Feelings. *Psychological Bulletin, 127*(2). https://doi.org/10.1037/0033-2909.127.2.267

Loucks, E. B., Crane, R. S., Sanghvi, M. A., Montero-Marin, J., Proulx, J., Brewer, J. A., & Kuyken, W. (2022). Mindfulness-Based Programs: Why, When, and How to Adapt? *Global Advances in Health and Medicine, 11*, 216495612110688. https://doi.org/10.1177/21649561211068805

Love, T. M. (2014). Oxytocin, motivation and the role of dopamine. *Pharmacology Biochemistry and Behavior* (Vol. 119). https://doi.org/10.1016/j.pbb.2013.06.011

Loy, D. (2001). The Happiness Project: Transforming the Three Poisons that Cause the Suffering We Inflict on Ourselves and Others (review). *Buddhist-Christian Studies, 21*(1). https://doi.org/10.1353/bcs.2001.0018

Loy, D. (2003). *The Great Awakening: a Buddhist Social Theory*. Wisdom Publications.

Lupyan, G., & Clark, A. (2015). Words and the World: Predictive Coding and the Language-Perception-Cognition Interface. *Current Directions in Psychological Science, 24*(4). https://doi.org/10.1177/0963721415570732

Lutz, A., & Thompson, E. (2003). Antoine Lutz and Evan Thompson. *Journal of Consciousness Studies, 9–10*.

MacMullen, R. (2012). *Feelings in History*. CreateSpace Independent Publishing Platform

Marković, D., Gläscher, J., Bossaerts, P., O'Doherty, J., & Kiebel, S. J. (2015). Modeling the Evolution of Beliefs Using an Attentional Focus Mechanism. *PLoS Computational Biology*, *11*(10). https://doi.org/10.1371/journal.pcbi.1004558

Maturana, H. R., & Poerksen, B. (2004). *From Being to Doing*. Carl-Auer.

Maturana, H. R., & Varela, F. J. (1992). *The Tree of Knowledge: The Biological Roots of Human Understanding* (Revised Edition). Shambala Publishers.

McEwen, B. S., Bowles, N. P., Gray, J. D., Hill, M. N., Hunter, R. G., Karatsoreos, I. N., & Nasca, C. (2015). Mechanisms of stress in the brain. *Nature Neuroscience*, *18*(10). https://doi.org/10.1038/nn.4086

McNamee, S., & Hoskings, D. M. (2011). *Research and Social Change*. Taylor and Francis Ltd.

McNamme, S., & Gergen, K. J. (1999). *Relational Responsibility*. Sage Publications.

McParlin, Z., Cerritelli, F., Friston, K. J., & Esteves, J. E. (2022). Therapeutic Alliance as Active Inference: The Role of Therapeutic Touch and Synchrony. *Frontiers in Psychology*, *13*. https://doi.org/10.3389/fpsyg.2022.783694

Mendonça, D., Curado, M., & Gouveia, S. (2021). *The Philosophy and Science of Predictive Processing*. Bloomsbury Publishing.

Merton, R. C., & Bodie, Z. (2005). The Design of Financial Systems: Towards a Synthesis of Function and Structure. *SSRN Electronic Journal*. https://doi.org/10.2139/ssrn.313651

Metzinger, T. (2013). The myth of cognitive agency: Subpersonal thinking as a cyclically recurring loss of mental autonomy. *Frontiers in Psychology*, *4*(DEC). https://doi.org/10.3389/fpsyg.2013.00931

Metzinger, T. K. (2017). The problem of mental action: Predictive control without sensory sheets. *Philosophy and Predictive Processing*.

Mezo, P. G., Callanan, T. S., Radu, G. M., & English, M. M. (2018). Irrational Beliefs and Self-Management as Separable Predictors of Anxiety and Depression. *Journal of Rational-Emotive and Cognitive-Behavior Therapy*, *36*(2). https://doi.org/10.1007/s10942-017-0280-4

Michael, M. T. (2020). Unconscious Emotion and Free-Energy: A Philosophical and Neuroscientific Exploration. *Frontiers in Psychology*, *11*. https://doi.org/10.3389/fpsyg.2020.00984

Miller, M., Kiverstein, J., & Rietveld, E. (2020). Embodying addiction: A predictive processing account. *Brain and Cognition*, *138*. https://doi.org/10.1016/j.bandc.2019.105495

Mirza, M. B., Adams, R. A., Parr, T., & Friston, K. (2018). Impulsivity and active inference. *Journal of Cognitive Neuroscience*, *31*(2). https://doi.org/10.1162/jocn_a_01352

Molnar, A., & Loewenstein, G. (2022). Ideologies Are Like Possessions. Psychological Inquiry, 33(2), 84–87. https://doi.org/10.1080/1047840X.2022.2065129

Molnar, A., & Loewenstein, G. F. (2021). Thoughts and Players: An Introduction to Old and New Economic Perspectives on Beliefs. *SSRN Electronic Journal*. https://doi.org/10.2139/ssrn.3806135

Moutoussis, M., Shahar, N., Hauser, T. U., & Dolan, R. J. (2018). Computation in Psychotherapy, or How Computational Psychiatry Can Aid Learning-Based Psychological Therapies. *Computational Psychiatry*, *2*(0). https://doi.org/10.1162/cpsy_a_00014

Nair, A., Rutledge, R. B., & Mason, L. (2020). Under the Hood: Using Computational Psychiatry to Make Psychological Therapies More Mechanism-Focused. *Frontiers in Psychiatry*, *11*. https://doi.org/10.3389/fpsyt.2020.00140

Nave, K., Deane, G., Miller, M., & Clark, A. (2020). Wilding the predictive brain. *Wiley Interdisciplinary Reviews: Cognitive Science* (Vol. 11, Issue 6). https://doi.org/10.1002/wcs.1542

Ng, A., & Soo, K. (2017). *Numsense!: Data Science for the Layman.*

Nguyen, D., Naffziger, E. E., & Berridge, K. C. (2021). Positive affect: nature and brain bases of liking and wanting. *Current Opinion in Behavioral Sciences* (Vol. 39). https://doi.org/10.1016/j.cobeha.2021.02.013

Nussbaum, M. C. (2012). Who is the happy warrior? Philosophy, happiness research, and public policy. *International Review of Economics* (Vol. 59, Issue 4). https://doi.org/10.1007/s12232-012-0168-7

Nutt, D., Erritzoe, D., & Carhart-Harris, R. (2020). Psychedelic Psychiatry's Brave New World. *Cell*, *181*(1). https://doi.org/10.1016/j.cell.2020.03.020

O'Reilly, J. X. (2013). Making predictions in a changing world-inference, uncertainty, and learning. *Frontiers in Neuroscience*, *7 JUN*. https://doi.org/10.3389/fnins.2013.00105

Ondobaka, S., Kilner, J., & Friston, K. (2017). The role of interoceptive inference in theory of mind. *Brain and Cognition*, *112*. https://doi.org/10.1016/j.bandc.2015.08.002

Owens, A. P., Allen, M., Ondobaka, S., & Friston, K. J. (2018). Interoceptive inference: From computational neuroscience to clinic. *Neuroscience and Biobehavioral Reviews* (Vol. 90). https://doi.org/10.1016/j.neubiorev.2018.04.017

Pal, D. (20106) *Ratnagiri Alphonseo Orchard: Bayesian Decision Analysis*. Ivey Publishing.

Panksepp, J., Lane, R. D., Solms, M., & Smith, R. (2017). Reconciling cognitive and affective neuroscience perspectives on the brain basis of emotional experience. *Neuroscience and Biobehavioral Reviews* (Vol. 76). https://doi.org/10.1016/j.neubiorev.2016.09.010

Parr, T., Pezzulo, G., & Fruition, K. J. (2022). *Active Inference: The free Energy Principle in Mind, Brain, and Behavior*. The MIT Press.

Parr, T., Rees, G., & Friston, K. J. (2018). Computational Neuropsychology and Bayesian Inference. *Frontiers in Human Neuroscience*, *12*. https://doi.org/10.3389/fnhum.2018.00061

Paulus, M. P., Feinstein, J. S., & Khalsa, S. S. (2019). An Active Inference Approach to Interoceptive Psychopathology. *Annual Review of Clinical Psychology*, *15*(1), 97–122. https://doi.org/10.1146/annurev-clinpsy-050718-095617

Pearl, J., & MacKenzie, D. (2018). *The Book Of Why*. Basic Books.

Pennycook, G., & Rand, D. G. (2019a). Lazy, not biased: Susceptibility to partisan fake news is better explained by lack of reasoning than by motivated reasoning. *Cognition*, *188*. https://doi.org/10.1016/j.cognition.2018.06.011

Pennycook, G., & Rand, D. G. (2019b). Who falls for fake news? *Cognition* (Vol. 188).

Pennycook, G., & Rand, D. G. (2021a). The Psychology of Fake News. *Trends in Cognitive Sciences* (Vol. 25, Issue 5). https://doi.org/10.1016/j.tics.2021.02.007

Pennycook, G., & Rand, D. G. (2021b). The Psychology of Fake News Why Do People Fall for Fake News? *Trends in Cognitive Sciences*, *25*.

Pepperell, R. (2018). Consciousness as a physical process caused by the organization of energy in the brain. *Frontiers in Psychology*, *9*(OCT). https://doi.org/10.3389/fpsyg.2018.02091

Pessiglione, M., & Delgado, M. R. (2015). The good, the bad and the brain: Neural correlates of appetitive and aversive values underlying decision making. *Current Opinion in Behavioral Sciences* (Vol. 5). https://doi.org/10.1016/j.cobeha.2015.08.006

Petitmengin, C. (2011). Describing the experience of describing? *Journal of Consciousness Studies*, *18*(1).

Petitmengin, C. (2017a). Enaction as a Lived Experience: Towards a Microgenetic Neurophenomenology Light or mild neurophenomenology. *Constructivist Foundations*, *12*(2).

Petitmengin, C. (2017b). Enaction as a lived experience: Towards a radical neurophenomenology. *Constructivist Foundations* (Vol. 12, Issue 2).

Petitmengin, C., & Bitbol, M. (2009). The validity of first-person descriptions as authenticity and coherence. *Journal of Consciousness Studies*, *16*(10–12).

Petzschner, F. H., Glasauer, S., & Stephan, K. E. (2015). A Bayesian perspective on magnitude estimation. *Trends in Cognitive Sciences* (Vol. 19, Issue 5). https://doi.org/10.1016/j.tics.2015.03.002

Petzschner, F. H., Weber, L. A. E., Gard, T., & Stephan, K. E. (2017). Computational Psychosomatics and Computational Psychiatry: Toward a Joint Framework for Differential Diagnosis. *Biological Psychiatry*, *82*(6), 421–430. https://doi.org/10.1016/j.biopsych.2017.05.012

Petzschner, F. H., Weber, L. A., Wellstein, K. v., Paolini, G., Do, C. T., & Stephan, K. E. (2019). Focus of attention modulates the heartbeat evoked potential. *NeuroImage, 186*. https://doi.org/10.1016/j.neuro-image.2018.11.037

Pezzulo, G. (2012). An Active Inference view of cognitive control. *Frontiers in Psychology, 3*(NOV). https://doi.org/10.3389/fpsyg.2012.00478

Pezzulo, G., & Friston, K. J. (2019). The value of uncertainty: An active inference perspective. *Behavioral and Brain Sciences* (Vol. 42). https://doi.org/10.1017/S0140525X18002066

Pezzulo, G., Zorzi, M., & Corbetta, M. (2021). The secret life of predictive brains: what's spontaneous activity for? *Trends in Cognitive Sciences* (Vol. 25, Issue 9). https://doi.org/10.1016/j.tics.2021.05.007

Pine, D. S. (2017). Clinical Advances From a Computational Approach to Anxiety. *Biological Psychiatry* (Vol. 82, Issue 6). https://doi.org/10.1016/j.biopsych.2016.09.020

Pollard-Wright, H. (2020). Electrochemical energy, primordial feelings and feelings of knowing (FOK): Mindfulness-based intervention for interoceptive experience related to phobic and anxiety disorders. *Medical Hypotheses, 144*. https://doi.org/10.1016/j.mehy.2020.109909

Powell, T. C. (2014). Strategic management and the person. *Strategic Organization, 12*(3). https://doi.org/10.1177/1476127014544093

Prosser, A., Friston, K. J., Bakker, N., & Parr, T. (2018). A Bayesian Account of Psychopathy: A Model of Lacks Remorse and Self-Aggrandizing. *Computational Psychiatry, 2*(0). https://doi.org/10.1162/cpsy_a_00016

Quintana, D. S., & Guastella, A. J. (2020). An Allostatic Theory of Oxytocin. *Trends in Cognitive Sciences* (Vol. 24, Issue 7). https://doi.org/10.1016/j.tics.2020.03.008

Rabeyron, T., & Finkel, A. (2020). Consciousness, Free Energy and Cognitive Algorithms. *Frontiers in Psychology, 11*. https://doi.org/10.3389/fpsyg.2020.01675

Rabeyron, T., & Massicotte, C. (2020). Entropy, Free Energy, and Symbolization: Free Association at the Intersection of Psychoanalysis and Neuroscience. *Frontiers in Psychology, 11*. https://doi.org/10.3389/fpsyg.2020.00366

Raglan, G. B. (2014). Decision Making, Mindfulness and Mood: How Mindfulness Techniques can Reduce the Impact of Biases and Heuristics through Improved Decision Making and Positive Affect. *Journal of Depression and Anxiety, 04*(01). https://doi.org/10.4172/2167-1044.1000168

Rahman, T. (2018). Extreme overvalued beliefs: How violent extremist beliefs become normalized. *Behavioral Sciences, 8*(1). https://doi.org/10.3390/bs8010010

Ramstead, M. J. D., Friston, K. J., & Hipólito, I. (2020). Is the free-energy principle a formal theory of semantics? From variational density dynamics to neural and phenotypic representations. *Entropy*, *22*(8). https://doi.org/10.3390/E22080889

Ramstead, M. J. D., Hesp, C., Tschantz, A., Smith, R., Constant, A., & Friston, K. (2021). Neural and phenotypic representation under the free-energy principle. *Neuroscience and Biobehavioral Reviews* (Vol. 120). https://doi.org/10.1016/j.neubiorev.2020.11.024

Raviv, S. (2018). The Genius Neuroscientist Who Might Hold the Key to True AI. *Wired.*

J Rawls. (1999). *A Theory of Justice.* Belknap Press.

Reb J. and Atkins W.B. Eds. (2015) *Mindfulness in Organizations – Foundations, Research, and Applications.* Cambridge University Press.

Reb, J., Allen, T., & Vogus, T. J. (2020). Mindfulness arrives at work: Deepening our understanding of mindfulness in organizations. *Organizational Behavior and Human Decision Processes* (Vol. 159). https://doi.org/10.1016/j.obhdp.2020.04.001

Reb, J., Junjie, S., & Narayanan, J. (2012). Compassionate Dictators? The Effects of Loving-Kindness Meditation on Offers in a Dictator Game. *SSRN Electronic Journal.* https://doi.org/10.2139/ssrn.1612888

Reb, J., Narayanan, J., & Ho, Z. W. (2015). Mindfulness at Work: Antecedents and Consequences of Employee Awareness and Absent-mindedness. *Mindfulness*, *6*(1).

Reb, J., Young, J.H., and Cheah S. M. (2023). *Better Decision-making through Mindfulness-based Strategic Awareness Training.* Case Study, Singapore Management University.

Rollwage, M., Dolan, R. J., & Fleming, S. M. (2018). Metacognitive Failure as a Feature of Those Holding Radical Beliefs. *Current Biology*, *28*(24). https://doi.org/10.1016/j.cub.2018.10.053

Roney, P. & Rossi, A. (2021). Sloterdijk's Anthropotechnics. *Angelaki - Journal of the Theoretical Humanities* (Vol. 26, Issue 1). https://doi.org/10.1080/0969725X.2021.1863583

Ross Ashby, W. (2004). Principles of the self-organizing system. *E:CO Emergence: Complexity and Organization,6*(1–2). https://doi.org/10.1007/978-1-4899-0718-9_38

Rouault, M., Drugowitsch, J., & Koechlin, E. (2019). Prefrontal mechanisms combining rewards and beliefs in human decision-making. *Nature Communications*, *10*(1). https://doi.org/10.1038/s41467-018-08121-w

Rouault, M., McWilliams, A., Allen, M. G., & Fleming, S. M. (2018). Human Metacognition Across Domains: Insights from Individual Differences and Neuroimaging. In *Personality Neuroscience* (Vol. 1). https://doi.org/10.1017/pen.2018.16

Rubin, S., Parr, T., da Costa, L., & Friston, K. (2020). Future climates: Markov blankets and active inference in the biosphere. *Journal of the Royal Society Interface* (Vol. 17, Issue 172). https://doi.org/10.1098/rsif.2020.0503

Ruff, C. C., & Fehr, E. (2014). The neurobiology of rewards and values in social decision making. *Nature Reviews Neuroscience* (Vol. 15, Issue 8). https://doi.org/10.1038/nrn3776

Rutledge, R. B., Skandali, N., Dayan, P., & Dolan, R. J. (2014). A computational and neural model of momentary subjective well-being. *Proceedings of the National Academy of Sciences of the United States of America, 111*(33). https://doi.org/10.1073/pnas.1407535111

Sadeh, N., & Bredemeier, K. (2021). Engaging in risky and impulsive behaviors to alleviate distress mediates associations between intolerance of uncertainty and externalizing psychopathology. *Journal of Personality Disorders, 35*(3). https://doi.org/10.1521/pedi_2019_33_456

Safron, A. (2020). *Integrating Cybernetic Big Five Theory with the Free Energy Principle: A new strategy for modeling personalities as complex systems Cognitive and Neural Correlates of Apophenia Across the Openness-Psychosis Continuum View project Personality and Neural Correlates of Social Affiliation View project.* https://doi.org/10.31234/osf.io/653wp

Solomon, R., & Flores, F. (2001). *Building Trust in Business, Politics, Relationships, and life.* Oxford University Press.

Sapolsky, R. M. (2015). Stress and the brain: Individual variability and the inverted-U. *Nature Neuroscience* (Vol. 18, Issue 10).

Schaefer, G. O., & Savulescu, J. (2017). Better Minds, Better Morals: A Procedural Guide to Better Judgment. *Journal of Posthuman Studies, 1*(1). https://doi.org/10.5325/jpoststud.1.1.0026

Schroeder, J., & Epley, N. (2020). Demeaning: Dehumanizing others by minimizing the importance of their psychological needs. *Journal of Personality and Social Psychology, 119*(4). https://doi.org/10.1037/pspa0000199

Schwartenbeck, P., FitzGerald, T. H. B., Mathys, C., Dolan, R., Wurst, F., Kronbichler, M., & Friston, K. (2015). Optimal inference with suboptimal models: Addiction and active Bayesian inference. *Medical Hypotheses, 84*(2). https://doi.org/10.1016/j.mehy.2014.12.007

Schwartenbeck, P., FitzGerald, T., Dolan, R. J., & Friston, K. (2013). Exploration, novelty, surprise, and free energy minimization. *Frontiers in Psychology, 4*(OCT). https://doi.org/10.3389/fpsyg.2013.00710

Schwartz, B., Ward, A., Monterosso, J., Lyubomirsky, S., White, K., & Lehman, D. R. (2002). Maximizing versus satisficing: Happiness is a matter of choice. *Journal of Personality and Social Psychology, 83*(5). https://doi.org/10.1037//0022-3514.83.5.1178

Schwengerer, L. (2019). Self-Knowledge in a Predictive Processing Framework. *Review of Philosophy and Psychology, 10*(3). https://doi.org/10.1007/s13164-018-0416-1

Scoblic, J. P. (2020). Strategic foresight as dynamic capability: A new lens on knightian uncertainty strategic foresight as dynamic capability. *Harvard Business School.*

Serra, D. (2021). Decision-making: from neuroscience to neuroeconomics—an overview. *Theory and Decision*, *91*(1). https://doi.org/10.1007/s11238-021-09830-3

Seth, A. (2021). *Being You: A New Science of Consciousness*. Faber & Faber.

Seth, A. K. (2019). From Unconscious Inference to the Beholder's Share: Predictive Perception and Human Experience. *European Review*, *27*(3). https://doi.org/10.1017/S1062798719000061

Seth, A. K., Wanja Wiese, C., Gutenberg-, J., Metzinger, T., & Windt, J. M. (2014). The Cybernetic Bayesian Brain. *Open MIND*, *35*.

Shadlen, M. N., & Roskies, A. L. (2012). The neurobiology of decision-making and responsibility: Reconciling mechanism and mindedness. *Frontiers in Neuroscience*, *APR*. https://doi.org/10.3389/fnins.2012.00056

Sharot, T., & Garrett, N. (2016). Forming Beliefs: Why Valence Matters. *Trends in Cognitive Sciences*, *20*(1), 25–33. https://doi.org/10.1016/j.tics.2015.11.002

Sims, M., & Pezzulo, G. (2021). Modelling ourselves: what the free energy principle reveals about our implicit notions of representation. *Synthese*, *199*(3–4), 7801–7833. https://doi.org/10.1007/s11229-021-03140-5

Smith, R., Friston, K. J., & Whyte, C. J. (2022). A step-by-step tutorial on active inference and its application to empirical data. *Journal of Mathematical Psychology*, *107*, 102632. https://doi.org/10.1016/j.jmp.2021.102632

Smith, R., Lane, R. D., Nadel, L., & Moutoussis, M. (2020). A Computational Neuroscience Perspective on the Change Process in Psychotherapy. In *Neuroscience of Enduring Change*. https://doi.org/10.1093/oso/9780190881511.003.0015

Smith, R., Ramstead, M. J. D., & Kiefer, A. (2022). Active inference models do not contradict folk psychology. *Synthese*, *200*(2), 81. https://doi.org/10.1007/s11229-022-03480-w

Sobhani, M., & Bechara, A. (2011). A somatic marker perspective of immoral and corrupt behavior. *Social Neuroscience*, *6*(5–6). https://doi.org/10.1080/17470919.2011.605592

Solberg, E., Traavik, L. E. M., & Wong, S. I. (2020). Digital Mindsets: Recognizing and Leveraging Individual Beliefs for Digital Transformation. *California Management Review*, *62*(4). https://doi.org/10.1177/0008125620931839

Solms, M. (2021). *The Hidden Spring*. Profile Books.

Solms, M., & Friston, K. (2018). How and why consciousness arises: Some considerations from physics and physiology. *Journal of Consciousness Studies*, *25*(5–6).

Spinelli, E. (2005). *The Interpreted World: an introduction to phenomenological psychology* (2nd Edition). Sage Publications.

Stanley, S. (2012). Intimate distances: William James' introspection, Buddhist mindfulness, and experiential inquiry. *New Ideas in Psychology*, *30*(2). https://doi.org/10.1016/j.newideapsych.2011.10.001

Stephan, K. E., Manjaly, Z. M., Mathys, C. D., Weber, L. A. E., Paliwal, S., Gard, T., Tittgemeyer, M., Fleming, S. M., Haker, H., Seth, A. K., & Petzschner, F. H. (2016). Allostatic Self-efficacy: A Metacognitive Theory of Dyshomeostasis-Induced Fatigue and Depression. *Frontiers in Human Neuroscience*, *10*. https://doi.org/10.3389/fnhum.2016.00550

Stephan, K. E., Petzschner, F. H., Kasper, L., Bayer, J., Wellstein, K. v., Stefanics, G., Pruessmann, K. P., & Heinzle, J. (2019). Laminar fMRI and computational theories of brain function. *NeuroImage* (Vol. 197). https://doi.org/10.1016/j.neuroimage.2017.11.001

Sterling, P. (2014). Homeostasis vs Allostasis. *JAMA Psychiatry*, *71*(10), 1192. https://doi.org/10.1001/jamapsychiatry.2014.1043

Sterling, P. (2018). Point of View: Predictive regulation and human design. *ELife*, *7*. https://doi.org/10.7554/eLife.36133

Sterzer, P. (2016). Moving forward in perceptual decision making. *Proceedings of the National Academy of Sciences of the United States of America* (Vol. 113, Issue 21). https://doi.org/10.1073/pnas.1605619113

Sterzer, P., Adams, R. A., Fletcher, P., Frith, C., Lawrie, S. M., Muckli, L., Petrovic, P., Uhlhaas, P., Voss, M., & Corlett, P. R. (2018). The Predictive Coding Account of Psychosis. *Biological Psychiatry* (Vol. 84, Issue 9). https://doi.org/10.1016/j.biopsych.2018.05.015

Sterzer, P., Mishara, A. L., Voss, M., & Heinz, A. (2016). Thought insertion as a self-disturbance: An integration of predictive coding and phenomenological approaches. *Frontiers in Human Neuroscience*, *10*(OCT2016). https://doi.org/10.3389/fnhum.2016.00502

Stewart. S. III, & Wright, J. (2019). *The Economic Impact of Closing the Racial Wealth Gap*. McKinsey & Company.

Strack, F., & Deutsch, R. (2004). Reflective and impulsive determinants of social behavior. *Personality and Social Psychology Review*, *8*(3). https://doi.org/10.1207/s15327957pspr0803_1

Swanson, L. R. (2016). The predictive processing paradigm has roots in Kant. *Frontiers in Systems Neuroscience*, *10*(OCT). https://doi.org/10.3389/fnsys.2016.00079

Swinkels, M. (2020). Beliefs of political leaders: conditions for change in the Eurozone crisis. *West European Politics*, *43*(5). https://doi.org/10.1080/01402382.2019.1635802

Szczepanik, J. E., Brycz, H., Kleka, P., Fanslau, A., Zarate, C. A., & Nugent, A. C. (2020). Metacognition and emotion – How accurate perception of own biases relates to positive feelings and hedonic capacity. *Consciousness and Cognition*, *82*. https://doi.org/10.1016/j.concog.2020.102936

Tabor, A., Thacker, M. A., Moseley, G. L., & Körding, K. P. (2017). Pain: A Statistical Account. *PLoS Computational Biology* (Vol. 13, Issue 1). https://doi.org/10.1371/journal.pcbi.1005142

Tamir, M., & Gutentag, T. (2017). Desired emotional states: their nature, causes, and implications for emotion regulation. *Current Opinion in Psychology* (Vol. 17). https://doi.org/10.1016/j.copsyc.2017.06.014

Tappin, B. M., & Gadsby, S. (2019). Biased belief in the Bayesian brain: A deeper look at the evidence. *Consciousness and Cognition* (Vol. 68, pp. 107–114). Academic Press Inc. https://doi.org/10.1016/j.concog.2019.01.006

Tart, C. T. (1987). *Waking Up*. New Science Library.

Tart, C. T. (1990). Extending mindfulness to everyday life. *Journal of Humanistic Psychology*, *30*(1). https://doi.org/10.1177/0022167890301005

Titova, L., & Sheldon, K. M. (2022). Happiness comes from trying to make others feel good, rather than oneself. *Journal of Positive Psychology*, *17*(3). https://doi.org/10.1080/17439760.2021.1897867

Tottenham, N., & Gabard-Durnam, L. J. (2017). The developing amygdala: a student of the world and a teacher of the cortex. *Current Opinion in Psychology* (Vol. 17). https://doi.org/10.1016/j.copsyc.2017.06.012

Tsakiris, M. (2017). The multisensory basis of the self: From body to identity to others. *Quarterly Journal of Experimental Psychology*, *70*(4). https://doi.org/10.1080/17470218.2016.1181768

Tsakiris, M., & de Preester, H. (2019). *The Interoceptive Mind: From homeostasis to awareness*. Oxford University Press.

Tuchman, B. W. (1984). *The march of Folly*. Time Warner Books.

Tversky, A., & Kahneman, D. (1974). Judgment under uncertainty: Heuristics and biases. *Science*, *185*(4157). https://doi.org/10.1126/science.185.4157.1124

van de Cruys, S., & van Dessel, P. (2021). Mental distress through the prism of predictive processing theory. In *Current Opinion in Psychology* (Vol. 41). https://doi.org/10.1016/j.copsyc.2021.07.006

van der Linden, S., Roozenbeek, J., Maertens, R., Basol, M., Kácha, O., Rathje, S., & Traberg, C. S. (2021). How Can Psychological Science Help Counter the Spread of Fake News? *Spanish Journal of Psychology*. https://doi.org/10.1017/SJP.2021.23

VanderWeele, T. J. (2019). Suffering and response: Directions in empirical research. *Social Science and Medicine* (Vol. 224). https://doi.org/10.1016/j.socscimed.2019.01.041

VanderWeele, T. J. (2020). Activities for flourishing: An evidence-based guide. *Journal of Positive Psychology and Wellbeing*, *4*(1).

Varela, F., Thompson, E., & Rosch, E. (2017). *The Embodied Mind: Cognitive Science and Human Experience* (Revised Edition). The MIT Press.

Varela, F. J. (1996). Neurophenomenology: A methodological remedy for the hard problem. *Journal of Consciousness Studies, 3*(4).

Varela, F. J. (1999). *Ethical Know-How*. Stanford University Press.

Varela, F., & Shear, J. (1999). *The View From Within: First Approaches to the Study of Consciousness*. Imprint Academic.

Veissière, S. P. L., & Stendel, M. (2018). Hypernatural monitoring: A social rehearsal account of smartphone addiction. *Frontiers in Psychology, 9*(FEB). https://doi.org/10.3389/fpsyg.2018.00141

Vohs, K. D. (2010). The mere thought of money makes you feel less pain. *Harvard Business Review, 88*(3).

Wager, T. D., Kang, J., Johnson, T. D., Nichols, T. E., Satpute, A. B., & Barrett, L. F. (2015). A Bayesian Model of Category-Specific Emotional Brain Responses. *PLoS Computational Biology, 11*(4). https://doi.org/10.1371/journal.pcbi.1004066

Wang, H., Kim, M., Normoyle, K. P., & Llano, D. (2016). Thermal regulation of the brain-an anatomical and physiological review for clinical neuroscientists. *Frontiers in Neuroscience* (Vol. 9, Issue JAN). https://doi.org/10.3389/fnins.2015.00528

Wiese, W. (2018). *Experienced Wholeness: Integrating Insights from Gestalt Theory, Cognitive Neuroscience, and Predictive Processing*. MIT Press.

Wiese, W. (2020). The science of consciousness does not need another theory, it needs a minimal unifying model. *Neuroscience of Consciousness, 2020*(1).

Wiese, W., & Friston, K. J. (2022). AI ethics in computational psychiatry: From the neuroscience of consciousness to the ethics of consciousness. *Behavioural Brain Research, 420*. https://doi.org/10.1016/j.bbr.2021.113704

Wiese, W., Metzinger, T., Hohwy, J., Clark, A., Anderson, M. L., Bruineberg, J., Bucci, A., Grasso, M., Burr, C., Butz, M. v., Dewhurst, J., Dolega, K., Downey, A., Drayson, Z., Fabry, R. E., Fink, S. B., Zednik, C., Gladziejewski, P., Harkness, D. L., … Wiese, W. (2017). Philosophy and Predictive Processing. *Philosophy and Predictive Processing*.

Wilkinson, S., Deane, G., Nave, K., & Clark, A. (2019). Getting warmer: Predictive processing and the nature of emotion. *The Value of Emotions for Knowledge*. https://doi.org/10.1007/978-3-030-15667-1_5

Williams, D. (2021). Socially adaptive belief. *Mind and Language, 36*(3). https://doi.org/10.1111/mila.12294

Winograd, T., & Flores, F. (1987). *Understanding Computers and Cognition: A New Foundation for Design*. Addison - Wesley Professional.

Yoshida, W., Seymour, B., Friston, K. J., & Dolan, R. J. (2010). Neural mechanisms of belief inference during cooperative games. *Journal of Neuroscience*, *30*(32). https://doi.org/10.1523/JNEUROSCI.5895-09.2010

Yufik, Y. M. (2013). Understanding, consciousness and thermodynamics of cognition. *Chaos, Solitons and Fractals*, *55*. https://doi.org/10.1016/j.chaos.2013.04.010

Yufik, Y. M., & Friston, K. (2016). Life and understanding: The origins of "understanding" in self-organizing nervous systems. *Frontiers in Systems Neuroscience*, *10*(DEC).

Acknowledgments

Gratefulness is a two-way street. I have a lot to be thankful for and often I have also been on the receiving side of thankfulness. "If you only knew how much you inspired me back in 2010 @HSG St Gallen[1]. Your ideas have been my guiding stars ever since," a former student, now a partner of a law firm in Stockholm, wrote to me recently, years after I taught his class. Over the years, I have received similar notes, most recently, a gratitude note from one of my students from South Africa. Nothing can give me more satisfaction and encouragement than knowing that I have helped people advance through the vicissitudes of life. It is so rewarding.

On the other hand, I have also been the beneficiary of advice, care, and love. To all who have been so generous toward me, I would like to dedicate this book and offer my thankfulness. I will mention only a few of them, as they are so many.

My high school teachers, Angel y Doris, are amongst those I keep in thankful memory for their iconoclast advice. "Seek out problems in life," they told me, "it is the only way to learn and grow." I will also always be grateful to Mr. Helmut Maucher (RIP), the Chairman and CEO of Nestle, for the three pieces of advice he gave me on how to navigate professional life as a foreigner in Switzerland; they were critical to any success I have achieved. He said: "As a foreigner, you will be more exposed to adverse situations than locals. Therefore, you need to have a thick skin and a calm, non-reactive mind. Get a job where you can produce measurable financial results so you can prove your performance, and thirdly, don't get involved in internal company politics."

My two doctoral advisors, John Aram and Richard Boland, strongly motivated and encouraged me to keep developing and cultivating what they considered a strong ability of mine: connecting ideas from diverse fields and integrating them into a coherent discourse and argument.

My two bosses at UBS, Zurich, Dr. Thomas Krayenbuehl and Karl Janjoeri (RIP), have had a profound, positive influence on my life path - two outstanding people with different biographies: one a lawyer, book author, cello player, lieutenant colonel and member of the general staff of the Swiss army; the other more empirical, with an extraordinary ability for risk management; both highly cultivated polyglots, committed to guiding me with care and courage to become a member of UBS senior management.

I owe great thankfulness to the ideas, theories, and work of Karl Friston, Klaas Enno Stephan, and Howard Raiffa (RIP), my Bayesian decision-making professor at Harvard. The intellectual input of this book has its origin in the work of many people, but this trio of scientists has been most influential.

I also thank the other dynamic trio: Monika, Roberta and Francesca. My wife, Dr. Monika Young, was the first to read the manuscript and helped me improve its readability; Roberta Cerini expertly and

---

1 HSG stands for the University of Saint Gallen, Switzerland's prominent School of Business, Law and Social Science.

artistically captured the essence from my rough sketches and converted them into beautiful, precise illustrations of what I intended to express. And Francesca Poggi captured the book's spirit and created an evocative and inviting-to-read layout.

Special thanks also to Professor Jochen Reb at the Singapore Management University, a specialist in decision making who, upon reading MBSAT's first book, has become my academic partner and friend, introducing the program in Asia and to the government of Singapore, where MBSAT is part of the world-wide recognized national skill-building program.

A person who has been of great support for this book is Monica Rogers, my editor at Wiley Blackwell. The monthly conversations we have had during the past three years were very important to me during this lonely time writing the book.

Finally, I dedicate this book to my students of the past, present, and future, my clients, friends, and all fellow human beings wishing to improve their lives and engaging on a path toward less Free Energy and more flourishing.

To my entire family thanks for your patience during the three intense years I spent working on this book.

Index

V

volatility, 347

Volatility, Uncertainty, Complexity, and Ambiguity (VUCA), 5–6, 28, 347

W

walking mindfully, 199-200